Custom List Box

 A list box with more features and functions than Visual Basic's list box.

Here are the new features in this list box:

- *Multiple Selection.* You can select more than one item at a time.
- *Clear List.* A fast command for removing all the items from a list box.
- *Searching.* MicroHelp's list box provides commands for searching a list box.
- *Tab Stops.* You can place tab stops inside list boxes for aligning text.
- *Multiple Columns.* List boxes can also have multiple, scrolling columns, like the File Manager's file list box.

Common Dialog Boxes

When Microsoft introduced Windows 3.1, they also introduced a number of common dialog boxes for opening and saving files, selecting printers, printing, choosing fonts, and choosing colors. They even work in Windows 3.0!

MicroHelp provides the "glue" commands that let you to add these dialogs to your own programs.

File Open and File Save As Dialogs

The File Open dialog box looks like this:

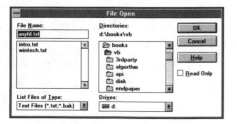

Using this dialog box is much simpler than trying to build a similar dialog box in Visual Basic.

Print and Print Se...

The Print and Print Se... standard way to selec... as landscape vs. portrai... printing.

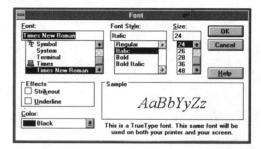

Font Selection Dialog

You can use this dialog box to let your users select fonts, sizes, and styles.

Color Selection

Add color selection to your programs.

Using any of these dialog boxes is much easier than building such dialog boxes yourself. And they're also standard!

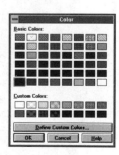

MicroHelp Files on the Disk:

MHDEM200.VBX	Design-time file
MHDEM200.VBR	Run-time version
COMMDLG.DLL	Common dialog

Continued on inside back cover...

Computer users are not all alike.
Neither are SYBEX books.

We know our customers have a variety of needs. They've told us so. And because we've listened, we've developed several distinct types of books to meet the needs of each of our customers. What are you looking for in computer help?

If you're looking for the basics, try the **ABC's** series. You'll find short, unintimidating tutorials and helpful illustrations. For a more visual approach, select **Teach Yourself,** featuring screen-by-screen illustrations of how to use your latest software purchase.

Running Start books are really two books in one—a tutorial to get you off to a fast start and a reference to answer your questions when you're ready to tackle advanced tasks.

Mastering and **Understanding** titles offer you a step-by-step introduction, plus an in-depth examination of intermediate-level features, to use as you progress.

Our **Up & Running** series is designed for computer-literate consumers who want a no-nonsense overview of new programs. Just 20 basic lessons, and you're on your way.

We also publish two types of reference books. Our **Instant References** provide quick access to each of a program's commands and functions. SYBEX **Encyclopedias** and **Desktop References** provide a *comprehensive reference* and explanation of all of the commands, features, and functions of the subject software.

Our **Programming** books are specifically written for a technically sophisticated audience and provide a no-nonsense value-added approach to each topic covered, with plenty of tips, tricks, and time-saving hints.

Sometimes a subject requires a special treatment that our standard series doesn't provide. So you'll find we have titles like **Advanced Techniques, Handbooks, Tips & Tricks,** and others that are specifically tailored to satisfy a unique need.

We carefully select our authors for their in-depth understanding of the software they're writing about, as well as their ability to write clearly and communicate effectively. Each manuscript is thoroughly reviewed by our technical staff to ensure its complete accuracy. Our production department makes sure it's easy to use. All of this adds up to the highest quality books available, consistently appearing on best-seller charts worldwide.

You'll find SYBEX publishes a variety of books on every popular software package. Looking for computer help? Help Yourself to SYBEX.

For a brochure of our best-selling publications:

SYBEX Inc. 2021 Challenger Drive, Alameda, CA 94501
Tel: (510) 523-8233/(800) 227-2346 Telex: 336311
Fax: (510) 523-2373

SYBEX

SYBEX is committed to using natural resources wisely to preserve and improve our environment. As a leader in the computer book publishing industry, we are aware that over 40% of America's solid waste is paper. This is why we have been printing the text of books like this one on recycled paper since 1982.

This year our use of recycled paper will result in the saving of more than 15,300 trees. We will lower air pollution effluents by 54,000 pounds, save 6,300,000 gallons of water, and reduce landfill by 2,700 cubic yards.

In choosing a SYBEX book you are not only making a choice for the best in skills and information, you are also choosing to enhance the quality of life for all of us.

Learn Programming and Visual Basic with John Socha

Learn Programming and Visual Basic™ with John Socha

John Socha

SYBEX®

San Francisco • Paris • Düsseldorf • Soest

Acquisitions Editor: Dianne King
Developmental Editor: Gary Masters
Editor: Richard Mills
Tech. Editors: John Barrie, Business & Technology Development; Michael Warren
Word Processors: Ann Dunn and Susan Trybull
Book Designer: Lucie Živny
Screen Graphics: Cuong Le
Typesetter: Dina F Quan
Proofreader/Production Assistant: Lisa Haden
Indexer: Ted Laux
Cover Designer: Ingalls + Associates
Cover Photographer: David Bishop

Library of Congress Card Number: 92-61132
ISBN: 0-7821-1057-6

Manufactured in the United States of America
10 9 8 7 6 5 4 3 2 1

To Michele, for being Michele

Acknowledgments

This book is all Paul Yao's fault. Paul Yao is a Windows programming expert, who, among other things, teaches Windows programming classes all over the world. He was writing a new class and used me as a guinea pig. During one of these sessions (which often strayed from the point), he showed me a copy of Visual Basic, which had just been released a week earlier. I was hooked! I got so excited that I called my agent, Bill Gladstone, and said I wanted to write a book about Visual Basic.

This led to a meeting with Rudolph Langer and Dianne King of SYBEX, who were both really interested in this book (but I guess that's obvious since you're reading this). I'd like to thank Rudy and Dianne for letting me do this book.

Whenever an author thanks his editors, he always says something like, "It was a pleasure working with...." But in my case, it really was a pleasure to work with my editors: Gary Masters and Richard Mills. Gary, the developmental editor, helped me shape this book to be what it is now, and he helped me figure out how to keep it from being too long (I never thought I'd have *that* problem). We also wasted far too much time chatting on the telephone about lots of things other than this book.

And special thanks to Richard Mills for doing a file (er, that is "fine") job editing this book. He started editing the book before I finished writing it, which I thought would be a problem: "What if I want to make changes to earlier sections as a result of things I do later?" But in reality, his editing in the earlier chapters helped me change my writing so he wouldn't have to do much editing in later chapters. This was good for me and for him: No author likes to see his or her writing changed, and it's hard work editing a book.

SYBEX had two technical reviewers for this book: Michael Warren and John Barrie. They both did a great job and had some really good suggestions that I was able to incorporate into this book.

Michele Leialoha, who's not what we call a "computer person," read the first few chapters to make sure they weren't over a beginner's head. I'd also like to thank her for her love and support throughout this project.

To all the people on the MSBASIC forum of CompuServe: Thanks! I learned a lot about what people were having problems with from this forum, and I also got a lot of ideas for the Toolbox part of this book. There are so many people there who were helpful that I can't list them all. But a big thanks to everyone. And especially thanks to Jonathan Zuck, who answers an unbelievable number of questions every day. How do you do it, Jonathan?

Three people, and their companies, provided the software included with this book, and to them I'm grateful. In alphabetical order by last name, they're Don Malin of Crescent Software, Joe Modica of Sheridan Software Systems, and Mark Novisoff of MicroHelp. All of their products are great, and thanks guys for letting me include some of your software with my book.

Contents at a Glance

Introduction   *xxvi*

Part one: Introduction to Visual Basic

Chapter 1:	Starting with Basic	**3**
Chapter 2:	Learning about Variables and Values	**27**
Chapter 3:	Drawing on the Screen	**45**
Chapter 4:	Building Programs	**61**
Chapter 5:	Adding a Menu Bar	**87**
Chapter 6:	Using Array Variables to Save Lines	**103**
Chapter 7:	Building a Clock Program	**133**

Part two: Building Larger Programs

Chapter 8:	Approaches to Designing and Building Programs	**173**
Chapter 9:	Building Address Book's Interface	**191**
Chapter 10:	Reading and Writing Address Books	**219**
Chapter 11:	Working with Multiple Records	**255**
Chapter 12:	Searching, Printing, Sorting, and Deleting	**293**

Part three: Toolbox of Advanced Techniques

Chapter 13:	Overview of Advanced Techniques	**303**
Chapter 14:	Writing Programs That Work with All Displays	**311**
Chapter 15:	Toolbox for Controls	**345**
Chapter 16:	Toolbox for Forms	**371**
Chapter 17:	Toolbox for Drawing	**387**
Chapter 18:	Toolbox for Fonts	**413**
Chapter 19:	Toolbox: Miscellaneous	**433**
Appendix A:	Installing Visual Basic and the Companion-Disk Files	**455**
Appendix B:	Using the Commercial Software on the Companion Disk	**461**

Index   *469*

Table of Contents

Introduction   *xxvi*

Part one: Introduction to Visual Basic   xxx

Chapter 1: Starting with Basic   3

Starting Visual Basic   3
    Exiting Visual Basic   4
What Is Programming?   4
Using the Immediate Window   6
    Showing the Immediate Window   6
    Typing in the Immediate Window   7
Leaving Run Mode   9
The Print Command   10
The Making of a Basic Command   11
Doing Arithmetic   17
    The Calculator Functions   17
    Quotient and Remainder   18
    Exponentiation   19
    Complex Equations   20
Related Tools   22
Summary   23

Chapter 2: Learning about Variables and Values   27

What Are Variables?   27
    Where Are Variables?   30
    Naming Variables   30
Values and Types   32
    More about Types and Numbers   35
    Exploring the Limits on Numbers   37

Scientific Notation 40

Related Tools 41

Summary 42

Chapter 3: Drawing on the Screen 45

Drawing in a Window 45

Drawing and Twips 47

A Peek at Objects and Forms 50

More Explorations in Drawing 52

Exploring the Step Keyword 52

The CurrentX and CurrentY Properties 53

Related Tools 56

Summary 57

Chapter 4: Building Programs 61

Building Your First Program 61

Anatomy of an Event Handler 63

A Multiline Program 65

A Look at Event-Driven Programs 66

Building a Sketch Program 67

Drawing Lines to Follow the Mouse 68

Choosing the Event 68

Writing Event Code 71

Clicking to Draw 72

Saving Sketch 72

Opening Your Sketch Project 75

The If..Then Command 76

Boolean Expressions (Conditions) 77

The Else Part of If..Then 79

Boolean Operators 80

Finishing Sketch 82

Related Tools 84

Summary 84

Chapter 5: Adding a Menu Bar   87

Building a Menu Bar   87

Creating the Menu Title   88

Controls and Control Names   89

Creating the Exit Item   91

Adding Code to a Menu Item   92

Adding the Erase Menu Item   92

Completing the Menu Bar   93

Inserting Separating Lines in Menus   94

Adding Control Arrays   94

Changing the Line Width   96

Checking Menu Items   98

Summary   101

Chapter 6: Using Array Variables to Save Lines   103

Designing a New Sketch   103

Array Variables   105

Defining Form Variables   107

Saving Points in Sketch   109

Redrawing Forms   111

Redrawing Sketch's Lines   113

The For..Next Command   114

Remembering Separate Lines   116

Remembering the Line Widths   120

Printing Your Picture   121

Creating an EXE Program   123

The Final Sketch Program   124

Related Tools   127

Summary   129

Chapter 7: Building a Clock Program   133

Designing Icon Clock   133

Working with Icons   134

Drawing in an Icon   135
Setting the Caption   136
Reading the Clock   137
Using Timers   138
Creating a Timer   139
Setting the Timer   140
Showing the Time   142
Using Time Functions   143
Getting Information from Date Serial Numbers   146
Drawing the Clock Face   147
Setting the Icon   148
Drawing the Clock Hands   149
Minimizing Icon Clock   152
Showing One Second Hand   154
Drawing with Color   154
Using Xor to Erase a Line   155
Drawing the Hour and Minute Hands   160
Related Tools   167
Summary   168

Part two: Building Larger Programs   170

Chapter 8: Approaches to Designing and Building Programs   173

How to Design Programs   173
Detailed Specifications   174
Programming as Evolution   174
In-Between Approaches   175
The Approach We'll Use Here   175
Designing the User Interface   176
The Initial Design   177
Writing a Feature List   178

Drawing the Screens   181

Building Programs   183

    Add Features First, Test Later   183

    Add, Test, Redesign   184

What Is Good Design?   186

Summary   187

Chapter 9: Building Address Book's Interface   191

Creating the Controls   191

    A Step-by-Step Approach   193

    Creating Control Arrays   194

    Saving Your Work   201

    Creating a Program Manager Icon   201

Overview of Controls and Properties   203

    Text Boxes   203

    Labels   204

    Command Buttons   204

    Combo Boxes   204

    Form Properties   206

Bringing Address Book to Life   207

    Controlling the Tab Order   207

Setting Up the Combo Boxes   209

    The Method of Methods   210

    Initializing the cboPhone Combo Boxes   211

Related Tools   215

Summary   215

Chapter 10: Reading and Writing Address Books   219

Working with Disk Files   219

    Creating a Disk File   221

    Writing to a File   223

    Reading Files   226

    Closing Files   228

Reading and Writing the Address Book   229

Packaging Data: User-Defined Types   231

Defining New Types   231

The Global Module   233

Designing an AddressInfo Type   234

Fixed-Length Strings   236

Writing and Reading Compound Variables   238

Removing Trailing Spaces   242

Using On-line Help   243

Creating New Subroutines   244

Subroutines and Variables   247

Creating the DBClose Subroutine   248

Creating DBRead and DBWrite Subroutines   248

Related Tools   250

Summary   251

Chapter 11: Working with Multiple Records   255

Creating Modules   255

Using Subroutine Parameters   260

Modifying the Database Module   263

Modifying DATABASE.BAS for Multiple Records   264

Adding Multirecord Support to DBOpen   264

Testing Your Code   266

Creating a DBLen( ) Function   268

Modifying DBRead   270

Modifying DBWrite   271

Adding Comments to DBClose   272

Adding Multiple Records to the Form   272

Adding Form-Level Variables   273

Modifying GetRecord   273

Creating Empty Records   276

Modifying SaveRecord   277

Noticing Changes to Records   278

Creating the Menu Bar   280

Adding New Records   282

Navigating through Records   284

Enabling the Exit Menu Item   286

Supporting Cut, Copy, Paste, and Undo   287

Related Tools   289

Summary   290

Chapter 12: Searching, Printing, Sorting, and Deleting   293

Searching   293

Printing Addresses   296

Sorting Addresses   297

Deleting Addresses   298

Summary   298

Part three: Toolbox of Advanced Techniques   300

Chapter 13: Overview of Advanced Techniques   303

Visual Basic–Only Techniques   303

Custom Controls   304

DLLs and Windows Functions   304

The Declare Statement   305

Translating between C and Visual Basic Types   306

Chapter 14: Writing Programs That Work with All Displays   311

Understanding Screen Resolution   311

Printer Resolution   312

Display Resolution   312

How Screen Size Affects Density   312

Magazine Advertisements: What Do They Mean?   314

What Are Logical Inches?   315

Defining a Logical Inch 316

Can I Have Sharper Images? 317

How Visual Basic's Objects Change Size 318

Twips and the Height of Text 318

How the Heights of Controls Vary 319

How to Adjust Your Programs 321

How to Work with Combo Boxes 322

How to Work with List Boxes 322

How Pictures Change 323

Text and Pictures 326

Colors 328

Summary of Rules 328

The ClockCal Example 330

Control Arrays 331

How Resizing Works 332

How ClockCal Works 333

The ClockCal Form 335

The Code for ClockCal 337

Chapter 15: Toolbox for Controls 345

Progress Bars 345

How to Use UpdateProgress 346

How UpdateProgress Works 346

The Code 347

Drawing Shadows around Controls 348

The Code 349

Checking Text Box Input 350

Discarding Characters 350

Limitations of Using KeyPress 351

Checking Simple Floating-Point Numbers 352

Checking Other Types of Inputs 354

Limiting the Number of Characters in Text Boxes   355
How to Use LimitLength   355
How It Works   355
The Code   356
Overtype Mode in Text Boxes   356
An Example   357
Password Text Boxes   358
How to Use Password Fields   358
How It Works   359
The Code   360
Supporting an Edit Menu   361
How It Works   362
Keyboard Shortcuts   364
Setting Default and Cancel for 3-D Buttons   365
Hiding the Controls on the Left Side   367
Quickly Clearing a List Box   368
Using MhTag   368
Using Windows Functions   368

Chapter 16: Toolbox for Forms   371

Adding Lines to a Form   371
Notes   372
Centering Forms   372
How to Use CenterForm   372
Notes   373
How It Works   374
The Code   374
Sizing Forms Using Inside Dimensions   374
How to Use ResizeInside   375
Notes   375
How It Works   375

The Code   377

Limiting a Form's Size   377

   Keeping the Width Constant   378

   Setting a Minimum Size for a Form   378

   Notes   378

Resizing a Form's Controls   379

   Resizing a Text Box   380

   When to Resize Controls   381

   Moving Controls   381

   Sample Program   381

Showing a Start-up Screen   382

   Using a Start-up Screen   383

   Creating a Sub Main   383

   Adding a Start-up Screen to Sub Main   384

Chapter 17: Toolbox for Drawing   **387**

Fast Line Drawing   387

   How Polyline Works   389

   Global Definitions   389

   Sample Program   390

   Drawing on a Printer with Polyline   390

   Using Nonpixel Scaling Modes   391

   Notes   391

Fast Ruler Drawing   392

   How Ruler Works   392

   The RULER.BAS Module   394

   Sample Program   395

Drawing Filled Polygons   396

   How Polygon Works   397

   Global Definitions   398

   Sample Program   398

Polygon Fill Modes   399

Drawing on a Printer with Polygon   400

Using Nonpixel Scaling Modes   400

Notes   400

Adjusting DrawWidth on Printers   401

Calculating the Width of a Pixel   402

Ratio of Screen to Printer Pixel Size   404

Printing Using the Screen Pixel Mode   404

How to Use APISCALE.BAS   405

How Pixel Scaling Works   405

The Code   406

Using Twip Scaling with API Calls   408

How to Use APISCALE.BAS   408

How Twip Scaling Works   409

The Code   409

Chapter 18: Toolbox for Fonts

Chapter 18: Toolbox for Fonts   **413**

Font Name Problems   413

Using Standard Names   413

Putting Helv and Tms Rmn Back into the FontName List   414

Asking for a Font by TextHeight   416

A Brief Primer on Fonts   416

How to Use FindFontSize   417

How It Works   417

The Code   418

Setting Font Names Reliably   419

The Simple Solution   420

Background Information on Fonts   420

Adding FONTNAME.BAS to Your Project   421

Using FONTNAME.BAS   423

How Font Matching Works   424

How GetMatchingFont$ Works   424

The Code   426

Chapter 19: Toolbox: Miscellaneous   433

Multimedia Sound   433

How to Use sndPlaySound   433

The Definitions   435

Running DOS Programs   435

The Basics of Shell   435

Running Special DOS Commands   436

Running DOS Programs in the Background   436

Waiting Until a DOS Program Finishes   439

Building Very Large Programs   439

A Quick Introduction to Memory   440

Error Messages   440

Visual Basic's Limits   441

Limits in the Debug Version of Windows   443

The Valuable System Resources   443

Other Limited Resources   446

Checking the DOS and Windows Versions   446

How It Works   447

The Code   448

Finding a Program's Directory   449

How to Use It   450

The Code   450

Sample Program   451

Notes   452

How It Works   452

Appendix A: Installing Visual Basic and the Companion-Disk Files   455

Installing Visual Basic   455

Installing the Companion-Disk Files   459

Appendix B: Using the Commercial Software on the Companion Disk 461

Where to Put the VBX Files 462

Crescent Software Files 463

MicroHelp Files 465

Sheridan Files 466

Index 469

Introduction

Have you ever wanted to create your own programs but found it hard to learn how? Or have you wanted to write Windows programs but found Windows to be difficult to program? Visual Basic has changed all that.

For the first time, writing programs and creating screens is actually fun and simple. After reading this book, you'll be able to create programs in hours that would take an experienced, professional programmer days or weeks to write in any other computer language. So even if you're only interested in writing programs for yourself, Visual Basic is the way to do it. And you won't need a degree in computer science or any background in programming.

In this book I'll teach you how to program in Visual Basic, which other Visual Basic books also do. But I'll cover material you won't find in other books: I'll teach you how to design and *build* real programs, using an address book program as a real-world example. Unlike the authors of most Visual Basic books, I actually have a number of years' experience as a software developer: I designed and wrote the best-selling Norton Commander (the parent of Norton Desktop for DOS), sold by Symantec.

What I'd like to do in this introduction is to give you an overview of this book and a better idea of why I think this book is for you.

Can You Write Real Programs in Visual Basic?

You may have been wondering if you can write real programs in Visual Basic. Absolutely! I've already seen a number of real programs written in Visual Basic, and many corporations are investing heavily in using Visual Basic to write in-house applications. Why? Because they can write their programs in far less time and less expensively using Visual Basic.

I've been a professional programmer since 1985, and I've never been able to write programs as quickly as I can now that I'm using Visual Basic. Furthermore, as you'll see in this book, you can do almost anything in Visual Basic that you can do with any other language.

☞ **Please send me the items checked below:**

System requirements: 386SX or better, CD-ROM Drive, MS-DOS 5.0 or higher with 2MB of memory, Windows™ Version 3.0 MME or higher with 4MB of memory, Mouse. Music and Audio Support : Sound card with DAC. Supports standard sound cards.

☐ *King's Quest VI* CD – Originally $79.95 **Now $39.95** 8330210200		$ _____
☐ *King's Quest V* CD – Originally $69.95 **Now $39.95** 8330610200		$ _____
☐ *Inca* CD – Originally $69.95 **Now $39.95** 8350210200		$ _____
☐ *King's Quest VI* Hint Book 0030300209 Reg. $9.95 - only $4.95		$ _____
☐ *King's Quest V* Hint Book 0030700209 Reg. $9.95 - only $4.95		$ _____
☐ *Inca* Hint Book 005130209 Reg. $9.95 - only $4.95		$ _____

SALES TAX: CA -7.75%; IL, TX- 6.25%; MN, PA - 6%; MA - 6%; WA - 6% $ _____

S&H: Single game add $4.00 U.S. or $5.00 Canada. Add $2.00 for each additional game ordered. No S&H on hint book(s) when ordered with game order. Add $1.50 for hint book(s) if ordered separately.(Canadian customers are responsible for GST tax and any special Poste fees. DO NOT INCLUDE WITH PAYMENT TO SIERRA.) $ _____

TOTAL $ _____

Offer expires 5/31/94

Who Is This Book For?

Regardless of your level (from beginner to more experienced programmer), there are sections in this book you'll find useful.

If You Are a Beginner

The first two parts of this book are devoted entirely to those who have never written a program before, or who don't know the Basic language. I use a gentle, visual, and interactive approach to teaching Basic. You'll start out in the first chapter with very simple, one-line Basic programs. And you'll learn each new concept through real examples that you can run and experiment with. I won't overload you with details, so you'll be able to learn just a few concepts at a time.

In Part II you'll build an address book program that makes it easy to keep your address book up-to-date. This program is both useful for learning programming and useful in its own right.

Once you've finished reading the first two parts of this book, you'll be ready to write your own programs. You'll find the rest of this book a valuable resource and reference, and you can go back and read individual chapters to answer specific questions you have.

If You Are a Programmer New to Basic

If you're already a programmer, but you're new to Basic and Visual Basic, you'll probably want to skim the first few chapters. You'll also find the later chapters in the book an invaluable resource of code and ideas.

If You Are a Basic Programmer New to Visual Basic

If you're already a Basic programmer, but you've never worked with Visual Basic, you can skim the first few chapters. You'll probably discover that Visual Basic programming is very different from writing programs in other versions of Basic (such as Quick Basic). This is because Visual Basic is, well, visual: You draw the interface, then write code to bring the interface to life. Many Quick Basic programmers, on the other hand, are used to building the interface later in the project rather than at the start. I think you'll find the visual approach to be quite useful once you get the hang of it. You'll also find the rest of the book invaluable as a reference and as a source for code and algorithms to handle Windows-specific tasks.

If You Are an Advanced Programmer

Part III and the companion disk are useful to *all* programmers. Anyone who wants to learn programming will find their job easier if they have a number of "components" they can use and modify for their needs. Part III has a number of hints, techniques, and advanced information, as well as an entire library of code that you can use in your own programs. All this code is included on the disk at the back of this book.

The disk also contains a number of fully functional custom controls and functions you can use in your own programs. These are commercial quality and were provided by three companies as samples of their Visual Basic add-on products: Crescent Software, MicroHelp, and Sheridan Software Systems (more on these libraries later).

What's in This Book?

As I mentioned before, this book has a lot of material that you'll find useful even after you've finished reading. This is both a beginner's first book *and* a collection of tools for *all* Visual Basic programmers. You'll find a bunch of free, fully functional commercial software on the companion disk, which makes it, by itself, worth the price of this book.

Parts I–II: Tutorial for Beginners

If you've never programmed before, this is the book for you. I start out with a slow, gradual pace to teaching you about programming, the Basic language, and Visual Basic. Each chapter contains as few new concepts as possible so you're not overwhelmed. Successive chapters build on the material you learned in previous chapters, so you'll find yourself working with more and more advanced material, perhaps without even realizing just how much you've learned.

You'll also learn how to go about writing a program. I'll show you how to develop your idea and how to start your project once you have the idea. You build programs, one step at a time, by starting with simple pieces and gradually adding more and more to your program. This technique, called *stepwise refinement,* is the technique most professional programmers use when they write programs, so you'll be learning the techniques of the pros.

Part III: The Toolbox

Once you've learned how to write programs in Visual Basic, you'll find the material in Part III very useful. You'll find a number of tools and techniques you can use directly in your own programs or modify for your needs. Using the tools in this book is a lot easier than figuring out how to do these things yourself.

I've tried to provide techniques and code that solve real-world problems. As a commercial software developer, I have a good understanding of what kinds of problems you'll run into using Visual Basic, and I've tried to include as many solutions and techniques to address these problems as I could. I think you'll find the reference part of this book worth the price, all by itself.

What's on the Disk?

The disk at the back of this book contains code and tools that you'll be able to use in your own programs. Here are some of the things you'll find:

Examples. You'll find code for the examples in this book.

Code Libraries. You'll find code libraries from Part III of this book, so you don't have to type in any of the code.

Custom Controls. There are a number of custom controls (which you'll learn about later in the book) that you can use in your own programs. These custom controls are fully functional samples from commercial software libraries (provided by Crescent, MicroHelp, and Sheridan) and by themselves are worth the price of this book. You're free to use this software in any programs you create.

Full Documentation. Each company provided documentation for its software. This documentation was too long to fit into this book, so I've included these files on the disk as Windows Write files that you can print out.

Part one

Introduction to Visual Basic

In this part you'll learn basic programming concepts so that you can move on to building useful programs with Visual Basic. In the first two chapters you'll learn what programming is and how to use arithmetic functions, variables, values, and types. In Chapter 3, you'll learn how to draw lines on the screen with Visual Basic. In Chapter 4, you'll build your first Visual Basic Program, Sketch, and in Chapter 5 you'll learn how to add a menu bar to it. In Chapter 6, you'll learn how to use array variables. Finally, in Chapter 7, you'll put all your basic knowledge together to create a clock icon.

Chapter 1

Featuring

Introducing Visual Basic

Using the Immediate Window

Learning Simple Basic Commands:
Beep, End, and Print

The Basics of Command Syntax

Computer Arithmetic and
Precedence

Starting with Basic

In this chapter we're going to get off to a quick start. After I cover some introductory material to make sure we're all starting in the same place, we'll get straight to the business of learning about programming.

Your first journey into programming will be relatively easy, and you won't need to learn a lot before you actually write some very short Basic programs. Each program will be one line long, and you'll be able to *run* these programs directly from within Visual Basic, so you'll see what they do. You'll be pleasantly surprised at how much fun learning Basic can be.

First, though, we need to cover a few preliminaries.

Starting Visual Basic

The first thing you'll want to do is make sure you've installed Visual Basic. If you haven't already done so and you want a little more help than you'll find in Microsoft's manual, you can find further details in the Appendix. Return here when you're finished with it.

At this point you should have a program group called Microsoft Visual Basic, which is created by the Setup program. This program group should look something like the one in Figure 1.1 when you open it.

(Notice the small clock icon at the lower left? This is a small program that displays the current time. It's like the CLOCK.EXE program that's part of Windows, but it looks a lot nicer and has a second hand. Not only that, it's written completely in Visual Basic, and you'll find the entire program later in this book! You'll also find an enhanced version on the disk included with this book.)

Figure 1.1:

After installing Visual Basic, you should have a program group that has the Visual Basic icon in it.

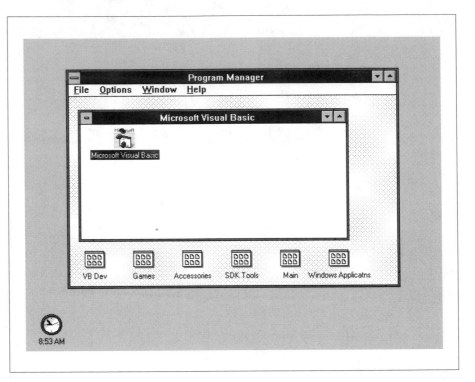

Double-click on the Microsoft Visual Basic icon to start Visual Basic. You'll then see a screen like the one shown in Figure 1.2, which you'll become quite familiar with in a few chapters.

Exiting Visual Basic

If you've used other Windows programs, you probably already know how to exit from Visual Basic. But in case you're new to Windows, here's how: Pull down the File menu (press Atl+F) and select the Exit item (X).

What Is Programming?

In the next few chapters, you'll learn that programming in Visual Basic consists of writing instructions that tell Visual Basic what steps you want it to perform. Programmers tend to use several names to refer to such instructions;

Figure 1.2:

You should see a screen like this one when you first start Visual Basic. (The Program Manager's Minimize on Use option in the Options menu was used to get its windows out of the way after starting Visual Basic.)

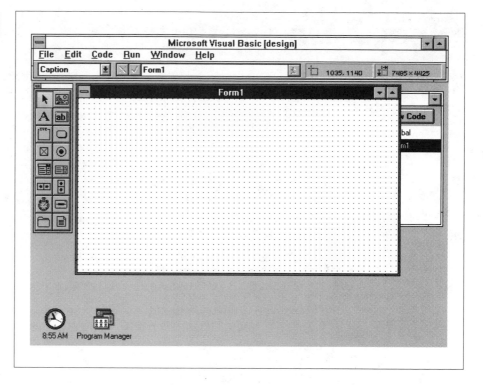

statements, instructions, commands, and *code* are the most common. In this chapter I'll usually refer to them as *commands.*

You'll also see the term *programming language.* There are a number of programming languages, including Basic, C, Pascal, and Assembly Language, that you can use to write programs. In a sense, these languages are like different spoken languages because each one has its own grammar and set of words. And different languages have their strengths and weaknesses. Many professional programmers (including the ones at Microsoft) write their programs using the C language because of its power and flexibility. C, however, tends to be difficult to learn, and writing Windows programs in C takes a lot of work. Of all the languages I've ever worked with, Visual Basic is the easiest to learn and use.

In this chapter you'll learn about three commands in the Basic language, using something called the Immediate window in Visual Basic. This window lets you enter commands and run them right away. *Running* a command simply means that you tell Visual Basic to actually *do* the steps you've asked it to follow.

Using the Immediate Window

When you started Visual Basic, you probably noticed that Visual Basic uses a number of windows—four, to be exact. We're going to ignore all these windows for now because we'll be working entirely within a fifth window for the rest of this chapter. (We'll start to use the other windows in Chapter 3, where you'll learn how to draw lines in the large window called Form1.)

The fifth window is called the *Immediate window,* which you'll use to write one-line programs. It's called the Immediate window because it allows you to type in *commands* (parts of a program) that Visual Basic will run immediately. If this doesn't make sense, don't worry; it will become quite clear after a couple of examples.

Showing the Immediate Window

Before you can work with the examples, though, you have to find out how to open the Immediate window. This, as it turns out, is quite simple. Here are the steps:

1. Press F5, or pull down the Run menu and select Start. This tells Visual Basic to switch from *design mode,* which you'll use later to design programs, to *run mode,* which you use to actually run programs.

2. Press Ctrl+Break, or pull down the Run menu and select Break. This brings the Immediate window to the front and makes it the active window.

You should now see an Immediate window like that shown in Figure 1.3.

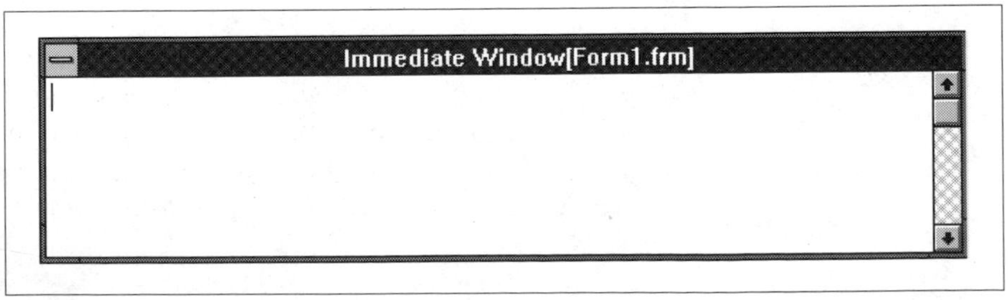

Figure 1.3:

The Immediate window. The blinking insertion point in the upper-left corner shows where text will appear as you type.

Immediate Window[Form1.frm]

Key Concept: The Immediate Window

The Immediate window is a great way to test new commands because you can type a command and immediately see the result. Since you'll be using it often, here are the steps for showing the Immediate window:

1. Press F5, or select the Start item from the Run menu.

2. Press Ctrl+Break, or select the Break item from the Run menu.

Typing in the Immediate Window

The Immediate window is very much like a text editor because characters appear as you type, and you can use the mouse to select and edit what you've typed. But the Immediate window differs from a text editor in one very important way: When you press the Enter key, the Immediate window does more than just move the insertion point to the next line—it also tries to *run* what you've typed.

To understand this more clearly, you'll enter a very simple Basic command, called Beep, that emits a sound from your computer. Try entering this command now. Simply type **Beep** and press the Enter key (see Figure 1.4). The insertion point moves to the next line and your computer makes a sound.

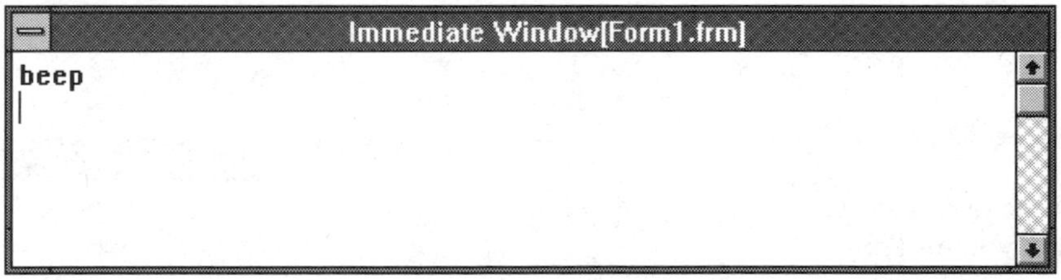

Figure 1.4:

The Immediate window after entering the Beep command, which tells Visual Basic to generate a beep sound.

```
Immediate Window[Form1.frm]
beep
|
```

The first time I entered a command like this (which was a number of years ago), I remember being quite excited. There's something very exciting about typing a word on your computer and having it respond with an action. Programming, once you get the hang of it, can be very addicting.

Reference: Beep Command

The Beep command tells Visual Basic to emit a sound from its speaker.

Since you'll be using the Immediate window rather heavily to test out new commands, let's spend a few minutes exploring some other aspects of this window. First, press the Backspace key. This causes the insertion point to move back to the previous line. If you press Backspace again, you'll delete the letter *p* at the end of *Beep*. Type *p* again, then press Enter. Visual Basic beeps again.

OK, now let's explore even further. Click the left mouse button between the two *e*'s so the insertion point looks like this:

be|ep

Then press the Enter key. Notice that instead of moving *ep* to the next line as you might expect, Visual Basic again emits a beep. In other words, pressing Enter in the Immediate window tells Visual Basic to run the command on the line that contains the insertion point.

Let's explore one final aspect of the Immediate window before we move on. You can also edit previous commands. Let's say you made a mistake when typing in the Beep command and typed *Beeo* instead of *Beep*. When you press the Enter key, Visual Basic displays an alert box to let you know that you made a mistake, as shown in Figure 1.5. At this point, the message probably seems mysterious. As it turns out, it actually isn't all that mysterious. In essence, it means that Visual Basic couldn't find a command with the name you typed.

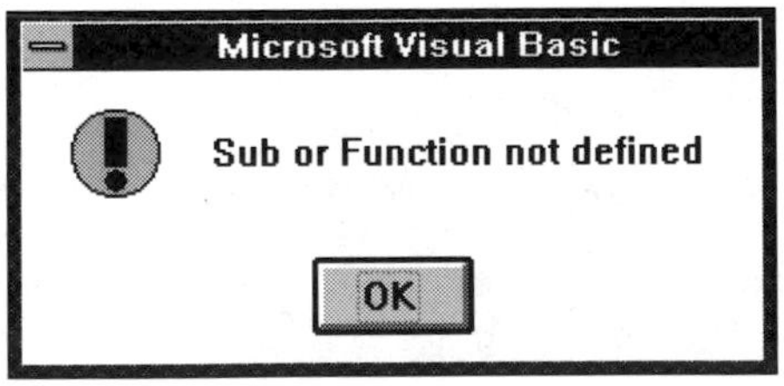

Figure 1.5:

You'll see this alert box if you mistype a command, such as typing *Beeo* instead of *Beep*. Basically, it means "huh?"

You can press Enter to dismiss this alert box. Then you can edit what you typed, either with the mouse or with the cursor keys. When you're finished making corrections, press Enter to run the corrected command.

Leaving Run Mode

The next command you'll learn about is called the End command, which tells Visual Basic to stop running a program. In other words, End tells Visual Basic to switch back from run mode (which you're in whenever you can see the Immediate window) to design mode.

Reference: End Command

The End command tells Visual Basic that you're finished running your program. Visual Basic returns to design mode when it executes this command.

Try entering this command now. Type **End** in the Immediate window, and press the Enter key. You'll notice that the window disappeared from the screen and Visual Basic is now back in design mode. By the way, you can tell which mode you're in by looking at the top of the screen. When you're in design mode, the top line on the screen should read

Microsoft Visual Basic [design]

The word in square brackets, [design] in this case, indicates which mode is currently active. If you enter run mode again (press F5), you'll notice that the mode changes to [run]; when you press Ctrl+Break to show the Immediate window, it switches to [break]. I'll discuss these three modes when you graduate from using just the Immediate window.

You can also use the pull-down menus rather than the End command to exit from programs: Pull down the Run menu and select the End item.

You've now learned how to use two simple Basic commands, Beep and End. You've learned just about everything there is to know about them. In the next section, I'll discuss a more interesting command that can do a number of things.

Visual Basic's Modes

Visual Basic has three modes, and during the course of reading this book, you'll work with all three. You can tell which mode is currently active by looking at the word in square brackets at the top of the screen: Microsoft Visual Basic [design].

[design]	Appears while you're designing programs
[run]	Appears while Visual Basic runs the current program
[break]	Appears while the program is stopped, which allows you to use the Immediate window

You'll use it quite a bit in your explorations of the Basic language, as well as in programs that you write.

The Print Command

In this section you'll learn about the Print command, which you'll use to explore how Basic handles arithmetic.

Be sure the Immediate window is visible, because you're going to use this window to learn about the Print command. The first thing we'll do is have Print display a number. If you type **Print 10**, you'll see the following:

```
print 10
 10
 |
```

Notice that 10 appears after you press Enter, and then the insertion point moves down another line.

Now let's try something a little more involved: Let's add two numbers together. Type **Print 11+23**. Notice that Print did the arithmetic and just "printed" the answer:

```
print 11+23
 34
 |
```

How Print Got Its Name

The name Print is a little misleading. Most people think of printing as the act of sending output from a computer to a printer. The Print command, on the other hand, sends it to the screen. So why is it called Print and not Display? The reasons are entirely historical.

The Basic language was originally created by two professors, John G. Kemeny and Thomas E. Kurtz, at Dartmouth College between 1963 and 1964. At that time people worked with large, mainframe computers rather than personal computers. These computers filled large, air-conditioned rooms with very expensive equipment. To communicate with such computers, you used a teletype rather than a CRT screen. So whenever a program sent output to the user, it was actually printed on a piece of paper, rather than displayed on a screen. And this is why Kemeny and Kurtz chose the name Print rather than Display for this command.

The name Basic is an acronym, which stands for Beginner's All-purpose Symbolic Instruction Code, and most of the time it is written in all uppercase letters: BASIC. In the case of Visual Basic, however, Microsoft chose to change the spelling to mixed case.

The Making of a Basic Command

So far you've been working with very simple Basic commands. Beep and End are the simplest commands you can type: They're only one word long. In a sense, these commands are like one-word sentences in the English language, like "Run!"

But one-word sentences don't convey much meaning; to communicate effectively with your computer, you need to build longer sentences. For longer sentences, however, we need rules that tell us how to combine words. For spoken languages, these rules make up what is called grammar. For programming languages, on the other hand, they make up what is called *syntax* (computer scientists rather than linguists chose the word *syntax*), and they describe how to combine various elements to form a command.

Arguments and Delimiters

Whenever you have more than one argument, you'll need to separate the arguments somehow so Visual Basic will know where one argument ends and the next begins.

Visual Basic has definite rules on what characters you can use to separate arguments. In the Print example, a space was used, but you can also use a comma or a semicolon in a Print command. These characters, which you use to separate arguments, have a special name: *delimiters*. They're called this because they delimit, or set the boundaries, between two arguments next to each other.

Here is a list of the delimiters you can use in the Print command (other commands use other delimiters):

Delimiter	What It Does in Print
;	Displays one value after the other, with no gap between them. Print always puts a space in front of positive numbers and a minus sign (without a space) in front of negative numbers.
space	Same as a semicolon. Actually, Visual Basic converts a space internally to a semicolon.
,	Moves to the next tap stop before displaying the next value.

Any command you write must have at least one word, which is called the *keyword*. Keywords are the names given to commands, such as Beep, End, and Print (you'll learn other keywords as well).

Commands can also include additional information, such as the equations you asked Print to calculate and display. These equations are known as *arguments*. The syntax rules, then, tell us how to combine keywords and arguments. For Print, there is a syntax rule that says the keyword must appear first, followed by arguments. This is correct:

print 10+2

This is incorrect:

10+2 print

There is also a syntax rule that says you can display the results of several equations by using one Print command. You do this by typing a space between each of the arguments (equations):

print 10+2 3
  12 3
  |

You can also place a comma between the 10+2 and the 3 to tell Print to move over to the next tab stop after it displays the first result:

print 10+2, 3
  12   3
  |

There is one major difference between English grammar and Basic syntax: Unlike English, the Basic programming language is very precise. So a given Basic command has one, and only one, meaning. (A single English sentence

Why We Don't Program in English

Have you ever wondered why you have to learn a programming language like Basic rather than write your programs in English? It's because computers are very dumb, and they can't understand the subtleties of English. Computers are like idiot savants: They can perform amazing feats of computation, but they have no idea what they're doing or what it means.

The English language is ambiguous, at best, and some sentences have a number of meanings. And even we, as humans, don't always understand a sentence correctly. So computer scientists created programming languages, like Basic, in which each "sentence" you write has one, and only one, meaning. Of course, you might not understand Basic's rules and therefore write the wrong sentence, but that's another issue altogether.

Language Syntax

print [*expression* [{**;**|**,**| }*expression*] ...]

Here is a chart that shows you what the different parts of a syntax description mean:

command	Words in bold are words that you type as you see them. These are the *keywords* that exist in the language, such as Print.
expression	Italic type indicates additional information you need to supply to the command. For example, you might substitute 3+4 for *expression* in the Print command.
[*something*]	Anything you see in square brackets is optional. You don't type the brackets—they indicate only that what appears inside the brackets is optional.
{*a* | *b*}	The braces indicate that you must choose from one of the options separated by the vertical bar, |. You must choose one, and only one, of these options. In this example, you must choose either *a* or *b*. In the Print command, the braces indicate that you must choose a semicolon, a comma, or a space.
...	An ellipsis indicates that you can repeat an element. In the Print command, this means you can combine any number of expressions in one Print command.

can have many meanings, which allows us to write poetry but would make it difficult for the computer to figure out what we want.) Another difference is that each Basic command has its own syntax rules, whereas English tends to have general rules for the entire language rather than for specific words.

Let's use the Print command again to make this clear. The syntax for the Print command looks like this:

print *expression* [{;|,| } *expression*] ...

What this means (I'll show you how to read it in a minute) is that you can display the results of one or more equations, which are called *expressions* in computer-science jargon. You separate expressions, when you have more than one, with a semicolon, a comma, or a space. We saw how this worked in the last two examples.

Now let's take a look at how to read this syntax. First, you'll notice that the Print command appears in bold letters. Anything you see in bold letters, such as **print**, is known as a keyword, which is a command in the Basic language. You type it in as you see it.

Words that appear in italics, such as *expression,* are placeholders for other pieces of information. In this case, you supply an expression, which can be a number, an equation, or, and we haven't covered this yet, a string of characters that you want Print to display.

You'll notice that syntax descriptions often include some special characters. The square brackets, [and], for example, indicate parts that are optional. So the second expression here is optional. The braces, { and }, and vertical bars, |, are used to show choices. When you see something like {;|,| }, it means you must choose one of the options separated by the vertical bars. So in the {;|,| } notation, your options are a semicolon, a comma, or a space. In other words, you must use one of these three characters between expressions in the Print command. And finally, the ellipsis, ..., indicates that you can repeat this process; in other words, you can have one, two, three, or more expressions in one Print command.

What's the difference between an argument and an expression? The answer is subtle. An expression is a value or an equation by itself. In other words, 10 + 2 and 3 are both expressions. An argument, on the other hand, is a value that you use in a command to supply information to that command (see Figure 1.6). This means that an expression used in a Print command is also an argument to the Print command. It's a little confusing now, but you'll get the hang of it after a few more chapters.

Figure 1.6:

An example of an expression, showing the parts of a Basic command

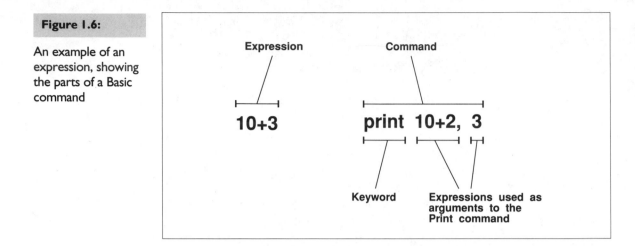

Reference: Print Command

The Print command displays numbers and strings of characters (more on this later) on the screen. In this chapter we're using Print only within the Immediate window, but we'll use it in other windows later in the book.

Print can display multiple *expressions*. If you have more than one expression, separate them with spaces, semicolons, or commas (commas tell Print to move to the next column before printing the next expression; spaces or semicolons tell Print not to move before printing the next expression).

print
Without any parameters, Print displays a blank line.

print *expression*
Displays the expression on the screen.

print *expression* [{;|,| }*expression*] ...
You can display more than one expression with a single Print command by separating each expression from the previous one with a semicolon, a space, or a comma.

Doing Arithmetic

You've probably already guessed that in addition to adding numbers, you can subtract, multiply, and divide them. Table 1.1 shows a list of arithmetic *operators,* which are the symbols, like +, that you use between numbers.

Table 1.1:

Visual Basic's Arithmetic Operators

Symbol	Meaning	Example	Result
+	Addition	10+3	13
−	Subtraction	10−3	7
*	Multiplication	10*3	30
/	Division	10/3	3.333333
\	Integer Division	10\3	3
^	Exponentiation	10^3	1000
Mod	Remainder (modulo)	10 mod 3	1

You can also put a minus sign in front of a number to type a negative number, for example, −23.

There are probably a few operators in Table 1.1 that are either new to you or a little different from what you're used to working with. Arithmetic is very important in programs, as you'll see as you learn to write programs. Let's spend a few minutes going through each of these operators so you understand what they do and how to use them.

The Calculator Functions

Most simple electronic calculators provide only four functions: addition, subtraction, multiplication, and division—so you're certainly used to the +, −, *, and / symbols. The only difference from what you might be used to is the multiplication symbol. Some people (usually scientific types) use one of the following forms to indicate multiplication:

2 × 3

2 · 3

2 3

None of these forms work in Basic—you must use the form 2 * 3. And the same thing applies for division: You can't use 2 ÷ 3—you must type 2 / 3.

Quotient and Remainder

Two of the operators, \ and Mod, provide functions that you may not have thought about since grade school, so I'll review them very quickly. When you first learned division, you learned that 7 / 3 = 2 with a remainder of 1. In other words, you can divide 3 into 7 evenly only two times, with one left over. Of course, now that you've gotten past grade school you know that 7 / 3 = 2.33333..., which is exactly the result Print displays:

print 7/3
2.333333
|

But what if you want to get only the whole part of this division? Or what if you want only the remainder? Both these operations are things you'll want to do from time to time when you're writing a program, and Basic has two operators designed to return exactly these two parts.

The first operator, \, is called the *integer division* operator. What this means is that the result returned will always be a whole number (like 1, 2, 3, ...) rather than a fractional or mixed number (like 2.3). In computer jargon, such whole numbers are called *integers*. In other words, \ produces an integer that is the whole part of the division:

print 7 \ 3
2
|

(By the way, you can put spaces between the numbers and operators, as I've done in this example. Sometimes such spaces make it easier to read a complex equation.)

Another operator, called Mod, calculates only the remainder of a division. For example, if you want to display the remainder of 7 / 3, you type

print 7 mod 3
I

|

That's all there is to it. The Mod operator gets its name from the mathematical operation called *modulo,* which calculates the remainder of a division.

Now, just for the fun of it, I'm going to show you something a little ahead of time: Print can display more than one result at a time, and it can also show strings of characters enclosed by double-quote characters:

print 7 \ 3 "remainder" 7 mod 3
2 remainder I

|

As you can see, the command neatly displays the result of dividing 3 into 7, just as you wrote it when you were in grade school.

I've now discussed all the operators in Table 1.1 except for the exponential operator. Let's look at it next.

Exponentiation

Exponentiation is an operator you may not use very often, if ever. But programmers sometimes use it, so a few words are in order so you'll recognize it when you're reading someone else's program. You probably learned about the exponentiation operator in algebra when you were learning about powers, and you probably saw something like this:

$$10^2$$

This means ten to the second power, or 10 * 10. The way we write this in Basic is 10^2, as you can see in this example:

print I0^2
I00

|

Now that you've learned all the arithmetic operators, there are actually two more issues we should cover, which aren't very interesting but you'll need to know: operator precedence and parentheses.

Complex Equations

The next concept that we're going to look at will probably take a little while to get used to, but it's a very important subject because almost all programs deal with equations of one form or another (although your equations could be as simple as adding numbers). You can use several operators in a simple expression to create a complex equation.

If you use more than one operator in a single equation, it's not always obvious how Basic will handle the calculation. For example, if you have an equation with both addition and multiplication, such as 3 + 4 * 5, you know from algebra class that you have to multiply (4 * 5 = 20) before you can add (3 + 20 = 23):

```
print 3 + 4 * 5
 23
 |
```

What happens, however, when you mix the \ integer division operator with, for example, multiplication?

Most programming languages use a concept known as *precedence* to determine which operators are more important. Operators with higher precedence, such as multiplication in the example above, are calculated before operators with lower precedence, like addition. Table 1.2 shows all the arithmetic operators from Table 1.1, grouped by precedence. The most important (highest precedence) operators are at the top of the table.

These rules take a little while to get used to, and you can often make a mistake. For example, you might expect the integer division operator \ to be on equal footing with normal division, and expect the result of 3 \ 2 * 2 to be 2. But as you can see from Table 1.2, this isn't the case. In fact, multiplication has the same precedence as regular division, but a higher precedence than integer division. So Basic calculates 2 * 2 before doing the integer division.

I made this mistake once and it took me a while to find my error. If you're at all in doubt about what order Basic will use in such a calculation, use

	Operator	Meaning
Table 1.2:	∧	Exponentiation (to the power of)
	−	Minus (negative) sign
Operator Precedence	*, /	Multiplication, division
	\	Integer division
	Mod	Remainder
	+, −	Addition, subtraction

Rules:

Highest precedence first: Basic first calculates operators that appear higher in this table (such as 4 * 5 in 3 + 4 * 5).

Left to right: If two operators are at the same level (such as * and /), Basic starts with the leftmost operator, then moves to the right (such as calculating 2 + 3 first in 2 + 3 + 4).

Parentheses: You can override these rules using parentheses, such as (3 + 4) * 5 to force Basic to calculate 3 + 4, and then multiply by 5.

parentheses to tell Basic how to calculate the result. So instead of writing 3 \ 2 * 2, write (3 \ 2) * 2.

If you have a really complex equation, you might want to use more than one set of parentheses, like this: 1 / ((3 + 4) * (2 + 5)), which is the same as

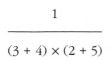

$$\frac{1}{(3 + 4) \times (2 + 5)}$$

As you can see, a lot of parentheses can become a bit complicated, and you'll want to make sure you put them in the right place.

One final note before I close this chapter. You might have noticed in Table 1.2 that there are two − signs: one for subtraction and one for a negative sign. The negative sign is a little different from all the other operators, which

Matching Parentheses

As you've seen, some equations can have a lot of parentheses in them. How can you make sure you have the correct number of left and right parentheses?

The pros use a method called counting parentheses. You go through the equation counting parentheses. But you count in a very special way. Each time you see a left parenthesis, (, you count up. And each time you see a right parenthesis,), you count down. If you start with 1 for the first left parenthesis, you should have a count of zero at the end of the equation. If you don't, you're missing a parenthesis. If your final number is 1, you need another right parenthesis. And if your final number is −1, you need another left parenthesis.

Let's look at an example that is incorrect. If you count parentheses in the following equation, you won't end with a count of zero:

$$1 / ((3 + 4) * (2 + 5)$$

Here is what you'll end up with when you count this equation: 1, 2, 1, 2, 1. The final 1 means you're missing a right parenthesis.

work with two expressions, such as 3 + 4. The negative sign, on the other hand, modifies just one expression: −(2 + 3) returns the result −5. You can also write something like 3 + −2, which means 3 + (−2) and equals 1.

Related Tools

Because Visual Basic is such a rich language, I won't be covering every aspect of Visual Basic in this book. But to help you explore Visual Basic on your own, you'll find a section called Related Tools at the end of each chapter. In this section you'll find a list of commands and features related to the ones you learned about in the chapter. You might find some of these commands of interest, and you can explore them on your own.

I should warn you, however, that sometimes (and often near the beginning) these related tools will use knowledge you don't have yet. So if you don't understand this section now, you will later, after you've read more of the book.

Tab Stops In this chapter you briefly used the comma to display two numbers in different columns. You can also use the Tab function for more control over which column Visual Basic moves to between items you want to display on a line. For example, "print 1 tab(15) 2 tab(30) 3" displays a 2 in column 15 and a 3 in column 30, which produces a display very much like "print 1,2,3."

Format$ Command You'll want to use this command if you want more control over how your numbers appear than you get with the Print command. For example, if you're displaying money information, you might want to display the number 2.3 as $2.30 (with a dollar sign and two decimal places). Format$ will do that for you, and much more. Right now Format$ may seem like an advanced command, but by Chapter 7, where you'll use Format$ to display time information, you'll know enough to be able to use it yourself.

Exp—e to the x Power This is a rather advanced function related to exponentiation. Many people working in the sciences often need to calculate powers of the constant e (which is related to natural logarithms). You can calculate e^2 by writing Exp(2). There are many other such functions you might also find useful, such as Log and Sqr (square root).

Summary

We've covered a lot of introductory material in this chapter, and you've actually learned three Basic commands. Here is a summary of what you've learned so far:

Starting Visual Basic. You learned how to start and exit Visual Basic.

Immediate Window. The Immediate window is a window you'll use quite heavily in the next few chapters to learn about new Basic commands. Press F5 to enter run mode; then press Ctrl+Break to show the Immediate window and make it active.

The Beep and End Commands. These two commands are very simple. Beep emits a sound from your computer; End tells Visual Basic to exit run mode and return to design mode.

Arithmetic and the Print Command. We spent much of the chapter using the Print command to learn about Basic's arithmetic operators, and we also took a quick look at how you can send text strings to your screen.

Precedence. You learned about the precedence of operators, which determines what order Basic will calculate expressions when you have a complex equation.

In the next chapter you'll learn about *variables,* which let you give names to numbers and other pieces of information.

Chapter 2

Featuring

What Variables Are

Values and Types

Introduction to Strings and String Operators

Learning about Variables and Values

In this chapter I'm going to talk about some things at the heart of all but the simplest of programs. They're called *variables* and *values*. Variables, as you'll see shortly, are places that store numbers and strings of characters. These numbers and strings are values.

You may wonder why you have to learn about variables and values. Why can't you just graduate to building windows and dialog boxes? Well, nearly every program you write, no matter how small, will have to use variables and values. Programs aren't very useful if they don't do anything, and programs you build in Visual Basic won't be able to do anything unless you use variables and values. That's why you have to learn about them before you can move on to the fun stuff.

You'll also learn much more about strings of characters and the operators that you can use to work with strings.

What Are Variables?

Variables are places where you can store numbers and strings, which you'll do often in programs to keep track of intermediate results. The easiest way to demonstrate this idea is with an example.

Make sure you have Visual Basic running and the Immediate window is visible and active (press F5 to enter run mode, followed by Ctrl+Break). Then, type the following line in the Immediate window and press Enter:

```
n=2
|
```

What does this mean, and what did it do?

The equal sign is a new command called the *assignment operator,* which saves a value in part of your computer's memory (it's not an equation; see the sidebar later in this chapter called "Equal Is Not Equal—It's Assignment"). You'll soon see where it saves this value. But first, let's make sure this number is actually in memory.

You can use the Print command to display the value stored in a variable simply by supplying the variable's name:

```
print n
 2
|
```

As you can see, the value of 2 is still in *n*.

NOTE

In case you're wondering, I chose to use the letter *n* here because it's short for the word *number.* Programmers sometimes use a single letter, like *n,* for a name rather than spell it out. In most of this book, I'll use more descriptive names, but for now, using a single letter makes the examples a little simpler.

Notice that the *n* = 2 line is still in the Immediate window. You might be wondering what would happen if you edited this line to something like *n* = 3. Would this change the value of *n*? The answer is yes, and no. If you change this line, then press the Enter key while the insertion point is still in the line, Visual Basic *will* change the value of *n*. But if you move the cursor to another line *without pressing Enter,* Visual Basic won't change the value of *n*. Here's why.

The text you see inside the Immediate window is merely a string of characters as far as Visual Basic is concerned. It only treats this text as a command when you press the Enter key, at which point Visual Basic runs the command. So the moral of the story is this: Previous commands inside the Immediate

Reference: = Command

The = command is an assignment operator. It assigns a value to a variable:

name **=** *expression*

Assigns the value of *expression* to the variable called *name*

window are merely text until you press the Enter key. And pressing Enter only runs one command—the line that contained the insertion point when you pressed Enter.

The next thing you'll do is really interesting. Let's say you want to add 3 to the value already in *n;* in other words, you want to add 3 to 2 and put this result back into *n*. How do you do this? By writing *n = n + 3*, as you can see here:

```
n = n + 3
print n
 5
 |
```

It worked. (I added some spaces around the = sign to make this statement more readable. Basic doesn't care whether you use spaces.)

Equal Is Not Equal—It's Assignment

The equal sign in programming languages is very different from the equal sign in algebra. In algebra, *num = num + 3* is an equation with one unknown: *num*. (This particular equation doesn't have a solution.) Basic, on the other hand, treats the equal sign as a command.

Here's what happens in the Basic language. When Basic sees an equal sign, it looks on the right side of the equal sign and calculates the value of the expression it finds there (*num + 3*, which results in 5 because *num* is currently 2). Then Basic assigns this value to the variable num, which appears on the left side of the equal sign.

Because this can be a little confusing, some programming languages actually use a left-pointing arrow for assignment, like this: *num ← 2 + 3*. The Pascal language uses := rather than =, as in *num:= 2 + 3*.

Where Are Variables?

The simple answer is that variables are stored in memory. Each program in Windows has its own areas of memory that it uses and works with. Visual Basic, for example, has a number of pieces of memory that it uses for itself and the programs you write. Some of this memory is available for storing variables.

What happened when you typed *n* = 2? First Visual Basic looked through its memory for a variable named *n*. One didn't exist, so Visual Basic *created* a new variable with the name *n*. This variable only exists while you're running a program: Visual Basic "forgets" all variables whenever you leave run mode. So if you type End to exit run mode, then press F5 and Ctrl+Break again, you'll discover that *n* no longer has the value 2:

```
n=2
end
```

Then press F5 and Ctrl+Break, and type the following:

```
print n
 0
 |
```

Why did Print display a 0 rather than telling us that *n* doesn't exist anymore?

It turns out that Visual Basic defines a new variable for you automatically whenever it sees a name it hasn't seen before. So when you typed Print *n,* Visual Basic automatically defined a variable called *n*. But since you didn't assign a value to *n,* it had the value 0. All new variables are set to 0 until you assign a value to them.

NOTE

All new variables are set to 0 until you assign a value to them.

Naming Variables

The only variable name you've used so far is *n*. But you can actually use much longer, and more descriptive, variable names. The sidebar "Naming Variables" gives the rules you must follow when naming variables.

Here are some examples of names that are allowed, using these rules:

lastName	Mixed case, starting with a lowercase letter
first_Name	Underscore in the name
NumNames	Mixed case, starting with an uppercase letter
Name3	Includes a number that isn't the first character
München	Uses an international character: ü
last_Name_3	Combines several of the elements above

Here are examples of names that are not allowed:

1Name	Variables cannot have names that start with a number.
beeP	Variables cannot have the same name as a Basic keyword. Basic ignores the case of a word, so *beep, Beep,* and *BEEP* are all considered to be the same keyword.

Naming Variables

Variable names can be almost anything you want, as long as you follow these rules:

Length. Names can be up to 40 characters long.

Characters. You can use any upper- or lowercase letters, numbers, and the underscore (_) character. But the first character *must* be a letter. Letters can include international letters like ü, but not symbols such as @.

No Keywords. You can't use names like Print or Beep, or even beep, because these are keywords in the Basic language. Nor can you use any other Basic keywords as variable names. Visual Basic has many keywords, so it's best to check names that you want to use against the words listed in the *Language Reference* manual included with Visual Basic.

As you can see, you have quite a bit of freedom in choosing variable names. I'll have more to say about variable names and how to choose them later when we start writing programs. For now, though, let's work with small, simple names because the names really aren't important yet. We're more interested in the concepts of variables and values.

Values and Types

Most of the examples until now have dealt with numbers, but you did work briefly with what's known as a *string* in Chapter 1. There you wrote the following command:

print 7\3 "remainder" 7 mod 3

which generated the following output:

2 remainder 1
|

The text "remainder" is called a string because it's a *string of characters*. You must enclose strings in Basic with a pair of double-quote marks to tell Basic that the characters are a string rather than a variable name.

Reference: Strings

Strings are strings of characters that you work with in Basic. Whenever you write a string in a Basic command, you must surround all the characters with double-quote marks (one on each end):

"any string of characters"

You can use any character inside a string. However, if you want to place a double-quote character (") itself in a string, you must write it twice for each time you want it to appear in the string. For example:

print "A double-quote "" character"
A double-quote " character

What happens if you try to assign such a string to a variable called *s*?

s = "remainder"

You'll see a warning message like the one in Figure 2.1. Why doesn't Basic like this command? And what is a "type mismatch"?

Figure 2.1:

You'll see this warning message box when you try to assign a string to a numeric variable.

Figure 2.1:

You'll see this warning message box when you try to assign a string to a numeric variable.

```
┌──────────────────────────────────────────────┐
│   ┌────────────────────────────────────┐      │
│   │ ▬     Microsoft Visual Basic        │      │
│   ├────────────────────────────────────┤      │
│   │   ⊙     Type mismatch               │      │
│   │                                     │      │
│   │            ┌────────┐               │      │
│   │            │   OK   │               │      │
│   │            └────────┘               │      │
│   └────────────────────────────────────┘      │
└──────────────────────────────────────────────┘
```

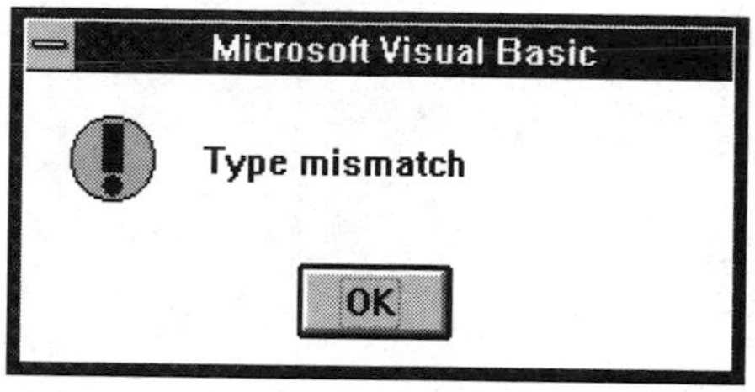

It turns out that every value has a specific type—for example, a string or a number. And variables also have types. The variables you've been working with have been numeric variables. But "remainder" is a string, rather than a number. And Basic won't let you assign a string value to a numeric variable. So what do you do?

You must tell Basic that the variable is a string rather than a numeric variable. Adding a dollar sign ($) to the end of a variable name signals Basic that the variable is a string. So if you type *s$* = "remainder" rather than *s* = "remainder", you're telling Basic that it's working with a string variable called *s$* rather than a numeric variable called *s*:

```
s$ = "remainder"
print s$
remainder
|
```

You might be wondering if you can have both a variable *s* and a variable *s$* at the same time. A curious thing happens when you switch from using a variable *s* to a variable *s$*. If you type

print s, s$

to see the value of these two variables, you'll see a warning message like the one shown in Figure 2.2. In other words, Basic permits only one variable called *s*, whether you write it as *s* or as *s$*.

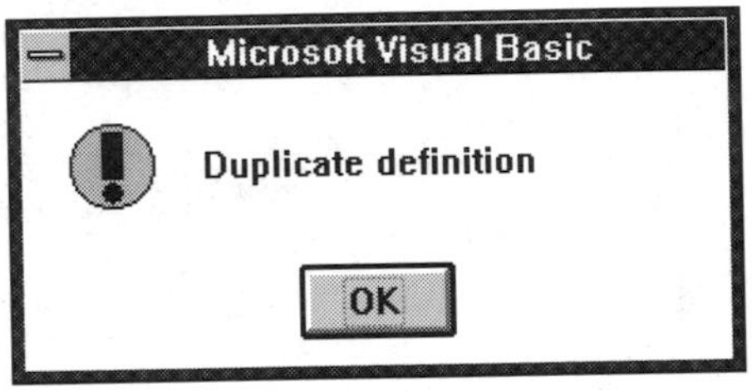

Figure 2.2:

Visual Basic doesn't allow two variables with the same name—even if they are different *types*.

You might also be wondering if a single variable can contain both a string and a number. The answer is no. Variables in Basic can only contain one value at a time, and each variable, such as *s* or *s$*, can contain only one type of value. So *s* always contains a number, and *s$* always contains a string. (Some languages, like LISP, actually do allow you to assign multiple values to a single variable, but not Basic.)

While we're on the subject of strings, there is one operator you can use on strings. The + operator *concatenates* two strings, which means it creates a new string by combining the two strings. Here's an example that shows exactly how the process works; notice the use of the different variables:

```
s1$ = "Text in"
s2$ = " two parts."
s$ = s1$ + s2$
```

Reference: String Concatenation with +

When placed between two strings, the + sign creates a third string that contains both the other strings:

```
sCombined$ = s1$ + s2$
```

This command creates a string *sCombined$* that contains *s1$* followed by *s2$*.

```
print s$
Text in two parts.
|
```

This example creates two string variables, *s1$* and *s2$,* and assigns part of a sentence to each variable. The third string, *s$,* is a combination of *s1$* and *s2$* using the + operator. String concatenation is really quite easy and very useful. (Note that I put a space before "two" in *s2$* to prevent "in" and "two" from being combined as "intwo.")

More about Types and Numbers

You've now seen two different types of variables and values: numbers and strings. In fact, there are actually five different types of numbers. How's that? Calculators get by with just one type of number, so why do computers need five?

Floating-Point Numbers

You'll often read and hear about *floating-point* numbers in connection with computers. So let's take a couple of minutes to learn exactly what they are and why they're called floating-point numbers.

Any number with something after the decimal point is called a floating-point number. Thus, both 1.1 and 3.14159 are floating-point numbers.

The reason it's called a *floating*-point number is a little more subtle. All floating-point numbers are represented inside your computer as whole numbers. Another piece of information tells your computer where the decimal point should be in a number. Because the decimal point can move left or right, depending on the actual number (for example, 123.4, 12.34, and 1.234), it can *float* around in the number.

The digits in the number make up what is known as the *mantissa* (you don't need to remember this). The information on the location of the decimal point is known as the *exponent.* For example, the number 12.34 has a mantissa of 1234 and an exponent of −2, which means the decimal point has to be moved two places to the left.

This question is a little hard to answer because it has a lot to do with the microprocessor inside your computer. For the most part, computers have very limited native abilities to perform mathematical calculations. The 80386 microprocessor, for example, can multiply integers, which are whole numbers such as 1, 200, etc. But to multiply two floating-point numbers, such as 1.3 and 6.87, someone had to write a small program telling the computer how to do this calculation. In the case of Visual Basic, these programs were written by Microsoft. But if Microsoft did the work for us, why do we need other types of numbers?

The answer has to do with speed. The native arithmetic provided by your computer for working with integers is much faster than the floating-point arithmetic provided by Visual Basic. When you're writing programs, the difference in speed can be very important. Almost all programs written by professional programmers make very heavy use of the native arithmetic to make their programs run more quickly. You'll see examples of this speed difference later in the book.

Bytes and Numbers

Your computer's memory is divided into many small storage locations called bytes (most computers running Windows, for example, have at least 4 megabytes of memory). Each byte can hold a single character of information. So a string of characters requires one byte for each character, plus a few extra bytes that keep track of how many characters are in the string. For example, the string "word" is six bytes long: four bytes for the characters and two bytes to keep track of the *length* in characters of the string.

You might guess that numbers would require one byte for each digit in the number, but there's actually a much more efficient way to store numbers. As it turns out, a single byte can represent any number between 0 and 255. Two bytes together can represent any positive number between 0 and 65,535. In actual practice, half the numbers are defined as negative, producing a range of −32,768 to 32,767, which is exactly the range allowed by an Integer type. In other words, an integer is exactly two bytes long.

For now, simply be aware that Visual Basic uses several different types of numbers. Table 2.1 provides a list of all the types of values that are built into Basic. In this book you'll be working mostly with three types: Integer, Single, and String.

Table 2.1: Types of Variables and Values in Basic	**Type**	**Suffix**	**Range of Values**
	Integer	%	−32,768 to 32,767
	Long	&	−2,147,483,648 to 2,147,483,647
	Single	! (or nothing)	Largest number: $\pm 3.402823 \times 10^{38}$
			Smallest number: $\pm 1.401298 \times 10^{-45}$
	Double	#	Largest number: $\pm 1.797693134862315 \times 10^{308}$
			Smallest number: $\pm 4.94066 \times 10^{-324}$
	Currency	@	−922,337,203,685,477.5808 to 922,337,203,685,477.5807
	String	$	0 to about 65,535 characters

Notice how the ranges for numbers use rather strange values? Like −32,768 to 32,767 for integers? Why these particular limits?

Again, these limits are a result of the way your computer works. If you're interested, you'll find more information about this in the sidebar "Bytes and Numbers." The main thing we'll be concerned about in this book is the set of limits on the size of numbers. You want to be sure you don't work with numbers that are too large. Let's explore these size issues a little bit.

Exploring the Limits on Numbers

We're almost finished with the discussion of numbers, and soon we'll move on to more entertaining topics. Let's spend some time exploring numbers of different types and their limits. This will give you a better feeling for the ranges of numbers you can work with and will help you understand what happens when you pass the limits.

Let's do some more work in the Immediate window. First, let's create a new variable that's an integer. The variables you've been creating so far, such as *n,* have been of type Single because, as you can see from Table 2.1, all variables are of the type Single unless you specify otherwise. And this makes sense; variables of type Single act very much like numbers in a calculator.

To define the variable *n* as an integer, type the following:

n% = 5
|

You can verify that this worked correctly by typing

print n%
 5
|

That's all there is to defining *n%* as an integer.

NOTE

You need to be careful that you don't accidentally omit the % sign here. If you type *n%* = 5, followed by Print *n,* you've actually unintentionally redefined *n* as Single rather than Integer. The result is that *n* will be set to 0 since Basic treats *n* as a new variable.

WARNING

Be careful of using a command like Print *n%* = 5. If you expect this command to assign *n%* = 5, it won't. Instead, this command tests *n%* to see if it's equal to 5. It prints 0 when *n%* is not 5 and −1 when *n%* is equal to 5. You'll learn about this kind of command in Chapter 4, where you'll learn about *Boolean* expressions.

Now let's do some arithmetic so you can see how Integers behave differently than Singles. If you divide *n%* by 3, you would normally expect the answer to be 1.666667. But here, since *n%* is an Integer (whole number), the answer is 2:

```
n% = n% / 3
print n%
 2
 |
```

Why did this result in 2 rather than 1? Basic rounds the real answer, 1.666…, to the nearest whole number, which is 2.

Now let's see what happens when you multiply two large numbers. First, set *n%* to 30,000; then multiply this by 30,000 (note that Basic doesn't allow you to type commas between the thousands):

```
n% = 30000
n% = n% * 30000
 |
```

How Visual Basic Rounds Numbers

When you want to turn a fractional number into a whole number, the most accurate method is to round the number to the closest whole number. In other words, if the fractional part is above 0.5, you round up to the next highest number. If the fractional part is below 0.5, you round down. But what happens when the fractional part is exactly 0.5?

You may think that you should always round 0.5 up to the next highest number, but this isn't correct mathematically. Instead, you round up half the time and down the other half of the time. The rule is that you round up when the whole part of the number is odd and down when it's even. For example, 1.50 is rounded up to 2 (because 1 is odd) and 2.50 is rounded down to 2 (because 2 is even).

Let's see what happens if you always round up 0.5, rather than only when the whole part is odd. Let's say you're adding together a group of numbers that all end with 0.5: 1.5 + 2.5 + 3.5 + 4.5 = 12.0. If you round all these numbers up before adding them together, you get 2 + 3 + 4 + 5 = 14, which isn't correct. On the other hand, if you use the rule Basic uses, you get 2 + 2 + 4 + 4 = 12. The bottom line is that rounding up half the time gives more accurate answers than rounding up all the time.

You'll see the warning message box shown in Figure 2.3. *Overflow* means that the result is too large to fit into an Integer. In other words, the number *overflows* the size limits of an Integer.

Figure 2.3:

Whenever a result is too large for a type of variable, you'll see this warning message box.

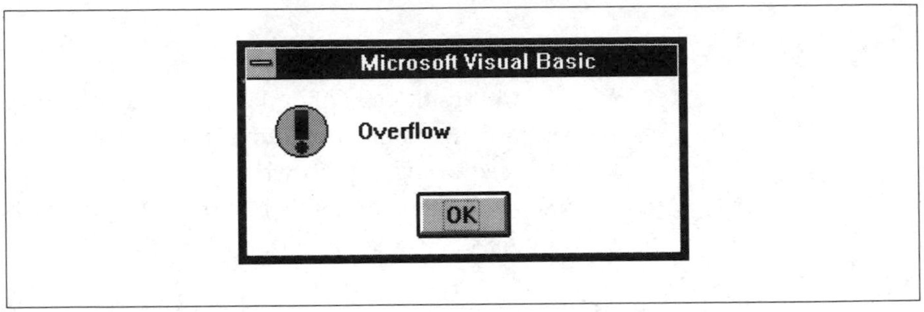

Another message you'll sometimes see is "Division by zero," which simply means you tried to divide a number by 0:

```
n% = 1/0
|
```

You might want to experiment a little with the limits on Integers before you move on.

Scientific Notation

Next let's look at what happens when you work with really large numbers using the variable *n,* which is of type Single. Numbers of type Single are floating-point numbers, which basically means that you can work with very small numbers, like 0.000001, as well as large numbers, like 10000.2. Notice that the decimal point "moved" between numbers.

First, set *n* to 1,000,000:

```
n=1000000
print n
 1000000
|
```

Multiply this by 1,000,000, which should result in 1 trillion (12 zeros). Here's what you'll actually see:

n = n * 1200000
print n
 1.2E+12
 |

The answer 1.2E + 12 is what's known as *scientific notation.* If you think back to grade school, you learned that you could write large numbers like 1.2×10^{12}. But this is impossible to write on a computer that can't use superscripts, so you must write it as 1.2E + 12. The E + 12 simply means that the number (1.2 here) is multiplied by 10 to the 12th power.

Now that we're done with our discussion of numbers, we can get back to having fun. In the next chapter, you'll learn some new commands that will let you draw on your screen.

Related Tools

Converting between Types Visual Basic has a number of functions (you'll learn about functions later in the book) that allow you to convert between the different types of numbers, and to convert between strings and numbers:

CCur	Number to Currency
CDbl	Number to Double
CLng	Number to Long
CSgn	Number to Single
CInt	Number to Integer; rounds to the nearest whole number
Fix	Number to Integer; truncates the fractional part
Int	Number to Integer; largest whole number less than or equal to number (3.2 → 3 and −3.2 → −4)
Str	Number to String
Val	String to Number

String Functions   Visual Basic has a very nice set of tools you can use to work with strings. These tools are a combination of functions and commands that allow you to search strings, break up strings into pieces, convert to upper- or lowercase, etc. Here's a brief overview of these functions:

InStr	Searches to see if one string is contained inside another.
Left$	Builds a new string that contains the first (leftmost) *n* characters from another string.
Mid$	Builds a new string that contains characters from the middle of another string. You can also use this function to replace part of a string with another string. Using InStr and Mid$, you can do search and replace operations.
Right$	Builds a new string that contains the last (rightmost) *n* characters from another string.
LTrim$	Builds a new string with any spaces at the start of the string removed.
RTrim$	Builds a new string with any spaces at the end of the string removed.
LCase$	Returns a copy of a string with all letters converted to lowercase.
UCase$	Returns a copy of a string with all letters converted to uppercase.
Len	Returns the length, in characters, of a string.

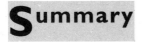

Summary

This chapter was filled with new material. I'll slow down a little in the next chapter, where you'll learn how to draw on your screen. Here's a quick review of the material in this chapter.

Variables are named locations in memory where you can store values. Each variable has a type that determines what you can store in it.

Values are pieces of information and can be numbers or strings. We spent quite a bit of time exploring the range of values that you can use with variables. For Integers, numbers can range from −32,768 to 32,767 (but you can't use the commas when you type the numbers in Basic).

Types. All of Basic's variables have specific types, and there are a total of six different types: one string type and five numeric types. In this book you'll work almost entirely with the Integer, Single, and String data types, but if you're writing scientific programs, you may need to use the Double type since it provides more precise results. (Note, however, that calculations with Double values are slower than calculations with Single values.) If you're writing financial programs, you might want to use the Currency type.

Chapter 3

Featuring

Drawing in a Window Using the
Line Command

Window Coordinate System
and *Twips*

Forms, Objects, and Properties

Drawing on the Screen

In this chapter you'll learn about a new window in Visual Basic: the Form1 window. You'll start drawing pictures inside this window using a couple of new commands in the Basic language. Through these commands you'll also learn about the coordinate system used by windows in Visual Basic.

Drawing in a Window

If you look at your screen when you start Visual Basic, you'll notice a window called Form1; it's probably the largest window. We're going to draw some lines in this window.

You'll want to make sure you have Visual Basic started, and the Immediate window is active and visible (press F5 then Ctrl+Break). You'll also want to make sure your Immediate window is about the same size and in the same location as the one shown in Figure 3.1 so it won't cover up much of the Form1 window. This is important since you'll be drawing in the Form1 window and don't want the Immediate window hiding Form1 (except for a small amount at the bottom, which is OK).

Visual Basic has a command called Line that lets you draw lines in windows. Line accepts several pieces of information (arguments) that tell it where the line should start and where it should end. Type the following Line command into the Immediate window:

```
line (100,100)-(1000,1000)
```

Figure 3.1:

The sample Line command draws a line about 1 inch long in the window Form1.

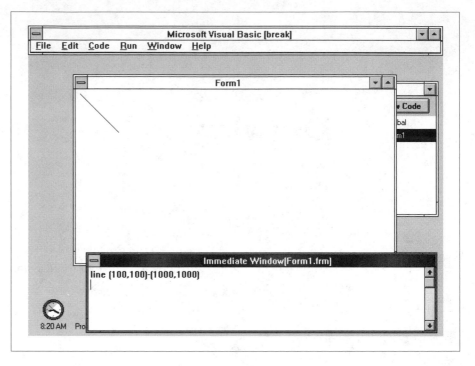

At this point you should see a line appear inside the window Form1, as shown in Figure 3.1.

There are a couple of things to notice here. First, this Line command has both a starting point and an ending point for the line. Each of these points is described by two numbers in parentheses. Now think about what the line looks like for a minute. Notice how the line goes from the upper left to the lower right? Is this what you expected?

The starting point is at (100,100), and the ending point is at (1000,1000). If this were the normal Cartesian coordinate system you learned in school, you'd expect to see the line start near the bottom-left corner of the window. And you'd expect the end of the line to be above and to the right of the starting point. So what's going on here?

It turns out that Microsoft Windows (and some other computers, like the Macintosh) uses an upside-down coordinate system, so the origin (0,0) appears in the upper-left corner of a window (see Figure 3.2).

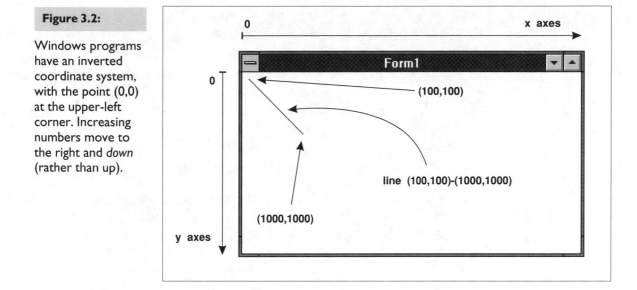

Figure 3.2:

Windows programs have an inverted coordinate system, with the point (0,0) at the upper-left corner. Increasing numbers move to the right and *down* (rather than up).

Drawing and Twips

You may also be wondering just how long the line is. You asked Visual Basic to draw a line that goes from (100,100) to (1000,1000). But what distance is this? The screen in Figure 3.1 is from a VGA display, which is 640 pixels wide and 480 pixels high. Obviously, then, the distance isn't measured in pixels because the line doesn't go 900 pixels down and across.

It turns out that the unit of measure is something defined by Windows as a *twip*. A twip is equal to ¹⁄₁₄₄₀ inch.

Let's try an example that allows us to actually measure the size of a twip, both on the screen and on the printer. First, you'll want to erase the line you just drew, which you can do with a new command called Cls, which stands for CLear Screen. Enter Cls into the Immediate window and you'll notice the line disappear from Form1. Then you'll use a slightly different form of the Line command that draws a box instead of a line:

```
cls
line (100,100)-(1540,1540),,b
|
```

Why Windows Are Upside Down

You're probably wondering, and rightly so, why the coordinate system is turned upside down in Windows. It is a result of how your monitor and the display adapter inside your computer work. Your computer's screen is very much like a television screen, only of higher quality and price. Both a television and your computer screen create an image by scanning electron beams across a phosphor screen. This beam moves from left to right and from top to bottom—the same as the way we read.

The image you see on your screen is also formed from a number of small dots, called *pixels* (short for *picture elements*). Your display adapter has a memory location for each pixel you can see on the screen. These memory locations appear in the same order as they're drawn on the screen. In other words, the top-left pixel is first in memory because it's drawn first on the screen, followed by the next pixel to its right. The lower-right pixel is the last pixel in memory.

The programmers at Microsoft who wrote Windows used this knowledge of how pixels are stored in memory to make Windows programs run faster. By inverting the coordinate system, they made calculating the memory address of a pixel just a little easier and therefore faster (because then you don't have to change the sign for locations on the *y*-axis).

(Be sure to type two commas before the *b* in the Line command.) Now you should see a small square on your screen. You've told Basic to make this box 1440 twips wide and high, which should be 1 inch. On my screen (which is a 14-inch VGA screen), this box comes out to be about $1\frac{1}{2}$" by $1\frac{1}{2}$". The letter *b*, by the way, is short for the word *box*.

NOTE

Since the screen on your computer could be any size from 12 inches (or even 9 inches for laptop computers) to 21 inches, the actual size of a pixel can vary considerably. Windows doesn't have any way of knowing how large your monitor is, so an "inch" (as in 1440 twips) may not be 1 inch long when you measure it on your screen. But as long as you work with twips in your programs as if they're

What's a Twip?

A twip is a unit of measure that Microsoft created, and it means a "twentieth of a point." A *point* is a unit of measure used in the typesetting world, which is equal to approximately $1/72$ inch. So a twip is equal to $1/1440$ inch and is measured in terms of points, not pixels.

The number of twips per pixel varies under Windows and depends on the type of display your computer has. On a normal VGA display, for example, a pixel is 15 twips wide and high. You'll find more information about twips and pixels later in this book.

real inches, anything you print out on paper will print at the correct size. (You'll find a much more detailed discussion of this entire issue in Chapter 14.)

Now let's see what happens when you try to print the sample box on the printer. It turns out that it's just as easy to draw on the printer as it is in the window Form1. All you have to do is put "Printer." in front of any Line commands. Then follow this up with a Printer.EndDoc command (which tells Windows that you're finished printing a document). If you have a printer connected to your computer, make sure it's turned on and ready; then try the following commands (Basic will take longer to run each of these commands):

```
printer.line (100,100)-(1540,1540),,b
printer.enddoc
```

After a little delay, your printer should print a page that has a box on it. And this box should be exactly 1 inch wide and high (there may be some small variation in size because not all printers are built exactly alike).

Reference: Cls Command

The Cls command clears the screen, which in this case means it clears the current form, or window. In this chapter, it clears the window called Form1. Cls takes no arguments.

Reference: Line Command

Line [[Step](*x1!, y1!*)**] – [Step]**(*x2!, y2!*)**[,[**color&**],B[F]]**

Draws a line in a window. Notice that you have a number of options you can use.

(*x1!, y1!*)

The starting point of the line, which is optional. If you leave the starting point out, Line continues drawing from the previous endpoint, as you'll see later in this chapter. Visual Basic uses numbers of type Single for the start points and endpoints (hence the ! after the arguments). You don't need to type the ! after each number.

(*x2!, y2!*)

Endpoint for the line.

color&

Allows you to use any color when you draw a line. You'll normally use a command called RGB to create these numbers, as you'll see later.

,B[F]

These two arguments allow you to draw a rectangle (B is short for box) or a filled rectangle (BF is short for box, filled).

Step

Tells Visual Basic that (*x1!,y1!*) or (*x2!,y2!*) are distances from previous positions, rather than positions themselves. In other words, the command Line (500,500)-Step(100,100),,B draws a box exactly 100 twips wide and high, with the top left at (500,500).

A Peek at Objects and Forms

Notice how we used exactly the same Line command on both the screen and the printer? As you'll see in the coming chapters, there are a number of *objects*

Key Concept: Objects

Visual Basic has a number of objects that you can work with, such as forms, the printer, and many others you'll see in coming chapters. Commands such as Line can actually work on different objects by putting the object's name in front of Line, such as Printer.Line. By default, commands like Line draw to the current form, which is Form1 in the examples.

in Visual Basic. And Visual Basic allows you to use the same command on different objects by putting the object name, followed by a period, in front of the command. What happens when you don't supply an object name?

If you take a look again at the Immediate window in Figure 3.1, you'll notice that the caption says

Immediate Window[Form1.frm]

The name in the square brackets (Form1.frm) gives you information on the current object—in this case it's telling you that the current object is a form (.frm) called Form1. This means that all commands, like Line, that draw in a window (also known as a *form* in Visual Basic's jargon) will be drawn in the window called Form1 when you don't supply an object name (like Printer).

This brief detour into printing is a little off the track, so let's get back on track and learn a little more about the Form1 window and drawing in it.

Key Concept: Forms

Visual Basic has its own jargon in addition to using much of the jargon from Windows. Because many programs are built out of a number of "forms," Microsoft chose not to call windows "windows" for programs written in Visual Basic. Instead, windows are called *forms*. The reference manual states that a form is "a window or dialog box that you create with Visual Basic."

More Explorations in Drawing

Our next subject is something you may already have stumbled upon. The question is this: What happens if you cover your window, then show it again? Will the line still be there? You might guess so, but let's find out what really happens.

Enter the following commands into the Immediate window:

```
cls
line (100,100)-(1540,1540)
|
```

This draws a line in the window Form1. Now drag the Immediate window so it covers the line you just drew. Release the mouse button, then drag the Immediate window back to the lower-right corner. Is the line still there? Nope.

Neither Visual Basic nor most Windows programs keep track of what you draw on the screen. Instead, they have to redraw a window every time something erases part of it. In other words, the programs you write have to redraw any lines each time you're informed that part of a window was erased. For now, though, we don't really care whether the lines we draw stay on the screen.

Exploring the Step Keyword

The Step keyword isn't actually a command by itself—instead it modifies the Line command. For this reason it's called a keyword rather than a command.

The Step keyword allows you to specify, for example, how wide a box will be without doing any arithmetic. For example, if you want a box 1 inch wide, you could write the command

```
line (100,100)-step(1440, 1440),,b
```

which draws a box exactly 1 inch wide and high (1440 twips = 1 inch). So in the case of the endpoint, Step means that the endpoint is (*width, height*) rather than (*x2, y2*). But what does Step mean for the starting point?

Type in the command above, then type in the following command:

```
line step(500,500)-step(1440,1440),,b
```

You know that the second part, Step(1440,1440), means that you want to draw a 1-inch box. But what does the first Step mean? The distance 500 twips is about ⅓ inch. And as you can see from Figure 3.3, the top left of this new box is about a third of an inch below and to the right of the previous box. In other words, the starting point of this new box is 500 twips down and to the right of the previous endpoint. How does Visual Basic keep track of the previous endpoint?

Figure 3.3:

This figure shows how the Step keyword works. For the endpoint, Step tells Line to treat (x2, y2) as a width and height instead of as coordinates. And for the starting point, Step tells Line to set the starting point to (x1, y1) twips from the previous endpoint.

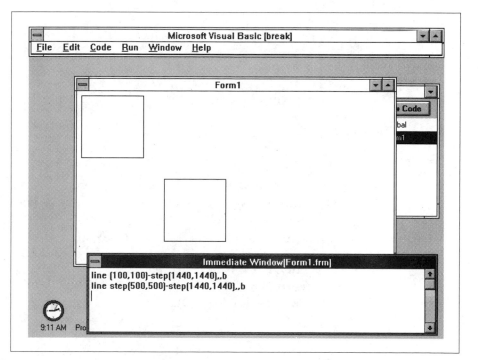

The CurrentX and CurrentY Properties

In the last chapter, you learned a lot about variables, which are areas in memory where you can store values. All the variables you saw in Chapter 2 were variables you created yourself. But Visual Basic also has another type of variable, called a *property,* that it creates itself. And there are two such variables that keep track of the previous location of something called the *pen,* which is a fictitious tool for writing on the screen.

Reference: CurrentX and CurrentY

The CurrentX and CurrentY variables are called *properties* and are of type Single. They keep track of the location of the writing pen. Each time you use a Line command, CurrentX and CurrentY will be set to the endpoint of the line after Visual Basic draws the line.

Let's see what the current values are for these two properties, called CurrentX and CurrentY:

```
print currentx, currenty
 3480        3480
 |
```

The endpoint for the last box you drew is something you can calculate easily. The first box ends at 100 + 1440 = 1540. So the endpoint of the second box will be 1540 + 500 + 1440 = 3480, and this is exactly what Visual Basic reports.

Try a simple experiment to see what happens if you change these numbers yourself. Use the command Line -Step(1440,1440),,B to draw a box 1 inch wide, with the upper-left corner located at the current location (CurrentX, CurrentY):

```
currentx = 100+1440+500
currenty = 100
line -step(1440,1440),,b
 |
```

You should now see a third box on your screen, to the right of the first box and above the second box. You can change the value of CurrentX and CurrentY just as easily as you change any other variable.

Knowing about CurrentX and CurrentY, and how they work, gives you a lot of freedom in how you write your programs. For example, if you want to draw a figure, like a triangle, it's much easier to use the Step keyword, as you can see in this example:

```
cls
line (1000,1000)-step(500,500)
```

What Property Means

The meaning of *property* as used by Visual Basic to describe variables like CurrentX and CurrentY is based on a different definition of property from the usual one. Here is the closest definition from Webster's dictionary: "a quality that defines or describes an object or substance."

CurrentX and CurrentY are thus properties (characteristics) attached to the form Form1 that describe the location of the drawing pen. As you'll see later, each form or other object in Visual Basic has a number of properties that you can use to change the way an object looks or behaves.

```
line -step(-500,0)
line -step(0,-500)
|
```

These commands draw a right triangle (see Figure 3.4), starting with the top at (1000,1000). The first line is drawn from (1000,1000) to a location 500 twips down and to the right of the starting point. The next Line command draws a line continuing from there to a location 500 twips to the left (the base of the

Figure 3.4:

This is the right triangle drawn by the three Line commands, using steps of 500 twips.

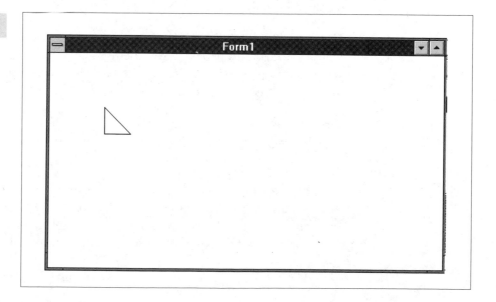

triangle). The final Line command draws a line back up (remember, the coordinate system is inverted, so -500 moves up, not down) to the starting point.

Before we leave this subject, let's try another simple experiment. I mentioned above that both CurrentX and CurrentY are defined by Visual Basic and are of type Single. What happens if you try to use these names as Integers by putting a % at the end? If you type

currentx% = 1
|

you'll see a warning message box from Visual Basic that says

Identifier can't end with type-declaration character

This means you don't have the freedom to change a variable's type when the variable is a property created by Visual Basic.

Related Tools

Circle   In addition to the Line command, Visual Basic also has a Circle command, which allows you to draw circles, ellipses, arcs, and pie segments. This command is rather complicated, but it can do a lot.

Colors   The Line and Circle commands can draw objects with different colors, which you'll do in Chapter 7. You use the RGB function to describe the color you want to use. You can also use the FillStyle and FillColor properties to tell Visual Basic how to fill boxes and circles.

Line Widths   You can change the width of lines you draw by using the DrawWidth property, which you'll learn about in Chapter 5. You can also change the color of these lines by using the ForeColor property.

Size of the Form   There are several properties you can read (and change) to get information on the current size of the form, in drawing units, and the left and top edges: ScaleWidth, ScaleHeight, ScaleLeft, and ScaleTop. These are very useful if you're trying to write a program that will use the full size of a form for any drawing you're doing. You can also change the ScaleLeft and ScaleTop values so the origin will be anywhere you want, rather than in the upper-left corner.

ScaleMode Property In this chapter you've been working with screen units measured in twips. But you can use the ScaleMode property to set the units to points ($\frac{1}{72}$inch), pixels, inches, millimeters, or centimeters.

Custom Scales You can create a custom scale that's anything you want by using the Scale command, which you'll do in Chapter 7. So you're not limited to working with just the modes provided by ScaleMode.

Printer There are several related commands you can use with the printer that I haven't talked about in this chapter: NewPage, which starts a new page, and Page, which is the number of the page you're currently drawing. The Page property is useful when you need to keep track of the page number, such as when you want to display "Page *nn*" at the bottom of each page.

Summary

You learned a number of things in this chapter about drawing inside a window, called Form1. And you also learned a little about printing and a new type of variable called a property. Here is a review of what we've covered here:

Line Command. The Line command allows you to draw lines inside a window. The coordinate system is inverted from the Cartesian coordinate system, and the unit of distance is called a *twip,* which is $\frac{1}{1440}$ inch.

Forms. Windows that you create with Visual Basic are called *forms.* You can tell which form a Line command will draw on by looking at the title in the Immediate window.

Printer. You can draw with the printer by using Printer.Line rather than Line by itself. The Printer.EndDoc command sends everything you draw to the printer.

CurrentX and CurrentY Properties. Visual Basic keeps track of the previous endpoint of a Line command by using the properties CurrentX and CurrentY. These are two variables created by Visual Basic for each form, and they're of type Single.

Objects. Visual Basic supplies a number of objects you can work with, such as Form1 and Printer. Commands like Line can draw lines on these different objects, and you tell Line which object to use by putting its name before Line: Printer.Line.

Property. Properties are special variables attached to objects, like forms, that allow you to change the way an object looks or works.

Chapter 4

Featuring

Events, Subroutines, and Functions

Building the Sketch Program

The If..Then Command and
Boolean Expressions

Saving and Loading Projects

Building Programs

At this point you're ready to roll up your sleeves and start writing some real programs in Visual Basic. By real programs I mean programs that will run by themselves, without your having to type commands in the Immediate window. In fact, we're only going to use the Immediate window to explore new commands.

The first program you'll build will beep when you click. After you've learned the basics with this simple beep program, you'll move on to build a real program. This program, called Sketch, will let you sketch lines inside a window. We'll spend the next two chapters building Sketch, and most of the work will be learning about new features in Visual Basic and how to write programs.

Building Your First Program

To start building your first program, exit from Visual Basic, then start it again. This will clear any changes you may have made.

Your first program will be a very simple, one-line program: It will show a window, called Form1, and exit as soon as you click in the Form1 window. To build this program, you're going to start working with another new window, called the Code window, that you'll use to write your programs. To display this window, double-click on the window called Form1. You should then see a window that is called Form1.frm (see Figure 4.1).

I'll explain what this window is all about in a minute. But first, let's try a simple experiment. Press the Tab key on your keyboard. This moves the insertion point to the right four spaces. Most programmers like to indent lines, as we'll do here. Indenting provides a visual clue about where groups of

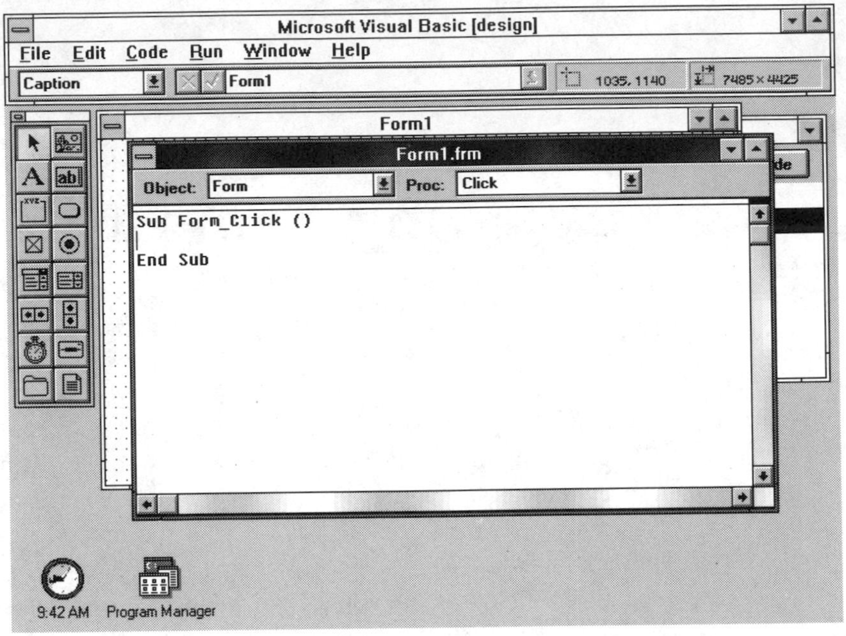

Figure 4.1:

To display Form1's Code window, called Form1.frm, double-click on the Form1 window (which is now behind Form1.frm).

instructions start and end. Here it won't make much difference, but it will in later chapters when you write longer programs.

Next type the word **beep** and you should see something like this:

```
Sub Form_Click ()
    beep
End Sub
```

Press F5 to run this simple program (but don't press Ctrl+Break because you won't be working with the Immediate window here). You'll see the window Form1 come to the front again. Also, notice that the caption at the very top of the screen reads

Microsoft Visual Basic [run]

This tells you that you're running this program.

Your program should beep every time you click inside the white part of the Form1 window. When you've had enough fun, quit this program and return to design mode by clicking on the Control box (the square icon in the upper-left corner of the Form1 window) and selecting the Close item from this menu, or simply double-click on the Control box.

We'll look at what happens in this small program in just a second. But first, you may have noticed something interesting. You typed the Beep command into the Code window using all lowercase letters, but this is what it now looks like:

```
Sub Form_Click ()
    Beep
End Sub
```

Visual Basic automatically capitalized the word Beep. As you'll see, Visual Basic automatically capitalizes all keywords in its language whenever you move to the next line or run the program.

Anatomy of an Event Handler

This small piece of code, which consists of three lines, is called an *event handler* because it handles mouse-click events inside the form. There are a number of different types of events in Windows programs. Clicking is an event. Pressing a key is an event. Even redrawing (or repainting) a window is an event. And Visual Basic allows you to write instructions for handling each of these events. In this example, you're handling the Click event, which means you're running the Beep command whenever you click inside the Form1 window.

An event handler consists of three parts: the event definition, any lines of code you write, and the End Sub line.

The first line defines the name of the event handler. In this case, Visual Basic has created an event handler called Form_Click( ). (In a minute we'll take a look at the rules Visual Basic uses to define event names. But first, let's finish

Events

Visual Basic programs are built around *events,* which are various things that can happen in a program. As you'll see in this book, there are a number of events that you can write code to handle—such as clicking, double clicking, painting (drawing a window), pressing a key, and moving the mouse.

Subroutines

Subroutines are small pieces of code that have a name. They begin with Sub *Name* and end with End Sub. Any lines of code you write must appear between the Sub statement and the End Sub statement. For example:

Sub *Name*
    [*statements*]
End Sub

These statements define a subroutine with the name *Name*. You can place as many statements as you want, or none at all, between the Sub and End Sub lines.

looking at the structure of this event handler.) The word Sub stands for *subroutine,* which is another piece of computer-science jargon. A subroutine is a small piece of code that stands as a separate package. This will become clearer later when you have more than one subroutine.

Subroutines must end with an End Sub statement. It's not actually a command, because it doesn't perform any action—it just marks the end of the subroutine. To make this clearer, let's look at how Visual Basic works with this subroutine. Whenever you click inside the Form1 window, Visual Basic automatically runs the code inside Form_Click( ). By the code inside, I mean any code that appears between the Sub Form_Click( ) and End Sub statements. In the example, this means Visual Basic runs the Beep command. After it finishes running that command, it sees the End Sub statement, which tells Visual Basic it's all done running this subroutine.

The name of this event procedure, Form_Click( ), has two parts (see Figure 4.2) separated by an underscore character (_). The first part of the name is the name of the object you're working with. For forms this name is always *Form.* For some reason, it never has the name of the form itself (in this case Form1). But as you'll see later, for other objects this part of the name will be the name of the object.

The second part of the name is the name of the event this subroutine will handle. In this example, you're handling the Click event for mouse clicks inside the form, so it's called Form_Click( ).

All subroutines end with the line End Sub.

Figure 4.2:

The various parts
of an event-handling
procedure

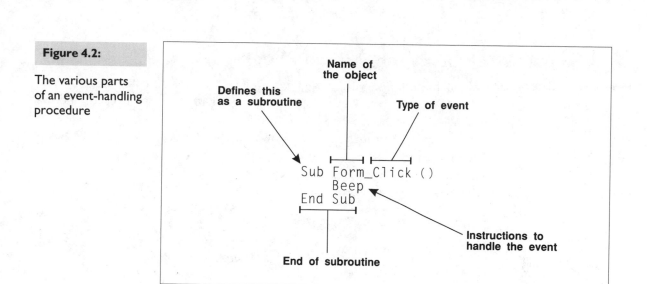

A Multiline Program

Let's make this program a little more interesting by adding another line to it. Use either the cursor keys or the mouse to move the insertion point after the *p* in *Beep,* then press the Enter key. Finally, type the word **end.** Your Click subroutine should now look like this:

```
Sub Form_Click()
    Beep
    end
End Sub
```

Now run the program and see what it does. Notice how it quits and returns to design mode as soon as you click the mouse? The End command, as you'll recall, tells Visual Basic to stop running the current program, which ends the current program and returns you to design mode. You may have noticed that Visual Basic capitalized the End keyword when you ran your program as it did Beep.

You'll also notice something potentially confusing. There are two Ends in this subroutine: the End command and the End Sub statement. The End in each case has a slightly different meaning. The End command, as you'll recall, ends the current program. The End Sub statement, on the other hand, simply marks the end of the current subroutine, which is similar to the way a period marks the end of a sentence.

A Look at Event-Driven Programs

Much of the time your program is "running" it's not actually doing anything. This is because your Visual Basic program has returned control to Windows. All Windows programs are built around what's known as the *event model* of programming. In this model, Windows watches your computer to see what's going on, and as soon as something interesting (an event) happens, Windows figures out which program the event belongs to, then sends that event off to the correct program (see Figure 4.3).

Figure 4.3:

This figure outlines the kind of event model used in Windows programs. In this model, your program only receives control and runs in response to events generated by Windows.

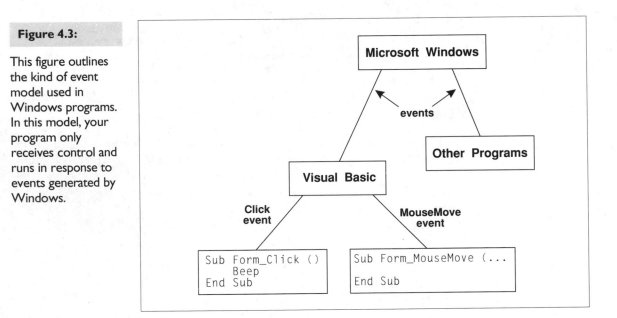

In this model your Visual Basic program, which beeps when you click on it, won't actually be running, in a sense, until you click in your Form1 window. At this point, Windows notices that the click belongs to a window owned by Visual Basic, so it sends the Click event to Visual Basic. Visual Basic, in turn, notices that the click is for your Form1 window, so it sends the event to your code in Form_Click( ), which beeps. When Visual Basic encounters the End Sub statement, it then returns control to Windows, to await the next event.

When you added the End command to Form_Click( ), you altered this picture a little. This command generates a "quit" message, telling Visual Basic that you want to quit your program. Visual Basic removes the program from the event-handling system and returns to design mode, where clicking in the Form1 window sends a message to Visual Basic rather than to your program.

All these concepts will become clearer in the next few chapters, where you'll continue to work with events. The concept of an event is one that most people have a little trouble learning at first. But once you get the hang of it, using events is a very nice, and simple, way to write programs. So hang in there.

Building a Sketch Program

Now we're going to change course. You're going to build your first real program, called Sketch, that will allow you to sketch on the screen. Figure 4.4 shows what this program will do once you finish it at the end of Chapter 5.

Think for a couple of minutes about where you're going to start building this program. So far you don't know very much about programming, so we'll start with the easiest thing you know how to do. In the last chapter you learned how

Figure 4.4:

Sketch lets you use the mouse to draw on the screen. It includes a pull-down menu that lets you erase the picture, change the width of the pen, and exit the program.

to draw lines. And in this chapter, you just learned how to attach some commands to an event. So the first thing you'll do is combine these two pieces so that you can draw lines inside this window as you move the mouse. This is very easy to do, but you'll run into a couple of simple problems that can be solved by using some new commands.

After you've polished the part of your program that draws lines as you move the mouse, we'll move on to adding the pull-down menu. This is remarkably easy, especially if you ever see how much work "real" programmers have to do to get menus running in *their* programs.

Drawing Lines to Follow the Mouse

Before you continue, you'll want to remove the two lines of code you added to Form_Click( ) at the start of this chapter. There are two ways to do this. First, you can quit Visual Basic and start over again. If you do this, you'll see a message like the one in Figure 4.5. This message box informs you that you'll lose the two lines of code you typed into Form_Click( ) if you don't save Form1.frm. Click on the No button—you don't want to save this Click program.

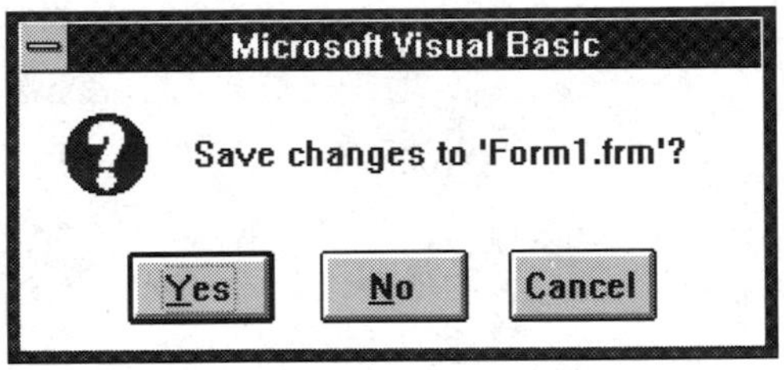

Figure 4.5:

You'll see this message box if you try to quit Visual Basic after you've entered some commands for Form_Click( ).

The other way you can remove these two lines is to delete them using the usual Windows methods for editing text. For example, you could use the mouse to select these two lines, then press the Delete key to remove them.

Choosing the Event

The Form_Click( ) event isn't the event you actually want to work with. Instead, you want to work with an event called Form_MouseMove. This event occurs whenever you move the mouse (big surprise, right?).

You get to this event by clicking on the down-pointing arrow in the combo box called *Proc:* in the Code window (Proc is short for *procedure,* which is another name of a subroutine). Figure 4.6 shows this combo box pulled down with the MouseMove event highlighted. Click on this event to show it in the window.

Figure 4.6:

Click on the down-pointing arrow for the Proc combo box to show the procedures (event handlers) available, then click on MouseMove to select this procedure.

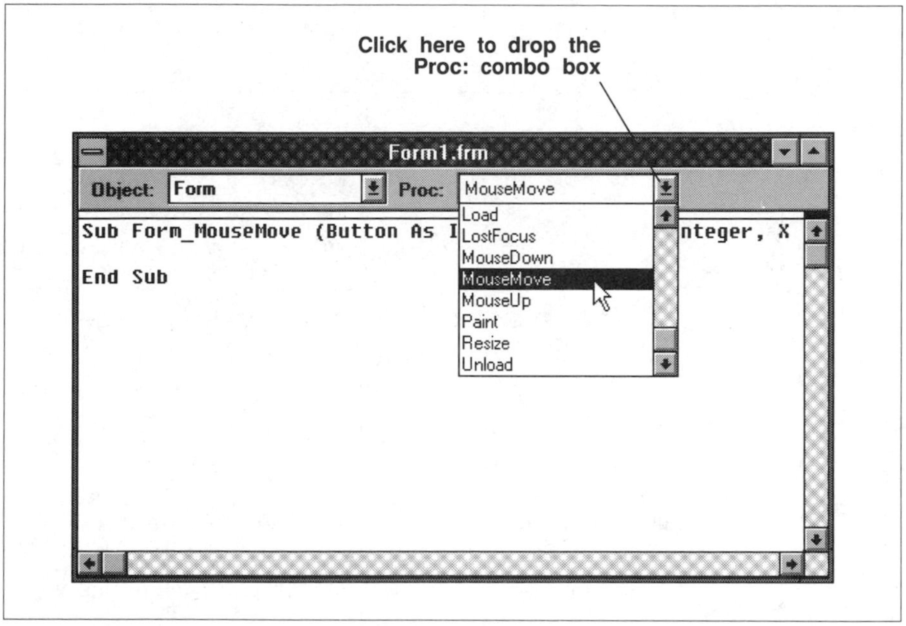

Click here to drop the
Proc: combo box

Form1.frm

Object: Form **Proc:** MouseMove

Load
LostFocus
MouseDown
MouseMove
MouseUp
Paint
Resize
Unload

Sub Form_MouseMove (Button As I   nteger, X

End Sub

Why It's Called the Proc Combo Box

You may have noticed that we changed which subroutine (event handler) we were looking at using the Proc combo box. If we're changing subroutines, why is this called Proc and not Sub? Good question.

The word *procedure,* as it turns out, is a more general name for a set of statements than the word *subroutine* or *function* (a function is like a subroutine, but returns a number or a string of characters). Because Proc is more general, Microsoft chose to call this combo box Proc, rather than something longer like Sub/Function.

If you use the horizontal scroll bar, you can see that the MouseMove event procedure actually has a number of arguments that it receives (these are the names inside the parentheses):

```
Sub Form_MouseMove (Button As Integer, Shift As Integer,
➤ X As Single, Y As Single)
```

Even though this is one line, I've written it as two lines so it will fit on this page.

NOTE

Lines of code in this book are restricted to about 65 characters because the page is not wide enough to fit more. So all the lines you write will not, for the most part, be longer than 65 characters. But Visual Basic often creates subroutine definitions that are longer than 65 characters. To make it clear that I had to write a single line as two lines, I'll always start continuation lines with a right-pointing arrow: ➤. So whenever you see lines like this, type them as one long line.

This subroutine definition includes four arguments. If you remember back to Chapter 1, you learned that the Print command can work with a number of arguments. Like Print, the MouseMove event handler also has some arguments it can receive:

Button   Gives information on which mouse button is pressed down. This will be 1 if just the left button is down, 2 if just the right button is down, and 3 if both buttons are down.

Shift   Gives information on which Shift keys (like Left Shift, Right Shift, Alt+Shift, or Ctrl+Shift) are currently down. You won't be using this information here.

X, Y   Gives information on where the mouse pointer is inside the window. You'll use these two numbers for the end-points of your lines.

Writing Event Code

Make sure you have the Form_MouseMove subroutine visible in the Code window, then type the following line of code into this window, between the Sub and End Sub lines:

```
Line -(X, Y)
```

(You can indent this line four spaces by pressing the Tab key.) Now press F5 to run this program. See how it draws lines to follow the mouse (see Figure 4.7).

Figure 4.7:

As you can see, the line followed the movements of the mouse; however, this program started by drawing a line from (0,0) to your mouse's location.

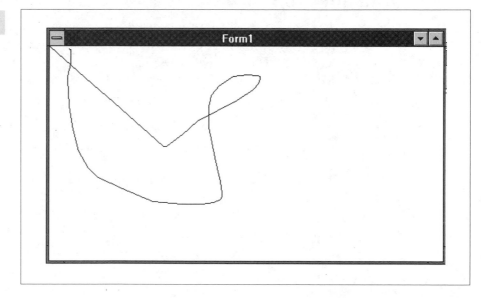

When you want to exit from this program, click on the Control box in the upper-left corner of the window and choose the Close item (or press Alt+F4).

There are a couple of problems with this program, which we'll fix next. First, notice how your Sketch program began by drawing a line from (0,0) to the mouse location. This happens because the Line -(X, Y) command draws lines from the last location. And since the "last location" is initially (0,0), the first line starts at (0,0). Second, we'd like Sketch to draw lines only when the mouse button is pressed.

Both of these problems are really easy to fix, and we could fix them at the same time. But it's actually better to fix one problem at a time, then test your solution. If you change too many things at one time, you may forget what you're doing and therefore forget to test a change you made. That said, let's start by changing Sketch so it won't start drawing until you click.

Let's think about what we need to do. We need some way to know when the mouse is down and only draw then. So let's try something to see what happens. If you look again at the arguments received in the MouseMove event subroutine, you'll notice one of them is called Button—it tells you which mouse button is pressed. How can you use this information?

Clicking to Draw

A command called If..Then will run a command (or set of commands) *only* if some condition is true; you can use this command to draw a line only if the left button is down. Before we look at all the details of If..Then and how it works, let's try it out in the program. Replace the current Line command in Form_MouseMove( ) with this command, which only draws lines when the left button is down:

```
If Button = 1 Then Line -(X, Y)
```

Then try running this program. Sketch should only draw lines when you hold down the left mouse button.

Now we need to cover some more theory, so let's save this project before continuing.

Saving Sketch

Visual Basic actually saves a number of files for each program you work on. Each program is called a *project* in Visual Basic's jargon. Each project consists of at least a project file, which has a .MAK extension and contains information on what other files belong to the project, such as forms like Form1.frm.

Forms are saved as separate files with the .FRM extension. The current form is called Form1, which isn't a very descriptive name. You'll want to change this to a more descriptive name before you save the project. The name Sketch jumps to mind.

You'll need to quit Sketch and return to design mode before changing the form's name. Make sure the Sketch form is active (click once on it), then click on the down-pointing arrow in the combo box near the top-left side of your screen (Figure 4.8 shows this combo box pulled down).

Figure 4.8:

To change the name of this form, pull down the combo box below the menu bar and choose the FormName item.

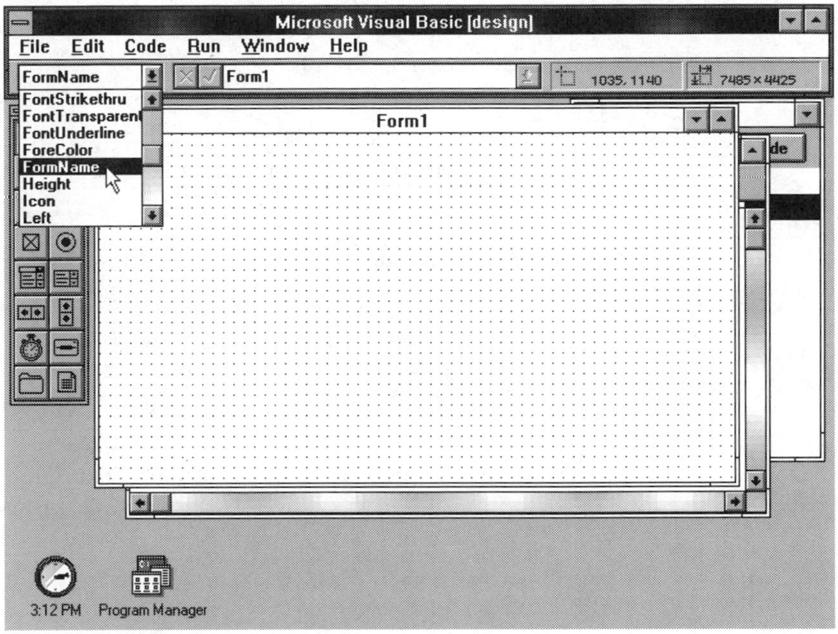

Once you've selected the FormName item, notice that the other combo box now reads Form1. This is the current name of your form, as you saw in the Immediate window. To change this name, simply type **Sketch** and press the Enter key (see Figure 4.9).

Incidentally, the combo box is in an area of the main window called the *Properties bar*. It's called this because it allows you to change various properties. The FormName item that you selected is a property of this form, just as CurrentX and CurrentY are also properties of this form. As you can see, there are a number of other properties you can also change using the Properties bar.

Figure 4.9:

The Properties bar after you've typed in a new form name

NOTE

You may have noticed that the CurrentX and CurrentY properties don't appear in this combo box. Why not? These properties are known as *run-time* properties, which means they only have meaning when you're running a program. On the other hand, the properties you see in this combo box are known as *design-time* properties. Some properties are both run-time and design-time properties, but only the design-time properties are shown in the Properties bar.

In addition to changing the form's name, you'll also want to change the caption in the window (which currently reads Form1) so it reads Sketch. To do this, again pull down the combo box (by clicking on the small down-pointing arrow) and select the Caption property (either click on it or use the cursor keys and press Enter). Then type **Sketch** and press Enter. Your Sketch window should now say Sketch, rather than Form1, at the top.

Now you're ready to save your project. You might want to first use the File Manager to create a directory called Sketch for all your Sketch files. Then pull down the File menu in Visual Basic and select the Save Project item. Visual Basic will first try to save the form Sketch (see Figure 4.10). Since you've already provided the form name, it supplies the name Sketch.frm. But you'll probably want to change the directory, as I've done in Figure 4.10, so the files won't be saved in Visual Basic's directory. Instead, as I mentioned above, you should save these files in a new directory you created for Sketch. Click on the OK button to save the form.

Figure 4.10:

When you ask to save the project, Visual Basic will first prompt you for the name and directory of the Sketch form.

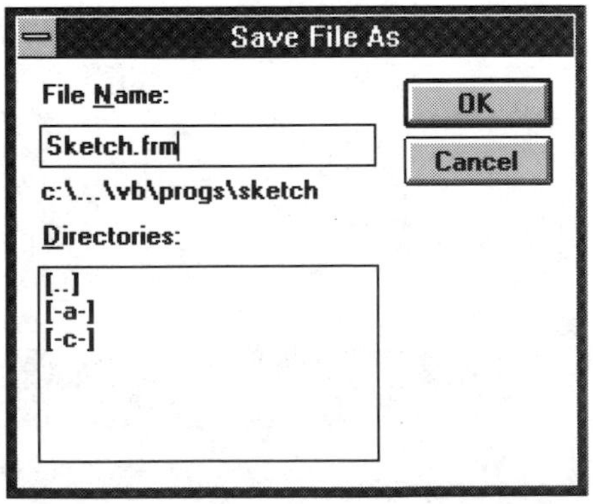

Next Visual Basic displays the Save Project As dialog box, with the default name Project1.mak for the project file. Type **Sketch.mak** and press the Enter key (the directory will already be the one where you stored Sketch.frm). And that's it. You've now saved Sketch, so you can exit Visual Basic, then load your project back into Visual Basic using the Open Project... item in the File menu.

Opening Your Sketch Project

When you start Visual Basic again, you'll want to know how to load your Sketch project back in. So quit from Visual Basic, then start over. Once you have Visual Basic running again, select the Open Project... item from the File menu. You'll see a dialog box like the one in Figure 4.11.

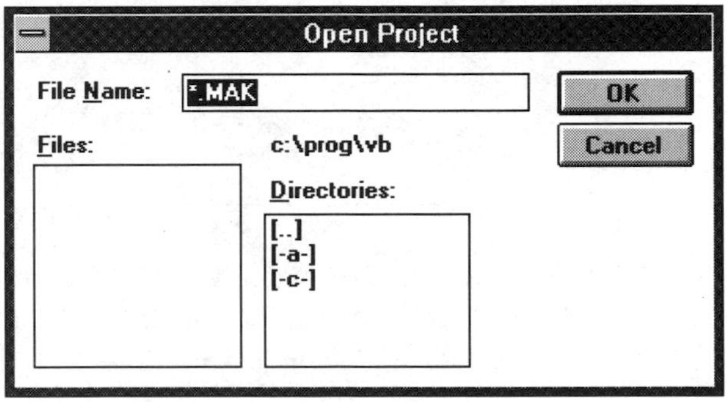

Figure 4.11:

This is the Open Project dialog box you'll see when you select the Open Project... item from the File menu. Notice how the current directory (c:\prog\vb) starts out with Visual Basic's directory.

You'll want to change the directory shown in this dialog box to the one you created for Sketch, at which time you'll see a file called Sketch.mak. Double-click on this file to load your Sketch project back into Visual Basic.

At this point you'll notice that the Sketch form (window) isn't visible (see Figure 4.12). Where did it go? For some reason, Visual Basic doesn't automatically open a form when you load a project. Instead, you have to open the form yourself.

You can open a form by clicking on the name SKETCH.FRM that appears below Global.bas in the Project window (you may have to select the Project Window item from the Window menu to make the Project window visible), then clicking on the View Form button. The Project window is the window on

Figure 4.12:

You'll see a screen like this one when you load your Sketch project back into Visual Basic. Simply double-click on the name SKETCH.FRM that appears inside the Project window (the window with the title SKETCH.MAK). (Note that you may have to select the Project Window item from the Window menu to make the Project window visible.)

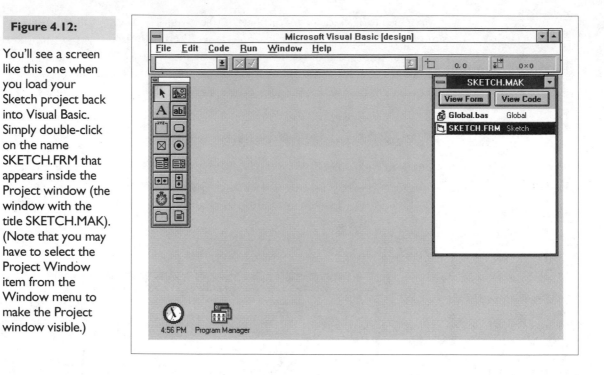

the right called SKETCH.MAK (you'll learn about the other file, Global.bas, in a later chapter). You can also open the Sketch form by double-clicking on SKETCH.FRM in the Project window.

The If..Then Command

Now that you've saved your project, I'll spend a few minutes on the theory behind the If..Then command. You've probably already figured out how the "If Button = 1 Then Line" command works, but let's try a few simple experiments anyway. Make sure you have the Immediate window visible and active, then enter the following command, which you'll use to test the If..Then command:

if 1=1 then print "True"
True
|

As you can see, the If..Then command checked to see if 1 = 1 and since it was (meaning that 1 = 1 is true), Visual Basic ran the command after Then: Print "True".

You can also try using this command with something you know isn't true, like 1 = 0:

if 1=0 then print "True"

You'll notice that Visual Basic completely ignores the Print "True" command, which is exactly what you want it to do. In other words, it only executes the Print command if the condition (1 = 0 in this last example) is true.

Boolean Expressions (Conditions)

You'll notice that the equal sign here is actually a test, rather than an assignment. Such tests are called *Boolean expressions* in the jargon of computer science. Although this name may sound somewhat intimidating, all Boolean really means is that an expression can be either true or false. In other words, it can only have one of two values.

There is also another piece of computer-science jargon, which should make a little more sense. When you use a Boolean expression like 1 = 0 in an If..Then statement, it's called a *condition*. In other words, If..Then runs a command only on the *condition* that an expression is true.

But how does Visual Basic represent true and false? Unfortunately, Visual Basic doesn't have True and False keywords, which would be very nice. Instead, it uses numbers to represent True and False.

Let's try some more tests with the Immediate window to see which numbers Basic uses. Since there are only two values, you can use two Print commands to display both of them:

print 1=1
−1
print 1=0
0

You can see from this reply that Visual Basic considers −1 to be true and 0 to be false. So if everything works as expected, you should be able to use numbers

Boolean Expressions

The term *Boolean* is named after an English mathematician named George Boole, who in the mid-1800s developed a type of mathematics called *Boolean algebra*. This type of algebra deals with values that are either true or false. It is invaluable for use with computers because computers work fundamentally with 0s and 1s (false and true) signals inside.

Because Visual Basic doesn't have a Boolean type, Boolean expressions return a number. The number 0 represents False, and −1 represents True. The reason Microsoft chose these numbers has to do with an operator called Not, because the expression Not True = False.

The Not operator, in turn, works with something called a bit, which is the smallest unit of storage inside your computer and is either 0 or 1. An Integer number, which is how True and False are represented, is built out of 16 of these bits. If you write the numbers for True and False as bits, you get this:

Boolean	Basic	Binary
False	0	0000 0000 0000 0000
True	−1	1111 1111 1111 1111

The Not keyword inverts all the bits in a number, changing 0s to 1s and 1s to 0s, which means that Not 0 = −1. This, of course, means that Not True = False, which is exactly what we want Not, True, and False to mean.

As to why Not 0 is negative, you learned in Chapter 1 that half the values in an Integer number are defined as being negative. The microprocessor inside your computer determines whether a number is negative by looking at the first digit in the binary number: All numbers that start with a 1 are negative numbers. So Not 0, which starts with a 1, will be a negative number, which happens to be −1.

as conditions just as easily as expressions. Here are the same Print commands as above, using numbers rather than expressions:

if −I then print "True"
True
if 0 then print "True"
|

The last thing we'll look at, in regard to Boolean expressions at least, is what happens when you use a number other than −1 or 0 in an If..Then command. You'll discover, as you can see in the example below, that If..Then actually treats any number other than 0 as true:

if 2 then print "True"
True
|

Another way to look at this is that 0 is false, and everything else is true. But a Boolean expression will *always* return either 0 or −1.

The Else Part of If..Then

The If..Then command is actually a very powerful command. So far we've only looked at the simplest case, where you run just one command if a condition is true. But you can also have If..Then run another command if the condition is false, as you'll see in the next example.

This example executes one command if a condition is true and another command if it's false:

if I=0 then print "True" else print "False"
False
|

You can see that all you have to do is add an Else keyword, followed by another command. The If..Then command is a very useful command that you'll use often in this book, so you'll learn more of the details in coming chapters.

Reference: If..Then..Else Command

You'll learn more about the If..Then..Else command and how to use all its pieces in following chapters.

If *condition* **Then** *command1* [**Else** *command2*]

There are several pieces to this command. The first piece, *condition,* is a test that the If command performs. If the result of this test is true, Visual Basic runs *command1;* otherwise it will do nothing or, when you have an Else, it will run *command2.*

If *condition1* **Then**
   [*statements*]
[**ElseIf** *condition2* **Then**
   [*statements*]]
[**Else**
   [*statements*]]
End If

When you want to run more than a single statement in any part of the If..Then command, you'll need to use this format, which places the statements on separate lines from the If..Then and Else keywords.

Boolean Operators

In addition to the simple = comparison that you've been working with so far, there are a number of other operators, as you can see in Table 4.1. Some of these operators should be fairly clear, but others, such as Xor, are more advanced, and I won't cover them until later chapters when you need them.

We will, however, take a quick look at the Or operator, which is quite useful when you have more than one condition and only need one condition to be true. For example, if you have the Boolean expressions 1 = 1 and 1 = 0, and you write (1 = 1) or (1 = 0), the result should be true because the first expression

Table 4.1:	Operator	Meaning
Boolean Operators	=	Equal to; returns True if the values on both sides are the same
	< >	Not equal; the values on the two sides differ
	<	Less than; True if the left side is less than the right side
	>	Greater than; True if the left side is greater than the right side
	<=	Less than or equal to
	>=	Greater than or equal to
	Not	Invert all the bits in the number to its right; Not 0 = −1
	Or	Bitwise Or
	Xor	Bitwise Exclusive Or
	Eqv	Equivalent
	Imp	Implication

is true. And if you try this using the Print command, you'll discover that it is, in fact, true:

```
print (1=1) or (1=0)
-1
|
```

The And operator is quite useful when you have multiple conditions that must all be true. The following two examples should give you a better idea of how And works:

```
print (1=1) and (2=2)
-1
print (1=1) and (1=2)
0
|
```

The first example returns True (−1) since both expressions are true, but the second example returns False (0) because the second expression (1 = 2) is not true.

One final word of advice. When you have a number of operators in one expression (there are two equal signs and one Or in the example above), it's a good idea to use parentheses to make sure that Basic correctly interprets what you write. If you're not intimately familiar with operator precedence (which you learned about in Chapter 1), you could easily write a statement that looked correct to you, but which Visual Basic calculated in an order different from what you might expect.

Finishing Sketch

Enough theory! Let's get back to our Sketch program and fix the problem we had. If you run Sketch again, you'll notice it draws a line from (0,0) to your mouse location when you first click. You'll also notice that you can't draw unconnected lines. This turns out to be the same problem.

All these extra lines appear because the Line -(X, Y) command draws a line continuing from the last point. In the last chapter, you learned that Visual Basic remembers the last point using the CurrentX and CurrentY properties and that they're set to 0 when you first start your program.

What you need to do, then, is set CurrentX and CurrentY to the location of the mouse when you first click. How do you do that? You use a new event called Form_MouseDown.

Visual Basic runs the code you write in this event subroutine whenever you click the mouse button, but not during the rest of the time you hold down the mouse button. (On the other hand, the Form_Click( ) event that you worked with before only runs when you click *and then release* the mouse button.) In other words, if you click and hold, then move the mouse, Visual Basic first runs MouseDown, then it runs MouseMove (and finally Click when you release the button). And this is exactly what you want. You'll set CurrentX and CurrentY to the mouse position (X, Y) inside the MouseDown subroutine.

NOTE

The MouseDown and Click events are quite different. Mouse-Down is called as soon as you click the mouse button. But Click is not called until you release the mouse button.

Make sure the Sketch form is visible, then double-click on this form to show the Code window. Next pull down the Proc combo box and select the Mouse-Down event. The following code is all you need to add:

```
CurrentX = X
CurrentY = Y
```

Once you've entered these two lines into Form_MouseDown, run your program and see how it works. You should now be able to draw lines without the initial line from (0,0). You'll also notice that Sketch now allows you to draw lines that aren't connected to one another.

Well, that was pretty easy. But there is one last problem. If you click and release the mouse button *without* moving the mouse, you'll notice that Sketch doesn't draw anything. It should draw at least a point, so let's add yet another command that will draw a point even if you don't move the mouse.

To draw a point, you'll use another Basic command called PSet, which stands for Point Set and draws a single point (pixel) on the screen. The command PSet(X, Y) will draw one pixel at (X, Y). Add this command to the Form_Mouse-Down subroutine, which should now look like this:

```
Sub Form_MouseDown (Button As Integer, Shift As Integer, X As
➤ Integer, Y As Single)
    CurrentX = X
    CurrentY = Y
    PSet (X, Y)
End Sub
```

Reference: PSet Command

[*object.*]**PSet** [**Step**](*x!*, *y!*)[,*color&*]

The PSet command draws a single point (pixel) at (*x!*, *y!*). You can also use the same Step keyword and *color&* argument used by the Line command.

The first line is too long to print as a single line, so I've wrapped it to two lines, with the ➤ character indicating that the second line is a continuation of the first line.

We've done as much work on Sketch as we're going to in this chapter, so you might want to save your work. You can use the Save Project command in the File menu to save the project file, as well as any other files (Sketch.frm) that you've changed. In the next chapter, you'll add a menu bar to your Sketch program.

Related Tools

Select Case This command is similar to the If..Then command. It's most useful when you have a single variable that you're testing against several values. In other words, if you want to run a different statement for different values in a variable, use this command.

Functions Functions, which you'll learn about later in this book, are very much like subroutines, except that they return a value (either a number or a string of characters).

Summary

You learned a lot about building real programs in this chapter, and you'll learn even more in the coming chapters.

Code Window. You'll use the Code window throughout the rest of this book to write your programs. You display this window by double-clicking in the Form window, which is called Form1 in new projects.

Events. Visual Basic programs are built around event subroutines that handle such events as clicking the mouse button, moving the mouse, and pressing a key. In this chapter you worked with the Click, Form_MouseMove, and Form_MouseDown event subroutines.

Sub. A subroutine begins with the word Sub and the subroutine's name. Event subroutines are formed from both the object name (such as Form) and the event name (such as MouseMove). Subroutines end with the line End Sub. Any lines of code you write must appear between these two sets of lines.

If..Then. The If..Then..Else command allows you to choose which code you want to run, based on the result of a condition. Conditions are Boolean expressions that result in a True or False. In the Basic language, True = −1 and False = 0, and Boolean expressions return numbers of type Integer.

Properties Bar. You saw how to use the Properties bar to change the FormName and Caption properties of your Sketch program, and how to save the project to disk.

Chapter 5

Featuring

Mnemonic Access Characters

Control Names and Menus

Using the Menu Design Window

Control Arrays

The Index Argument

Adding a Menu Bar

In this chapter you're going to add to the Sketch program by adding a menu bar. As you'll see, this is something that's quite easy to do, which means you won't have to learn as much new material in this chapter as in the previous chapters.

Building a Menu Bar

Because Visual Basic provides a visual tool (which is why it's called *Visual* Basic) for building menu bars, building them is very simple. Anyone who's ever written a program using a language like C or Pascal will tell you it's a lot more work using those languages.

If you don't already have Sketch loaded in Visual Basic, use the File Open Project… item from the File menu to open Sketch.mak.

To use this tool, you'll want to close the Code window (if you still have it open) so your Sketch form is visible and active. You might want to click once on it to make sure it's active. Next pull down the Window menu and click on the Menu Design Window item. This will bring up a window like the one shown in Figure 5.1.

This window lets you create an entire menu bar, with all the menus and items you want. There are only a couple of new concepts I'll be using here, which you'll learn shortly. First, let's quickly review the menu you'll create (see Figure 5.2). You'll actually start with a simpler menu called Draw, with a single menu item: Exit. This will allow you to get a menu up and running quickly, without learning everything you'll need to know for the full menu.

Figure 5.1:

You display the Menu Design window by clicking first in the Sketch window to make sure it's the active window and then selecting the Menu Design Window item from the Window menu.

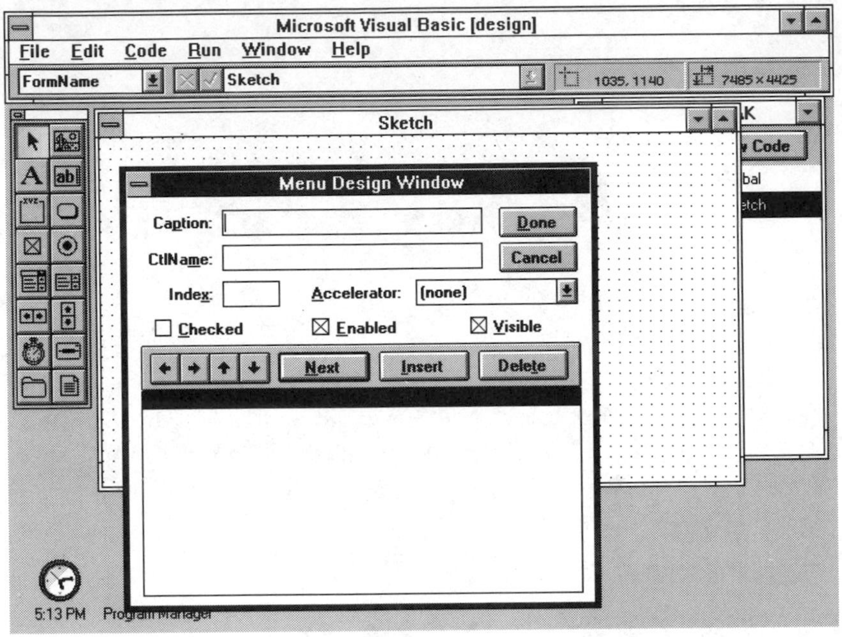

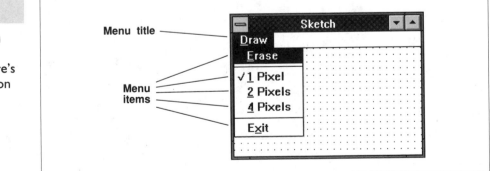

Figure 5.2:

The Draw menu you'll create. Notice that there's only one menu on the menu bar.

Creating the Menu Title

The first part of creating a menu is easy: Type in the name of the menu, which in this case is Draw. Notice, however, that the *D* in <u>D</u>raw is underlined. This tells Windows that you can use the Alt+D key combination to pull down this menu.

Such underlined letters are called *mnemonic access characters* in Windows jargon. This is quite a mouthful, but what it means is quite simple. Mnemonic characters are ones you can remember more easily than function keys, like F4, as shortcuts for some action. Such letters usually have some obvious connection to a longer name, such as the first letter. For example, when you think of Draw, the first sound you hear is the D sound. In other words, the letter *d* has a mnemonic connection to the word Draw.

Sometimes, however, you have two or more menus or menu items that start with the same letter, like File and Format in Word for Windows. In such cases, you'll have to use other rules to choose which letters to underline. See the sidebar "How to Choose Mnemonic Characters" for the rules that Microsoft suggests.

Windows, and therefore Visual Basic, uses an ampersand character (&) in front of a letter to mark that letter as a mnemonic access character. So to make the *D* in Draw the access character, type the following into the Caption text box of the Menu Design window:

&Draw

Next press the Tab key. This moves the insertion point to the next text box, called CtlName, which stands for *control name*.

Controls and Control Names

What's a control? It's a special type of object. You learned about objects in Chapter 3, when you looked at forms and the Printer object. There are also other types of objects in Visual Basic, and most of them appear inside forms. The menu bar and its items, for example, will appear inside your Sketch program (as soon as you finish building it). All objects that appear *inside* a form are called *controls*. All menus and all menu items are controls.

A control name, then, is the name you give to each control (object). In the CtlName field for your &Draw title, type the following:

menDraw

Here I'm using a naming convention I'll use throughout this book for the names of controls. I've put the letters *men* in front of Draw to indicate (to you, not Visual Basic) that this control name is the name of a menu.

How to Choose Mnemonic Characters

Microsoft has a number of suggestions on how to choose what letter to use for a mnemonic access character. These suggestions apply to all menu names, and to the names of all the menu items in any one menu. Here are the suggestions, in order of preference:

- **First Letter.** Use the first letter when you can. If you have more than one menu or item that starts with the same letter (such as File and Format), you'll have to choose a different mnemonic character for all but one name. You may also decide that another letter is more meaningful than the first letter, such as *x* for Exit. When you have a two-word title, you can also use the first letter in the second (or third) word. For example, many programs have a Save and a Save As... menu item. Notice that the *A* in Save As... is underlined.

- **Distinctive Consonant.** If you can't use the first letter, use a consonant that stands out. For example, the *t* in Format stands out more than the *r* or *m* because it's at the end of the word. On the other hand, the *b* in Ribbon is more distinctive than the *n*. There are no hard-and-fast rules.

- **Vowel.** If all else fails, use a vowel in the title. For example, Word for Windows has the following menus: File, Format, Tools, and Table.

You can see how Microsoft chose the *F* in File, the *t* in Format, and the vowels in Tools and Table by following all three rules. In all cases, you mark the mnemonic access character with an ampersand (&) in front of the character. For example, T&able marks the *a* in Table.

When you've finished typing in this control name, press the Enter key. This is the same as clicking on the Next button, which takes you to the next menu or item name.

Why do you have to provide a control name? So Visual Basic can provide an event handler for each menu and item. As you'll recall from Chapter 4, the name of an event handler is the object's name followed by the event name, such as Form_MouseMove. Here the names will look something like menDraw_Click( ). Even though you won't use this event, Visual Basic still requires you to give Draw a control name.

Creating the Exit Item

The next thing you'll create is the menu item Exit. First, type **E&xit** in the Caption text box, then press the Tab key. Next type **miExit** in the CtlName field (*mi* is a naming convention that tells you this is a "menu item"), but don't press the Enter key. First you need to tell Visual Basic that you want this to be a menu item rather than a menu. To do that, you'll need to click on the right-pointing arrow (see Figure 5.3).

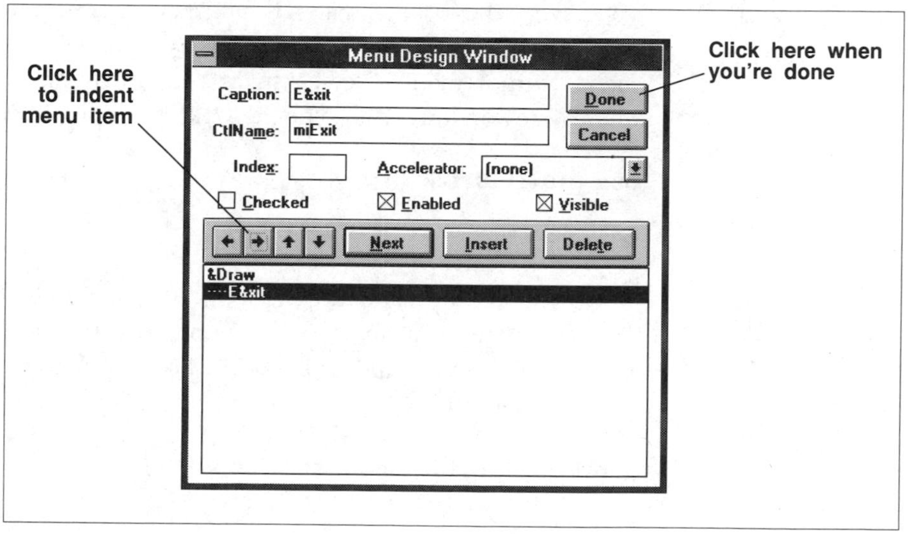

Figure 5.3:

Click on the right-pointing arrow to indent the Exit menu item so Visual Basic will know it's a menu item rather than a menu title. Then click on the Done button to finish editing the menu bar.

Finally, click on the Done button to close the Menu Design window. You'll notice that your Sketch window now has a menu bar, with a single menu called Draw.

Note

You may be wondering why I had you underline the *x* in Exit rather than the *E*. It turns out that Microsoft has a number of standard menu names and items, and Exit is one of these. If you look at most Windows programs, you'll notice they have a File menu with the last menu item being Exit.

Adding Code to a Menu Item

You're now ready to write some code to handle your new menu bar. The only menu item you have is Exit, which should exit your program. This is the same as double-clicking on the Control box in the upper-left corner of the window.

Each menu item has an event handler called *CtlName*_Click( ), which is called by Visual Basic whenever you click on a menu item. The control name you gave to the Exit menu item is miExit, so the event handler should be called miExit_Click( ). How do you get to this event handler? If you click on the Draw menu, then on the Exit item, Visual Basic displays the code for miExit_Click( ) in its Code window, which should look something like this:

```
Sub miExit_Click ()

End Sub
```

Do you know what code to put into this subroutine? When you select the Exit menu item, you simply want the program to exit, which means you want to use the End command. Type the End command into this subroutine and run your program.

```
Sub miExit_Click ()
    End
End Sub
```

Did selecting the Exit menu item work the way you expected it to?

Adding the Erase Menu Item

Let's go back and add another item to the menu. You'll add the Erase item, which simply erases whatever you've drawn into the Sketch form. If you remember back to Chapter 3, you learned about the Cls command, which erases a form. You'll use Cls here. But first, you have to add the Erase menu item.

Click on the Sketch form to make sure it's the active window. Then select the Menu Design Window item from the Window menu. At the bottom of this window, you'll see a list of the menus and items you've created so far; it should look something like this:

&Draw
....E&xit

Click on the second line, which is the one that reads E&xit. Then click on the Insert button just above this list. This will insert a new line (and therefore menu item) into your menu. It should look something like this:

&Draw
....
....E&xit

You can then click in the Caption text box and start typing (you'll have to click in the box because, as you can see, the insertion point won't be there until you click). Type **&Erase** for the caption, then press the Tab key and type **mi-Erase** for CtlName. Finally, click on the Done button. You should now have a menu bar with two items: Erase and Exit.

Finally, pull down the Draw menu and click on the Erase item. Then type the Cls command into the miErase_Click() event handler:

```
Sub miErase_Click ()
    Cls
Sub End
```

That's all there is to it! Now you have a simple menu bar that actually works. Try drawing in your Sketch window, then use the Erase command. Nice, huh?

Now you should save your project (using the Save Project item in the File menu) before you move on. In the next section, you'll add the menu items that allow you to change the width of the lines drawn in Sketch.

Completing the Menu Bar

In this section you'll add a total of five menu items to your menu: two separating lines and the three line-width menu items (1 Pixel, 2 Pixels, and 4 Pixels).

The first thing you'll want to do (can you guess?) is to bring up the Menu Design window. In the last section, you saw how to insert menu items before another menu item. You'll be using this technique to insert all five new menu items, so I won't step you through entering each and every menu item. But there are a couple of new techniques you'll learn.

Inserting Separating Lines in Menus

First, let's look at how you insert the two separating lines. If you type a hyphen (–) in the Caption text box, this tells Windows to draw a line across the menu. You'll also need to provide a control name for these two separating lines, even though you can't click on them. We'll use the names miLine1 and miLine2.

Go ahead and insert the first line, between your existing Erase and Exit menu items. Remember to set Caption to – and CtlName to miLine1.

Adding Control Arrays

Next add the three line-width menu items. The first one should have a caption of &1 Pixel and a control name of miPixel. But before you add the next menu item, there is another piece of information you'll want to add. If you look at the Menu Design window, you'll notice there is a text box labeled Index. Press the Tab key to move the insertion point into the Index box, then type **1**.

What's this for? It turns out you can create a number of menu items, or other controls for that matter, that are closely related to each other, and the Index field labels each control in a group. This will become clearer after an example, so let's continue creating the menu bar.

At this point your Menu Design window should look something like Figure 5.4. You can now enter the other two menu items and the final line using the information in Table 5.1 (which shows an index of 2 for the 2 Pixels item and an index of 4 for the 4 Pixels item).

Finally, close the Menu Design window by clicking on the Done button. You should now have a menu bar like the one shown in Figure 5.2. After doing all this work to build your menu, you might want to save your project. It's a good idea to save changes to your project often, in case Windows encounters the dreaded General Protection Fault (also known as a GPF, which was called a UAE in Windows 3.0), which most people encounter every now and then. GPFs result in a loss of all your work since the last time you saved your project.

Figure 5.4:

Your Menu Design window should look like this after you've entered the first line-width menu item, &1 Pixel. Notice that we've entered 1 (one) into the Index field.

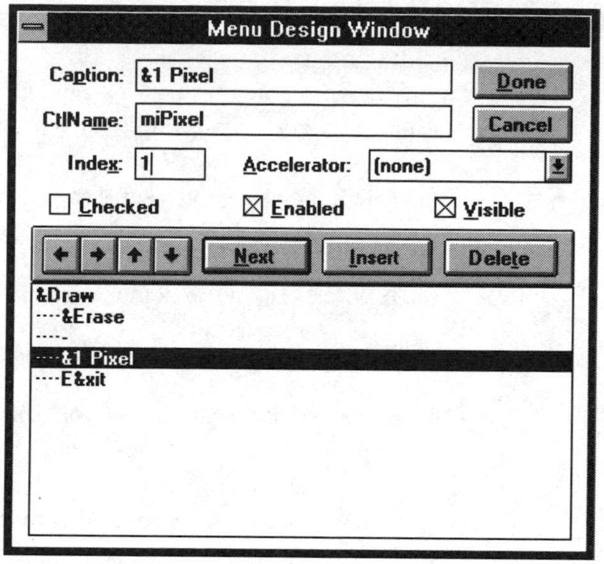

Table 5.1:

Menu Names and Control Names

Caption	CtlName	Index
&Draw	menDraw	
....&Erase	miErase	
....–	miLine1	
....&1 Pixel	miPixel	1
....&2 Pixels	miPixel	2
....&4 Pixels	miPixel	4
....–	miLine2	
....E&xit	miExit	

Notice that the Index field is blank for everything except the three *n* Pixel menu items. Also notice that the control name is the same for all three *n* Pixel menu items. The four dots (....) means that a caption is a menu item and shows the indent you'll see at the bottom of the Menu Design window.

Changing the Line Width

In the final section of this chapter, you'll add the code that allows you to change the width of your drawing pen. Once you see how it's done, you might want to add several more line widths to your program, by adding some more menu items.

Pull down the Draw menu and select the 1 Pixel menu item. The Code window should appear showing the following event handler:

```
Sub miPixel_Click (Index As Integer)

End Sub
```

There are two things different about this Click event handler. First, if you look at the Object: combo box, you'll notice it says miPixel( ). There are now two parentheses after the control name, indicating that we're dealing with a control array (which includes all three *n* Pixel menu items) rather than a single control.

You'll also notice that this event handler has an extra piece of information that you've never seen before: the "Index As Integer." What does this mean, and what's it used for?

The word Index is an argument to the Click event handler. Because you're now dealing with three controls that all have the same control name, you need some way to determine which menu item you clicked on. This is exactly what Index is for. It reports the value of the Index field from the Menu Design window. So Index will be 1, 2, or 4 because these are the three values you entered

Anatomy of an Argument

Any argument you see in Visual Basic appears in three parts:

ArgumentName **As** *Type*

The first part, *ArgumentName,* is the name of the argument and is Index in miPixel_Click. In the last chapter, you worked with the Button, Shift, X, and Y arguments in the Form_MouseDown event handler.

The next part, As, is one of Visual Basic's keywords, which tells you the next word will be the type of value this argument holds.

Finally, the variable's type can be Integer, Long, Single, Double, Currency, or String. See Table 2.1 for a refresher on types.

for the 1 Pixel, 2 Pixels, and 4 Pixels menu items. And you can now see why we chose to type 1, 2, and 4 into the Index field—these are the line widths we'll want to support.

The way to change the width of a line you draw is to use the DrawWidth property of a form. If you like, you can use the Immediate window to try out different line widths. Here are some examples you can try:

```
Line (0,0)-(1000,1000)
DrawWidth=2
line (500,0)-(1500,1000)
DrawWidth=4
Line (1000,0)-(2000,1000)
|
```

These commands will draw three lines, each with a different line width. The first line will be one pixel wide because Visual Basic initially sets DrawWidth to 1 when you run a program. The next line will then be 2 pixels wide, with the last line 4 pixels wide. Notice how the line widths are measured in pixels rather than twips, which is what the start points and endpoints are measured in. One of the things you'll discover about Visual Basic is that it's not consistent, which makes learning it a little more challenging.

By now you've probably figured out what code you need to put into the Click event handler, and you may even have tried it. Here's the code in its entirety:

```
Sub miPixel_Click (Index As Integer)
    DrawWidth = Index
End Sub
```

Reference: DrawWidth Property

The DrawWidth property of a form determines the width of lines that will be drawn on the form and is measured in pixels (*not* twips). By default, DrawWidth is 1 when you first start a program.

You can also change the default DrawWidth value for any form, which you do while you're in design mode. To do so, click on the form you want to change. Then pull down the Property combo box in the Properties bar and select the DrawWidth property. You can then type in a new number for the default DrawWidth.

That's all there is to changing the width of the drawing pen. Try running this program and changing the line width. Everything should work as advertised. But there is one last thing we'll add to this program before we end this chapter. If you look again at the menu in Figure 5.2, you'll notice that the current width has a check mark next to it. We're going to add yet another piece of code to keep this check mark up to date. As you'll see, this takes only two lines of code: one line to remove the current check mark and one line to check the new line width.

Checking Menu Items

Each menu item has a property called Checked, which controls whether or not a check mark will be drawn next to the menu item. By default, all menu items you create will not be checked. But you can easily check the correct menu item with this code:

```
Sub miPixel_Click (Index As Integer)
    miPixel(DrawWidth).Checked = 0        ' Uncheck current width
    DrawWidth = Index                     ' Change width of the pen
    miPixel(Index).Checked = -1           ' Check the new width
End Sub
```

Try this code, then we'll go back and see how it works (remember to save your project before you run your program). You'll notice that none of the menu items are checked initially; we'll fix this shortly. But once you select a width, it will be checked. And you can also change which width is checked.

Reference: Checked Property

Every menu item has a property called Checked that determines whether or not a check mark will be drawn next to it. The menu shown in Figure 5.2 has a check mark drawn next to the 1 Pixel menu item.

menName.**Checked = 0|-1**

Setting Checked to 0 removes the check mark, and setting it to -1 adds a check mark.

Now let's look at this code to see how it works. There are a couple of new concepts here that you'll learn about in the process.

Let's look at the first line:

```
miPixel(DrawWidth).Checked = 0        ' Uncheck current width
```

What does all this mean? Well, you know that DrawWidth tells you the current width of the pen. And you know that it can be 1, 2, or 4, since these are the values that Sketch can set DrawWidth to. You also know that you want to change the Checked state on the menu items for the current width. For example, if DrawWidth is 2, you want to uncheck the menu item called 2 Pixels. And that's what this command does. Let's now go through each part.

The miPixel control, as I mentioned, is a control array. This means that you have more than one control and that you can refer to each control in the array by a number. The number is the Index value that you typed into the Menu Design window. By writing miPixel(DrawWidth), you're telling Visual Basic that you want to work with the menu item with an Index value equal to DrawWidth.

This is also the first time you've changed a property on anything other than a form. As you'll recall from Chapter 3, properties are like variables, except that they're predefined by Visual Basic. All objects, such as forms, menu items, and the Printer object, have some properties. The Checked property you're using here is only available for menu items. You set a property by writing the menu item's name, followed by a period and the name of the property.

Control Arrays

The three menu items, 1 Pixel, 2 Pixels, and 4 Pixels, are a control array because you gave them all the same control name. You can refer to any control in an array using the following syntax:

CtlName(Index)

CtlName is the name of the control, and *Index* is the number that must match one of the Index values for a control in the array.

For a control array of menu items, the Index numbers can be any of the numbers you typed into the Index field of the Menu Design window.

Accessing Properties in Objects

You can read or change any property in an object, such as a menu item, using the following syntax:

ObjectName.Property

ObjectName is the name of the object (which can be a form, a control, or Printer), and *Property* is the name of the property that you want to set or read. Notice that you put a period between *Object-Name* and *Property*.

You can read a property by writing, for example, miPixel(1).Checked, and you can set it using the assignment operator: miPixel(1).Checked = 0.

The last part of this command is something called a *comment*. Comments are descriptions you can add to programs to make them easier to read in the future when you no longer remember what you were thinking when you wrote a program. Anything on a line that appears after a single vertical quote mark (') is treated by Visual Basic as a comment, which means Visual Basic will ignore everything after the quote mark.

You'll use comments often in all programs you write from here on. You can consider comments to be English-language descriptions of the Basic code you're writing. I can't say enough about using comments (and indeed, I'll say more in later chapters). Without comments, programs are very difficult to read. You'll probably be able to figure out what individual statements do, but you may not be able to figure out why the programmer wants to do something. Good comments should give you an idea of why the programmer (you) did something.

OK, now the only thing we have to do before we're finished is figure out a way to get the 1 Pixel menu item checked when our program first runs. This is really easy. Bring up the Menu Design window and click on the 1 Pixel menu item in the list at the bottom of the window. Then all you have to do is click on the check box called Checked. This will cause the 1 Pixel menu item to be checked initially.

The only thing left for you to do is to save your project. In the next chapter, you'll continue doing a little more work on Sketch, which will allow you to print out your sketches. In the process you'll learn even more about the Basic language.

In Chapter 7 you'll write another program, called Icon Clock, which produces the clock you have seen in the lower-left corner of the screens in this book.

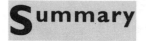

Summary

You're now finished writing your very first "real" Windows program. And you learned a great deal in the process.

Menu Design Window. You learned how to use the Menu Design window to add a menu bar to your programs. The only real trick is to make sure you're in design mode (not run mode) and that your window is active (you might have to click on it) before you select the Menu Design Window item from the Window menu.

Mnemonic Access Characters. You create mnemonic access characters by placing an & in front of the letter to be underlined.

Controls. Menus and menu items are all controls, which are objects that appear inside forms. Controls must have names.

DrawWidth. The DrawWidth property allows you to change the width of the drawing pen. This width is measured in pixels.

Control Arrays. Related controls (menu items) can be grouped into a control array. All menu items in a control array share the same control name, but each item must have a unique Index number. This number allows you to reference individual controls in a control array.

Checked. The Checked property for menu items allows you to check or uncheck items in a pull-down menu.

Chapter 6

Featuring

Defining Array Variables
Working with Arrays
The For..Next Command
Creating New Subroutines

Using Array Variables to Save Lines

The goal of this chapter is twofold. First, we're going to make some modifications to Sketch so it will remember all the lines you've drawn. This will allow us to add a Print command to Sketch, and it will also make it possible for Sketch to redraw your picture when part of its window is erased (such as by dragging another window over it). Second, you'll learn more about variables and writing Visual Basic programs. Variables are probably one of the most important aspects of any computer language, and they take a little getting used to. In this chapter you'll learn about some new forms of variables and how to work with them.

Designing a New Sketch

To redraw or print the figures, you'll need to be able to remember all the lines you drew. For that you'll use something called an *array*.

In the last chapter, you learned about control arrays. These are controls that are related and therefore all share the same name. You can also have a whole list of variables that all have the same name and are referenced using a number in parentheses (just as you referenced controls in a control array). Such variables are called arrays, and are very simple to work with, as you'll see shortly.

Here's an outline of what you need to do. First, you'll create two arrays, called saveX and saveY, in which you'll save all the points in the lines you've drawn. You'll also need a way to keep information on where one line ends and

A Word about Variable Names

You'll notice that I chose to use variable names, saveX and saveY, that start with a lowercase letter. But all the variables you've seen so far, like CurrentX, have started with an uppercase letter.

When you start to read other people's programs, you may find it difficult to tell the difference between properties and variable names. How can you tell if a name is a property or a variable name? Well, if all names start with uppercase letters, you can't. You'll have to look each name up in the *Language Reference* manual to see if it's in there. If, however, you start your variable names with a lowercase letter and all property names with an uppercase letter, you'll be able to tell at a glance whether a name refers to a variable or a property.

You'll also notice that I use an uppercase letter at the start of each new word, which makes reading variable names easier. For example, "longVariableName" is much easier to read than "longvariablename." (Of course, in languages like German you can have long names without mixed case, like "Damfschiffskapitänswitwe," which means "the widow of a steamship captain"—no kidding.)

the next line begins, and how thick each line is (remember that you can change the line thickness, so all lines may not have the same thickness).

I'd like to say a few words about writing programs. Whenever I have a program in mind I'd like to write, I think for a while about what I'd like this program to look like, and what I'd like it to do. Once I've figured that out, I don't sit down and write the entire program; that's a very difficult thing to do. Instead, I start with a simple piece and get it working. Then I add another piece. Adding one piece at a time is much easier than writing the entire program at once, because each piece is small and easy to work with. This process is known as *stepwise refinement,* and it's how most programmers write real programs.

What we're going to do with Sketch is start with a very simple piece. First, we'll write some code to keep a list of points as you draw them. Then we'll try to redraw these points when Sketch's window is erased. But here we'll just connect all the points we've stored without concern for where one line ends and the next begins, or the thickness of each line. We'll refine these additions later to add these "features."

So with that in mind, let's learn more about array variables so we can start to modify Sketch.

Array Variables

As you can see from the preceding discussion, two variables, saveX and saveY, will play an important role in your new version of Sketch. These variables will be arrays, so we can store a number of X and Y points in them.

To create an array variable, you have to define that variable, which also tells Basic how many "slots" the variables will have. For example, the definition

```
Dim saveX(1000) As Single
```

defines saveX as an array variable with 1000 slots, and it also says that each slot has the type Single (all slots must have the same type).

These "slots," by the way, are called *elements* of an array in computer-science jargon. So in the example above, there are 1000 elements in the saveX array.

Variable Arrays

A variable array is a group of variables that all have the same name and type. You define a variable array by placing a number in parentheses after the variable name. This number tells Visual Basic how many elements you want in the array. For example, Dim saveX(1000) tells Visual Basic that you want the array saveX to contain 1000 elements.

Each element in an array has an index value, which starts at 1 for the first element. You refer to elements in an array by putting the index value in parentheses after the name. For example, saveX(14) refers to the 14th element in the saveX array.

By the way, you can change the index of the first element in an array so it will be a number other than 1. There are two ways to do this, in case you're interested: You can use the To keyword (look up Dim in the *Language Reference* manual) or use the Option Base statement.

There are a number of new things in this statement (see Figure 6.1). First, you'll notice the Dim keyword, which tells Visual Basic that you're defining a variable. All the variables you've used so far have been defined *implicitly;* in other words, when you first used a variable, Visual Basic automatically defined it.

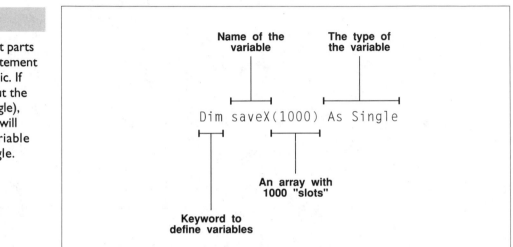

But array variables must be defined *explicitly* so Visual Basic will know how large to make the array (how many elements you want). The Dim keyword, therefore, explicitly defines a variable. (You can, and you will, use Dim to explicitly define any variable, not just arrays.)

You'll also notice the keywords As Single after the variable. The As keyword is a new keyword used to tell Visual Basic the variable type. In previous chapters, you always used special letters, like $ for a string, to define the type of a variable. But you have a choice. You can use either the type character (%, $, etc.) or As Single. Both of these statements have the same effect, except you must use the trailing $ in the second case, for example,

```
Dim someString As String
Dim someString$
```

Which form you use is really a matter of personal taste. If you look at other people's programs (which is a good way to learn, by the way), you'll notice some people tend to use As String, while others tend to use $. You'll also find

The As Keyword vs. Type Characters

Whether you use the As keyword or a type character to define a variable's type is really up to you. The table below lists the corresponding words and characters for all the types defined by Visual Basic:

Type Keyword	Type Character
As Integer	%
As Long	&
As Single	! or none
As Double	#
As Currency	@
As String	$

The only thing you have to remember when using the type character is that it becomes part of the name. So if you create a variable called someStr$, you must always write someStr$ with the trailing dollar sign.

people who use both methods for defining variables. So it's really up to you.

In this book, I'll mostly use the As String form of defining variables because I find it easier to remember words like String than characters like $.

Defining Form Variables

Getting back to the modifications to Sketch, you want to define two variables, saveX and saveY, in such a way that you'll be able to read and write these variables from several subroutines inside your form. (Normally variables are only available from inside the subroutine where they're defined.) In particular, you'll want to add points to saveX and saveY from inside both Form_Mouse-Move and Form_MouseDown. And you'll want to use these same points inside Form_Paint to redraw the picture whenever part of it is erased.

There is a special place where you can define such variables so they'll be available to all subroutines in a form. Make sure your Code window is visible (double-click on the Sketch form). Then click on the down-pointing arrow in the combo box called Object (see Figure 6.2). Finally, click on (general) at the top of this list.

The Object combo box allows you to switch between different objects in the form. You'll notice the Form object, as well as miErase and so on.

You'll notice this combo box lists all the objects (the form and controls) you created inside this form. It provides an easy way for you to move between the code for different objects inside a form. You'll probably find yourself using this combo box often to change from one object to another as you're writing programs.

The special entry at the top of this list, called (general), is used for things other than objects. The Proc combo box now reads (declarations), which means you're looking at the declarations part of the form. This is where you define variables you want to be available to all the code you write inside a form. (If you define a variable inside a subroutine, it's only available inside that sub-routine—see "A Word on Location of Variables.")

Once the (declarations) area is visible in your Code window, enter the following three lines:

```
Dim numPoints As Integer        ' Number of points saved
Dim saveX(1000) As Single       ' Saved X coordinates
Dim saveY(1000) As Single       ' Saved Y coordinates
```

A Word on Location of Variables

There are three places where you can define variables, and they each have a different effect:

Subroutine   When you define a variable inside a subroutine, it's only available when that subroutine is running. As soon as you exit the subroutine, Visual Basic forgets about that variable. Visual Basic creates the variable again the next time it runs that subroutine (with an initial value of 0 each time).

Form   When you define a variable in the (general) section of a form under (declarations), this variable is available to any subroutine inside the form.

Global   You can define variables in the global module (Global.bas in the Project window), which you'll do later in this book. Global variables are available anywhere in your program, rather than just in a form. This will become important when you begin to have programs with more than one form.

What happens when you define a variable inside a subroutine that has the same name as a form-level variable? In such cases, Visual Basic ignores the form-level variable. In other words, you won't be able to read or write the form-level variable in any subroutine where you've defined a subroutine variable with the same name.

Notice that comments are used to say what these variables are for. I'll use comments often, because even if you have a good name for a variable, you can always make it clearer with a comment.

Saving Points in Sketch

The next thing we'll do is modify MouseMove and MouseDown so they save points in these variables. To do this, we'll need to switch the current object back to the Form object; you should currently be looking at the (general) object. Pull down the Object combo box and select Form from this list. You should then see the Form_MouseDown event handler.

The MouseDown subroutine saves the starting point for a line, so let's add some code to save this point in saveX and saveY. Here is the new version of Form_MouseDown that saves these points in the arrays and draws the starting point:

```
Sub Form_MouseDown (Button As Integer, Shift As Integer, X As...
    CurrentX = X                       ' Start point for next line
    CurrentY = Y
    PSet (X, Y)                        ' Draw first point in line

    numPoints = numPoints + 1          ' The next free point
    saveX(numPoints) = X               ' Remember this point
    saveY(numPoints) = Y
End Sub
```

The three lines at the end of this subroutine are new, and you'll also notice I added comments to the other lines.

Next you'll want to modify MouseMove to save the endpoints of all the lines you draw. You can switch to the MouseMove subroutine by selecting it from the Proc combo box. Or you can use a new trick: Press the Page Down (or PgDn) key. This moves you to the "next" subroutine in the form. Using the Page Down and Page Up keys is a nice way to move quickly between all the subroutines in a form.

Here is the new version of Form_MouseMove, which is much like the new form of Form_MouseDown:

```
Sub Form_MouseMove (Button As Integer, Shift As Integer, X As...
    If Button = 1 Then                 ' Is the left button down?
        Line -(X, Y)                   ' Yes, draw a line

        numPoints = numPoints + 1      ' Next free point in array
        saveX(numPoints) = X           ' Remember this point
        saveY(numPoints) = Y
    End If
End Sub
```

You'll notice that this is a different form of the If..Then command here. In the last chapter we used a form of If..Then that fit on a single line. But here we're using the multiline version, which allows us to include a number of commands

> ## Keyboard Shortcut: Page Up and Page Down
>
> You can easily move between the subroutines in your form by using the Page Up and Page Down keys in the Code window. If you have long subroutines, these keys will scroll your subroutine one page at a time until you reach the top or bottom of the subroutine. The next Page Up or Page Down will then move you to the previous or next subroutine in your form.

in the Then part of the If statement. Thus, if Button = 1, Visual Basic will run all four lines between Then and End If.

I've also introduced another level of indenting. Programs are usually much easier to read (and therefore to write) if you use indenting to make it visually obvious how a program is built. Whenever you have some code that will be run if a condition is true, it's a good idea to indent it, as here, so it will be visually obvious that this *block* of code is at a different conceptual level than other parts of the code. You'll see many more examples of this in this book, as I'm very big on using indenting consistently to show how the program is built.

Now you can run your program to make sure there are no errors in what you've typed. It won't do anything different from the previous version since you're not using any of the points being saved, but at least you can make sure there isn't anything Visual Basic objects to, such as a typographical error.

Redrawing Forms

Most Windows programs have a way to redraw parts of a window that have been covered, then uncovered again. Whenever a part of a window is uncovered and therefore needs to be redrawn, Windows sends a *paint* message to that window telling it to redraw itself. Visual Basic works the same way.

Your form will receive a Paint event whenever your window (or part of it) needs to be redrawn. Pull down the Proc combo box and select Paint. This displays the Form_Paint event handler, which is responsible for redrawing your windows.

Let's try a simple experiment, which will give you an idea of when Form_Paint gets called. Put a Beep command inside Form_Paint to hear a beep whenever Visual Basic sends a Paint event to your program:

```
Sub Form_Paint ()
    Beep
End Sub
```

Now run this program. You'll hear a beep when Sketch starts running. This means you're asked to paint the window as soon as Sketch starts, which makes sense. After all, when Sketch starts, the window is blank (except for any controls you put in it, such as the menu bar).

Seeing Which Events Have Code

There is a nice feature of the Proc combo box you might be interested in. If you look at Figure 6.3, you'll notice that some of the lines in the Proc combo box are bold. The bold event handlers are the ones where you've added code, so you can tell at a glance which event handlers have code attached to them—in this case, MouseDown, MouseMove, and Paint.

Figure 6.3:

The Proc combo box uses bold characters to show which event handlers have code attached to them.

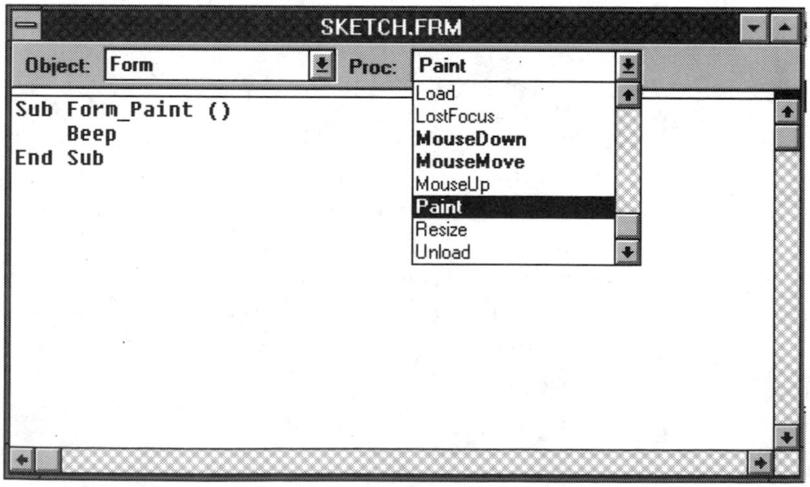

Next click on the Minimize button (the down arrow in the upper-right corner) to iconize Sketch. This simply makes the form invisible, so Visual Basic doesn't run Form_Paint. Finally, double-click on the iconized Sketch near the bottom of your screen. Sketch will return to a form and you'll hear a beep, telling you that Visual Basic sent a Paint message.

You might also want to try some other experiments on your own. Try covering part of Sketch's window with another window. Then uncover part of Sketch's window. Sketch should beep whenever part of Sketch becomes uncovered.

Redrawing Sketch's Lines

From the preceding example, you can see that you'll want to write code in Form_Paint to redraw the lines saved in the saveX and saveY arrays. For this, you'll need a new command called For..Next, which allows you to run a set of commands a number of times.

But before we get to the theory, here's the new Form_Paint that uses For..Next:

```
Sub Form_Paint ()
    PSet (saveX(1), saveY(1))          ' Draw first point in line
    For i = 2 To numPoints             ' Repeat numPoints - 1 times
        Line -(saveX(i), saveY(i))     ' Draw the i'th point
    Next i                             ' Go to the next point
End Sub
```

Now try running this program. See how nicely that works? This program will now redraw any lines you've drawn. Of course, there are a few things it doesn't do correctly, but we'll fix those problems next. For now we at least have some code that redraws something.

Let's take a close look at what this new subroutine does. The first line should be clear, since you've used PSet before. If you look at the MouseDown event handler, you'll notice that PSet draws the first point in a line. But you'll notice one difference from the MouseDown subroutine. In MouseDown, you set CurrentX and CurrentY to the mouse location, *then* you called PSet.

As it turns out, the first two lines in MouseDown aren't necessary because the PSet command automatically sets CurrentX and CurrentY after it draws a point. Now that you know this, let's go back and change MouseDown so it's a little cleaner (in other words, as simple as it can be):

```
Sub Form_MouseDown (Button As Integer, Shift As Integer, X As...
```

```
        PSet (X, Y)                     ' Draw first point in line

        numPoints = numPoints + 1       ' The next free point
        saveX(numPoints) = X            ' Remember this point
        saveY(numPoints) = Y
End Sub
```

OK, now that you've made Form_MouseDown a little simpler, let's get back to Form_Paint. As you just learned, the PSet command draws the first point in lines saved in the saveX and saveY arrays. But think about that for a second. When you first run Sketch, Visual Basic calls Form_Paint even though Sketch hasn't saved any points yet. So the first line, PSet (saveX(1), saveY(1)), tries to draw a point that hasn't been saved. What happens?

You learned earlier that new variables are set to 0, including all the elements in an array. So the first time Visual Basic runs Form_Paint, both saveX(1) and saveY(1) are set to 0. If you look very closely at your Sketch form when you run Sketch, you'll actually see a small dot in the upper-left corner of the window because of PSet (0, 0). That's one problem with this program, which you can fix very easily:

```
Sub Form_Paint ()
    If numPoints > 0 Then           ' Are there any points?
        PSet (saveX(1), saveY(1))   ' Yes, draw the first point
    End If

    For i = 2 To numPoints          ' Repeat numPoints - 1 times
        Line -(saveX(i), saveY(i))  ' Draw the i'th point
    Next i                          ' Go to the next point
End Sub
```

As you can see, I added an If..Then command to see if there are any points before trying to draw the first point.

Now let's look at the rest of this subroutine.

The For..Next Command

The rest of this subroutine relies on the new command For..Next. This command is a type of command called a *loop,* which allows you to run a set of commands more than once. There are actually several different types of loop commands, but we'll cover just For..Next here.

The For..Next command allows you to specify the number of times you want to run the commands inside the loop. It also uses a variable you supply as a *loop counter,* which starts with some value and counts up, adding 1 each time through the loop.

So when you write

```
For i = 2 To numPoints
    ...
Next i
```

you're telling Basic to set *i* to 2 before running any commands. The variable *i* will then be increased by 1 each time Basic sees the Next i statement. And finally, the To part of For tells Basic when to stop repeating the loop. As soon as *i* is greater than numPoints, Basic stops running this command.

Let's use the Immediate window for a few experiments to see exactly how the For..Next command works. Enter the following commands into the Immediate window:

```
for i = 1 to 3: print i: next i
1
2
```

Why I Use the Variable i

You're probably wondering why I chose to use a variable called *i,* rather than something more descriptive like *count.* Most programmers use the variable *i* whenever they need a counter, and if they need more than one counter, they also use *j, k, l,* and so on.

The reason for this is entirely historical, having to do with a programming language called FORTRAN. FORTRAN was one of the first popular computer languages and was (and still is) used by many scientists and other programmers. FORTRAN, unlike Basic, uses the first letter of a variable name to determine the type of variable. So any variable name that starts with *i* through *n* is defined to be an integer. Since most counters (like *i* in the For..Next loop) are integers, programmers use the letters *i* through *n* as loop counters.

Even though many programmers have never learned or used FORTRAN, this tradition of using *i* through *n* for loop counters persists even today. And it's not likely you'll see this practice disappear since it's passed on from one generation of programmers to the next.

```
3
print i
4
|
```

NOTE

Here I've used a new fact: You can place several commands on a single line by separating them with a colon, as in the first line of this example.

You can see that Basic ran Print i three times, with *i* starting at 1 and ending at 3. You can also see that *i* has the value of 4 after the For..Next command finishes.

Let's try another experiment. Let's see what happens when the To value is less than the initial value. Will Basic run the Print command once in this case, or not at all? To find out, enter the following command:

for i = 1 to 0: print i: next i
|

As you can see, For..Next won't run any of the commands inside its loop if the initial value is greater than the final value.

Enough theory. You can see from this short description of For..Next that Form_Paint will call Line for each line saved, starting with the second point. You'll also notice that For..Next won't draw *any* lines if numPoints < 2. For..Next will only draw lines if there are lines to be drawn.

Remembering Separate Lines

We've now managed to redraw all the lines we drew using the mouse. But we're not keeping information on where one line ends and the next line begins. So if you draw several separate lines (by releasing the mouse button between each line), your program will draw a single line, rather than the separate lines (see Figure 6.4).

To fix this problem, we'll need to add two more arrays to keep track of the starting and ending points of lines. We'll call these arrays lineStart and lineEnd, and we'll save enough room for 500 lines (which is a truly arbitrary number).

Figure 6.4:

This figure shows how the current version of Sketch connects separate lines when they're redrawn with the Form_Paint subroutine. This is because we're not keeping track of where one line ends and the next begins.

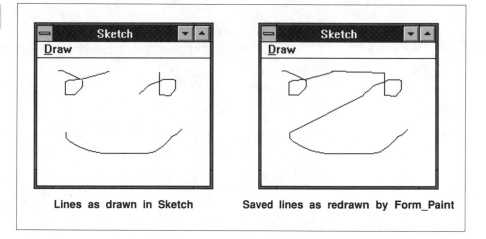

Lines as drawn in Sketch   Saved lines as redrawn by Form_Paint

Add these three lines to the (general) section of your form:

```
Dim numLines As Integer        ' Number of separate lines
Dim lineStart(500) As Integer  ' Start of each line
Dim lineEnd(500) As Integer    ' End of each line
```

Now you'll want to modify Form_MouseDown, Form_MouseMove, and Form_Paint to save and use these starting and ending points.

First let's modify Form_MouseDown so it will save the starting point (as well as an initial ending point). All the "points" you'll be saving in the lineStart and lineEnd arrays are actually indexes into the saveX and saveY arrays. Here are the changes to Form_MouseDown that save the starting index of each new line (add the three new lines at the end):

```
Sub Form_MouseDown (Button As Integer, Shift As Integer, X As...
    PSet (X, Y)                       ' Draw first point in line

    numPoints = numPoints + 1         ' The next free point
    saveX(numPoints) = X              ' Remember this point
    saveY(numPoints) = Y

    numLines = numLines + 1            ' Next free line
    lineStart(numLines) = numPoints ' Index of the first point
    lineEnd(numLines) = numPoints    ' Initially a single point
End Sub
```

Next we'll modify Form_MouseMove to update the index for the endpoint in a line. Each time Visual Basic calls MouseMove, we add another line segment

Reference: For..Next Command

The For..Next command runs a set of commands inside a loop a specific number of times.

> **For** *varName* **=** *initialValue* **To** *finalValue* **[Step** *increment***]**
>   *statements*
> **Next** [*varName*]

This command repeats *statements* between the For and Next lines. The variable *varName* starts at *initialValue* and increases by 1 (or by *increment*) each time through the loop. Basic stops running the loop when *varName* is greater than *finalValue*.

To make this command clearer, here is an English-language description of how Basic runs a For..Next command:

1. Set varName to initialValue.

2. If *varName* > *finalValue* Then we're all done.

3. Run *statements*.

4. *varName* = *varName* + 1 (adds *increment* rather than 1 if you use Step).

5. Go to step 2.

Note: If Step is negative, step 2 becomes "If *varName* < *final-Value*...." In other words, the values go down to *finalValue* rather than up to *finalValue*.

to the line we're drawing. Here's the new version of Form_MouseMove with one new line at the end:

```
Sub Form_MouseMove (Button As Integer, Shift As Integer, X As...
    If Button = 1 Then                  ' Is the left button down?
        Line -(X, Y)                    ' Yes, draw a line

        numPoints = numPoints + 1       ' Next free point in array
        saveX(numPoints) = X            ' Remember this point
        saveY(numPoints) = Y

        lineEnd(numLines) = numPoints' New ending index for line
```

```
        End If
End Sub
```

Finally, we'll need to modify Form_Paint to use this information. As you can see from the new version of Form_Paint below, Form_Paint needed more changes than the other two subroutines. In fact, this version is practically a new subroutine, so you might as well replace everything in Form_Paint with the code below rather than try to modify what you have now:

```
Sub Form_Paint ()
    For l = 1 to numLines          ' Draw each line
        aStart = lineStart(l)       ' Start index of this line
        anEnd = lineEnd(l)          ' End index of this line
        PSet (saveX(aStart), saveY(aStart))

        For i = aStart To anEnd      ' Draw parts of this line
            Line -(saveX(i), saveY(i))
        Next i
    Next l
End Sub
```

This new version of Form_Paint has two For..Next loops inside it. The outer loop (For l = 1 To numLines) runs the variable *l* from 1 to the number of separate lines you've drawn. The inner loop (For i = aStart To anEnd) draws all the parts of a single line.

I've added a couple of extra variables in this subroutine to make it a little easier to both write and read. By setting aStart to the starting index of a line and anEnd to the ending index for the same line, you can use these values in both the PSet command and the For..Next command, which means you don't have to write something like this:

```
PSet (saveX(lineStart(l)), saveY(lineStart(l)))
```

As you see, this line is hard to read because there are too many parentheses. Rather than write lines like this, I like to add a few lines of code to break long lines into several steps. So I find the following much easier to read (and to write):

```
aStart = lineStart(l)
anEnd = lineEnd(l)
PSet (saveX(aStart), saveY(aStart))
```

We've made quite a bit of progress so far. We only have a few things left to do in this chapter, and then we'll be done with Sketch. First, we'll want to modify Sketch so it will remember the thickness of each line. This isn't very hard to do, so you might want to try making this change yourself before reading the next section.

Then we'll have some fun. We'll add a Print menu item, then add some extra code that will allow you to print your drawings. Finally, we'll turn Sketch into an EXE file that you can run directly like any other program.

Remembering the Line Widths

If you haven't guessed yet, we don't have to do much to remember the thickness of each line. All we have to do, in fact, is add another array, called lineThickness, and then save the value of DrawWidth on each mouse click. Here are the changes you'll need to make.

Add this line to the (general) area of your form to declare the lineThickness array:

```
Dim lineThickness(500) As Integer    ' DrawWidth for each line
```

Next add this line to the end of your Form_MouseDown subroutine (on the line before the End Sub statement):

```
    lineThickness(numLines) = DrawWidth
```

Finally (yes, we're almost done adding this feature), add this line to Form_Paint immediately before the PSet command:

```
    DrawWidth = lineThickness(l)
```

(Make sure you type an el and not a one in the parentheses.)

And that's all there is to remembering the thickness of each line. Try this program and see how it works. (Remember to save your project, by pressing Alt+F V, before you run this program.)

Before we move on, there is one other small problem with our program. Do you know what it is? Have you tried all the menu items to make sure they work the way you expected?

It turns out that if you select the Erase menu item, Sketch doesn't forget all the points you've drawn, as it should. You can see this by drawing some lines, then minimizing and restoring your window. This will redraw the lines that should have been erased.

You'll want to modify miErase_Click so it clears all the lines you've drawn. You can do this simply by setting the numLines and numPoints variables to zero:

```
Sub miErase_Click ()
    Cls                      ' Clear the form
    numPoints = 0            ' Set to no points
    numLines = 0             ' Set to no lines
End Sub
```

In the next section, we'll modify Sketch so it can print your sketches, then we'll turn Sketch into a stand-alone EXE program you can run like any other program.

Printing Your Picture

Now that we've modified Sketch to redraw the picture, let's make one last change. We'll add another menu item, called Print, that will draw sketches on the printer. As you'll recall, you can draw on your printer simply by putting Printer. in front of each command.

Bring up the Menu Design window, then add another line and a Print menu item (see Figure 6.5).

Figure 6.5:

The menu item Print and the line that you'll want to add to your Sketch program. The control names should be miLine3 for the line and miPrint for the Print menu item.

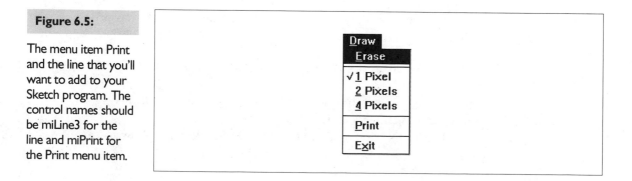

Once you've added miPrint to the menu bar, add the following code to miPrint_Click:

```
Sub miPrint_Click ()
    For l = 1 to numLines            ' Draw each line
        aStart = lineStart(l)        ' Start index of this line
        anEnd = lineEnd(l)           ' End index of this line
        Printer.DrawWidth = lineThickness(l)
        Printer.PSet (saveX(aStart), saveY(aStart))

        For i = aStart To anEnd       ' Draw parts of this line
            Printer.Line -(saveX(i), saveY(i))
        Next i
    Next l
    Printer.EndDoc
End Sub
```

You can see that this subroutine is identical to Form_Paint, except for the Printer. in front of each command that draws or changes properties (like DrawWidth). I also added a Printer.EndDoc command at the end of this subroutine. You need to use this command to tell the printer to print the page you've just drawn.

Your Sketch program should now be able to print anything you draw. Give it a try. Did you notice anything interesting? If you try different line widths, you'll notice the lines are much narrower on your printer. Why is this?

If you remember back to the last chapter, where you learned to change a line's width, you learned that line widths are measured in pixels, and the starting and ending points are measured in twips. What this means is that anything you draw on the printer, using points measured in twips, keeps the same size no matter what printer you print to. But line widths, since they're measured in pixels, are much smaller on high-resolution printers, like laser printers.

But what do you do if you want a line to keep its width in twips? The easiest thing to do for now is to modify the DrawWidth line in miPrint_Click like this:

```
Printer.DrawWidth = lineThickness(l) * 3
```

Multiplying by 3 is correct if you're using a laser printer, but it may not be correct for other printers. Figure 6.6 illustrates these ideas.

Later in this book you'll find a section that describes how to calculate the correct multiplier for any printer you use.

Figure 6.6:

DrawWidth set to 4 on both the screen and a laser printer. The lines won't be as thick on the printer because DrawWidth is measured in pixels, and pixels are smaller on a printer.

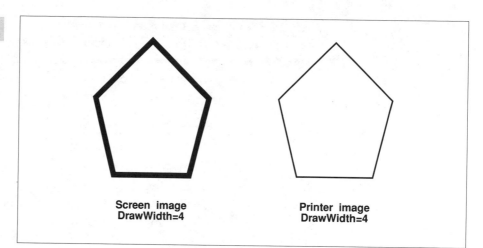

Creating an EXE Program

Now that you have a finished program that's fun to play with, you can turn this program into an EXE file, which you'll be able to run without starting Visual Basic. To create an EXE file, pull down the File menu and select Make EXE File…. You'll see the dialog box shown in Figure 6.7.

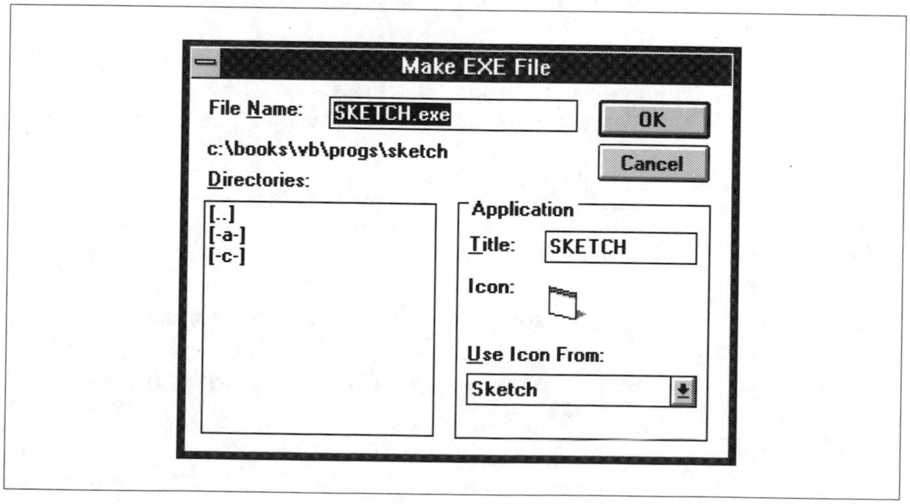

Figure 6.7:

You'll see this dialog box when you select Make EXE File… from the File menu. Simply click on OK to create SKETCH.EXE.

Press Enter (or click on OK) to create an EXE program called SKETCH.EXE. Now you can run Sketch from the File Manager, just as you can run any other Windows program. You can give a copy of this program to anyone you like, and they don't have to have Visual Basic on their computer. They do, however, need a copy of VBRUN100.DLL in their Windows directory.

NOTE

If you want to give your new EXE program to other people, you'll have to make sure they have a copy of the VBRUN100.DLL file in their Windows directory. Microsoft gives you permission to give a copy of this file to anyone, along with any programs you write in Visual Basic.

The Final Sketch Program

You've made a number of changes to your Sketch program, so in this section you'll find a full listing of Sketch, as it stands now. Table 6.1 shows all the captions, control names, and index values for the pull-down menu in your Sketch program.

The following lines should be in the (general) section of your form:

```
Dim numPoints As Integer          ' Number of points saved
Dim saveX(1000) As Single         ' Saved X coordinates
Dim saveY(1000) As Single         ' Saved Y coordinates

Dim numLines As Integer           ' Number of separate lines
Dim lineStart(500) As Integer     ' Start of each line
Dim lineEnd(500) As Integer       ' End of each line
Dim lineThickness(500) As Integer ' DrawWidth for each line
```

Here are all the event handlers in Sketch, in alphabetical order:

```
Sub Form_MouseDown (Button As Integer, Shift As Integer, X As...
    PSet (X, Y)                    ' Draw first point in line

    numPoints = numPoints + 1      ' The next free point
    saveX(numPoints) = X           ' Remember this point
    saveY(numPoints) = Y
```

Table 6.1:	Caption	CtlName	Index
Captions, Control Names, and Index Values for the Sketch Pull-Down Menu	&Draw	menDraw	
	....&Erase	miErase	
	....–	miLine1	
	....&1 Pixel	miPixel	1
	....&2 Pixels	miPixel	2
	....&4 Pixels	miPixel	4
	....–	miLine2	
	....&Print	miPrint	
	....–	miLine3	
	....E&xit	miExit	

```
    numLines = numLines + 1          ' Next free line
    lineStart(numLines) = numPoints  ' Index of the first point
    lineEnd(numLines) = numPoints    ' Initially a single point
    lineThickness(numLines) = DrawWidth
End Sub
```

```
Sub Form_MouseMove (Button As Integer, Shift As Integer, X As...
    If Button = 1 Then                ' Is the left button down?
        Line -(X, Y)                  ' Yes, draw a line

        numPoints = numPoints + 1     ' Next free point in array
        saveX(numPoints) = X          ' Remember this point
        saveY(numPoints) = Y

        lineEnd(numLines) = numPoints ' New ending index for line
    End If
End Sub
```

```
Sub Form_Paint ()
    For l = 1 to numLines             ' Draw each line
        aStart = lineStart(l)         ' Start index of this line
        anEnd = lineEnd(l)            ' End index of this line
        DrawWidth = lineThickness(l)
```

```
            PSet (saveX(aStart), saveY(aStart))

            For i = aStart To anEnd       ' Draw parts of this line
                Line -(saveX(i), saveY(i))
            Next i
    Next l
End Sub
```

```
Sub miErase_Click ()
    Cls                          ' Clear the form
    numPoints = 0                ' Set to no points
    numLines = 0                 ' Set to no lines
End Sub
```

```
Sub miExit_Click ()
    End
End Sub
```

```
Sub miPixel_Click (Index As Integer)
    miPixel(DrawWidth).Checked = 0   ' Uncheck current width
    DrawWidth = Index                ' Change width of the pen
    miPixel(Index).Checked = -1      ' Check the new width
End Sub
```

```
Sub miPrint_Click ()
    For l = 1 to numLines            ' Draw each line
        aStart = lineStart(l)        ' Start index of this line
        anEnd = lineEnd(l)           ' End index of this line
        Printer.DrawWidth = lineThickness(l) * 3
        Printer.PSet (saveX(aStart), saveY(aStart))

        For i = aStart To anEnd       ' Draw parts of this line
            Printer.Line -(saveX(i), saveY(i))
        Next i
    Next l
    Printer.EndDoc
End Sub
```

Related Tools

Array Lower Index The arrays in this chapter have a starting index of 1 and count up from there. You can also change the first index number for an array, in two ways. First, you can use the Option Base statement to change the lower bound from 1 to any other number. This will apply to all arrays. Second, you can use the To keyword when you define an array. For example, Dim a(−10 To 10) defines an array with index values that range from −10 to 10.

Array Bounds The UBound and LBound functions allow you to find out the lowest and highest index value for any array. For example, if you define an array with Dim a(−10 To 10), then LBound(a, 1) returns −10. For more details, see the *Language Reference* manual.

Erasing Arrays If you ever need to erase all the variables in an array (set them to 0 or to an empty string for String variables), you can use the Erase command. For example, to erase an array called A, you would type Erase A.

Dynamic Arrays Sometimes you may want to change the size of an array while your program is running. For such cases, Visual Basic has a type of array called a *dynamic array*. Dynamic arrays can change in size as your program runs.

You define a dynamic array by leaving out the size in the Dim statement. For example, Dim A( ) defines an array A as a dynamic array. To use this array, you need to set a size for the array using the ReDim command. This command erases any elements that might have been in the array and creates a new array of the size you ask for. The only problem with ReDim is that you can't change the size of an array without losing all the values stored in the array.

Loops In addition to the For..Next statement, Visual Basic supports several other loops. Each type of loop has its own advantages, so here is a summary of the types of loops in Visual Basic:

For..Next   Repeats a set of statements a specific number of times.

Here is the syntax:

For *counter* **=** *start* **To** *end* [**Step** *increment*]
    [*statements*]

Next [*counter*]

Do..Loop   Allows you to repeat a loop as long as (or until) a condition is true (like you'd use in If..Then). There are five forms, summarized below. Which form you use really depends on which is most convenient for solving a specific problem.

While..Wend   Works exactly like the Do While..Loop statement. I suggest you use Do..Loop instead since this is a more recent addition to the Basic language and is more flexible.

In general, it's best to use For..Next if you want to repeat some commands a specific number of times and to use the Do..Loop command whenever you need to test a condition to tell when you're finished running the loop. Here is a summary of the five versions of Do..Loop you might want to use and a discussion of how they're different:

Repeats *statements* as long as *condition* is True (could be zero times):

Do While *condition*
    statements
Loop

Repeats *statements* until *condition* is True (could be zero times):

Do Until *condition*
    statements
Loop

Repeats *statements* as long as *condition* is True (at least one time):

Do
    statements
Loop While *condition*

Repeats *statements* until *condition* is True (at least one time):

Do
    statements
Loop Until *condition*

Repeats *statements* forever:

Do
    statements
Loop

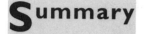ummary

This is the last chapter on the Sketch program. In the next chapter, you'll build a new program, which is the clock you see at the bottom-left corner of the screens in this book.

In this chapter you learned more about building Visual Basic programs. In particular, you learned the following:

Stepwise Refinement. You had your first introduction to building programs through stepwise refinement. With this technique you build a program one step at a time, and each step is a fairly small one. After each step, you test your program and see how it works. Building a program one small step at a time is much easier than trying to build too much at a time.

Array Variables. You learned about array variables, which are variables that share the same name and type. Each array consists of a fixed number of elements, and you get to any element using an index in parentheses. For example, saveX(9) returns the ninth element of the saveX array. You use the Dim keyword to define array variables.

Form Variables. Any variable defined in the (general) area of a form, which you get to using the Object combo box, is available to all subroutines inside a form. You defined several variables and arrays so they would be available to all your subroutines.

Form_Paint. Every time your program needs to redraw parts of its window because part of the window is being erased by another window, Visual Basic calls your form's Form_Paint event handler. You used this subroutine to redraw the lines in Sketch.

For..Next. You used the For..Next command to repeat a group of commands so you could draw all the lines you saved. For..Next allows you to specify how many times a group of statements (called a *code block*) should be run. It also uses a *counter variable,* which counts up from a starting value to an ending value. You used this counter as the index into the saveX and saveY arrays.

Creating EXE Programs. Finally, you turned your Sketch program into an EXE program that you can run just like any other Windows program (without using Visual Basic).

Chapter 7

Featuring

Working with Minimized Icons
Using Timers
Reading the Clock
Formatting Times
Custom Drawing Scales
Constants
Drawing in Color
Erasing Lines

Building a Clock Program

Building programs is what Visual Basic is all about, and that's exactly what you'll be doing in Part II of this book. In this chapter you'll build another small program, called Icon Clock, which displays the current time inside an icon. This is the small clock you've seen in the screen shots throughout this book.

As you're building this program, which is a little larger than the Sketch program, you'll learn more new concepts, and you'll also get a chance to gain more experience with ideas you learned in previous chapters.

In the next chapter, you'll start on a completely new program, called Address Book, that will take a number of chapters to build. Through this program, you'll learn more about the Basic language and building programs with Visual Basic. And you'll also learn more about how to go about building a program once you have an idea.

Designing Icon Clock

Before starting to build any program, you'll want to take at least a few minutes to think about what you want to build. Building a program without some game plan is quite hard to do because it's hard to know where to start.

The first thing to think about is what you want your program to look like and what you want it to do. Well, for Icon Clock, you already know what it looks like (see Figure 7.1). And you also have a pretty good idea about how it should work, since it works much like a real clock.

But there are a few things to review just to make sure we're all headed in the same direction. First, you'll notice that the program draws inside the icon. Very few programs draw inside an icon like this; most programs just let

Figure 7.1:

What you'll want Icon Clock to look like when you're done

11:50 AM

Windows show their default icon when they're minimized. But as you'll see in this chapter, it's actually very easy to draw inside an icon when you're using Visual Basic.

The icon you'll use is a blank clock face—everything you see in Figure 7.1 except for the clock hands—so you'll need to draw the clock hands yourself. Both the hour and minute hands are drawn in black, as two-pixel-wide lines. To make the second hand stand out like the clocks in kitchens, you'll draw the second hand in red rather than black.

Writing a program that does all this can be somewhat daunting unless you start with something simple, then work your way to a more and more complicated (and complete) program. As I mentioned in the last chapter, this process is known as stepwise refinement.

In this case we'll start with the very basics. We'll experiment with minimized programs to learn a little about how they work and how to draw in them. Then we'll move on to working with the caption underneath the clock. You'll learn how to get the current time from your computer and how to put it into the caption under the cursor.

Only then will we tackle the problem of drawing the clock hands inside the window and changing them every second. Now that we have a game plan, we can set to work, starting with minimized programs.

Working with Icons

As promised, the first thing we'll do is experiment with minimized programs and icons. Fire up Visual Basic with a new project (the default when you start Visual Basic), which will ensure that you have an empty window (form) called Form1. Next click on the Minimize button of the Form1 window to turn it into an icon (see Figure 7.2).

The icon used for Form1 is a generic icon that Visual Basic supplies to any new form you create. In a short while you'll see how to change this to an icon of your choosing, but for now we're going to work with this icon.

Figure 7.2:

If you click on the Minimize button of Form1, it will turn into an icon near the bottom-left corner of your screen. It should look like the icon labeled Form1 in this figure.

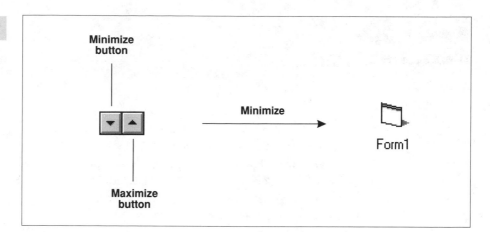

Drawing in an Icon

The first thing we'll do is experiment with drawing in this icon. From these simple experiments, you'll get an idea of how to draw the clock hands later in this chapter.

You've already done a bit of drawing inside forms—that's what the Sketch program was all about. But what happens when you minimize a form so it becomes an icon on the desktop? Can you still draw in it using the same commands?

Let's try a few experiments to see what happens. Keep Form1 minimized and press F5 followed by Ctrl+Break to show the Immediate window. You'll probably need to move the Immediate window up so it's not covering this minimized icon before you enter commands.

Enter this command and notice what happens to the icon:

line (0,0)-(300,300)

You'll see a new line from the upper-left corner of this icon to about its middle (see Figure 7.3). This tells you that you can use the Line command to draw inside an icon just as easily as you can draw inside a form.

But what happens when you try to clear this picture with Cls? Will it clear the entire picture? Try it:

cls

Figure 7.3:

The Line command

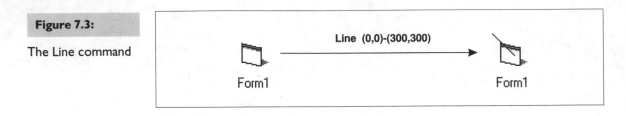

As you can see, the icon's still there but now the line's gone. The Cls command erases anything you draw inside an icon, but it doesn't erase the icon itself. This probably isn't exactly what you expected. I know the first time I tried a Cls with an icon I expected Visual Basic to erase the icon as well as the line I drew. But as you can see, it doesn't.

This is actually quite handy, because you don't have to write any code to draw the clock face itself. I've provided an icon for that. Then you're left just with the task of drawing the hands on the clock.

Now that you know how to draw inside an icon, let's move on to the next experiment: changing the caption underneath the icon.

Setting the Caption

If you remember back to Chapter 4, you learned that the title of a window is controlled by a property called Caption. You used the Properties bar to change the caption of the Sketch window to Sketch. But you can also change a window's caption using a command inside your program. All you have to do is assign a new string to the Caption property, like this:

```
caption = "testing..."
|
```

Try this out, and you'll see something like Figure 7.4. Changing a window's caption couldn't be easier. By the way, a window's caption appears inside the title bar when a window is normal size and underneath the icon when a window is minimized, as in Figure 7.4.

Figure 7.4:

Changing the caption on a minimized form

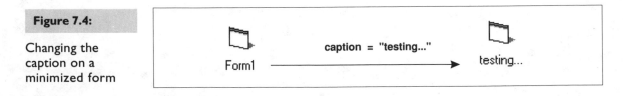

Incidentally, I know one professional programmer who spent several days figuring out how to change the caption in a program he was writing using a "real" programming language called C. Isn't it nice Visual Basic makes this so simple? You've now learned everything there is to know about changing the caption inside a Visual Basic program!

Reading the Clock

We're making fairly good progress doing our initial research. You now know how to draw inside the icon of a minimized program and how to set the caption below an icon. As soon as we figure out how to get the current time, we can actually start to write the program.

Visual Basic has a very special string called Time$ that will give you the current time. The easiest way to see how this works is to try an example, using the Print command to display the value of Time$:

```
print time$
13:48:43
|
```

And if you try this again after only a short pause:

```
print time$
13:49:22
|
```

You can see from these examples that Time$ isn't like other variables because each time you use it, it has a different value. In many ways, though, it acts like a variable. In fact, you can even assign a value to this "variable," which changes the time of the clock (you probably don't want to run this example because it will reset your clock to 1:20 AM):

```
time$ = "1:20"
print time$
01:20:04
|
```

You may have noticed from this example and the one above it that Visual Basic reports the time using a 24-hour format. I don't know about you, but I find it easier to read times with AM/PM, probably because this is what I've grown up with (the standard time display everywhere but the United States and Latin America is in the 24-hour format).

For now we'll use 24-hour time to build the program. Then later in this chapter I'll show you how to display the time using the AM/PM format.

Using Timers

Now you can go back to design mode (type **End** in the Immediate window or select End from the Run menu) to start building Icon Clock.

There is another window in Visual Basic that you'll use in this chapter. It's called the *Toolbox* (see Figure 7.5).

Restore the Form1 window to its normal size by double-clicking on its icon at the bottom of the screen. You'll use the Toolbox to create a new control inside this form, called a timer control. Timer controls have an event handler, called Timer, that you'll use to display a new time in the caption every second.

Figure 7.5:

You'll see the Toolbox on the left side of your screen. It allows you to create various types of controls on your form.

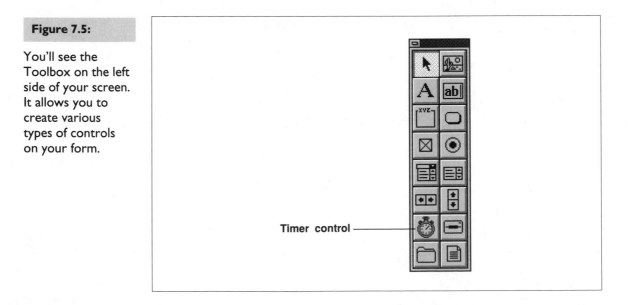

Creating a Timer

To create a timer, first click on the icon in the Toolbox that looks like a stopwatch (it's the one marked in Figure 7.5). This highlights the stopwatch, but it won't actually create the timer. To do that, you'll need to use the mouse.

Click with the mouse anywhere inside the Form1 window and hold down the button. Then drag the mouse down and to the right until you have a gray square about 1/2 inch on each side. When you release the mouse button, you'll see a small clock inside a box, as shown in Figure 7.6.

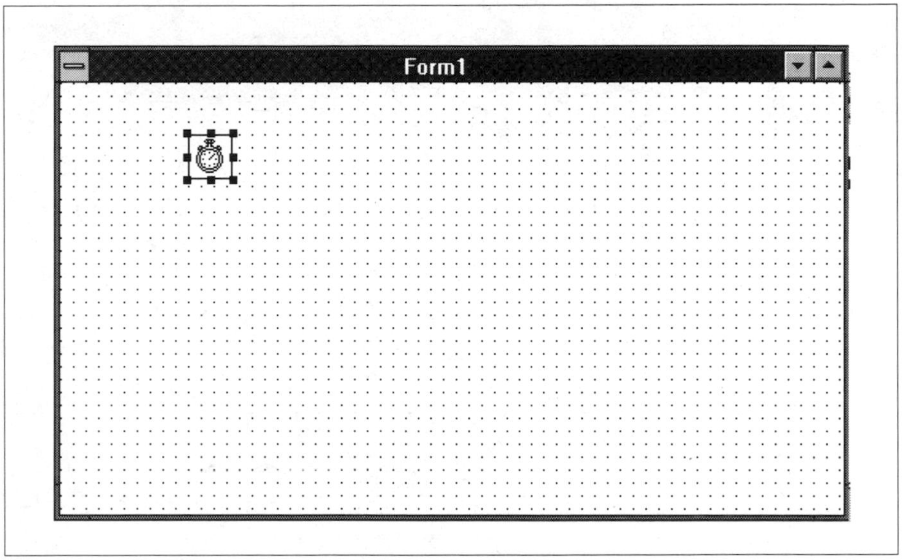

Figure 7.6:

Your form should look something like this after you create a timer object by clicking and dragging. The eight black squares along the outside of this timer are called handles and appear whenever you click on the object in design mode.

Before we move on, let's take a look at what we've got here. First of all, you've just created a new object, which is different from all the other objects you've been working with so far. You've only worked with Forms, Printer, and menu objects. But Visual Basic allows you to create a number of other objects, and you'll use many of them by the end of this book.

You'll notice that this object has a total of eight black squares around it. These squares are known as *handles,* because you can use them to change the size of objects. (As it turns out, the timer object is the only object that you can't change the size of.) If you don't see the handles around the timer, click on the timer inside the form.

Using the Toolbox to Create Objects

All the icons you see in the Toolbox (Figure 7.5) are objects you can create inside a form. You create any object by following these steps:

1. Click on the icon for the object you want to create (the timer in our example).

2. Click and drag to outline the area you want the object to cover. The timer object will always be the same size, but other objects can be different sizes.

3. Release the mouse button, and you'll see your new object.

Finally, take a look at the Properties bar (see Figure 7.7). You'll see that the control name for this new object is Timer1. Visual Basic automatically assigns a name to a new object, but as you can see, it may not be the most informative one. The control name does tell you it's a timer, but it gives you no idea about what you plan to do with the timer.

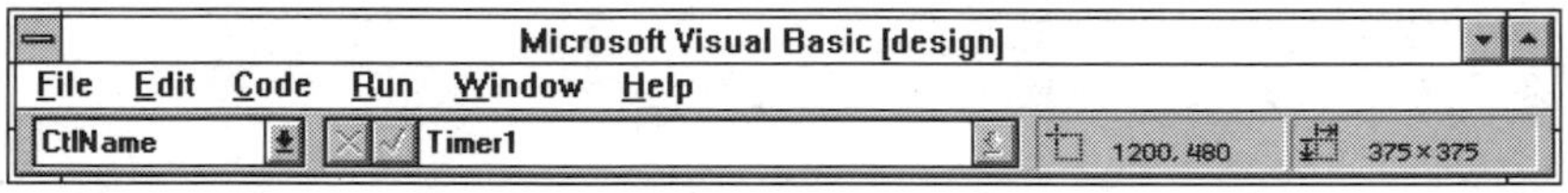

Figure 7.7:

The control name for the new timer object is Timer1.

Let's rename this control so it has a name that more closely resembles the function you intend to use it for. You're going to use this control to update your clock, so a better name might be something like Tick. Go ahead and change the CtlName property to Tick.

Setting the Timer

Your next step will be to run a very simple test program. I've mentioned before that it's best to work in very small steps, and I can't overemphasize the value of working with small pieces at one time. Instead of making all the changes so this timer will update the caption, all in one sitting, let's start with just making the timer beep every second.

There are two things you'll need to do to make your timer beep. First, you need to tell the timer how often to generate a Timer event. To do this, make sure your timer object has handles around it (by clicking on it), then pull down the Property combo box (the one that probably says CtlName now) and select the Interval property.

The initial interval will be 0, which means this timer will never generate a Timer event. You'll want to set this value to a number other than zero. But what number? What units are the intervals measured in?

Intervals are measured in milliseconds ($\frac{1}{1000}$ second), so if you want to generate a Timer event every second, you need to set this to 1000 milliseconds. To do this, simply type **1000** and press Enter (or you can select the 0 in the Properties bar, then type **1000**). You should now see the number 1000 in the Properties bar to the right of the Property combo box (see Figure 7.8).

Figure 7.8:

The Properties bar after changing the timer's interval to 1000.

Finally, double-click on the timer object inside your form. This will bring up the Code window, showing the Tick_Timer subroutine. Add the Beep command to this subroutine, so it looks like this:

```
Sub Tick_Timer ()
    Beep
End Sub
```

Now run this program. What you'll discover is that the timer object isn't visible in this window (it's only visible at design time), and your program should beep faithfully (or almost so; see the sidebar "The Timer Interval") every second.

Try experimenting with different interval values. Also, see what happens when you work with other programs while your Visual Basic program beeps away. For example, if you use the Program Manager (or File Manager) to run another program, you may discover that your program doesn't beep for a short while.

The Timer Interval

The Interval property tells a timer object how often to generate a Timer event and is measured in milliseconds ($\frac{1}{1000}$ second). But you don't, in fact, have this much control over how often your program receives Timer events, for a couple of reasons:

- Windows uses a timer inside your PC to determine how much time has elapsed since the last Timer event. But this internal timer only ticks 18.2 times every second, which is about 55 milliseconds. So you can never set the interval more accurately than 55 milliseconds.

- Windows won't always generate a Timer event as soon as the interval has elapsed, because Windows doesn't actually allow more than one program to run at a time. Instead, it lets one program process an event, then it lets the next program process an event, and so on. If you have a program that takes a long time to process an event, your program won't receive a Timer event until after that program finishes processing its event.

If this sounds confusing, just remember that your program will usually get a Timer event at about the right time, but sometimes it may take much longer than the interval value.

Showing the Time

Now that we've got the Timer event handler working, let's make it a little more interesting. In the next small program, we'll update the window's caption every second to display the current time. But before I show you the code, can you write it yourself?

Let's think about that for a minute. What you'll want to do is read the current time each second, then set the Caption property using this time. You've already learned all the pieces you need to build this program. All you have to do is put them together in the correct order, so give it a try.

Are you done yet? I'm now going to show you my solution to this problem. As you may have already guessed, the new version of Tick_Timer only requires a single line:

```
Sub Tick_Timer ()
    Caption = Time$
End Sub
```

Try out this program. Notice what happens when you minimize it? You'll see the caption flicker every second (unless you have a very fast computer). Flickering like this tends to draw your attention to the source of the flicker, which is great fun when you've just finished writing a program. But after a while, this kind of flickering bothers most people, especially when they're trying to work on something else. It can be downright distracting.

What can you do about this? Well, if you update the caption every minute instead of every second, you probably won't notice the flicker anymore. And this is exactly what Icon Clock does, as you can see in Figure 7.1.

The problem, though, is that Time$ always returns a time showing seconds. So you need some way to get a time that doesn't include the seconds.

Using Time Functions

To do this, you'll need to use some new commands in Visual Basic, and one of them is something called a *function*. A function is a command (or some code you write) that returns either a number or a string. Let's look at an example to make this clearer.

Functions in Visual Basic are very similar to the functions you learned about in math class. If you recall learning about the Sine and Cosine functions (which we'll use later in this chapter), these are mathematical functions that you can use to describe a circle. If you recall your geometry class, you'll remember that $\cos(0)$ equals 1. In fact, you can write this exact equation in Visual Basic, using the Immediate window:

```
print cos(0)
|
|
```

You can use functions very much the same way you use numbers or strings, so you can print the value returned by a function, assign it to a variable, and so on.

Visual Basic has other functions as well, including one called Now. The Now function returns the current time and date information in a single number, which Microsoft calls a *date serial number*. Microsoft doesn't say what the number actually means, but fortunately they do provide some other functions that take a date serial number apart. We'll use these other functions shortly, but first an example.

If you print the value of Now, you'll notice it's just a number and doesn't have any obvious connection to the current time or date:

print now
33645.5967013889
|

This number, by the way, has the type Double, which you'll need to keep in mind for later, when you define a variable to remember the value of Now at a single instant.

Visual Basic has four functions you'll use with the value returned by Now: one each to return the hour, minute, and second information, and one to nicely format the time.

Let's start first with the function that will nicely format the time reported by Now. This new function, called Format$, returns a string. It's a very useful and powerful function for formatting numbers of all kinds. Here you'll use just the part of this function that formats a date serial number using the AM/PM time display (rather than the 24-hour display) that doesn't show seconds. Try this command in the Immediate window:

print format$(now, "h:mm AM/PM")
9:55 AM
|

The Format$ function takes two arguments. The first one is a date serial number returned by the Now function. The second argument is a pattern that tells Format$ how you want the time formatted. If, for example, you want to display the time in 24-hour format rather than 12-hour format, you could use this string instead: "h:mm". Give this a try.

Reference: Now Function

The Now function returns a number of type Double called a *date serial number.* This single number contains all the information on the current time and date.

someVar = Now

Returns the current time and date information in a number of type Double

There are a number of functions you can use with the information returned by Now. Here are the functions you'll use in this chapter:

s% = Second(Now)

Returns the seconds, which is a number between 0 and 59

m% = Minute(Now)

Returns the minutes, which is a number between 0 and 59

h% = Hour(Now)

Returns the hours, which is a number between 0 and 23

s$ = Format$(Now, "h:mm AM/PM")

Returns the current time, using the U.S. 12-hour format (such as 9:55 AM)

Let's rewrite Icon Clock so it will use the Format$ command:

```
Sub Tick_Timer ()
    Caption = Format$(Now, "h:mm AM/PM")
End Sub
```

When you run this program, you'll notice the caption still flickers when your program is minimized, but now it displays the time in exactly the same format as in Figure 7.1. (Note: If you're in a country other than the United States, you may see the time displayed in your country's standard format instead.)

Now let's look at how to keep the caption from flickering. There are actually two approaches you can take. First, you could change the interval to 60,000, which is 1 minute. But since you'll want to draw a new second hand every second, this isn't the solution you'll use.

The second approach takes a little more work. We'll create a form-level variable, called lastMinute, that keeps track of the minute currently displayed. As soon as the current minute is different from lastMinute, we'll change the caption. If this sounds a little confusing, it will become clearer after a little more work.

Getting Information from Date Serial Numbers

Visual Basic has yet another function, called Minute, that returns the minute part of a date serial number. So if you type

print time$
9:58:04
print minute(now)
 58
 |

you'll see just the minutes part of the time. (The minutes will be different in this example if you wait too long between running these two commands.)

So here's what to do. First, define the variable lastMinute in the (general) section of your form:

```
Dim lastMinute As Integer        ' Last minute shown in caption
```

Next, we'll use this information in Tick_Timer:

```
Sub Tick_Timer ()
    Dim t As Double              ' The time information

    t = Now                      ' Get the current time
    min = Minute(t)              ' Get the current minute
    If min <> lastMinute Then    ' Update caption if new minute
        Caption = Format$(t, "h:mm AM/PM")
        lastMinute = min         ' Remember new current minute
    End If
End Sub
```

(If you changed the Interval property, make sure you set it back to 1000.) Try out this new program, then think about what it does before you read on.

There are a few things in this subroutine that may not be obvious. For starters, you'll notice I defined the variable *t* to be of type Double. Why did I do this? If you remove this definition, everything may appear to work correctly. But as you'll recall, the default type for new variables is Single, which can't contain as much information as a number of type Double (see Table 2.1). So you need to define *t* as Double to make sure you keep *all* the information returned by the Now function.

You'll also notice I used the variable name *t* to save the date serial number. Why didn't I use something more descriptive, like *time*? In this case you can't use the word *time* because Visual Basic already has a function called Time$; Visual Basic won't allow you to have a variable of the same name, so you have to use another name. We could use something long like dateSerialNumber, but since we're only going to be using this variable a couple of times, I've given it a very short name.

Let's look in detail at how this subroutine works. First, it assigns the value of Now to the variable *t*. I do this, rather than continue to use Now in the rest of the subroutine, to make sure you're working with a single time. If you don't do this, the time might change before Tick_Timer finishes.

Next it gets the minutes from this time and saves this value in the variable min. It then compares the value in min to the value in lastMinute. The symbols < > mean *not equal to*. So if min is not equal to lastMinute, Visual Basic runs the next two statements. In other words, it only updates the caption when min is different from lastMinute.

Finally, Tick_Timer updates the caption and saves the new minute it just displayed into the lastMinute variable. This ensures that it won't update the caption again until the minute changes.

Displaying the time in the caption was the easy part. Now for the hard part: drawing the hands on the clock face.

Drawing the Clock Face

Writing the rest of Icon Clock is a little more difficult because we'll be dealing with some trigonometry to draw the hands on the clock. Fortunately, there is something much simpler we can start with: changing the icon used for the minimized program.

Setting the Icon

The icon I use in this program is a special one I created using the Icon Works program that comes with Visual Basic. But you don't have to create this icon yourself because it's included on the disk at the back of this book. I'll show you how to use this icon in your own program.

Make sure you're in design mode, then click in your Form1 window to make it the active window. If your timer object has handles around it, click anywhere else in the form. This will ensure that your form, rather than the timer, is the currently selected object. Next pull down the Property combo box and click on Icon.

At this point you'll see (Icon) appear in the second box to the right, and you'll see a small button with three dots (...) to the right of this. Click on this button, and you'll see a dialog box like the one shown in Figure 7.9.

If you haven't installed the files from the disk at the back of this book, you'll need to do so now. Then use the Directories part of the Load Icon dialog box

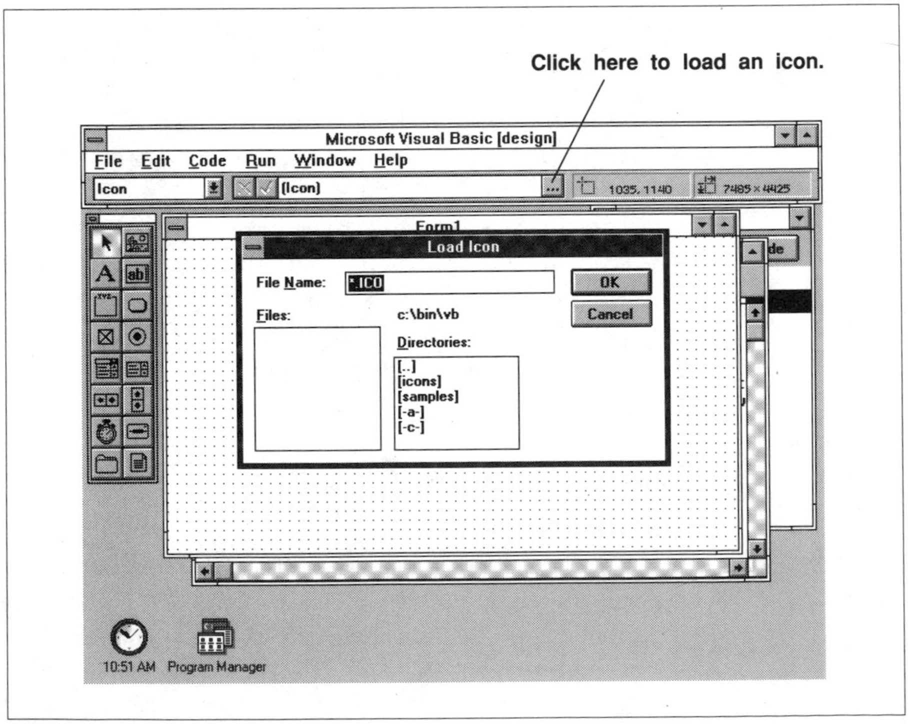

Figure 7.9:

The Load Icon dialog box. You can change drives and/or directories to load the Clckface.ico file.

to switch to the ICONCLCK directory. You'll find a file called Clckface.ico in this directory. Double-click on this file to load it into Visual Basic.

When minimized, your window should now look just like Icon Clock, except for the lack of hands. Our next project will be to draw the hands on the clock face.

Drawing the Clock Hands

Drawing the clock hands really isn't that hard to do, but it will take a much longer subroutine to do this than we've ever written before. We'll actually use several subroutines to do all the work.

Why does it take so much code? Well, for one thing, you'll be drawing three hands on the clock: the hour hand, the minute hand, and the second hand. And this is in addition to updating the caption, which you're already doing.

Let's start by drawing the second hand. Since it will move each second, we'll be able to see if it works correctly in all positions (and it will only take a minute). To do this, we'll need to review a little math, which is necessary to calculate where to draw the second hand. We'll be able to use the same code for both the hour and minute hands.

Figure 7.10 shows a blowup of the clock face, along with the hands drawn on the screen and a review of the trigonometry involved in drawing the second hand.

Figure 7.10:

This figure provides a brief review of the trigonometry we'll be using to draw the hands on the clock. We'll define the coordinate system to go from −16 to 16 since the icon is 32 pixels wide and high.

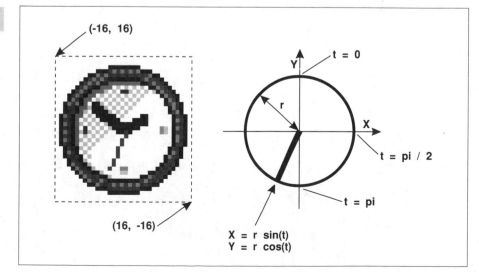

$X = r \sin(t)$
$Y = r \cos(t)$

Reference: Scale Command

The Scale command allows you to define a custom coordinate system for any form.

Scale [(x1, y1) – (x2, y2)]

Sets up a custom coordinate system, with the upper-left corner at (*x1, y1*) and the lower-right corner at (*x2, y2*)

If you don't provide any coordinates, Visual Basic resets the coordinates to the default coordinate system, with each unit equal to a twip, (0,0) at the upper-left corner, and Y increasing down.

If you remember the drawing you've done so far, you'll remember that (0,0) has always been in the upper-left corner, with increasing Y values moving *down* rather than up. But here you'll want to use a Cartesian coordinate system, with (0,0) at the center of the icon and increasing Y values moving *up*. How do you do this? You can fake it, by writing the equations to work with the standard coordinates. Or better yet, you can redefine the coordinate system so it's more to your liking.

It's easy to change the coordinate system; you use a command called Scale. This command lets you tell Visual Basic what numbers you want to use for the top-left and lower-right corners of your form. In the case of the icon, you'll use a range of numbers from –16 to 16, as you can see in Figure 7.10. Why these numbers?

Any icon for a minimized window in Microsoft Windows is 32 pixels (dots) wide and 32 pixels high. So by creating a coordinate system that spans the range from –16 to 16, we're creating a coordinate system where each unit is exactly one pixel wide. It's really not important in this case that each unit be one pixel wide, but we'll do it anyway since it really doesn't matter how large a unit is, as long as (0,0) is at the center of the icon.

Let's try a simple experiment using Scale. Start your clock program again and minimize it so you see just the icon. Then press Ctrl+Break to show the Immediate window, and enter these two commands:

```
Scale (-16, 16)-(16, -16)
Line (0, 0)-(10, 10)
```

This Line command draws a line starting at the center of your icon and ending 10 pixels up and to the right of the center (Figure 7.11).

Figure 7.11:

The effect of changing the scale, then drawing a line from (0,0) to (10,10)

1:29 PM

Now let's write the code to draw this second hand using the real time. Return to design mode, and make sure you're viewing the code for Tick_Timer( ). Then enter the following changes (notice I'm using the equations in Figure 7.10 to calculate the position of the second hand):

```
Sub Tick_Timer ()
    Const pi = 3.141592653      ' Define the value of pi
    Dim t As Double             ' The time information

    t = Now                     ' Get the current time
    sec = Second(t)             ' Get seconds, 0..59
    min = Minute(t)             ' Get the current minute, 0..59

    If min <> lastMinute Then   ' Update caption if new minute
        Caption = Format$(t, "h:mm AM/PM")
        lastMinute = min        ' Remember new current minute
    End If

    Scale (-16, 16)-(16, -16)   ' Set scale for clock icon
    x = 10 * Sin(sec * pi / 30) ' Calculate end of second hand
    y = 10 * Cos(sec * pi / 30)
    Line (0, 0)-(x, y)          ' Draw the second hand
End Sub
```

Then run this program.

You'll find two problems. First, this program starts out as a window rather than as an icon. You'll want to keep it as an icon. For now, minimize your program and see how it works. You'll then notice the other problem. Tick_Timer isn't removing the second hand after it draws it, so after a minute, your clock face will be filled with 60 second-hands.

Before we move on, there is a new keyword in this program: *Const*. The Const keyword defines a special type of variable, called a *constant,* which has a fixed value. In other words, you can never change the value of a constant.

Reference: Const Keyword

The Const keyword allows you to define constants in your programs. You can assign a name to a number or a string of characters:

Const *name* **=** *value*
Defines *name* to be a constant equal to *value*

I'll use Const whenever there's a constant value in a program, such as pi (which is written as π in mathematics but as pi in programs because you can't use Greek letters in programs).

Minimizing Icon Clock

Before tackling the problem of showing just one second hand, let's modify Icon Clock so it starts out as an icon rather than as a window. To do this we'll use another property of a form, called WindowState. WindowState can have three values:

0   Normal (default)

1   Minimized (just showing the icon)

2   Maximized (enlarged to the full-screen size)

Reference: WindowState Property

The WindowState property of a form tells you what state the window is currently in. You can also assign a value to this property to change the current window state.

The WindowState property can have any of these values:

0   Normal (default)

1   Minimized (shows as an icon)

2   Maximized (enlarged to full-screen size)

You can see that setting WindowState to 1 will minimize your program. But where should you do this? Should you set it to 1 on every clock tick? You can try that, but there are a couple of problems with this. First, your window won't be minimized right away; it will be minimized on the first clock tick, which will be 1 second after your program starts. Second, constantly minimizing your program can cause a lot of problems for other programs that are running (the reasons for this are quite complicated and subtle).

So where can you put the assignment? Well, there's another event handler, called Form_Load, that's only called when your form is first loaded. In other words, it's only called once at the start of your program (later, when you work with programs with multiple forms, you'll see that it's called whenever a form is loaded again).

Use the Object combo box to select Form, then select Load from the Proc combo box. Then enter WindowState = 1 into this event handler:

```
Sub Form_Load ()
    WindowState = 1                 ' Iconize the window
End Sub
```

Now your program will start out as an icon rather than as a form. However, it won't always remain an icon. If you click on the icon while your program is running, you'll see a Control menu pop up. This menu shows two items, Restore and Maximize, that can turn your icon back into a form. It's possible to remove these items, but we won't do it in this chapter.

But I'll give you a hint. There is a property called MaxButton that you can change while you're in design mode by using the Properties bar. Setting this to False removes the Maximize option from the Control menu.

Disabling the Restore option is much harder, and you have to use another event handler called Form_Resize to set WindowState back to 1. But, and this is important, you'll need to use an If statement to test WindowState, and only set WindowState to 1 if it's not already set to 1.

NOTE

You'll find a version of Icon Clock on the disk that comes with this book. That version has some more code in it to draw a form with some author information when you restore the window size.

Showing One Second Hand

We now have a program that starts out minimized, but we still have the problem with the second hand. Right now we're drawing the hand, but we're never erasing it, so we're filling the icon with black lines.

Think about this problem for a moment. How would you fix it? The first thing you need to do is identify exactly what the problem is; only then can you solve it. In this case, the problem is very simple. You're not erasing the previous second hand before you draw the new one, so you need a solution that erases this old second hand.

Right now you only know one way to erase anything. And that's using the Cls command. You also learned that the Cls screen automatically redraws the icon in your minimized program, so it erases everything *except* for the icon. In other words, the Cls command will erase only the second hand, since that's all you've drawn on top of the icon. Try adding Cls to your program, then run it. What happens now? (By the way, if you haven't made the change yet, here's how to do it. Put a Cls command in your Tick_Timer event handler on a line immediately before the Line command.)

At this point you'll notice that the second hand moves around the clock face. But the clock face flickers now, just as the caption flickered earlier in this chapter when you changed it every second. What we really want, then, is some way to erase the second hand without having to use the Cls command. In other words, we want some way to "undraw" a line. Which is exactly what we'll do after a brief side trip into colors.

Drawing with Color

At the start of this chapter, I promised that your second hand would be red, so let's learn how to change the color of the line. Doing this before learning a better way to erase a line may seem like we're getting off the track, but we're actually not. What you learn here will help make the next step clearer since the technique you'll use has to do with colors.

The Line command has an optional argument you haven't used yet. This argument allows you to draw lines with other colors. There is also a function, called RGB, that allows you to calculate a color number. RGB stands for red-green-blue because it takes three arguments: a red, a green, and a blue component. For a red line, you'll want to use 0 for green and blue, and 255 (the maximum value allowed for each part) for red.

Reference: RGB Function

colorNumber = **RGB(***redNumber***,** *greenNumber***,** *blueNumber***)**
Returns a color number, which you can use in the Line command to draw a line of any color

The red, green, and blue color numbers can be any number between 0 and 255. White is (255, 255, 255) and black is (0, 0, 0). The number returned by RGB is of type Long.

The RGB function builds color numbers used by the Line command and stands for red-green-blue, which are the primary colors used for television screens. If you remember back to your art classes in grade school (or later), you'll probably remember learning that the primary colors are red, yellow, and blue. So why do we use red, green, and blue here?

The primary colors you learned about in grade school are for *subtractive* colors, because if you use paint and combine all the primary colors, you'll end up with a very dark mess. On the other hand, when you're working with light rather than paint, you're working with *additive colors*. In this case the primary colors are red, green, and blue. This should be familiar if you've done any work with theater lighting, where you create a white spot by combing red, green, and blue spotlights.

Here is the new version of the Line command in Tick_Timer, which draws a red line (instead of the normal black line):

```
Line (0, 0)-(x, y), RGB(255, 0, 0)
```

Now your program should draw a nice red second hand.

Using Xor to Erase a Line

Now that you've learned about colors, you might guess that you could erase the line you drew before (without having to redraw the icon) simply by drawing a white line. You can try that, using RGB(255, 255, 255), but it will also erase anything on the clock face that wasn't white before. So we need another technique to undraw lines without erasing what was there before. Sounds like the impossible, but there is a way to do this.

Windows actually has a way to undraw lines, as long as you draw them properly. All the drawing you've done so far has simply drawn lines on top of other objects. But you can also draw lines by "inverting" dots on the screen. If you invert the dots twice, they end back at their original color. What this means is you can erase a line you drew by simply drawing that line a second time.

To see how this works, let's do some experiments with the Immediate window: Run your program and let it start ticking, then press Ctrl+Break to show the Immediate window. Next see what happens when you draw a line twice, without changing anything else:

```
cls
line (0,0)-(10,10)
line (0,0)-(10,10)
|
```

The first Line command will draw a line from the center, going up and to the right 10 pixels. The second Line command does the same thing, which is what you're probably used to.

Now let's add another command to this test. You'll use the DrawMode property to change the method used for drawing in a form. By default, Draw-Mode is set to 13, which tells Visual Basic to draw lines on top of anything on the screen. But here you'll set DrawMode to 10, which tells Visual Basic to use the inverting mode of drawing:

```
cls
print drawmode
 13
drawmode = 10
line (0,0)-(10,10)
line (0,0)-(10,10)
|
```

When you run the first Line command, you'll see a black line appear, just as before. But this time, the second Line command will erase the original line! And that's all there is to this trick.

Now let's take a look at how it works. First a comment. If you look in the *Language Reference* manual under DrawMode, you'll find a list of 16 different drawing modes you can use. You'll also find that the descriptions of the different drawing modes don't make much sense. And DrawMode 10, which is what you're using here, is called the *Not Xor Pen* mode. What does all this mean?

Well, it's a little hard to explain, especially because most professional Windows programmers don't fully understand all the different drawing modes. And you may not really want to understand *how* it works as long as you know it works. If you're interested, however, the sidebar on the DrawMode property will give you all the information you should need. And it will be here, waiting for you, if you ever need to learn more about DrawMode.

That said, you can now use DrawMode = 10 to display an erasable second hand. So now we need to figure out exactly how we're going to use this drawing mode. First we'll describe what we want to do in simple English. Then we'll try to describe it in a way that makes it easy to write this program. For the second way, we will be using something called *pseudo-code,* which is a cross between a programming language and English.

But I'm getting ahead of myself—first the English description. What you want to do here is draw the second hand. Then when you get the next Tick_Timer event, you'll want to erase the last second hand you drew, then draw a new second hand.

Sounds simple enough. But this is only the first step in solving the problem. In reality, there are a number of special conditions to look at, known as *boundary conditions*. You'll want to try to identify all the places where you might have to do something a little different. In other words, you want to find the boundaries of the problem.

For example, the very first Tick_Timer event you get after your program starts is slightly different from all the others. Why? Well, the English description of what you want to do says you'll want to erase the last line you drew before drawing the new second hand. But the first time you get a Tick_Timer event you haven't drawn a line yet. So there's nothing to erase, which means you'll want to handle this case a little differently. And this is exactly the type of thing you'll want to look for when you're looking for boundary conditions.

There are some other boundary conditions as well that you'll find later. But for now, the initial call to Tick_Timer is the only boundary condition you'll need to worry about.

Now let's rewrite the simple description of how to draw an erasable second hand, but this time in more detail, using pseudo-code. Here is what the solution will look like:

```
Tick_Timer( )
    If previous line Then
        Erase the previous second hand
    End If
    Draw the new second hand
```

As you can see, this is a cross between real Basic code and English. I'm using the Basic If..Then command, but for the condition and the statements I'm using an English-language description. This technique is a very powerful way to express your ideas in a way that's much easier to turn into a program.

Once you have this idea of what you're going to do, it's time to turn it into real code. Before I show you my solution, try writing a solution yourself; I'll give you a couple of hints. You'll need to keep track of where the last second hand was so you can erase it. And the obvious place (and best solution) for

Pseudo-code: The Tool of Pros

Pseudo-code is a very powerful tool for writing complex programs, and it's one you'll find many professional programmers (and professors as well) using, to try to express their ideas before they start to write programs. There aren't any hard-and-fast rules about how to express ideas in pseudo-code. The main idea is that you want to use some of the "control structures" like If..Then, but use English descriptions for other statements and even for the conditions that will appear in the If..Then statements.

When writing pseudo-code, you want to avoid defining things in too much detail, because that can easily get you bogged down in the trees so you can't see the forest. So write as simple a description as you can, then fill in the details later. If you're working with a very complex idea, you'll probably find yourself rewriting your pseudo-code several times, with a little more detail each time.

saving this information is in some form-level variables. OK, see if you can write this new Tick_Timer event handler yourself.

Now for my solution. First, I've created two variables, called lastX and lastY, to keep track of the endpoint for the second hand. Since the second hands always start at (0,0), this is all the information you'll need to keep track of the last second hand you drew. Put these two definitions into the (general) area of your form:

```
Dim lastX As Integer              ' Endpoint of last second hand
Dim lastY As Integer
```

Next, you need some way to let Tick_Timer know when there isn't a previous second hand for it to erase. I did this by setting lastX to a special value in the Form_Load event handler. I've chosen to use 999 because X for the second hand ranges between –10 and 10, so it can never be 999:

```
Sub Form_Load ()
    WindowState = 1               ' Iconize the window
    lastX = 999                   ' No previous second hand
End Sub
```

Finally, you need to modify Tick_Timer so it will erase the old second hand and remember the location of the new second hand. Since Tick_Timer is getting rather long, instead of showing you the entire event handler, I'll just show you the changes for the lines starting with the Scale command (which you won't change):

```
    Scale (-16, 16)-(16, -16)     ' Set scale for clock icon
    DrawMode = 10                 ' Set for erasable drawing
    red = RGB(255, 0, 0)          ' Define red color

    x = 10 * Sin(sec * pi / 30)   ' Calculate end of second hand
    y = 10 * Cos(sec * pi / 30)
    If lastX <> 999 Then          ' Erase any old second hand
        Line (0, 0)-(lastX, lastY), red
    End If
    Line (0, 0)-(x, y), red       ' Draw the new second hand

    lastX = x                     ' Save endpoint of new hand
    lastY = y
End Sub
```

Most of this new code should be fairly clear. There is one small trick I've pulled to cut down on any flicker you'll see in the second hand. You'll notice that I'm calculating the new x and y position *before* I erase the previous second hand. This allows the two Line commands to be as close together as possible. The closer together they are, the less time there will be no second hand at all on the screen. And trigonometric functions, such as Sin and Cos, tend to be rather slow.

In fact, you might want to try an experiment with this. If you move the three lines that erase the previous second hand (starting with If lastX <> 999) up two lines so they're before the x and y calculations, you'll notice that the second hand flickers slightly each time it's moved. The way I wrote them above, you won't see a flicker. Small differences like this can make the difference between a good program and an excellent program.

Drawing the Hour and Minute Hands

We're almost finished writing the Icon Clock program. We only have a couple of things left to add. First, and most obvious, we need to draw the hour and minute hands.

But there is also a slight glitch in the way our program works now. If you cover up part of the clock, then uncover it, you'll notice that the clock face will be erased, and Icon Clock may become confused about the previous second hand. It may leave behind a second hand. This happens because Visual Basic clears the entire clock face whenever you uncover part of the icon. This problem is a little tricky to fix, and we won't fix it here. But the version of Icon Clock on the disk accompanying this book fixes this problem, as well as adding a few more nice touches.

There is also a slight problem in which the old second hand sometimes stays behind. This happens now because the x and y variables are of type Single (since you didn't define them explicitly), whereas lastX and lastY are of type Integer. So it's possible for lastX to be different from the previous x as a result of rounding. You can fix this problem by defining x and y as Integer in Tick_Timer. Or you can redefine lastX and lastY so they're of type Single. Either solution will work.

As to adding the hour and minute hands, you'll find the new version of Tick_Timer below. You'll also need to add the variable lastHour to the (general) section of your form. There are a couple of other things I'll comment on. First, you'll notice a line that calculates a variable h. This line creates a fraction hour that includes the minute information, which allows the hour hand to move every minute. A real clock changes the position of the hour hand every minute, so it will be between two of the hour marks at 30 minutes past the hour.

You'll also notice I'm carefully changing the drawing mode between erasable mode (10) for the second hands and nonerasable mode (13) for the hour and minute hands. This allows you to have an hour and a minute hand such that the hour hand doesn't erase part of the minute hand. If you want to see what I mean, remove the line that sets DrawMode to 13.

You'll also notice that I set lastX to 999 when the hour or minute changes. This is because I erase the clock face whenever the hour or minute changes, so there won't be a previous second hand in such cases. The rest of this program should be familiar.

The final clock program has a single Timer control added to the form, called Timer1, with the CtlName Tick. The property for the form is Icon, with the setting Iconclock.ico.

Here are the definitions in the (general) part of your form:

```
Dim lastMinute As Integer        ' Last minute shown on clock
Dim lastHour As Integer          ' Last minute shown on clock

Dim lastX As Integer             ' Endpoint of last second hand
Dim lastY As Integer
```

```
Sub Form_Load ()
    WindowState = 1              ' Iconize the window
    lastX = 999                  ' No previous second hand
End Sub
```

```
Sub Tick_Timer ()
    Const pi = 3.141592653       ' Define the value of pi
    Dim t As Double              ' The time information
    Dim x As Integer             ' Use same type as lastX
    Dim y As Integer

    t = Now                      ' Get the current time
    sec = Second(t)              ' Get seconds, 0..59
    min = Minute(t)              ' Get the current minute, 0..59
    hr = Hour(t)                 ' Get hours, 0..23

    Scale (-16, 16)-(16, -16)    ' Set scale for clock icon
    '
```

```
' If the hour or minute has changed, update the caption,
' then remove all the hands and redraw them
'
If min <> lastMinute Or hr <> lastHour Then
    Caption = Format$(t, "h:mm AM/PM")
    lastMinute = min             ' Remember new current minute
    lastHour = hr
    Cls                          ' Clear all clock hands
    lastX = 999                  ' No previous second hand

    DrawWidth = 2                ' Draw 2-pixel-wide lines
    DrawMode = 13                ' Draw nonerasable lines

    h = hr + min / 60            ' Decimal hour, for hour hand
    x = 5 * Sin(h * pi / 6)      ' Endpoint of hour hand
    y = 5 * Cos(h * pi / 6)
    Line (0, 0)-(x, y)           ' Draw the hour hand

    x = 8 * Sin(min * pi / 30)' Endpoint of minute hand
    y = 8 * Cos(min * pi / 30)
    Line (0, 0)-(x, y)
    DrawWidth = 1                ' Set back to 1-pixel lines
End If

DrawMode = 10                    ' Set for erasable drawing
red = RGB(255, 0, 0)             ' Define red color

x = 10 * Sin(sec * pi / 30)      ' Calculate end of second hand
y = 10 * Cos(sec * pi / 30)
If lastX <> 999 Then             ' Erase any old second hand
    Line (0, 0)-(lastX, lastY), red
End If
Line (0, 0)-(x, y), red          ' Draw the new second hand

lastX = x                        ' Save endpoint of new hand
lastY = y
End Sub
```

You might want to create an EXE version of this program so you can run it. But I'd suggest using the version that comes on the companion disk, because it fixes a couple of boundary conditions I didn't address in this chapter. For example, the version on the disk will redraw itself properly when it becomes uncovered. It also has a nicer Program Manager icon.

Reference: DrawMode Property

The DrawMode property allows you to control how Visual Basic draws colored lines (and shapes) on your screen. This is a little like the difference between using watercolors and oil paints. With oil paints, you can paint one color over another color, and it will completely replace the old color. But watercolors don't work the same way: When you paint a watercolor over an existing color, the two colors blend together where they overlap to give you a third color.

Visual Basic has two drawing options similar to the painting examples, and it also has 14 other drawing modes. One of the nice things about computers is that you have much more freedom than you might have in the physical world. But it also takes a little while to understand all the nuances and meanings. You won't need to understand most of the material in this sidebar. But later, when you're ready to experiment, you'll find this sidebar to be a very useful reference, because much of this information isn't documented well anywhere else. We only use two modes in this chapter: 10 and 13.

Understanding all the DrawMode values takes quite a bit of work, and I wasn't able to find a good explanation in any of the books I looked at (including Microsoft's Windows programming reference manuals). Below you'll find a very complete description of each of the 16 modes supported by Visual Basic.

There are three groups of modes here (Mask, Inverse, and Merge) that are not at all simple, so I'd like to say a few words about them. But first, I'd like to point out which modes are the most commonly used in real programs, and give you an idea of what they do:

Type of DrawMode	DrawMode Numbers
Combining light	15
Draw over (replace old color)	13 (the default)
Erasable draw	10, 7, or 6

Figure 7.12 shows a color wheel for the additive colors (using light rather than paint). The inverse of any color on this wheel is the color on the opposite side of the circle. You can also see that bright colors are turned into dark colors when they're inverted.

The Merge and Mask groups use color information from both the pen and each pixel currently on the screen where the shape will be drawn. Colors in Windows have three components: red, green, and blue. The merge modes work with one pixel at a time and add together each color component from the pen color and the color of the pixel being drawn over. For example, if you draw a bright red pixel (RGB = 255, 0, 0) over a bright blue pixel (RGB = 0, 0, 255), you get a bright magenta pixel (RGB = 255, 0, 255). And drawing a green pixel on top of a bright magenta pixel gives you a white pixel. The merge modes act very much like combining the light from two lights with different colors.

The other group is the Mask group, which requires a little explanation. In the mask modes, either the pen or the current pixel color (or its inverse) is used as a mask. A mask, in this case, limits the amount of red, green, and blue in the final pixel drawn on the screen. For example, if the mask color is (127, 127, 0), the red and green components of the

Figure 7.12:

The left side shows which colors are the inverse of other colors. The right side shows how the brightness of a color changes when you invert it.

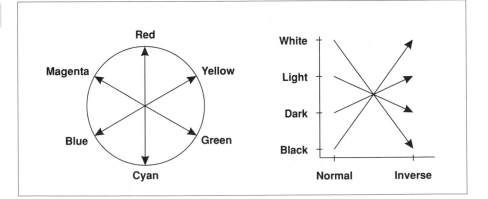

final pixel will be limited to 127 or less, and the blue component will be 0. For example, if you use a mask of (127, 127, 0) to mask bright magenta (255, 0, 255), you'll get a light red pixel (127, 0, 0).

These are the DrawMode values:

1　**Black.** Always draws in black. This ignores the pen color, and it draws over anything currently on the screen.

2　**Inverse of Merge.** Windows merges the pen and pixel colors, then draws the inverse of this on the screen.

3　**Mask Screen Using Inverse of the Pen.** Masks the colors on the screen, using the inverse of the pen color as a mask.

4　**Inverse Pen Color.** Draws using a color that's the inverse of the pen color.

5　**Mask the Inverse Screen.** Inverts the colors on the screen, then masks them using the pen color.

6　**Invert Screen.** In this mode, anything you "draw" will simply invert the colors on the screen. In other words, this mode ignores the pen color and just changes what's on the screen.

7　**Xor Draw.** Use this mode when you want to draw lines that you can erase by drawing them again. This mode will keep the correct color for lines you draw against a *black* background. Use mode 10 for a white background.

8　**Inverse of Mask Screen.** This mode displays the inverse of the colors displayed by mode 9. It uses the pen color to mask the screen color, then it inverts this color.

9　**Mask Screen.** Windows breaks the pen and pixel colors into red, green, and blue components, then "clips" the components so they're no larger than the RGB components of the pen. For example, if you mask a white pixel (RGB = 255, 255, 255) using a dark blue pen (RGB = 0, 0, 127), you get a dark blue pixel on the screen.

10   **Inverse Xor Draw.** Use this mode when you want to draw lines that you can erase by drawing them again. This mode will keep the correct color for lines you draw against a *white* background. Use mode 7 for a black background.

11   **Transparent.** Doesn't draw anything. You'll probably never need to use this mode.

12   **Merge Screen and Inverse of Pen.** Merges the inverse of the pen color with the screen colors. To draw any pixel, Windows first inverts the pen color, then it adds together (individually) the red, green, and blue components of these two colors. Windows does this for each pixel being drawn over.

13   **Pen Color (default).** Draws using the pen color. It draws over anything currently being shown.

14   **Merge Pen and Inverse of Screen.** Merges the pen with the inverse of the screen colors. To draw any pixel, Windows first inverts the pixel being drawn over, then adds together (individually) the red, green, and blue components of these two colors. Windows does this for each pixel being drawn over.

15   **Merge Pen and Screen.** Merges the color of the pen with what's currently on the screen. For each pixel drawn, Windows adds together each color component (red, green, and blue) of the pen color and the pixel being drawn over. For example, if you draw a bright red pixel (RGB = 255, 0, 0) over a bright blue pixel (RGB = 0, 0, 255), you get a bright magenta pixel (255, 0, 255). Drawing a green pixel on top of a bright magenta pixel gives you a white pixel. (If any component adds up to a number greater than 255, it's set to 255.)

16   **White.** Always draws in white. This ignores the pen color, and it draws over anything currently on the screen.

Related Tools

Format$ This command is very powerful and can format many types of numbers. For example, if you want to display money information, such as displaying 2.3 as $2.30 (with a dollar sign and two decimal places), this is the command for you. You'll find details in the *Language Reference* manual.

Time/Date Functions There are a number of time and date functions we didn't use in this chapter that you might find useful:

TimeSerial	Calculates a time serial number given the hour, minute, and second
TimeValue	Converts a string (such as "12:34PM") to a time serial number
Date$	Returns the current date in a string
DateSerial	Calculates a date serial number given a year, month, and day
DateValue	Converts a string (such as "3/6/92") to a date serial number
Day	Returns the day of the month (1..31) from a serial number
Weekday	Returns the day of the week, between 1 (Sunday) and 7 (Saturday), from a serial number
Month	Returns the month (1..12) from a serial number
Year	Returns the year part of a serial number (1753..2078)

Trigonometric Functions In this chapter you learned about the Sin and Cos functions. Visual Basic also provides the Tan (tangent) and Atn (arctangent) functions.

Scale-Related Properties When you set a custom scale, you can use the ScaleWidth and ScaleHeight properties to get the current width (in drawing units) and height of your form. You can also get the coordinates of the top and left edges using ScaleLeft and ScaleTop.

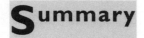ummary

You covered a lot of ground in this chapter, but you should now have a much better understanding of how to write programs. In the next chapter, we'll start all over again with a new program. This program, however, will be larger, so you'll get a chance to learn how to write large programs. It will also be a useful program, and one you'll probably want to change.

Here's what we covered in this chapter:

Designing Programs. You learned more about writing programs using stepwise refinement and planning ahead. It's always a good idea to think about what you want your program to look like and how you want it to work before you start programming. You also learned about using pseudo-code to design programs. Pseudo-code is a cross between English and Basic. Finally, you learned about boundary conditions, which are parts of your program where you need to handle a special case. You looked at the case where you wanted to erase the previous line, but there wasn't a previous line to erase.

Drawing inside Icons. You can draw inside an icon just as easily as you can draw inside a form. You can also change the caption below a minimized program by setting the Caption property to any string.

Timers. You learned how to create a timer object and how to write code in the Timer event that will run every so many milliseconds. The timer interval is set by selecting the timer object on the form, then setting the Timer property using the Properties bar.

Reading the Time. You can use the Time$ string to get a string that shows the current time in 24-hour format. You can also use Format$(Now, "h:mm AM/PM") to display a string with the time in 12-hour format. The functions Hour, Minute, and Second will break a time serial number, returned by the Now function, into the hour, minute, and second parts of the time.

WindowState and Form_Load. The WindowState property allows you to minimize your program when you first start it. You do this by setting WindowState in the Form_Load event handler, which runs once when your form first loads (and before it appears on the screen).

Const Keyword. The Const keyword allows you to define constants in your programs. These are like variables in that they have a name, but they have a single value and can't be changed.

Color. The RGB function allows you to draw lines using any color. You provide a red, green, and blue component, and each component can be between 0 and 255 (0 is no color, and 255 is full color). RGB(0, 0, 0) is black, and RGB(255, 255, 255) is white.

DrawMode. Setting DrawMode to 10 allows you to draw erasable lines. The normal drawing mode (13) writes nonerasable lincs.

Part two

Building Larger Programs

In this part you'll build on the knowledge you gained in the first seven chapters. In Chapter 8, you'll learn some different approaches to designing programs and developing a user interface. In Chapters 9–12 you'll work on creating a full-fledged application—an address book that can keep track of names, addresses, and phone numbers. You'll build the interface, learn how to work with disk files and multiple records, and learn how to sort and print addresses.

Chapter 8

Featuring

How to Design Programs
Designing User Interfaces
Building Programs

Approaches to Designing and Building Programs

In this chapter we're going to start building a large Visual Basic program, which is useful for a number of reasons. First, by building a large program, you'll see firsthand how programmers go about designing and building real programs. You'll also learn a number of new techniques you'll find useful in writing your own programs.

The first thing I'll do is spend some time talking about how you go about designing programs. As you'll see, there are a number of different approaches you can take; I'll take just one approach in this book, which is the one that works best for me (but it may not be the best approach for you).

After several pages of philosophy and approaches, we'll get down to the actual work of designing a large program, which will be an address book program that you can use to keep track of names and addresses, and to print them out. Since we'll be building this program for the next few chapters, you'll be able to change anything you don't like, or add features you think are missing. Let's begin by looking at how you start to build a large program.

How to Design Programs

There are a number of schools of thought on the "correct" way to design and build programs. Some people believe you should write very detailed specifications of any program before you write a single line of code or spend any time at all behind your computer. Other people believe that programming is an incremental process that constantly evolves, and that you should start writing *something* as soon as you can. I'll spend a few paragraphs explaining these approaches in more detail, and then I'll present the approach I use myself, which is the approach we'll use in the next few chapters.

I should mention that there is no one correct method for writing programs, although you're likely to run into programmers and managers who do believe there is but one correct approach. What this really means is that each person has their own approach that they find most comfortable, and if you're working for someone else, you may have to use the approach they like rather than your own.

Still, by understanding the different approaches to designing programs, you'll be able to use different techniques even if you have to follow the "one correct approach" to software design.

Detailed Specifications

The idea behind using detailed specifications is that you want to completely design your program before you write any code, which allows you to work out all the complicated interactions in a program before you've worked yourself into a hole. If you just start writing the program, you may discover that you've headed off in the wrong direction, so it's important to think things through first.

Design specifications vary considerably in the amount of detail you'll find, but they usually contain a description of what problems your program should solve and how it should solve them. Specs also usually contain drawings of what the different screens in your program should look like. And the really detailed specifications contain a list of all the modules (and sometimes even subroutines and functions) that will be in the program, along with a description of what they should do and what conventions will be used to call the subroutines and functions.

Programming as Evolution

Other people believe that you only need the idea for a program before you start to work on the program. In this approach, you start writing something as soon as possible, then modify your design as you go along. In a sense, this is an evolutionary approach. Your design will be very fluid. To managers, this is a scary approach because they won't know what they have until it's finished. But if you're working on a program for your own use, or if you're building the next great *fill-in-the-blank* all by yourself, this may be a good approach.

In-Between Approaches

In between these two approaches are many variations of the two basic approaches. When you're working with other people on a project, you'll have to have some type of design specification. But how detailed these specifications are really depends on a number of factors, including how many programmers are working on the program, how many other people are involved in the project, the philosophy of the managers involved, and so on.

My own preference, when I'm working on commercial software rather than small programs for my own use, is to write a design specification that's about five pages long. This document usually lists the features that should be in the finished program, with a short one- or two-paragraph description of each feature. I also spend some time talking about the general philosophy of the program and how the features should work together. I don't tend to include any screen designs, module lists, or other details below the level of a feature list. This works well for my way of designing programs, which is closer to the evolutionary approach than the detailed design approach.

The Approach We'll Use Here

My own opinion is that if you go too far in writing specifications, you'll lock yourself into a design that may not work well. I've discovered that you often don't know the real problems you're trying to solve until you've tried out some of your ideas on the computer. There have been times when I had a clear idea of "the best way" to solve a problem, only to discover that my solution had many problems when I actually implemented it. If I'd been compelled to keep my original approach, I would have ended up with a program that wasn't very easy to use and wasn't very reliable. The moral of the story is that you often learn the real problems that you're trying to solve only after you've done a few experiments.

Designing the User Interface

Every program has a user interface, particularly Visual Basic programs. The user interface is the part of the program you see on the screen, and the part that responds to your key presses and mouse clicks. Because of the way Visual Basic itself is designed (in other words, because of its user interface), designing the user interface for your own programs is quite different from the way it's done in other computer languages, so I'd like to spend a few paragraphs talking about these differences.

Most programmers don't start with the user interface (the look and feel of the screens) when they start to work on a program. Instead, they tend to start working on the code inside the program that does the hard (and for many programmers, interesting) work.

For example, to build the Address Book program, many programmers would start by writing the code that handles working with the disk file used to store names and addresses. Why would they start there? The answer has a lot to do with history.

If you look at most programming languages (and systems), they don't offer many tools for building the user interface. For example, if you want a window with a button in it, you have to write quite a bit of code before you can get such a program to work. This is very different from Visual Basic. In Visual Basic you can build the same program in a matter of minutes (if that long) and have it running without writing a single line of code. And that's why Microsoft calls their product *Visual* Basic.

Because other languages require so much work to build an interface, programmers tend to tackle the "easy" part first—they start with the "core" part of the project. But for a new programmer, this can be a very difficult approach. At this point you know enough to be able to write very simple programs, but you haven't learned yet how to read and write disk files. So even though we could start the Address Book project by working with disk files, it may not be the best approach.

One problem with leaving the user interface for last is that it tends to get the least amount of attention. Most programmers start to run out of energy by the time they get to the end of a project, so if they save the user interface until the end, they don't have much time (or interest) left for creating a good interface.

But there are other reasons it's not a good idea to leave the user interface for last. The first idea and design you have for a user interface may not be a very good one. Often you'll find that you have to actually try out your ideas before you discover how they feel. And you may discover that other people have problems using a design you come up with. If this happens, the best thing to do is try to figure out why other people have problems with your design, and then try some other ideas. Leaving the interface until the end won't give you time to experiment.

Other parts of your program may also need to change if you change your idea of the interface. If you work on the interface first, you can design the rest of your program to fit the interface. But if you design the interface last, you're really designing the interface to fit the rest of your program, which isn't a very good solution.

All that said, people who start a new program by working on the user interface generally design better programs than people who leave the user interface until last. And Visual Basic makes designing the user interface first much easier.

So for the Address Book project, we'll start by thinking about the user interface—both what it should look like and how people will interact with it.

The Initial Design

One final comment before we start to design the Address Book program. Anytime you create a design for a program, you should consider the design to be preliminary (as I've mentioned before), and you should allow yourself the freedom to change the design as you learn more about your program through building it.

Let's take a look at what we want the Address Book program to do and how we want it to work. When I design a program, the very first thing I do is to come up with a short list of features I want in my program. In a sense, these are a set of objectives I have for the finished program. I also come up with some initial ideas for the user interface; these are usually sketches I draw on paper and file away in a folder that I create for each program I have in mind.

For a simple program like an address book, it may not seem like there are many features we'll want in it. After all, we simply want to keep a list of names and addresses. But computer programs, unfortunately, aren't as simple as the paper analogies we're used to. When we have a paper address book, there are a number of features already built into this physical book.

First of all, you'll notice you have a number of pages in the book that are divided into sections, corresponding to the letters of the alphabet. We all know from experience that these sections are based on last name (although some people actually use first names rather than last names). Each page is also divided into sections, usually with ruled lines in each address, plus some boxes for phone numbers. All these elements, in a sense, are features.

Now let's take a look at how we'll want to transfer these ideas over to the computer. But first, a word of warning. Computers work with information very differently from the way we do, and things that might work well on paper may not be the best solutions when we try to implement them in a computer program.

For example, with an address book program, it doesn't really make sense to draw individual pages, with a number of addresses on each page, which you have to flip through on the screen. What makes more sense is to use your computer's ability to search for and find names. So instead of flipping pages looking for a name, you could type in the name of the person you're looking for. The computer would then search for that person and display their address and phone numbers.

Writing a Feature List

So we're going to create a new design that uses your computer's abilities to its best. The first thing we'll do, as I mentioned above, is write down a list of *features* we want in this program. These features are sort of a list of what we want our program to be able to do. Here's how we'll build this list. First, I'll talk you through the thinking process I followed to come up with a feature list. And then I'll present the final list.

When you're writing a feature list, you'll often need to write down things that may seem obvious. Even though they're obvious, someone else might not think about doing it in the same way. For example, it's clear that we want to be able to type in names and addresses. But it isn't clear how you enter this information. Most address book programs I've seen and worked with have a number of fields marked First Name, Middle Initial, Last Name, Address Line 1, Address Line 2, City, State, and Zip Code. Figure 8.1 shows an example of what this might look like.

Figure 8.1:

Many address book programs require that you enter an address into separate fields.

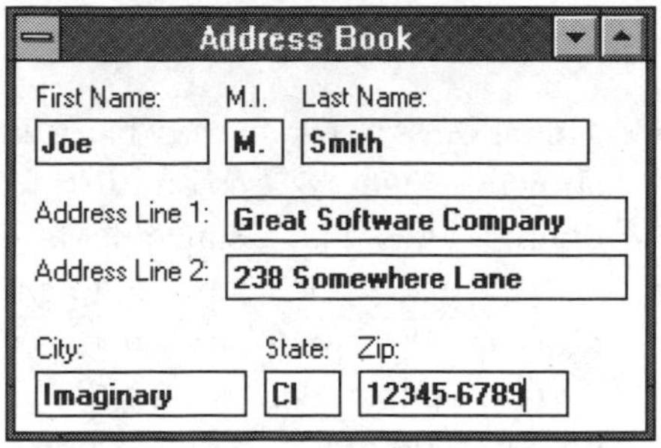

You might be wondering, and rightly so, why you have to enter the parts of an address in separate fields. Why can't you simply type

Joe M. Smith
Great Software Company
238 Somewhere Lane
Imaginary, CI 12345-6789

The reason most programs look like Figure 8.1, rather than the address above, is entirely historical. Most address book programs are built on top of *database programs,* which are a type of software designed specifically to store and retrieve data. By chopping addresses into separate fields, it's possible for the database to perform a number of functions, such as sorting on last names, printing out address labels grouped by zip code (which gives you lower rates for bulk mail), listing people in a certain city, and so on.

In other words, the choice of a data entry form like the one shown in Figure 8.1 has much more to do with how a program is written than how you interact with it. In the address book program we'll build here, I chose to take a very different approach to entering names and addresses. I wanted to be able to just type in names, so instead of having a number of text fields, I chose to have a single field for the entire name and address, which allows you to type in the address in any form. This is particularly useful for foreign addresses because they often have a very different format, such as this:

Joe M. Smith
"Hartley Cottage"
17 Beacon Place
Waymouth WA8 2ST

Dorset
ENGLAND

This address would be very hard, if not impossible, to type into the address form shown in Figure 8.1, so our first "feature" is that we want to be able to type the entire address into a single field.

We'll also want to be able to type in phone numbers of different types. I've chosen to allow up to four phone numbers. And each phone number can be of a different type, such as fax, home, office, and car phone. I also like to be able to write notes that go along with a name and an address, which is very useful for people I don't have much contact with, or for keeping track of why I'm talking to someone.

For this address list to be really useful, however, you need to be able to use these names and addresses after you've typed them in. There are several ways you can do this. First, you might want to print out your address list so you can find names. Of course, you'll want these names to be in alphabetical order, so you'll need to make sure you have some way to sort the names. And if you're working with your computer, rather than a printed list, you'll want to be able to type in a name (first or last or company) and have your computer search for the name, which is a lot easier than searching through a printed list.

Now that we've thought through the feature list, we can write it down as a bulleted list. The following list is the one I used when I wrote the address book program included here. You can see that it's basically a sketch of where we're going to head, and it leaves a lot of details unspecified.

- **Name and address.** We'll use an input box that allows you to type multiple lines, which will allow you to type the address any way you want (most programs require you to enter the first name, last name, middle initial, first address line, etc., in separate fields).

- **Phone numbers (up to four).** We'll also want to keep track of what each phone number is for, such as fax, home, office, or car phone.

- **Notes.** I often want to write notes along with a name and address so I can remember small facts about a person (such as spouse's name, children's names, etc.)

- **Printing.** We'll want to be able to print out the address list so you can take it along in your briefcase.

- **Searching.** You should be able to search for any person by name or company name. For this feature we'll search the entire address information.

- **Sorting.** This may seem obvious, but we'll want to sort the names in alphabetical order. And as you'll see, this will actually take quite a bit of work.

Drawing the Screens

Once I have a preliminary feature list put together, I draw some sketches of what I want the screen to look like. Figure 8.2 shows the sketch I drew for the main screen, which shows what you'll see most of the time when you're running the Address Book program.

Figure 8.2:

Here is the pen sketch I drew for the address book program before I started building the program on my computer.

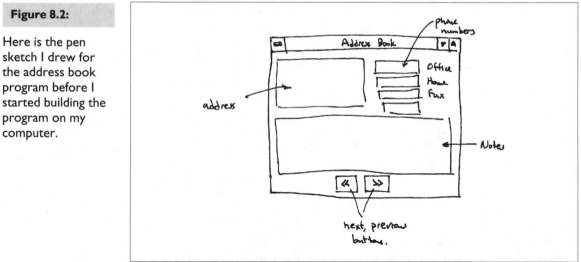

These sketches aren't exact drawings, so I usually end up making some small changes between the drawing and the actual program when I'm finished. I also tend to change, remove, and add features to the program as I gain experience using it. Often my best ideas appear only after I've started to build the program, and they are usually triggered by something that happens while I'm using what I've built so far. For example, Figure 8.3 shows the actual screen you'll end up with after the next few chapters.

The Address Book program you'll have at the end of the next few chapters. This is fairly close to the sketch in Figure 8.2, but there are some differences.

As you can see, there are a few differences between this screen and the sketch in Figure 8.2. Most of the changes are rather small, and you'll see them appear as you build the program. But I'll say a few short words here about the changes. First, you'll notice a menu bar, which isn't in the sketch. This menu bar provides a number of small functions we'll be adding later on in the development process. We'll initially build the Address Book program without a menu bar.

You'll also notice a few text fields under the notes area. On the left side is a display that shows you how many addresses are currently in the file. The 12/11 means that we're adding a 12th address, but it hasn't been saved yet to the file (it's saved automatically when you're finished making changes).

You'll also notice two dates on the right side. The top date shows the date that you initially created an address in the file. The lower date shows when you last changed an address. I find this information useful for keeping track of how old my information is, which is useful when I have two addresses for someone and I'm not sure which is more current.

Building Programs

Just as there are a number of ways to design programs, there are also a number of ways to go about building large programs. I'd like to spend a few paragraphs talking about the different approaches.

Add Features First, Test Later

Most software companies start with a detailed design specification, which they then hand over to a team of programmers. This team of programmers then writes code to implement all the features in the program. Once all the features are implemented, the software goes into a testing phase called *alpha* testing. In alpha testing, most of the features are implemented, more or less, but many of them aren't working correctly. The idea is that the program will be far enough along so you can start to work with it and identify any problems with the design.

The problem, however, is that alpha testing starts fairly late in the development cycle, so by the time you get to alpha testing, it's hard to make any major changes in your design. If you do have to make major changes, you may have

The Origin of the Term "Bug"

One of the first modern-day computers to be built was the Harvard Mark I computer, which was built in the early 1940s. One hot day in the summer of 1945, the Mark I computer mysteriously failed. After a careful search, the programmers found the remains of a moth blocking an electrical relay inside the circuitry of the computer. They extracted the remains with a pair of tweezers and taped it into the logbook that they kept for their work on the Mark I computer for the U.S. Navy. Grace Hopper (who found the bug) recalled, "From then on, when the officer came in to ask if we were accomplishing anything, we told him we were 'debugging' the computer."

The term stuck, and today a bug is some type of failure in a computer program. Programmers *debug* programs by looking for the problem and fixing it. A program that has a large number of design or reliability problems or both is said to be a *buggy* program.

to throw out large chunks of the program, which will cause major delays in the release of your software. Not good.

The next stage of testing is called *beta* testing. During this phase of testing, all the features should be working correctly, but there are usually a large number of *bugs* left in the program that keep it from working reliably. The last phase of development is a mad scurry to eradicate all the bugs in the program, which often takes several months (some companies have spent six months or more just trying to fix all the bugs in a program).

Add, Test, Redesign

In contrast (and many programmers and managers don't agree with me on this one), I believe you should start alpha testing as soon as possible, and usually within a few months of starting development (as opposed to a year or more down the line). I also believe that each alpha release of the program should be very reliable. The only difference, then, between an alpha release and the final program (in my scheme) is that not all the features will be implemented yet. But any features that are implemented should be reliable.

When I'm building a program, I start by implementing some core features. I implement and carefully test these features so that I'll have a debugged and reliable program when I finish the first part. This initial program won't be very useful because it won't have many features implemented, but it will allow me to start using the program as quickly as possible.

I then start to add other features. And each time I add a feature, I test it to make sure that it works correctly under all cases and that it "feels" right. In other words, I start my usability testing very early in development. The earlier you

Allegory

I've had the opportunity to beta-test software for a number of companies (they almost never let outsiders see alpha software). I can't remember how many times I've heard the following when I reported a problem: "That's a really good idea! But at this point, it's too late for us to make any changes like that." In other words, even though the beta-test period should allow you to change your design, in reality it's almost always too late.

Allegory

When I was a junior in college, I was taking a Plasma Physics exam, and partway through the exam my professor (Prof. Sheshadri) came over and said, "Stop. You're writing too quickly and making too many mistakes. Slow down and do everything slowly and carefully. You'll finish sooner and make fewer mistakes." And he was right.

I've remembered his words of advice ever since, and I believe they're true for almost everything you do. They're certainly true for programming.

start such testing, the easier it is to change your mind about how you want your program to work.

Oftentimes I'll first implement a feature partway to get a sense for how it will feel and work, but before I've invested much time handling all the special cases that will make the feature fully functional and reliable. By doing my testing early on, I can easily make major changes to my design without affecting the final schedule. But more important, because I'm doing all the reliability testing as I'm writing the program, rather than during the beta-test period, I'm doing all the work on each problem while it's still fresh in my head.

I used this very approach when I was developing the Norton Commander, which is a program designed to make DOS easier to use. After about a month, I had a program I could work with, but it didn't do very much. After about two or three months I had a program that was actually somewhat useful, and I put it into alpha testing and had several other people using the program in their normal work. The final program wasn't finished until about a year later, so I had a full year to do reliability and usability testing, and I got valuable feedback on my design very early on, when it was still easy to make changes.

What's most interesting about this approach, however, is that there really wasn't much of a beta-test period. The total beta-test period lasted about one month, which is very short in the computer industry. But the best part is that there were no major bugs in the Norton Commander. Version 3.0, which was the last release I worked on, was on the market for over two years without any major bugs being reported.

What Is Good Design?

There is no single answer to this question. In many ways, good design is a matter of opinion, which means that it's very important that you test your designs out on other people. And unless your program is designed for other programmers, you should try out your programs on real users: people who don't have any programming or technical experience, but who would use the program you're writing.

When you do test your programs on users, you'll probably be frustrated. They won't understand how to use your program the way you do, and they'll make mistakes. When they do make mistakes, don't correct them. If you correct someone and explain the right way to do things, you're not really testing your program—you're simply teaching someone how to use it.

So when a user has problems with your program, resist the urge to teach. Instead, try to ask questions so you can understand why they're having problems with your design. This is very hard to do because you first have to admit that the design you worked so hard on may have some flaws. But if you do open your mind and try to find out why someone is having problems with your design, you can learn a lot. And you'll then be able to think about how you could improve your design to make it easier to learn and use. The thing to remember is that any design, no matter how good, can be improved.

There are several ways to learn good design. One way is to work with as many different Windows programs as you can, so you can learn from other programmers. Programs written by Microsoft are considered by many to be the *de facto* standard for user interface design, but even Microsoft doesn't always do a good job. Still, they spend a lot of time and effort on testing and redesigning the programs in usability labs, so you'll probably learn a lot from their programs.

Another good source of information is books. There are many books about user interface design, and about program design in general. I have my own favorites, which I've listed below.

Norman, Donald A. *The Design of Everyday Things*. New York: Basic Books, 1988. If you read only one book from this list, read this one. It should open your eyes to the problems that ordinary people have with common, everyday designs. And it should give you some insight into how to build designs that get around these problems.

Heckel, Paul. *The Elements of Friendly Software Design*. Second edition. Alameda, Calif.: SYBEX, 1991. This book is a useful book to read to gain a better understanding of the things you should think about when you're designing user interfaces.

Laurel, Brenda, ed. *The Art of Human-Computer Interface Design*. Reading, Mass.: Addison-Wesley, 1990. This book is a collection of papers and articles published on user interface design and is a very good book to have around. It has much more information about graphical environments (like the Macintosh and Windows) than the two books above, and covers far more ground.

Brooks, Frederick P., Jr. *The Mythical Man-Month*. Reading, Mass.: Addison-Wesley, 1975. Anyone developing computer software should read this book. You'll learn a lot about why it's difficult to use classical management techniques with software projects.

Microsoft Corp. *Microsoft Windows User Interface Style Guide*. Seattle: Microsoft.

Summary

This chapter was more philosophical than other chapters in the book, but it's good to know more about designing programs. Here is a quick review of the material in this chapter:

Specification. You'll probably want to write some type of design specification for any programs you write, except for very small programs. Such documents can be anywhere from a page or two to a hundred pages (although I don't agree with the value of such detailed specifications).

User Interfaces. Learning how to design good user interfaces is very important, and it's something not everyone can become an expert at. And you certainly can't become an expert in a vacuum. Interact with other people and see how they interact with your programs. Ask questions, and don't succumb to the temptation to explain to your testers how to use your program. You should also read some books like the ones I listed above.

Building Programs. Just as there are many opinions on how you should design a program, there are also many opinions on how you should build your programs once you have a design. I tend to view a program as a living entity that has a soul of its own. My job is to learn what that soul is and redesign and write my program to best bring out that soul. This is a very evolutionary process, rather than a straightforward coding task.

Testing. It's very important that you test your programs, and I'll have much more to say about this in Chapter 10, where we'll really get down to the work of building the Address Book program. There is an art to testing your programs, which begins with being skeptical about whether your program really works correctly.

Address Book Design. We spent some time in this chapter writing a short design specification for the Address Book program we'll build in the next few chapters.

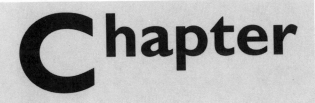

Chapter 9

Featuring

Creating Controls

Creating a Program Manager Icon
for Your Projects

New Controls: Text Boxes,
Labels, Command Buttons, and
Combo Boxes

Controlling Tab Order

Methods

Setting Up Combo Boxes

Building Address Book's Interface

In this chapter we're going to start building the Address Book program we designed in the last chapter. As you'll recall, we sketched a design for Address Book and wrote down a short list of features we want to put into the program. In this chapter we'll work mainly on the user interface, the part of the program that you see. We'll start by drawing all the controls onto the form and setting their properties. Once we have all the controls, we'll start bringing Address Book to life by adding some code. We'll then continue this process in the next few chapters by bringing more and more of Address Book to life.

Creating the Controls

The way you go about building a program in Visual Basic is really quite different from the way you'd do it in any other language. In Visual Basic, you start by drawing controls on a form, which can take quite a bit of work, but doesn't involve writing a single line of code. In most other languages, creating the user interface is something programmers do much later because it requires writing quite a bit of code. In other words, drawing the user interface in Visual Basic is a *lot* simpler than writing code to create the same interface.

As you can see in Figure 9.1, there are a total of 18 controls we'll draw on this form, not including the menu bar, which we'll add in a later chapter.

There are a number of ways you can go about drawing the controls on a form to match the design in Figure 9.1. First, you could just draw all the controls

Figure 9.1:

These are all the
controls we'll add
to the main form.
Notice the control
names for each
control (except for
the labels, which
won't change).

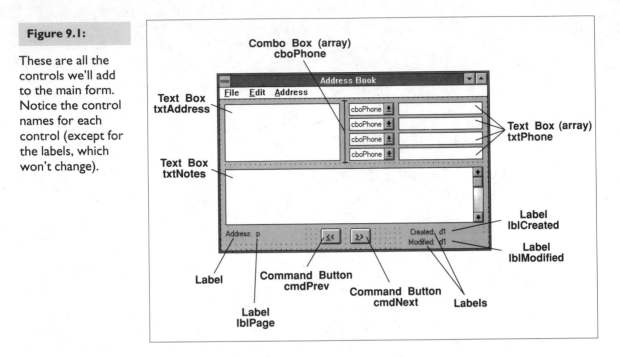

on the form, then align them and set their sizes later. Or, you could draw each
control in place and set its size before you draw the next control. I tend to do
a little of both, and I keep moving the controls around on the form until everything looks nice. I do a lot of experimenting.

It's a good idea to experiment so you can get an idea of what works and
what doesn't. But it's also a little frightening. What happens if you have a
nice design, and then you start changing it? How can you get back to a previous
design you preferred? The way I solve this problem is to save a copy of the
form after I have a design I like. You can use the File Manager in Windows to
make a copy of the .FRM file. Then if you decide later that you really want to
go back to a previous design, you'll still have a copy of the .FRM file you liked.

You'll probably settle on an approach to drawing controls that works best
for you after you've worked with Visual Basic for a while. Here I'm going to go
through the steps of drawing each control and setting its size and location
before you go on to the next control. You can do this because I've already spent
some time experimenting with the sizes and locations of the controls.

NOTE

You're free to make your controls any size you want and place them wherever you want on your form—Address Book will work correctly no matter where the controls are or how large they are. So feel free to redesign the look of Address Book if you like. The only thing you'll need to ensure is that all the control names and other properties (except Left, Top, Width, and Height) match the ones in Table 9.1 later in this chapter.

A Step-by-Step Approach

In the detailed instructions below, I'll include the size and location of each control so you can make these controls the same size as in Figure 9.1. All these sizes will be in twips, because that's the default measurement scale used by Visual Basic.

There are two ways you can set the location and size of a control. First, you can use the information shown in the Properties bar (see Figure 9.2). While you drag controls around on the form and resize them, the Properties bar tells you the size of the control and the location of its top-left corner.

NOTE

There is a small bug in Visual Basic that sometimes causes the height readout in the Properties bar to be slightly off. In these cases the Height property will always be correct. For example, the height

Figure 9.2:

The Properties bar, with Top, Left, Width, and Height values for selected object txtAddress

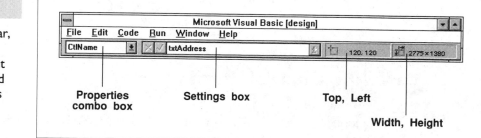

readout for txtAddress may sometimes be 1335 rather than the correct 1380. The width readout, on the other hand, always seems to be correct.

Your other option is to directly set the Top, Left, Width, and Height properties of a control. Doing so will change the size and location of a control to match the numbers you type in.

Both of these methods work very well, so which one you choose really depends on your own preference.

As you'll recall from Chapter 7, you draw controls on a form by clicking first on the control in the Toolbox (see Figure 9.3) that you want to draw. Then click and drag inside the form to tell Visual Basic where and how large you want the control.

Figure 9.3:

Visual Basic's Toolbox allows you to add controls (objects) to your forms.

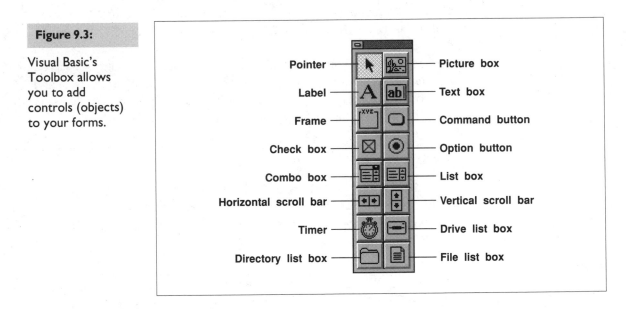

Creating Control Arrays

Before you draw any controls on the form, I need to say a few words about control arrays. As you'll recall from Chapter 5, control arrays are groups of controls that all have the same name; you use the Index property to distinguish

Keyboard Shortcuts in the Properties Bar

There are a number of very useful keyboard shortcuts you can use to help you navigate the Properties bar (these are documented in the on-line help, but since they're hard to find I've summarized them here):

F2	**Activate Settings Box.** This is a quick way to activate the Settings box when the form is currently active. You can then use the keyboard to edit the setting in this box.
Ctrl+*alpha*	**Select Property.** Select the property that starts with the letter *alpha* in the Properties combo box. Pressing Ctrl+*alpha* again selects the next property that starts with the same letter.
alpha	**Change Setting.** Typing any character when the form is active will change the value in the Settings box. For settings like Caption, pressing a key inserts that character and activates the Settings box. If the Settings box is a combo box, typing a letter selects the first option that starts with the letter (or number) you typed.
Esc	**Cancel Changes.** Cancels changes you've made to the setting.
Enter	**Accept Setting.** Accepts the changes in the Settings box and reactivates the form.
F4, Alt+↓	**Drop Combo Box.** Pulls down the active combo box (after you press F2, for example). If the Settings box has a ... button at the end, pressing one of these keys is the same as pressing the ... button.

between the controls in a control array. The Address Book program uses two control arrays: one for the Phone combo boxes (which tell you whether a number is a home, office, fax, or car phone) and one for the phone-number text boxes.

To create a control array of combo boxes, all you have to do is give each control the same control name and assign a value to the Index property for each control. In Table 9.1 you'll find all the information you need to create control arrays, but I've removed a lot of the redundant information.

Table 9.1:	Object	Property	Setting
Properties for Each Control in the Address Book Program	**Form**	BorderStyle	1 – Fixed Single
		BackColor	&H00C0C0C0&
		Caption	Address Book
		FormName	Address
		Height	4020
		MaxButton	False
		Width	6615
	Text Box	CtlName	txtAddress
		FontBold	False
		Left	120
		Height	1380
		MultiLine	True
		Top	120
		Width	2775
	Combo Box (array)	CtlName	cboPhone
		FontBold	False
		Index	0
		Left	3120
		Style	2 – Dropdown List
		Top	120
		Width	1095
	cboPhone(1)	Index	1
		Top	480

	Object	Property	Setting
Table 9.1: Properties for Each Control in the Address Book Program (continued)	cboPhone(2)	Index	2
		Top	840
	cboPhone(3)	Index	3
		Top	1200
	Text Box (array)	CtlName	txtPhone
		FontBold	False
		Height	300
		Index	0
		Left	4320
		Top	120
		Width	2055
	txtPhone(1)	Index	1
		Top	480
	txtPhone(2)	Index	2
		Top	840
	txtPhone(3)	Index	3
		Top	1200
	Text Box	CtlName	txtNotes
		FontBold	False
		Left	120
		Height	1335
		MultiLine	True

Table 9.1:	Object	Property	Setting
Properties for Each Control in the Address Book Program (continued)		ScrollBars	2 – Vertical
		Top	1680
		Width	6255
	Label	BackColor	&H00C0C0C0&
		Caption	Address:
		FontBold	False
		Height	255
		Left	120
		Top	3120
		Width	615
	Label	BackColor	&H00C0C0C0&
		Caption	p
		CtlName	lblPage
		FontBold	False
		Height	255
		Left	840
		Top	3120
		Width	1095
	Label	Alignment	1 – Right Justify
		BackColor	&H00C0C0C0&
		Caption	Created:
		FontBold	False
		Height	255
		Left	4440
		Top	3120
		Width	735

Object	Property	Setting
Table 9.1: Properties for Each Control in the Address Book Program (continued)		
Label	BackColor	&H00C0C0C0&
	Caption	d1
	CtlName	lblCreated
	FontBold	False
	Height	255
	Left	5280
	Top	3120
	Width	1095
Label	Alignment	1 – Right Justify
	BackColor	&H00C0C0C0&
	Caption	Modified:
	FontBold	False
	Height	255
	Left	4440
	Top	3360
	Width	735
Label	BackColor	&H00C0C0C0&
	Caption	d2
	CtlName	lblModified
	FontBold	False
	Height	255
	Left	5280
	Top	3360
	Width	1095
Command Button	Caption	&<<
	CtlName	cmdPrev
	Height	375

	Object	Property	Setting
Table 9.1:		Left	2400
		Top	3120
Properties for		Width	495
Each Control in			
the Address			
Book Program	**Command Button**	Caption	&>>
(continued)		CtlName	cmdNext
		Height	375
		Left	3120
		Top	3120
		Width	495

For example, in the entries for the combo boxes, the first seven lines list all the properties you'll need to set for the first control in the array, as well as the other three controls in this array. The six size lines that follow list the properties that are different for the last three controls in this array. When you create the controls in an array, make sure you set all the properties for all the controls in the array.

There's a simpler way you can do this. Create the first control in an array and set all its properties to the values in Table 9.1. Then click on this control and press Ctrl+Ins (or select Copy from the Edit menu) to copy this control to the Clipboard. Next press Shift+Ins (or select Paste from the Edit menu) to paste a copy of this control on your form. Finally, move this new control from the upper-left corner (where pasted controls appear) into place (or set the Top and Left properties), and set the Index property.

Now you'll want to create all the controls shown in Figure 9.1. You can use the information in Table 9.1 to create a form that looks exactly like the one shown in Figure 9.1, or you can try to create the form yourself, without using any of the information in the table.

When you're all finished creating these controls, there is one last thing you'll want to do. You'll notice that all six text boxes currently contain the text *Text1,* which is the default text you'll see in each text box when you run Address Book. This initial string isn't very useful, and you'll probably want all the text boxes to be empty. What you'll want to do, then, is set the Text property of each control to nothing. How do you do this?

The easiest way to clear the default text in a text box is as follows: First, click on a text box and select the Text property in the Properties bar. Then press the spacebar, Backspace, and Enter. This has the effect of setting the default text to nothing. You can also use the mouse to select the property value in the Properties bar, then press Backspace to delete it. Finally, press Enter to accept this change.

Make sure you set the Text property for all six text boxes to nothing. You'll see the default text inside each text box, so it's easy to tell when you've cleared the default text.

Saving Your Work

Be sure you save your project, by choosing Save Project from the File menu, after you've created all these controls (or even before that). When Visual Basic prompts you for the project and form names, use ADDRESS.MAK and ADDRESS.FRM.

Creating a Program Manager Icon

Because you'll be working a lot with this project in the next few chapters, you may want to create an icon in Program Manager for this project. Then you can start Visual Basic and have it load your project just by double-clicking on the icon. Setting up such an icon isn't very hard, but it may not be obvious how you do so.

First you'll want to decide which Program Manager window (program group) you want your icon to appear in. Make sure this window is active, then select New... from the File menu in the Program Manager. Next press Enter to create a new program item. You'll see a dialog box like the one shown in Figure 9.4 (the Windows 3.0 dialog box is a little simpler).

This dialog box allows you to create Program Manager icons that run a program, but what we want to do is to start the Address Book project. In other words, what we really want to do is to run Visual Basic and have Visual Basic load your project for you. You can do just that by providing a command line that runs Visual Basic (VB.EXE) followed by the name of your project file as a parameter.

Figure 9.4:

This dialog box allows you to create an icon to launch Visual Basic with your Address Book project.

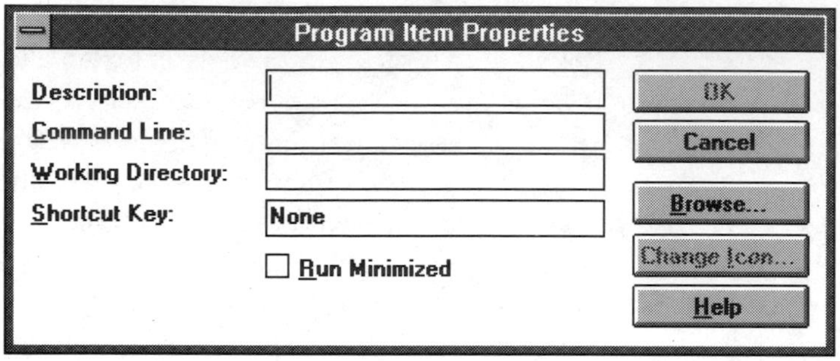

Program Item Properties

Description:

Command Line:

Working Directory:

Shortcut Key: None

☐ Run Minimized

OK

Cancel

Browse...

Change Icon...

Help

For example, let's say you installed Visual Basic in the directory C:\PROG\VB and you saved your project in a directory called C:\FILES\ADDRESS. You would then enter the following information into the three fields in the Program Item Properties dialog box:

Description	Address Book
Command Line	c:\prog\vb\vb.exe c:\files\address\address.mak
Working Directory	c:\files\address

The name that will appear below the icon in the Program Manager is the name you put in the Description field, which I've chosen to call Address Book.

The next field, Command Line, tells the Program Manager what program to run when you double-click on the icon. In this case it will run VB.EXE and tell Visual Basic to load the file ADDRESS.MAK into it after Visual Basic starts.

The Working Directory text box isn't available in the Windows 3.0 dialog box. This item allows you to specify which directory will be the current directory when your program first starts. Under Windows 3.0, the current directory would be the same as Visual Basic's directory—C:\PROG\VB in this example. But since Address Book will be creating files, it's really better to have the current directory be the same as your project's directory. This ensures that any files Address Book creates will be in its, rather than Visual Basic's, directory.

NOTE

When you run a program, the Windows 3.0 Program Manager always sets the current directory to that program's directory. So the current directory for projects you run from within Visual Basic would use Visual Basic's directory as the current directory. But any programs you turn into EXE files, then run as EXE files, will have *their* directory as the current directory. In other words, programs will have one of two current directories, depending on whether you run them from within Visual Basic or as stand-alone EXE files. This is the reason we want to use the Working Directory field to change the current directory.

Overview of Controls and Properties

Address Book contains several controls you haven't used before, so I'd like to take some time to cover these new controls and the meaning of some of the properties connected with them.

Text Boxes

The first new type of control is the text box, which provides a simple text input field. You can type any text into such fields, but you can't change the font, style, or size of individual characters—all characters in a text box share a single font, style, and size. So you can't use a text box to implement a word processor, but you can use it to edit simple text.

Address Book uses two variations on the text box: single line and multiline. The single-line text boxes allow you to type in only one line of text. If you press the Enter key inside a single-line text box, Visual Basic will simply beep. This is the default for Visual Basic's text boxes.

You can also create multiline text boxes by setting a text box's MultiLine property to True. After you make this change, your text box will support many lines of text. You can even add a scroll bar to a text box by setting the ScrollBars property to a value other than 0 – None. For example, the txtNotes text box has the ScrollBars property set to 2 – Vertical to add just a vertical scroll bar to the text box (you can also add a horizontal scroll bar, or both vertical and horizontal scroll bars).

If your text box doesn't have a horizontal scroll bar, Windows automatically word-wraps long lines just as a word processor does. Text boxes are really quite powerful, and you'll probably use them in many of your own projects.

Labels

Anytime you want to display text on a form without the ability to edit it, you'll want to use a label control. Address Book contains a total of six labels: three act as titles and the other three are used to display information, such as the date that you created an address book entry. In a later chapter we'll write some code that sets the Caption properties of lblCreated and lblModified to show the dates when each address was created and last modified.

Labels have a property called Alignment that allows you to control how text will be formatted inside its box. You can choose between flush left (the text starts at the left side), centered (the text is centered left-to-right inside the box), and flush right (the lines of text touch the right, rather than left, side of the label box). All Visual Basic labels are left-aligned when you first create them. I've set the Created and Modified labels to right-justified, as you can see in Figure 9.1.

Command Buttons

We'll use two command buttons to show the previous and next address in your address book. Each command button has a Click event that you'll use in a later chapter. For now all you'll need to do is set the Caption property and CtlName. As with menu items, you can place a & in a command button's caption to create a mnemonic access character. When you set the caption of cmdPrev to &<<, pressing Alt+< is the same as clicking on this button.

Combo Boxes

Address Book has four combo boxes that allow you to select the type of phone number that appears in each of the txtPhone text boxes. These combo boxes allow you to choose from a list of options, which I've set to Home, Office, FAX, Direct, and Car because these are the common types of telephone numbers. You'll be able to add your own types of phone numbers if you want.

The names in these combo boxes, by the way, are names you add to a list with lines of code you write. You can't set up a list of names as you design your program. Instead, you have to write some code that will set the names in each combo box when Address Book first starts. You'll learn how to do this later.

The one property you'll need to set for the combo boxes is Style, which you'll want to set to 2 – Dropdown List. There are three types of combo boxes you can use in your programs, but we'll only use the Dropdown List style here.

New Properties

There are several new properties that Address Book uses:

Control	Property	Meaning
Many Controls	FontBold	Determines whether the font will be shown in bold. I've set this to False in all controls except for the command buttons.
Form	BackColor	Sets the background color used for the form.
	BorderStyle	Controls what type of border your window will have: whether it's fixed or resizable, and whether it has a thin or wide line
	MaxButton	Determines whether your form will have a Maximize button.
Combo Box	Style	Controls which type of combo box you'll get—there are three types.

Control	Property	Meaning
Command Button	Caption	The name you'll see on the button. You can include a & in the name to create a mnemonic access character.
Labels	Alignment	Controls how the text inside a label is aligned: left-justified, centered, or right-justified.
	BackColor	Sets the background color used for the form.
	Caption	The text you see inside the label.
Text Box	MultiLine	Controls whether text boxes can have more than one line of text.
	ScrollBars	Allows you to add scroll bars to multiline text boxes.
	Text	Contains all the text you type into a text box. We'll use it later to get and set the text for each address.

Form Properties

There are also several new properties we'll use in the form. The BackColor property changes the color used for the background (as opposed to the foreground, which is the color used for the characters and lines). I've set the background color to light gray, which is more appealing than the standard all-white background. It also means that the white areas show you quite clearly where you can make changes. Any text with a gray background provides information and can't be changed.

The standard border for Visual Basic's forms allows you to change the size of a form. In this case, however, we don't want to be able to change the size of the form while Address Book is running. I've designed Address Book to be one, and only one, size. I've also changed the BorderStyle property so the border won't have resizing corners. You do this by setting BorderStyle to 1 – Fixed Single.

Whenever you change the border style so you don't have resizing corners, you'll probably want to remove the Maximize button as well, which is exactly what the MaxButton property controls. I've set MaxButton to False so you won't have a Maximize button (this also removes the Maximize option from the Control menu).

Bringing Address Book to Life

You should now have an Address Book program you can run, but it doesn't do very much. Go ahead and run your program and experiment with typing text into the text fields. You'll notice you can type multiple lines of text into both the txtAddress and txtNotes text boxes, and you can use the Enter key to start new lines in these text boxes. On the other hand, Visual Basic beeps whenever you press Enter inside one of the phone-number text boxes.

Controlling the Tab Order

Now try using the Tab key to move between the different controls. Each time you press the Tab key, a different control in your program will receive the *focus*. The control with the current focus is the control that responds to keys you press on your keyboard. In other words, the focus refers to which control has the keyboard's focus of attention.

For example, when a text box has the current focus, anything you type will appear inside the text box. When a command button has the focus, pressing the spacebar has the same effect as clicking on that control with the mouse.

Not all controls are capable of receiving the focus from the keyboard. Labels, for example, can respond to mouse clicks, but *not* to keyboard events, so labels will never receive the current focus. The controls in Address Book that can receive focus are the text boxes, the combo boxes, and the command buttons.

Each time you press the Tab key, Visual Basic uses a property called Tab-Index to determine which control should receive the focus next. Whenever you create new controls on a form, Visual Basic assigns TabIndex values to each one, starting with 0 and counting up. If you created the controls in the order shown in Table 9.1, you'll probably notice that the Tab order is fairly reasonable.

But what if you decide you want to change the Tab order? How can you do this? All you have to do is change the TabIndex property for each control.

Here's how you would set up a Tab order. Click on the control you want to receive the focus when your program first starts, and set its TabIndex property to 0. Then click on the next control and set its TabIndex property to 1, and so on. Visual Basic will automatically adjust all the other TabIndex values if some control already has the TabIndex value you assign to a control.

Here is the TabIndex order I suggest for Address Book:

CtlName	TabIndex
txtAddress	0
txtPhone	1–4
txtNotes	5

Reference: TabIndex Property

Visual Basic uses the TabIndex property to determine which control will receive the focus next when you press the Tab key. Here's how it works. Every time you press the Tab key, Visual Basic looks at the value of TabIndex for the control that currently has the focus. Then it scans through the controls looking for the next highest TabIndex number. If this new control can accept the keyboard focus, Visual Basic moves the focus to this control. Otherwise it looks for the next higher TabIndex value, until it finds a control with a higher TabIndex value.

Once there are no more controls with higher TabIndex values, Visual Basic starts over with 0 and looks for the first controls with a TabIndex of 0 or higher that can accept keyboard input.

When you first load a form, the control with the lowest TabIndex (usually 0) that can accept keyboard input will receive the focus.

CtlName	TabIndex
cmdPrev	6
cmdNext	7
cboPhone	8–11

You'll notice I set the cboPhone combo boxes so they're last in the list. This order will make it easy for you to type in address and phone numbers using the default phone types (which will be Home, Office, and FAX for the first three combo boxes). If you don't like this Tab order, you can easily change it to anything you want.

Setting Up the Combo Boxes

The combo boxes we're using here are called *drop-down lists* because whenever you click on the down-pointing arrow, you'll see a list of options; these are the only options you can choose from (the other two types of combo boxes allow you to type in any text you want).

I mentioned before that we'll want the phone combo boxes to have the following options: Home, Office, FAX, Direct, and Car. As it turns out, it's also a nice idea to include a sixth option: a blank entry. Why do you want to include a blank entry? So you can have no label at all next to lines that will be blank. If you look at Figure 8.3 again (which shows what Address Book will look like when we're finished writing it), you can see that the bottom-most combo box is blank, which is possible because the last option is a blank.

Figure 9.5 shows what we want the phone combo boxes to look like when the list is dropped down. As you can see, all six possibilities are in this combo box, in the order I wrote them above. You can put these entries in any order: I chose to put them in the order that made the most sense to me. But you may

Figure 9.5:

The cboPhone combo boxes will look like this when you click on the down-pointing arrow.

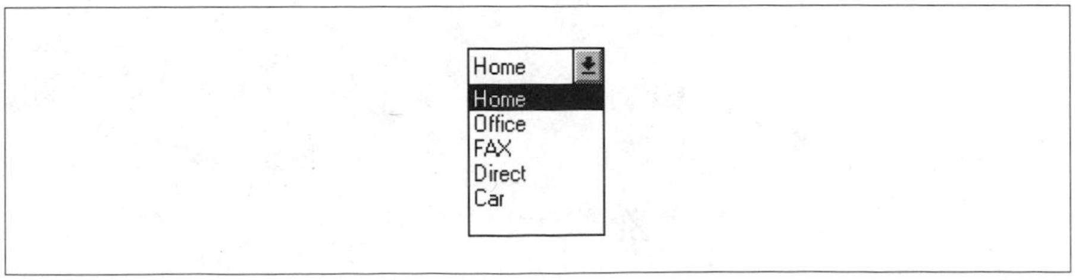

decide, for example, that you want the Office, Direct, and FAX numbers to appear before the Home number. It's entirely up to you.

Let's look at how you create this list in a combo box. Each combo box has a list of items you can select from. But when Visual Basic first creates a combo box (when it first loads a form), there are no entries in this list. So you, the programmer, have to add these items to the list.

When do you add items to the list? In this case the items will never change, so you can load the items into the list whenever your form is loaded into memory. As you saw in Chapter 7, the Form_Load event is called by Visual Basic every time a form is loaded. This is the best place to write code that will fill in the combo box's list, which we'll do next.

The Method of Methods

But first, we need to cover another piece of jargon. Visual Basic has a number of commands you can apply to its objects. For example, you write Form1.Line to draw a line on the form called Form1. Form1 is an object, and the Line "command" is actually called a *method*. Many other objects also have methods, and the reason they're called methods has to do with a branch of computer science called *object-oriented programming* (no, you don't have to remember this part),

What Are Methods?

Methods are very much like subroutines, only different. Each object defined by Visual Basic (such as timers, text boxes, and so on) has a set of properties, events, and methods that are defined as part of the object. So in a sense, a method is really a subroutine attached to an object by a period. You call a method like so:

object.method
Runs the "subroutine" called *method* on the control (or form or printer) called *object*

For example, to add an item called "Red" to a combo box called myCombo, you would write

myCombo.AddItem "Red"

Reference: AddItem Method

The AddItem method allows you to add items to a combo box's list of possibilities (which you'll see when you click on the down-pointing arrow).

control.**AddItem** *item$* [, *index%*]

Adds the item in *item$* to the control (which can be a combo box or a list box, which you haven't used yet). The optional parameter, *index%,* allows you to control where the item will be added in the list. Without this parameter, Visual Basic always adds the item to the end of your list.

You use the RemoveItem method to remove items.

---

or OOP as it's often known. In the world of OOP, functions that act on objects are called methods, rather than subroutines. They're called methods so it's clear that they're connected with a specific object instead of being a general-purpose subroutine.

Enough theory. Combo boxes, like any other object in Visual Basic, have a number of methods you can use to control them. One of these methods is called AddItem, which adds a single item to your combo box. For example, if you have a combo box called myCombo and you want it to have two choices, Red and Green, you can write these two lines of code to add these two items to the combo box's drop-down list:

```
myCombo.AddItem "Red"
myCombo.AddItem "Green"
```

Initializing the cboPhone Combo Boxes

The Address Book program has four different combo boxes you need to initialize using the AddItem method, and each combo box needs to have six items added to it. You need code that looks something like this:

```
cboPhone(0).AddItem "Home"
cboPhone(0).AddItem "Office"
cboPhone(0).AddItem "FAX"
```

```
cboPhone(0).AddItem "Direct"
cboPhone(0).AddItem "Car"
cboPhone(0).AddItem ""
cboPhone(1).AddItem "Home"
cboPhone(1).AddItem "Office"
        .
        .
        .
```

The problem with this approach is that you need a total of $6 \times 4 = 24$ lines of code to add six items to each of the four combo boxes. That's a lot of code!

Fortunately, you can use the For..Next command you learned in Chapter 6 to reduce these 24 lines of code to just 8, as you can see here:

```
Sub Form_Load ()
    For i = 0 to 3
        cboPhone(i).AddItem "Home"
        cboPhone(i).AddItem "Office"
        cboPhone(i).AddItem "FAX"
        cboPhone(i).AddItem "Direct"
        cboPhone(i).AddItem "Car"
        cboPhone(i).AddItem ""
    Next i
End Sub
```

Add this code to the Form_Load event handler in your form and run Address Book. You should now have four combo boxes, each with a list of these six items.

NOTE

It's a good idea to save your program before you run it in case your computer crashes (it happens) while you're running your program. It can be really frustrating to lose work, even if it's only five minutes' worth. The easiest way to save your project is to press Alt+F V.

There is one small problem: All four combo boxes are initially empty, even though they now have the correct list of items. Fortunately, combo boxes have a property, called ListIndex, that you can set to tell it which item each combo box should currently have selected. When you first create a combo box, List-Index is set to −1, which means that no item is currently set in the combo box.

Reference: ListIndex Property

The ListIndex property of a combo box allows you to select which entry in the drop-down list will be used in the combo box. Combo boxes start with ListIndex = −1, which means that no entry is currently selected. You can set it to any value between 0 and the number of items in the list − 1 as long as you have at least one item in the list.

Value	Meaning
−1	No item selected.
0	The first item will be selected.
1	The second item will be selected.
$n - 1$	The last item will be selected, when there are n items in the list.

If you look in the Properties combo box when you have one of the cbo-Phone objects selected (in design mode), you'll notice there's no ListIndex property. Why not?

ListIndex is missing because it's a property you can only read and set at run time, not at design time. All the properties you've worked with till now were properties you could set at design time, and many of them, but not all, you could also set at run time. But, as you've just discovered, there are some properties you can only set at run time.

The reason you can only set ListIndex at run time is very simple. ListIndex can never be set to a value larger than the number of items in the list. And as you've discovered, the list is empty until your code adds some items to the list during the Form_Load event handler. In other words, the only allowed value for ListIndex is −1 (nothing selected) until you add some items to the list. At design time it doesn't really make sense to assign a value to ListIndex; this is why Microsoft defined ListIndex as a run-time-only property.

Add the last four lines of code below to your Form_Load event handler so they appear *after* the For..Next loop:

```
    . . .
    Next i

    cboPhone(0).ListIndex = 0        ' Set these combo boxes to
```

```
        cboPhone(1).ListIndex = 1        ' Home, Office, FAX, and blank
        cboPhone(2).ListIndex = 2
        cboPhone(3).ListIndex = 5
End Sub
```

These lines must appear after the For..Next loop so the combo boxes will have entries you can select. If you put these lines before the For..Next loop, you'll get an "Invalid property value" error message from Visual Basic because the only ListIndex value that's valid for an empty list is −1.

Your program should now look like Figure 9.6. Address Book is looking more and more like a real program. And you really haven't done that much work yet (believe it or not).

Figure 9.6:

Your version of Address Book should now look like this. Notice the combo boxes show the correct titles.

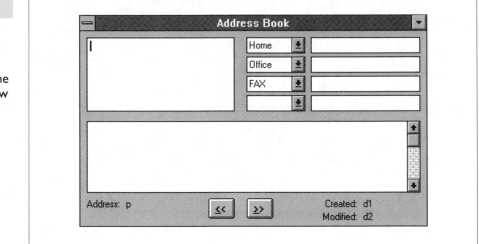

You'll notice the three information labels haven't been filled in yet (the ones that read p, d1, and d2). You won't start to use these labels until a later chapter, once you start to read and write addresses to disk.

Actually, when I originally designed and started to write Address Book, I didn't even have these labels in the program. I didn't add them until later in my design. You may recall that they're not in my pencil sketch, shown in Figure 8.2. As you begin to write your programs from your initial specifications, you'll often have new ideas about what you want your program to do. You'll almost always find yourself adding or changing features in your program, as is the case with the three labels, which will report information on the current address.

Related Tools

RemoveItem The RemoveItem method allows you to remove items from combo or list boxes that you added with AddItem.

ListCount You can use the ListCount property (read-only, and available only at run time) to get the number of items in a combo box's drop-down list.

MinButton This property allows you to control whether your form has a Minimize button (it also controls whether the Control menu has a Minimize item).

ControlBox You can remove the Control menu (and box) entirely by setting this property to False.

Font Properties There are a number of font properties, whose names all start with *Font,* that you can use to control the appearance of characters in text boxes, combo boxes, labels, and many other controls.

TabStop If you don't want the Tab key to be able to move to one of your controls (such as the cboPhone combo boxes), you can set TabStop to False. This property is called TabStop because it controls whether the focus can stop on a control when you press the Tab key.

Summary

At this point you have a user interface that is functional, but the Address Book program doesn't do very much right now. The next step, which you'll take in the next chapter, is to read and write all the information to a file on your disk.

Here's what you learned in this chapter:

Drawing Controls. The Properties bar provides size readouts you can use to set the sizes of your controls. You can also set the Height, Width, Left, and Top properties using the Properties bar.

Program Manager Icon. You learned how to create a Program Manager icon for your project, which is an easy way to start your projects.

Text Boxes. The text box control allows you to create text-entry sections in your forms. These text boxes can be limited to a single line of text, or you can allow multiple lines by setting the MultiLine property to True. You can also use the ScrollBars property to add scroll bars to any text box.

Labels. These controls are useful anytime you want some text on your form that you don't need to be able to edit. You can use labels both for static labels and for information readouts. Address Book has three readout labels you'll use later to show information about the current address.

Command Buttons. Visual Basic makes it very easy to add command buttons to your programs.

Combo Boxes. These controls are the ones you spent the most time on in this chapter. You learned how to add items to the lists attached to combo boxes using the AddItem method, and you learned how to select an item in a combo box using the ListIndex property.

Tab Order. The TabIndex property allows you to determine which control will receive the keyboard focus when you press the Tab key. Visual Basic looks for the control with the next-highest TabIndex that can accept keyboard input and sets the focus to that control. Shift+Tab moves the focus backward through the same list.

Methods. Methods are like subroutines, but they're defined as part of an object. A method is a predefined subroutine that you call using the *control.method* convention we used here.

 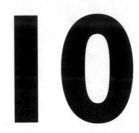

Chapter 10

Featuring

Creating, Reading, and Writing
Disk Files

Random-Access Files

User-Defined Variable Types

The Global Module

Fixed-Length Strings

Using On-line Help

Creating New Subroutines

When Variables Are Visible

Reading and Writing Address Books

The next step in building the Address Book program is to write addresses to a disk file and read them back later. To do this, you'll need to learn several new concepts. But rather than cover everything at once, we'll go one step at a time so you can try out each new concept before you move on.

Here's the basic plan. First we'll look at how you read and write disk files. You'll see that it's fairly easy to do. But it won't be easy to write all the data Address Book needs to write because Visual Basic can only write a single type of data (Integer, String, etc.). So what you'll have to do is create a new type that packages all this data into a single, new variable, which you'll then be able to read and write.

At the end of this chapter you'll have a program that can save a single address to the disk. Each time you start Address Book, it will show this address. But you won't be able to add more than one address. For that, you'll need to do some more work, which we'll do in the next chapter.

Working with Disk Files

If you know anything about working with disk files from using other languages, the first thing you should do is forget everything you know. Visual Basic works with disk files a little differently from many other programming languages. In some ways, Visual Basic is simpler than other languages, and in some ways it's more confining.

The best way to understand Visual Basic's approach is to think about arrays of variables. You used arrays of variables in Chapter 6, where you used the array *saveX* to save the points in Sketch. It was defined like this:

```
Dim saveX(1000) As Single
```

This statement defines *saveX* as an array of 1000 elements of Single. You refer to these elements using an index (or offset). So saveX(9) refers to the tenth element of this array (since saveX(0) is the first element).

When it comes to disk files, Visual Basic has a number of ways it can work with them. We'll be using the *random access* method, which allows you to treat a disk file as an array. You'll then be able to write elements to this file and read them back in any order simply by providing the index for the element you want to read or write.

If these concepts seem a little confusing, hang in there. It's not that difficult, and a couple of examples should make it clear. We'll start with a small test program that doesn't do very much at all. When you're trying to learn some new concepts, it's often easier to write a small test program than it is to try your new ideas in a program you're currently writing.

We could start to add some test code to Address Book, but there are a couple of problems with doing so. First, if you're writing a test program, the simpler

Random-Access Files

Visual Basic provides a number of *modes* for reading and writing disk files. The mode called *random access* allows you to treat the disk file as if it contains an array of *records*.

There are a couple of differences between variable arrays and random-access files. First, variable arrays have elements, while random-access files have records. They're really the same idea, but Microsoft gave them different names. Second, variable arrays usually start with element number 0, while the first record in a random-access file is record 1. Third, random-access files can grow to any length—you're limited only by available disk space, and you don't have to define the size ahead of time. Variable arrays, on the other hand, are limited in size to about 64K.

the program, the easier it is to understand everything that's happening. If your program doesn't work the way you expect, you won't have much code to understand, so it should be easier to understand what's going wrong. Second, your ideas of what kinds of changes you want to make to your program often change after you've learned the new concept. If you start to change your program before you know, for example, how disk files work, you may discover later that there are better ways you could have changed your program. For these reasons, we'll work first with a very small test program.

Creating a Disk File

The first thing you'll need to do is create a disk file. Once you've created the file, you'll want to *open* the file so you can read from it, or write to it. As you'll see, Visual Basic handles both these functions with a single command: Open.

Save any changes you've made to Address Book, then select New Project from the File menu to start a new project. Next open the Code window and enter these three lines into the Form_Load event handler:

```
open "\test.dat" as #1
beep
end
```

You'll notice that Visual Basic shows the code you just typed into Form_Load as follows:

```
Sub Form_Load ()
    Open "\test.dat" For Random As #1
    Beep
    End
End Sub
```

Visual Basic added the "For Random" to the Open command. We'll look at what all this means in a minute. For now, suffice it to say that Open will open a file called \TEST.DAT, or create it if it doesn't already exist. I chose to use the root directory for the new file so this file will be easy to find. If you don't put a \ in front of the name, it may not be clear where Visual Basic will create the file (we'll look at this in more detail shortly).

Run this program. It will start, create the file \TEST.DAT, beep, and finally exit (I put the Beep command in this program so you would have some feedback that it ran). You should now see a new file in your root directory called TEST.DAT (use the File Manager to check this out, as in Figure 10.1), and this file should have a length of 0, because you haven't written anything to it yet.

Reference: Open and Close Commands

The Open command allows you to open files on your disk.

Open *file$* [**For** *mode*] [**Access** *access*] [*lock*] **As** [#]*filenumber%* [**Len** = *reclen%*]

Opens a file called *file$*, or creates the file if it doesn't exist (new files always have a length of 0). There are a number of optional parameters you can use to control how Visual Basic will open a file, but we'll only use a few of them here:

For Random

We'll use the random-access mode for reading and writing files, which will treat disk files as an array of records (the first record is always 1).

As [#]*filenumber%*

Specifies which file number you'll want to use to refer to the file after you open it. In this chapter I use #1, but the best way to assign a file number (as you'll see later) is with the FreeFile function.

[Len = *reclen%*]

Specifies how long each record is in the random-access file. The default is 128 bytes; we'll change it later to be the size of the address book type.

Whenever you open a file, you should also close that file when your program finishes with it by using the Close command.

Close [[#]*filenumber%*]] [,[#]*filenumber%*]]...

Closes a file that you opened with Open. If you don't provide any file numbers, Close will close all the files you opened in your program. However, it's usually better to explicitly close each file you opened.

Figure 10.1:

The Open command creates an empty file in your root directory called TEST.DAT.

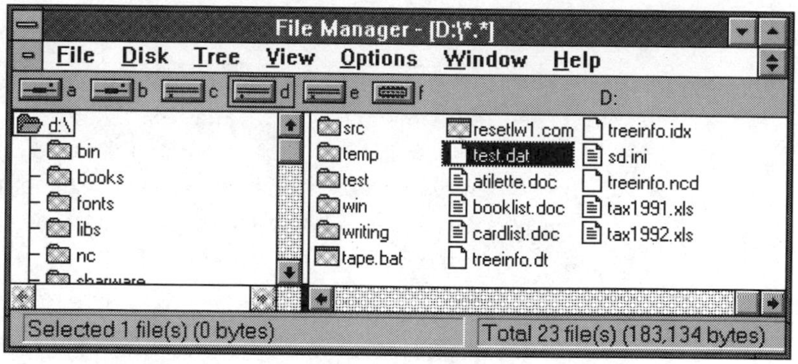

Before we move on, let's take a closer look at the Open command. The name of the file you want to open is a string, which means it must be enclosed in double quote marks. Next is the "For Random" that Visual Basic added to the Open command. What this means is that we'll be able to read or write any element in the disk file. In other words, we can read or write elements in any order, which is usually called *random access* by computer scientists.

Finally, the "As #1" is an element that Visual Basic needs for some bookkeeping. Once you open a file, you'll need to be able to refer to it. Since you can open more than one file at a time, Visual Basic needs to assign a *file number* to any file you open. In this case we simply used 1 (later I'll show you a better way to assign file numbers). The # in front of the file number is optional—I've included it because it's easier to tell that this number is a file number, which will be more important later.

Writing to a File

Now that you've managed to open a file, let's see how you can write to this file. You'll want to use the Put command (there is a Write command, but it doesn't work for random-access files). The Put command writes a single element to a disk file.

NOTE

By the way, computer scientists call these *records* rather than elements. A record is exactly like an array element, but it refers to the "elements" in disk files. In other words, memory arrays have elements, and disk file arrays have records.

The Put command writes variables, rather than raw data, to a disk file. Put can't directly write a string or a number. Instead, you need to create a variable first, then write this variable. So you'll need to add two commands to Form_Load: one to set a variable and one to call the Put command.

Here is the new version of Form_Load:

```
Sub Form_Load ()
    Open "\test.dat" For Random As #1
    test$ = "This is a test file."
    Put #1, 1, test$
    Beep
    End
End Sub
```

Run this program now. Your TEST.DAT file should be 22 bytes long (you can verify this using the File Manager). How can you see what's inside this file? By using DOS, of all things.

Start a DOS window and use DOS's TYPE command to display the contents of this file:

```
D>type \test.dat
¶ This is a test file.
D>
```

Reference: Put Command

The Put command writes a record to a file you've opened for random access (using For Random).

Put [#]*filenumber%***, [***recordnumber&***]***, recordvariable*

Writes a single variable to a record in the disk file. The first parameter, *filenumber%*, is the file number that you used in the Open command. The *recordnumber&* variable specifies which record you want to write (the first record is always 1). Finally, *recordvariable* is the variable you want to write to the file.

You can see that the string we created, "This is a test file.", is in the file. But there are also two characters that appear before the string. Why are they there? After all, you didn't put them there. The reason is quite simple.

Visual Basic keeps two bytes (characters) at the start of each string so that it can keep track of how many characters are in each string. The paragraph mark, ¶, is a DOS character with a value of 20 (every character you see has a value associated with it called its *ASCII value*), and the space is actually a character with value 0. If you count the characters in "This is a test file." you'll find there are 20 characters. The ¶ followed by a space tells Visual Basic that the string has 20 characters in it.

Let's now take a closer look at the Put command. The first two parameters refer to the file and record and numbers, respectively. In other words, the #1 means that you're writing to file number 1. And the second 1 means you're writing the first record in the file. If you think back to Chapter 6, where you worked with arrays, the first element in an array was element 0. But here, the first record in a file is record 1. Why did Microsoft use 0 in one case and 1 in the other? Who knows. There are a number of such inconsistencies in Visual Basic.

Characters and ASCII Values

Every character you see on your screen has a number associated with it, between 0 and 255 (the range of values you can represent with a single byte). The way numbers are assigned to characters is specified by a document called the American Standard Code for Information Interchange, or ASCII for short (pronounced "askee").

ASCII really only defines the values for letters, numbers, and the standard punctuation marks and symbols you find on U.S. keyboards, and uses the numbers between 32 and 127. Special characters such as ¶ and foreign-language characters such as ü are defined as *extended ASCII* characters. There is no broad standard for how numbers are assigned to these characters. IBM PC–compatible computers have one standard, and Windows has a different standard (Windows has some functions that convert strings of characters between the DOS standard and the Windows standard). So the assignment of 20 to ¶ was defined by IBM.

Reading Files

Now that you have a disk file with some data in it, let's look at how you can read this data back into your program. But first, let's think about what you'll want to do. What will you do with the data once you read it back into your program? Right now, this program writes some data and then quits immediately.

One solution, which nicely heads back to the Address Book program, is to use a text box to display the data you read back into your program. Then, you can also add some code that will write any changes you make in this text box back to your \TEST.DAT file. We'll rewrite this test program so you can type in text that will be saved to the disk, which is exactly the way we'll want Address Book to work.

Once again, instead of making all these changes at once, we'll want to make one small change at a time, then test the change. If you try to change too much at once, you may find yourself getting lost. Or worse, you may forget to test some changes you make. Good programmers test everything they write very carefully; you can never test your program too much.

The first thing you should do is remove the Beep and End commands from the Form_Load event. Then run your program again. Instead of running only briefly, now it will show an empty form on your screen. Double-click on the Control box in the upper-left corner to close the form and return to design mode.

Now add a text box to your program. This text box can be any size you want, and it can be anywhere on your form. The only thing that's important about this text box is its CtlName property, which should be Text1.

Finally, you'll want to change the code in Form_Load so it reads, rather than writes, data to the test file, which you do using the Get command. But how do you get this string into the text box?

All text boxes have a property called Text that refers to any string inside a text box. You can read this property to get the current string from a text box. And you can change the text inside a text box by assigning a string to this property.

This new version of Form_Load will read the first record in \TEST.DAT and assign the string to your text box:

```
Sub Form_Load ()
    Open "\test.dat" For Random As #1
    Get #1, 1, test$
    Text1.Text = test$
End Sub
```

Run this new program and see what happens. You should see something like Figure 10.2, and you'll be able to make any changes to the text inside the text box. But this test program won't save any of these changes back to the disk file.

Let's make another small change to this program so it will save any changes you make in the text box, which is easy to do using the Form_Unload event handler. This event is called whenever your form is *unloaded* from memory—in other words, whenever you double-click on the Control box (or select Close from the Control menu). By calling Put in the Form_Unload event handler, you can write the Text property of the text box back to your \TEST.DAT file:

```
Form_Unload (Cancel As Integer)
    test$ = Text1.Text
    Put #1, 1, test$
End Sub
```

That's all there is to it. Now your test program should save any changes you make to the text box, and load the modified string back into your program when you run it again.

Reference: Get Command

The Get command reads a record from a file you've opened for random access (using For Random).

Get [#]_filenumber%_, **[**_recordnumber&_**]**, _recordvariable_
Reads a single record from a record in the disk file into a variable. The first parameter, _filenumber%_, is the file number that you used in the Open command. The _recordnumber&_ variable specifies which record you want to read (the first record is always 1). Finally, _recordvariable_ is the variable you want to read from the file.

NOTE

Using this technique for reading and writing files, the length of your strings is limited to 126 characters. Later you'll see how to use the Len parameter of Open to change this limit.

Reference: Form_Unload Event

The Form_Unload event handler will run whenever you unload a form from memory. For simple programs with just one form, this happens whenever you quit your program.

Sub Form_Unload (*Cancel* As Integer)

Runs whenever you quit your application or otherwise unload a form.

Cancel

Set this parameter to True (−1) to prevent your form from being unloaded. This is useful when you display a dialog box asking if the user wants to quit without saving changes. If the user says no, set Cancel = −1 and your program will continue to run.

Closing Files

You're now almost ready to add reading and writing to the Address Book program. But first, there is one small detail that we should cover. In all the tests you've done so far, you've been opening a file, but you may have noticed that you never closed the file. Consider what would happen on your desk if you kept opening file folders but never closed them and put them away. Pretty soon your desk would become very cluttered (maybe that's what my problem is!). So you need to close file folders and put them away when you're done with them. (Of course, some people have assistants to clean up after them.)

In the same way, you should close Visual Basic's files after you're done with them. If you don't, Visual Basic will clean up for you when your program finishes. But it's better to explicitly close the files rather than rely on Visual Basic to clean up after you. So add a Close 1 to your Form_Unload event handler:

```
Form_Unload (Cancel As Integer)
    test$ = Text1.Text
    Put #1, 1, test$
    Close #1
End Sub
```

This closes file number 1, which is the file number you opened in Form_Load.

Reading and Writing the Address Book

If you think about this simple test program and what you want Address Book to do, they're fairly close (big surprise, right?). The test program allows you to save any changes in a text box, which is the same type of thing you want Address Book to do. The difference, of course, is that Address Book will be able to read and write more than a single address. And it will also save more than a single text box (it needs to save the phone numbers, the notes, and so on for each record).

We'll add all these features in sections later in this chapter and in other chapters. For now, though, let's modify Address Book so it remembers the contents of the address text box.

But first, let's think about where the address book file should be. You certainly don't want to keep it in your root directory, as your test program did; it's a good idea to place as few files as possible in your root directory. So where can you keep it? The best place to keep the address book file is in the same directory as your program, which is usually the *current directory*.

Whenever you create a file without a path name in front of it, such as AD-DRESS.DAT, the file will be created in the current directory. But the question (and problem) is: Which directory is the current directory?

In the last chapter I had you set up a Program Manager icon for your Address Book project. At that time I mentioned that you should fill in the Working Directory field of the Program Item Properties dialog box with the directory that contains your ADDRESS.MAK project file. When you set this field, you tell the Program Manager that you want this to be the current directory when you start your project.

If you don't use this field (or if you have Windows 3.0 or you open your project with the Open Project... item from the File menu), the current directory probably won't be the same as your ADDRESS.MAK file; it will probably be the same directory as VB.EXE, but it could be the same as the last project you worked on if it had a different current directory.

The bottom line is that you should always open your Address Book project using its icon to make sure it will always look in the same place for its files.

Now that we have that out of the way, let's modify Address Book so it saves the contents of the txtAddress text box. You'll want to quit Visual Basic, then double-click on your Address Book program to start Visual Basic again with your project loaded. Before I show you the code, can you guess how you want to modify Address Book? Go ahead and make the changes.

OK, now that you've given it a try yourself, here's the code that I wrote to modify Address Book. First, let's look at the changes I made to Form_Load. Rather than show you the entire Form_Load subroutine, I'll just show you the changes with ellipses (...) showing previous code that I'm not showing again:

```
...
    Next i

    Open "address.dat" For Random As #1
    Get #1, 1, temp$              ' Read text from disk file
    txtAddress.Text = temp$       ' Set address to first record

    cboPhone(0).ListIndex = 0     ' Set these combo boxes to
...
```

Then you'll need to add three lines to Form_Unload to save anything you type into the txtAddress text box:

```
Sub Form_Unload (Cancel As Integer)
    temp$ = txtAddress.Text       ' Get the new text
    Put #1, 1, temp$              ' Save it back to the file
    Close #1                      ' Close the data file
End Sub
```

Is this what your code looked like? How does your Address Book program work? It should now remember anything you type into the address text box—it won't remember anything you type into other text boxes. If your program doesn't work this way, check your changes and see how they compare to my changes.

Once you have your program working, you'll be ready for the next step (but save your project first). I'm going to show you how you can write records that include all parts of the address: the address, phone numbers, phone-number types, notes, and creation and modification dates.

Packaging Data: User-Defined Types

You're probably wondering how you can write multiple variables into each record. It would be really simple if you could write Put #1, 1, address$, notes$, and so on. But that doesn't work; the Put command only writes one variable in each record.

You have to use another approach. And the approach that works best is to use something called a *user-defined type*, which allows you to "package" several variables into a single, new variable. You do this by creating a new variable type (in Chapter 2 you learned that Visual Basic has six types of variables: five numeric types plus strings).

Defining New Types

Here's how it works. Visual Basic has a keyword called Type that allows you to define new types of variables. You'll use Type, for the most part, to create "compound" variables, where each variable actually contains several pieces. Since this can be a little confusing, let's look at an example.

In Chapter 6 you created two arrays to hold the X and Y parts of lines you wanted to remember in Sketch. Using the Type command, you can instead create a single, compound variable that contains both the X and Y part in a single variable. These "parts" are known as *elements*, and you get to each element using the following notation:

variableName.elementName

For example, if you have a variable called *save* that's defined as a compound type with an *x* and a *y* element, you can set each element like this:

```
save.x = 10
save.y = 20
```

Now let's look at how you go about creating compound variables. The first thing you'll need to do is create a user-defined type, which is a description of what you want to be inside each of your compound variables. The Type description includes the name you want to use for your new type, as well as one line for each element in the type, as you can see in this example that defines a Point type:

```
Type Point
    X As Single
    Y As Single
End Type
```

The first line says you're defining a type called Point, while the second and third lines define the elements that will be in the type. You can have any number of elements, and they can all be different types, as you'll see below.

Reference: Type Statement

The Type statement allows you to define new types for creating compound variables (variables with one or more components inside).

> **Type** *typeName*
>   *elementName* **As** *type*
>   .
>   .
>   .
> **End Type**

Defines a new variable type, with the name *typeName*. Every variable of this type will have at least one element, *elementName*. You can have any number of elements in a user-defined type.

You create variables of new types using the Dim statement, just as with regular types like Single or Integer. To read the value of an element or to change its value, you use the variable name followed by a period and the element name:

> *varName.elementName*

Use this syntax to read or write any element in a compound variable that you create with a user-defined type.

Once you've defined such a type, you can use this new type name (Point in the example above) to declare new variables. For example, you can declare an array called *save* with this statement:

```
Dim save(1000) As Point
```

The only question left is: Where do you put the Type declaration? Do you put the Type statements into the (declarations) section of your form? Nope. For some reason, Visual Basic is very picky about where you define new types, and you can't define new types inside forms. Instead you must define new types in the *global module*.

The Global Module

If you look at your Project window again (Figure 10.3), you'll notice two files listed in this window. One of them, Global.bas, is a file you didn't create. If you look on your disk in your Address Book directory (using the File Manager), you'll notice there's no file called Global.bas. So what's this file doing here?

Each new project that Visual Basic creates will always have a file called Global.bas listed in the Project window, but this "file" will only be saved to the disk after you've put something into it. Furthermore, you can't remove this file from your project. Obviously, this is a special file.

Figure 10.3:

The Project window shows the names of all the files (forms and modules) included in your project.

ADDRESS.MAK

View Form   View Code

Global.bas   Global
ADDRESS.FRM Address

All the projects we've worked with so far have used a single form file. But more complex and larger Visual Basic programs use a number of forms, as well as a number of *modules*. Modules are somewhat like forms because they can have code inside them. But they don't have a form attached to them—they're just used for holding code. You'll see later in the next chapter why that's useful (since we'll create a module).

There is also one very special module in every project called the *global* module. This module is used only for defining global types and *global variables,* which are like form variables that you defined in the (declarations) section of your form in Chapter 6, except that global variables can be seen in *all* forms and modules (this hasn't been an issue yet because we haven't put more than one form into any project).

To display the global module, you double-click on the Global.bas file in the Project window, which I'll show you in more detail later.

Designing an AddressInfo Type

You're almost ready to define an AddressInfo type that will package all the data Address Book needs to save and read for each record (address) in the file. Before you actually define the type, let's take a look at all the pieces you'd like to save.

The Address Book form has a total of 10 input fields you'll want to save: the address, the four phone types, the four telephone numbers, and the notes. You'll also want to save the creation and modification dates for each record in your file. There are 12 pieces of information, all together, that you'll want to save.

Now let's look at what types of information you'll want to save (String, Integer, etc.). The address and notes will obviously be strings, so you'll need two String types. But what about the telephone numbers? Do you want to save them as strings or numbers?

I've chosen to save telephone numbers as strings for a very good reason. I have a number of friends in Europe, and the telephone numbers there look very different from numbers in the United States. But even in the United States, there are some variations in how to write telephone numbers. Here, for example, are some numbers you might write:

(310) 555-1212   A telephone number without an extension

(800) 555-1212 x123   A telephone number with an extension

011 49 2134 33 44 55   A telephone number in Germany

As you can see, saving these numbers as strings is a lot easier than saving them as numbers. So we'll save the four telephone numbers as strings, for a total so far of six strings.

You have a couple of choices about how you save the type (Home, Office, etc.) in the phone-type combo boxes: You can save them as numbers (the value of the ListIndex property), or you can save them as strings. There are advantages and disadvantages to each approach. Saving them as numbers is very easy, but if you later change your mind about the order of the items in the phone type's list, you also have to change all the numbers in your address book file. On the other hand, if you save the types as strings, then later change the names of some of the strings, you have to change all the affected names in your address book file—so it's really not clear which approach is best. Therefore, since saving the ListIndex property is a little easier, we'll use this approach. Add four integers to the list of elements in the AddressInfo type.

Finally, you'll want to save the dates of creation and last modification. These are numbers you'll get from the Now( ) function you used in Chapter 7, which you'll recall returns a number of type Double. So add two Doubles to the list.

Here is a summary of all the data types you'll need in your AddressInfo type:

Type	How Many	What For
String	1	Address text
Integer	4	Phone-type combo boxes (ListIndex)
String	4	Telephone numbers
String	1	Notes text
Double	1	Creation date
Double	1	Last modification date

You might expect, then, that you can write something like this to define the type:

```
Type AddressInfo
    address As String
    types(4) As Integer
```

```
        phones(4) As String
        notes As String
        created As Double
        modified As Double
End Type
```

But this doesn't work for several, somewhat frustrating, reasons.

First, for some reason Visual Basic doesn't allow you to have arrays inside types. (Microsoft's BASIC Professional Development System, a DOS product, *does* allow arrays inside types.) What this means is that you have to provide a different element for each combo box and each telephone-number text box:

```
        type1 As Integer
        type2 As Integer
        type3 As Integer
        type4 As Integer
        phone1 As String
        phone2 As String
        phone3 As String
        phone4 As String
```

This is most inconvenient! Unfortunately, until Microsoft adds arrays to Visual Basic, you don't have much choice in the matter. You'll have to write one element in the type for each element of the array you want.

Fixed-Length Strings

The other problem is a little more subtle. All the string variables you've worked with so far have been variable-length strings. They can be almost any size you want, large or small (strings can never be larger than 65,533 bytes long, however). But this presents a problem when you're writing records to a disk file (or reading them back).

Visual Basic doesn't allow you to read or write compound variables that contain variable-length strings (for an explanation, see the sidebar "Random-Access Files and Variable-Length Strings"). Instead, you have to use what's known as a fixed-length string. Fixed-length strings are strings that always have the same length, and they're defined like this 20-character long string:

```
Dim fixedString As String * 20
```

The "* 20" identifies the string as a 20-character long string. Remember before how the string you wrote to the test file began with a 2-byte length count?

Fixed-length strings don't have a length count. Instead, you define their length when you define the string. And because each string has no length count, any "empty" slots at the end of the string will be filled with spaces. For example, setting fixedString = "Word" will set the variable *fixedString* to "Word" followed by 16 spaces (20 − 4).

There are a couple of other issues about fixed-length strings we'll need to cover later. But you now know enough to modify your Address Book program so it reads and writes more information than before.

First, double-click on the Global.bas file in your Project window. You should see an edit window appear with the caption Global. Type the following into the Global window:

```
Type AddressInfo
    address As String * 160        ' The address
```

Random-Access Files and Variable-Length Strings

Visual Basic isn't always consistent, and it certainly isn't consistent in the way it handles variable-length strings and random-access files.

As you saw earlier in this chapter, Visual Basic makes it very easy to read and write variable-length strings (in other words, strings you define As String). But this is only true as long as such strings are shorter than a record (which is 128 bytes, unless you use the Len parameter in Open).

On the other hand, you can't create a user-defined type that has a variable-length string, then write variables of this new type to random-access files. If you try it, you'll get an error message from Visual Basic: "Record with variable-length String not allowed."

Why this restriction? Well, it's not really a restriction. Instead, this "restriction" is a result of the way computer scientists often view database files. In the database world, nonrelational databases have a number of records in them. Each record is divided into one or more fields, and the length of each field is fixed. This is exactly how Visual Basic's Put and Get commands work with random-access files and user-defined types. To fit the standard database model, you'll need to define the strings in your records as fixed rather than variable-length.

```
        notes As String * 300              ' Notes field

        type1 As Integer                   ' Four telephone types
        type2 As Integer
        type3 As Integer
        type4 As Integer

        phone1 As String * 25              ' Four telephone numbers
        phone2 As String * 25
        phone3 As String * 25
        phone4 As String * 25

        created As Double                  ' Date record was created
        modified As Double                 ' Date record last modified
End Type
```

Notice the order in which I wrote these elements? The order you use really isn't important, as long as you don't change it after you start to create an address book file. The data on the disk will be stored within each record in exactly the same order as you write it (see Figure 10.4), so if you later change the order of the elements, your data won't be read back in correctly.

In case you're wondering where the strings lengths came from, they're really just arbitrary numbers. I chose 160 for the length of the address field because the longest address I have in my files (including the company name, division name, and the person's title) is about 130 characters long. I added an extra 30 characters just to be safe. In the same spirit, the longest telephone number I have in my files is 20 characters long, so I set the length of these fields to 25. Finally, the 300-character length of the notes field is really arbitrary. I wanted to keep it small to keep the size of my address-book file small (since each notes field will use 300 characters, even if you leave it blank). Setting the size to 300 characters allows about three full lines of text, or a number of shorter lines, which is enough for my needs.

Now close the global module (by double-clicking on its Control box) to get its window out of the way. You should also save your project (press Alt+F V). When you do this, Visual Basic will display the Save File As dialog box for Global.bas. Press Enter to accept the standard name: Global.bas.

Writing and Reading Compound Variables

Let's take a look at what you'll need to change in Form_Load and Form_Unload to read and write compound variables. Here is a summary of the changes

Figure 10.4:

Variables created by user-defined types are written directly to a disk record, byte-for-byte.

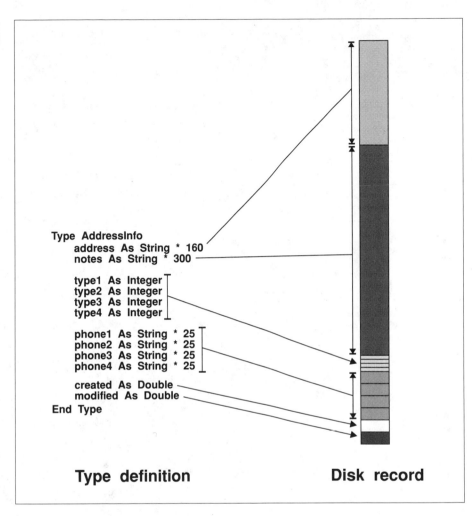

```
Type AddressInfo
    address As String * 160
    notes As String * 300

    type1 As Integer
    type2 As Integer
    type3 As Integer
    type4 As Integer

    phone1 As String * 25
    phone2 As String * 25
    phone3 As String * 25
    phone4 As String * 25

    created As Double
    modified As Double
End Type
```

Type definition   **Disk record**

you'll need to make, which I'll describe in more detail below:

1. Define a variable called *addr* that has the type AddressInfo.

2. Specify the length of a record in the Open command so Visual Basic will know how long your records are.

3. Read in the *addr* record.

4. Transfer the values from *addr*'s elements to your form's controls.

5. In Form_Unload, transfer the values from the form back into the *addr* variable.

6. Write the *addr* record back to disk.

Each one of these changes is actually fairly simple, so let's go through them one at a time (I'll present the new Form_Load and Form_Unload subroutines in their entirety at the end of this section).

The very first thing you have to do is define a variable called *addr* that has the type AddressInfo. Define this variable in the Form_Load subroutine (later we'll think about how all the code should really be organized) so it looks like this:

```
Dim addr As AddressInfo
```

Next you'll want to modify the Open statement in Form_Load so it defines the length of each record, which you do like this:

```
Open "address.dat" For Random As #1 Len = Len(addr)
```

Reference: Len( ) Function

The length function tells you how large a variable is, in bytes. For string variables, it tells you how many characters are in the string.

Len(*strVar$*)

Reports the number of characters in the string *strVar$*. Note that this isn't the size of the variable in bytes; rather, it's the number of characters in the string.

Len(*varName*)

Reports how many bytes are used to store the variable called *varName*. This is very useful when used with variables of user-defined types in the file Open command.

Note: Be careful not to use Len with a type name, as this won't give you a correct value. You need to define a variable of that type, then use Len on the variable.

The Len parameter tells Visual Basic how large each record is in the file you're opening. Here the function Len(addr) calculates the size, in bytes, of the variable *addr*, which means you don't have to calculate the size of each record yourself. In fact, it's better not to calculate the size yourself—letting Visual Basic do it for you is much safer, because Visual Basic won't make a mistake. It's also a lot easier to let Visual Basic do all the work.

Next you'll want to modify the Get statement along with the statement that sets the Text property of text boxes (you'll want to make sure you remove any lines that refer to the variable *temp$*). Here's the new Get statement, along with statements to read the address and the first telephone number:

```
Get #1, 1, addr               ' Read first record from file
txtAddress.Text = addr.address  ' Transfer the address field
txtPhone(0).Text = addr.phone1  ' Transfer first phone number
```

I've written code to read only two fields of the record, as test code. The idea is to keep your code as simple as possible until you have something that works. Only then should you add all the remaining code. This approach makes it much easier to track down problems, since you'll tend to discover them sooner.

You'll need to make one last change, to Form_Unload, before you try these changes in your program. Replace the first two lines in Form_Unload (the assignment and the Put statements) with these lines:

```
Dim addr As AddressInfo

addr.address = txtAddress.Text
addr.phone1 = txtPhone(0).Text
Put #1, 1, addr               ' Save changes back to file
```

Now try your new program. Does it work correctly? It should save anything you write in the address field and the first telephone field. Does it work this way? If not, check your Form_Load and Form_Unload subroutines to make sure they're correct. Here are the correct versions:

```
Sub Form_Load ()
    Dim addr As AddressInfo

    For i = 0 To 3
        cboPhone(i).AddItem "Home"
        cboPhone(i).AddItem "Office"
        cboPhone(i).AddItem "FAX"
        cboPhone(i).AddItem "Direct"
        cboPhone(i).AddItem "Car"
```

```
        cboPhone(i).AddItem ""
    Next i

    Open "address.dat" For Random As #1 Len = Len(addr)
    Get #1, 1, addr                ' Read first record from file
    txtAddress.Text = addr.address ' Transfer the address field
    txtPhone(0).Text = addr.phone1 ' Transfer first phone number

    cboPhone(0).ListIndex = 0        ' Set these combo boxes to
    cboPhone(1).ListIndex = 1
    cboPhone(2).ListIndex = 2
    cboPhone(3).ListIndex = 5
End Sub
```

```
Sub Form_Unload (Cancel As Integer)
    Dim addr As AddressInfo

    addr.address = txtAddress.Text
    addr.phone1 = txtPhone(0).Text
    Put #1, 1, addr                ' Save changes back to file
    Close #1                       ' Close file before exit
End Sub
```

Removing Trailing Spaces

There is one small problem that's very easy to fix. Run your program again, then use the cursor keys to move within the address or the first phone-number text box. You'll notice there are a number of spaces at the end of each field. Why? Since all the strings in the *addr* variable are fixed-length fields, assigning

```
txtAddress.Text = addr.address
```

places all the trailing spaces in the text box. Wouldn't it be nice if there were a simple way to remove all these spaces? Well, there is. Visual Basic has a number of functions for working with strings, and one of them, called RTrim$( ), removes trailing spaces from a string. You can remove the trailing spaces in your program by changing two lines in Form_Load:

```
txtAddress.Text = RTrim$(addr.address)
txtPhone(0).Text = RTrim$(addr.phone1)
```

Now run your program again and you'll notice there are no trailing spaces.

Using On-line Help

You're probably getting to the point where it's hard to remember all the statements and functions you've learned, much less the syntax for each instruction. Fortunately, there's a very quick way to get information on these commands. To see how it works, switch to the Form_Load subroutine in your Code window, then position the insertion point anywhere inside the RTrim$ function you just added. Next, press the F1 key. This will bring up a Help window that shows information on the command (see Figure 10.5).

There are a couple of useful shortcuts you can use once you have the Help window visible. First, Help allows you to jump between related items very easily. You'll notice two underlined strings in Figure 10.5: *LTrim$* and *example*.

Figure 10.5:

Pressing F1 at any time will display Visual Basic's on-line help, which is a quick way to refresh your memory on how a command works.

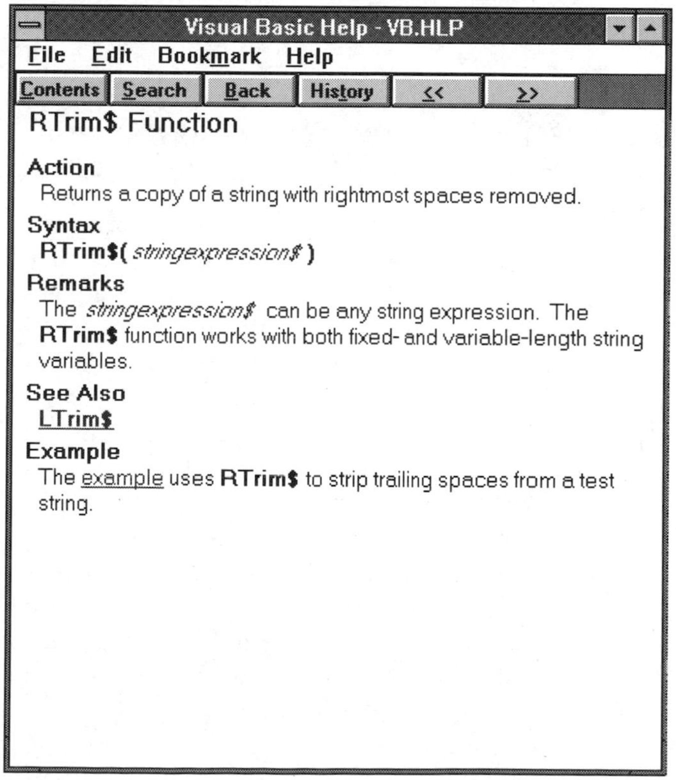

```
┌─────────────────────────────────────────────────┐
│ ─        Visual Basic Help - VB.HLP        ▼  ▲ │
│  File   Edit   Bookmark   Help                   │
│ ┌────────┬────────┬──────┬────────┬─────┬─────┐ │
│ │Contents│ Search │ Back │History │  << │  >> │ │
│ └────────┴────────┴──────┴────────┴─────┴─────┘ │
│  RTrim$ Function                                 │
│                                                  │
│  Action                                          │
│   Returns a copy of a string with rightmost      │
│   spaces removed.                                │
│  Syntax                                          │
│   RTrim$( stringexpression$ )                    │
│  Remarks                                         │
│   The stringexpression$ can be any string        │
│   expression. The RTrim$ function works with     │
│   both fixed- and variable-length string         │
│   variables.                                     │
│  See Also                                        │
│   LTrim$                                          │
│  Example                                         │
│   The example uses RTrim$ to strip trailing      │
│   spaces from a test string.                     │
│                                                  │
└─────────────────────────────────────────────────┘
```

If you click on either of these items, Help will show you information on related items. You can then click the Back button to return to where you were.

You can also search for keywords in the help file. To do this, click the Search button at the top of the help screen, then start typing a word that you want to look for. Help will show you the first keyword that matches what you've typed so far. Click on the Show Topics button to see the related topics. For example, to find the help screen on the Open statement, do the following:

1. Click on the Search button.

2. Type **open.**

3. Click on the Show Topics button.

4. Double-click on the Open Statement item in the lower list.

As you can see, using on-line help can be much faster than looking up commands in your Visual Basic *Language Reference* manual, especially if you don't remember (or know) the name of a command.

Creating New Subroutines

You now have an address book program that remembers just two fields, out of a total of ten different fields. Remembering the other text fields is really quite simple. See if you can write the code yourself before I present my solution. Remembering the ListIndex property for each of the phone-type combo boxes is also very simple. Try adding this code as well.

The changes I suggested you make are a little different from the ones we'll make together. If you add all the code in Form_Load and Form_Unload to load and save a single record, you'll notice that these two subroutines are becoming rather long. And the Form_Load subroutine is also doing a number of tasks: It's initializing the combo boxes, opening the database file, reading in the first record, and setting the fields in your form.

In general, it's best to keep your subroutines short and to have each subroutine perform a single function. But, you ask, how do you do this? By using a feature of Visual Basic we haven't explored yet, which allows you to create new subroutines, with your own names and parameters.

Let's start by creating a new subroutine called DBOpen, which stands for Database Open; programmers often use DB as an abbreviation for *database*.

To create this new subroutine, first make sure your Code window is visible and active. Then choose the New Procedure... item from the Code menu, and type **DBOpen** in the Name text box of the dialog box that appears (see Figure 10.6).

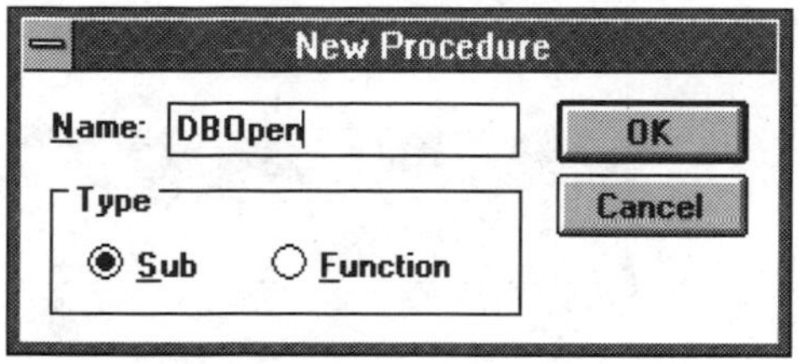

Figure 10.6:

Choosing the New Procedure... item from the Code menu displays this dialog box, which allows you to define new subroutines.

Your Code window should now show a new, empty subroutine called DBOpen. Enter the following code into this subroutine:

```
Sub DBOpen ()
    Dim addr As AddressInfo

    Open "address.dat" For Random As #1 Len = Len(addr)
End Sub
```

Finally, switch back to the Form_Load event (select the Form object from the Object combo box, then select the Load event from the Proc combo box), and change the Open command in Form_Load to this line:

```
DBOpen                          ' Open the database file
```

This line looks very simple, and it is, but it's something new: It is a command that calls the subroutine DBOpen that you just created. DBOpen then runs until it's finished doing all its work, at which time Visual Basic continues to run the code in Form_Load. In other words, you can move code into a subroutine, then run that code by writing the name of the subroutine—there's a small caveat I'll talk about shortly.

NOTE

To view your own subroutines inside the Code menu, first select the (general) section from the Object combo box in the

Code window. Next pull down the Proc combo box and you'll see a list of all the subroutines you created yourself. Selecting any of these subroutines will take you to its code. Figure 10.7 shows the Proc combo box with four new subroutines.

Figure 10.7:

The Proc combo box showing the four new subroutines you'll create in this chapter.

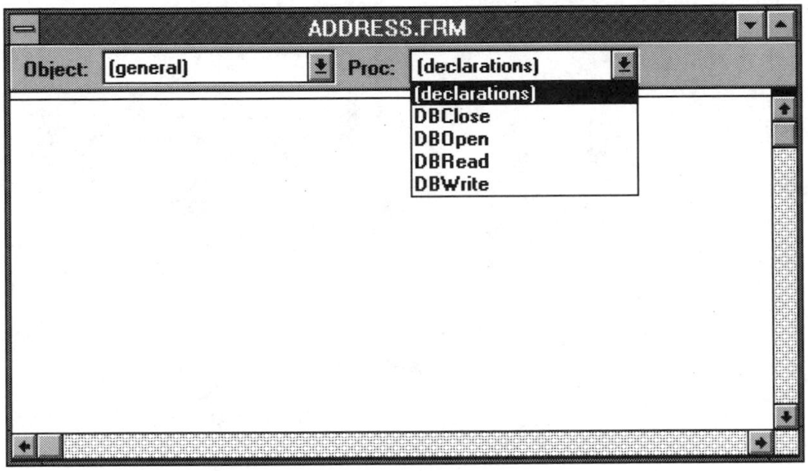

Why did I create such a short subroutine? The answer is that I have some ideas about how I like to organize programs, based on my experience writing commercial software. And I'm heading toward reorganizing Address Book along these lines. Here's a quick overview of what I have in mind and where we're headed.

I usually like to organize my programs into different "modules" that each perform a different function. All the subroutines in any module are related in terms of the type of function they provide. In the case of Address Book, you can draw a fairly clear distinction between the database side of the program (the part that works with the disk file) and the user-interface (or form) part of the program. What I plan to do, then, is to separate these two areas of the program into two distinct modules.

Creating the DBOpen function was the first step toward creating such a module. We'll also need several other subroutines in the module, namely, DBClose, DBRead, and DBWrite. You'll notice I put a DB in front of each of these names. Programmers often like to put a short two- or three-letter mini-description in front of all the subroutines and functions in a module; this makes it easy to tell that these functions all belong to the same module.

By the way, by the time we're finished writing DBOpen in Chapter 11, it will be a little longer than what you see here.

Subroutines and Variables

There is one small detail about subroutines that can be a little confusing the first time you run into it. You'll notice that I defined the variable *addr* in the DBOpen subroutine, even though it was already defined in Form_Load. Why did I do this? Because any variable you define in one subroutine won't be available to any other subroutine.

The best way to understand this is with an illustration, showing when variables are available and when they're not. For example, let's say you have a form-level variable called *someVar*, and you have two subroutines, Form_Load and DBOpen, that each define a variable: *addr1* and *addr2* respectively (see Figure 10.8). Let's take a look at where each of these variables will be visible.

Figure 10.8:

Form-level variables are available to *all* subroutines. But subroutine-level variables are only available to the code within the subroutine where that variable is defined.

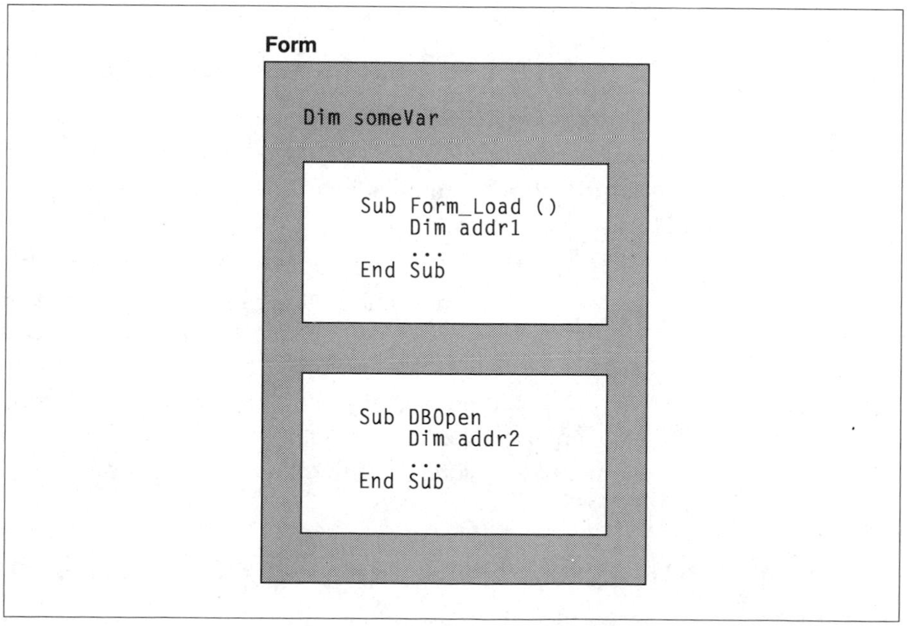

```
Form

  Dim someVar

      Sub Form_Load ()
          Dim addr1
          ...
      End Sub


      Sub DBOpen
          Dim addr2
          ...
      End Sub
```

The variable *someVar* is visible to any code inside both Form_Load and DBOpen, because it's defined as a form-level variable. As you'll recall from Chapter 6, any variables defined in the (declarations) section of a form will be visible in every subroutine and function inside the same form.

On the other hand, the variables *addr1* and *addr2* are each defined inside a subroutine. What this means is that these variables are visible only to the other statements inside the same subroutine. So if Form_Load calls DBOpen, none of the code inside DBOpen will see the variable *addr1* because this variable was defined in Form_Load, not DBOpen. Here is a chart that summarizes which variables will be visible in each subroutine:

Subroutine	someVar	addr1	addr2
Form_Load	✓	✓	
DBOpen	✓		✓

The thing to remember is that what determines whether a variable will be visible is not what happens when you run your program but where you write the lines of code.

Creating the DBClose Subroutine

Any module with an Open subroutine should also have a Close subroutine to balance the Open subroutine. Let's move the Close command from the Form_Unload event handler into its own subroutine:

1. Replace the Close #1 statement in Form_Unload with DBClose.

2. Create a new subroutine called DBClose (use the New Procedure... item from the Code menu) that contains Close #1.

You should now have a new version of Address Book that uses subroutines to open and close the database file. Save your project, then try this new program. Does it work correctly? If it doesn't, check your work carefully.

Creating DBRead and DBWrite Subroutines

The last thing we'll do in this chapter is move the code that reads and writes individual records into separate subroutines. This new code will read and write all the text and combo box data, so you'll have an Address Book program that remembers all the fields. The only things it won't remember, at this point, are the creation and modification dates.

At this point you probably have a pretty good idea about what the DBRead and DBWrite subroutines should look like, so I'll simply show them here along with the new versions of Form_Load and Form_Unload:

```
Sub Form_Load ()
    For i = 0 To 3
        cboPhone(i).AddItem "Home"
        cboPhone(i).AddItem "Office"
        cboPhone(i).AddItem "FAX"
        cboPhone(i).AddItem "Direct"
        cboPhone(i).AddItem "Car"
        cboPhone(i).AddItem ""
    Next i

    DBOpen                          ' Open the database file
    DBRead                          ' Get the first record
End Sub
```

```
Sub Form_Unload (Cancel As Integer)
    DBWrite                         ' Write record back to file
    DBClose                         ' Close the file
End Sub
```

```
Sub DBRead ()
    Dim addr As AddressInfo

    Get #1, 1, addr                 ' Read first record from file
    txtAddress.Text = RTrim$(addr.address)
    txtNotes.Text = RTrim$(addr.notes)

    txtPhone(0).Text = RTrim$(addr.phone1)
    txtPhone(1).Text = RTrim$(addr.phone2)
    txtPhone(2).Text = RTrim$(addr.phone3)
    txtPhone(3).Text = RTrim$(addr.phone4)

    cboPhone(0).ListIndex = addr.type1
    cboPhone(1).ListIndex = addr.type2
    cboPhone(2).ListIndex = addr.type3
    cboPhone(3).ListIndex = addr.type4
End Sub
```

```
Sub DBWrite ()
    Dim addr As AddressInfo

    addr.address = txtAddress.Text
    addr.notes = txtNotes.Text

    addr.phone1 = txtPhone(0).Text
    addr.phone2 = txtPhone(1).Text
    addr.phone3 = txtPhone(2).Text
    addr.phone4 = txtPhone(3).Text

    addr.type1 = cboPhone(0).ListIndex
    addr.type2 = cboPhone(1).ListIndex
    addr.type3 = cboPhone(2).ListIndex
    addr.type4 = cboPhone(3).ListIndex

    Put #1, 1, addr                        ' Save changes back to file
End Sub
```

When you make all these changes and run Address Book, you'll notice one slight anomaly: All the phone-type combo boxes now say Home. How did this happen? When you wrote out records before, you never set any values in the addr.type*n* fields, which means they were all 0 (all new variables have their values set to 0). Since cboPhone(i).ListIndex = 0 shows the first item in the list (Home in this case), all the combo boxes will say Home.

This, by the way, falls under the heading of boundary conditions. Later when we write code that allows you to add new addresses to the database, we'll have to write code that sets the initial values for the four phone-type combo boxes.

Related Tools

Deleting and Renaming Files Visual Basic has two commands for deleting and renaming files. The Kill command deletes a file (or a group of files), and the RmDir command deletes an empty directory. The Name command renames a file or a directory.

File Information There are several functions you can use to obtain information on files. The LOF function returns the size of an open file, in bytes. We'll use it in the next chapter to determine how many records are stored in a file.

Another function, Loc, returns your current location in the file. This is the number of the last record you read or wrote.

Binary and Sequential Files　Visual Basic provides two other modes for opening files: binary and sequential. Binary access mode allows you to read and write groups of bytes anywhere in the file. This mode gives you the most control over a file, but requires a lot of work. Sequential files allow you to read a file from start to finish, one line at a time. This is useful if you want to read lines of text, but you don't need to go backward through the file.

Sequential File Functions　Print # or Write # allows you to write lines, and Input # or Line Input # allows you to read lines.

Binary Files　You use the Get and Put statements to read and write data to a binary file.

Unload Command　The Unload command allows you to unload a form from within your program. This is very useful when your program uses multiple forms and you need to remove a form as a result of clicking on an OK or a Cancel button in a form.

**LTrim$**　This function allows you to remove leading spaces from a string, just as RTrim$ removes trailing spaces.

Summary

You learned a lot in this chapter and made a number of changes to Address Book. In the next chapter we'll continue to work on Address Book. We'll modify Address Book so it can read and write more than one record. In the process we'll also make some more changes to the organization of Address Book so it will be nicely modularized.

Here is what you learned:

Open and Close. You used the Open command to create a new address book file and then to open it so you could read and write to the file. You should always close any files you open.

Random-Access Files. The type of file you worked with in this chapter is a random-access file, which is like an array of records in a disk file. This "array" starts with record 0 and can grow to any size.

Put and Get. These commands allow you to read and write single records in any disk file.

User-Defined Types. The Type command allows you to define new variable types. These new types are compound types, because they contain one or more elements. In other words, you can create a variable that "packages" a number of pieces of information into a single variable. This is very useful for reading and writing records, where each record contains all the information you want to store, along with an address.

The Global Module. All Type declarations must appear in the global module, which is called Global.bas for new projects. You can change this name to anything you want when you save the global module or use the Save File As... item from the File menu.

Fixed-Length Strings. Whenever you create a user-defined type with strings that you want to write to a disk file, all the strings must be fixed-length strings. This restriction is a result of the way records are defined.

On-Line Help. If you want help on a command or function, place the cursor on that command in your Code window and press the F1 key. This will display a help screen with information on that function. You can also search help for keywords by clicking the Search button near the top of the Help window.

Creating New Subroutines. You can create your own subroutines by selecting New Procedure... from the Code menu whenever you have a Code window visible and active. Then simply type in the name you want to use for your new subroutine (or function).

Subroutines and Variables. Any variables you define in a subroutine will only be visible to lines of code that appear inside that same subroutine. For example, if subroutine A calls subroutine B, any variables inside A won't be visible to code inside B. The best way to understand this is to think of boxes within boxes. Any variable defined inside a box is only visible to code written inside the same box (Figure 10.8 shows this).

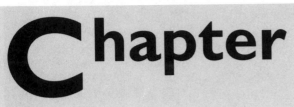 **Chapter 11**

Featuring

Creating Modules

Using Parameter Subroutines
You Create

Creating a Separate Database
Module

Debugging and Testing Programs

Creating New Functions

Reading and Writing Multiple
Address Records

Adding a Menu Bar to Address
Book

Cut, Copy, Paste, and Undo in
Text Boxes

Working with Multiple Records

I'm going to change the approach somewhat in this chapter and the next one. You're almost finished reading the tutorial part of this book. The remaining parts contain more advanced information and hints and techniques you can use in your own programs. What I'd like to do in this and the next chapter is to give you as much information and show you as much code as possible. So instead of taking you through all the steps of adding the rest of Address Book's features, I'm going to present the code, then describe how it works.

By taking this approach I'll be able to show you more examples of code. The best way for you to learn how to program is to see examples of other people's programs. It's also useful to see the techniques people use in building larger programs. By adding new features to Address Book, you'll gain insight into how I go about writing larger programs (you may find that other programmers use different approaches).

In this chapter we're going to continue building Address Book. First, we'll extend Address Book so it can work with more than one record. In the process, we'll fill out some of the other details, such as saving the creation and modification dates, and displaying information on which record we're looking at.

Creating Modules

In the last chapter you created a set of four subroutines that in a sense are in a module of their own. Visual Basic also has its own type of module, which is a file that contains nothing but code. Right now your project has two files in it: the Address Book form and the global module. You can also add other forms to your project, as well as other modules, although new modules are quite different from the global module.

The global module can't contain any code: It can only contain type definitions, global variables (we don't have any), and a few other things we won't get into until later. On the other hand, new modules you create are more like forms without any objects. In other words, they contain subroutines you create as well as module-level variables. What we're going to do here is make a greater separation than we already have between the form code and the DB module.

This approach is called *modular design,* and the idea is that it's much easier to write a larger program if you divide it into modules. Each module should be self-contained, and its connections to other modules should be as simple as possible. The database module we'll build will have just four subroutines (DBOpen, DBClose, DBRead, and DBWrite) and one function (DBLen). All the rest of the work will be handled internally by the database module.

With that said, let's create a new module. Select the New Module item from the File menu. This will create a new module in your project, called Module1.bas. It will also display a Code window with the caption Module1.bas.

Next, display the Code window for your form. If it's not already visible, click on ADDRESS.FRM in your Project window, then click on the View Code button. This will bring up the Code window for your Address form. You may want to move one of your windows so the Address.frm and Module1.bas Code windows don't overlap.

Next, display the procedure DBOpen. Use the mouse to select all the text from this form (see Figure 11.1), then choose Cut from the Edit menu. Finally switch back to the Module1.bas Code window and select Paste from the Edit menu. These steps first remove the DBOpen subroutine from your form, and then put it into the new module you just created.

At this point your form should not have a DBOpen subroutine: It's now in your new module, and DBOpen should be the only subroutine in this module. Run your program and make sure it still works correctly. Finally, select Save Project from the File menu to save these changes. You'll see a File Save As dialog box asking you where you want to save the new Module1.bas file. Type **database** then press Enter to save this file as DATABASE.BAS.

Next you'll want to move the other three DB subroutines from your form to your module. Here's how to do this:

1. Use the mouse to select the DB subroutine in your form's Code window.

Figure 11.1:

Your project should look something like this after you create a new module and select DBOpen in your form.

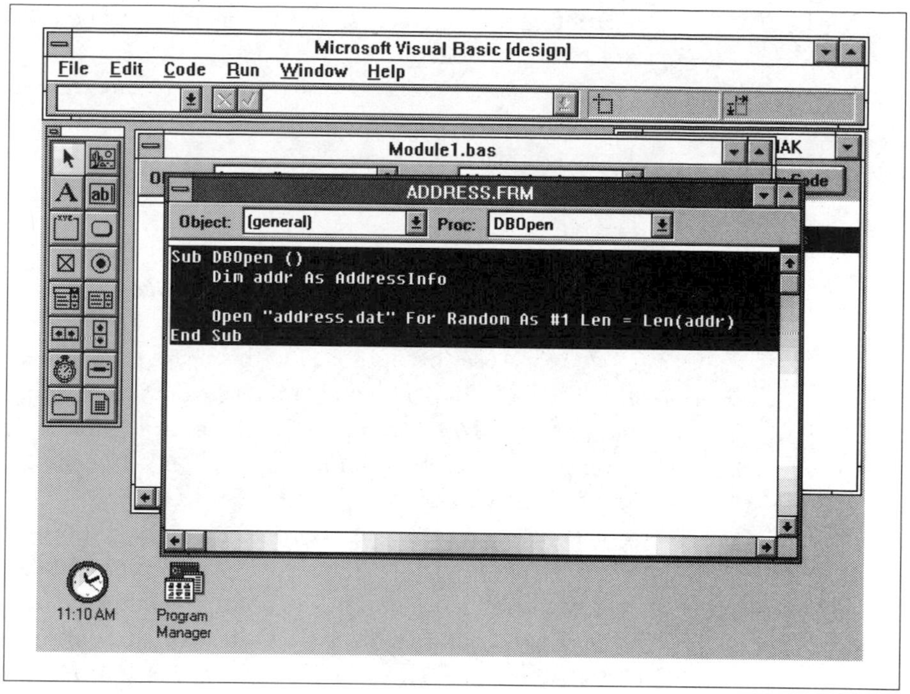

```
┌────────────────────────────────────────────────────────────┐
│                Microsoft Visual Basic [design]          ▼ ▲ │
│  File   Edit   Code   Run   Window   Help                   │
│ ┌──────────────┐ ⊠ ✓                        ⌐┐       ⌐┘     │
│ └──────────────┘                                            │
│ ┌───┬───┐ ┌──────────────── Module1.bas ──────── ▼ ▲│AK  ▼ │
│ │ �k │ 🔲│ │ O                                     ──────Code│
│ ├───┼───┤┌──────────────── ADDRESS.FRM ────────────── ▼ ▲ │ │
│ │ A │ab││                                                 │ │
│ ├───┼───┤│ Object: [(general)      ▼]  Proc: [DBOpen    ▼]│ │
│ │🗔 │ ◉ ││ ┌──────────────────────────────────────────┐▲  │ │
│ ├───┼───┤│ │Sub DBOpen ()                             │   │ │
│ │🖼 │📑 ││ │    Dim addr As AddressInfo               │   │ │
│ ├───┼───┤│ │                                          │   │ │
│ │🔲│ ⬓ ││ │    Open "address.dat" For Random As #1 Len = Len(addr)│ │
│ ├───┼───┤│ │End Sub                                   │   │ │
│ │⏱ │ ⊟ ││ │                                          │   │ │
│ ├───┼───┤│ │                                          │   │ │
│ │🗀 │📄 ││ │                                          │▼  │ │
│ └───┴───┘│ └──│◄──────────────────────────────►│──────┘   │ │
│ ◄────────└──────────────────────────────────────────────┘ │
│                                                             │
│ 🕚                                                          │
│ 11:10 AM  🏢                                                │
│           Program                                           │
│           Manager                                           │
└────────────────────────────────────────────────────────────┘
```

2. Select Cut from the Edit menu to remove your subroutine from the form.

3. Click on your Database.bas module's Code window, then use the Proc combo box to show the (declarations) section.

4. Select Paste from the Edit menu to paste your DB subroutine into the Database.bas module.

Now try running your program. Does it work? Nope. Visual Basic displays an "Element not defined" dialog box and then shows the DBRead subroutine in the Code window. What's going on?

The problem is with this line in DBRead:

```
txtAddress.Text = RTrim$(addr.address)
```

Here's what's happened. Visual Basic knows that *txtAddress* must be either a control or a variable with a user-defined type. It knows this because of the

.Text after the name *txtAddress*. But it couldn't find a variable or control called *txtAddress*. Why not?

Anytime you create a control in a form, such as *txtAddress* in the Address form, that control belongs to the form where you created it, and it won't be visible directly anywhere outside that form. To gain access to such a control, you need to tell Visual Basic which form that control resides in. For example, you can fix the line above by writing

```
Address.txtAddress.Text = RTrim$(addr.address)
```

We won't use this approach in this chapter. As I mentioned above, modules should be as independent as possible from the other parts of your program. If you put an *Address.* in front of each control name in this module, you'll have a complex, rather than simple, connection between this module and the form. So what can you do?

The best solution is to keep the interface between form and module as simple as possible, by making some changes to DBRead and DBWrite, and adding two new subroutines to your form: GetRecord and SaveRecord. The idea is that DBRead and DBWrite should read or write information into a variable of type AddressInfo. Then the statements that transfer information between this variable and the controls of your form should be in the subroutines GetRecord and SaveRecord in your form.

Rather than go into all the details of how you make these changes (you've learned all these methods already), I'll simply present the finished subroutines.

Referencing Controls inside Other Forms

As mentioned in the text, you can gain access to any control inside any form by writing the form's name, a period, and the control's name:

formName.controlName

Refers to a control called *controlName* inside the form called *formName*

Note that this only works for controls or properties inside a form. You can't reference form-level variables inside other forms.

First, here are the new subroutines you should create in your form:

```
Sub GetRecord ()
    Dim addr As AddressInfo

    DBRead addr                    ' Read one record

    txtAddress.Text = RTrim$(addr.address)
    txtNotes.Text = RTrim$(addr.notes)

    txtPhone(0).Text = RTrim$(addr.phone1)
    txtPhone(1).Text = RTrim$(addr.phone2)
    txtPhone(2).Text = RTrim$(addr.phone3)
    txtPhone(3).Text = RTrim$(addr.phone4)

    cboPhone(0).ListIndex = addr.type1
    cboPhone(1).ListIndex = addr.type2
    cboPhone(2).ListIndex = addr.type3
    cboPhone(3).ListIndex = addr.type4
End Sub
```

```
Sub SaveRecord ()
    Dim addr As AddressInfo

    addr.address = txtAddress.Text
    addr.notes = txtNotes.Text

    addr.phone1 = txtPhone(0).Text
    addr.phone2 = txtPhone(1).Text
    addr.phone3 = txtPhone(2).Text
    addr.phone4 = txtPhone(3).Text

    addr.type1 = cboPhone(0).ListIndex
    addr.type2 = cboPhone(1).ListIndex
    addr.type3 = cboPhone(2).ListIndex
    addr.type4 = cboPhone(3).ListIndex

    DBWrite addr                    ' Write record back to file
End Sub
```

These two subroutines should be fairly clear. The only new twist I've added is in the calls to DBRead and DBWrite. You'll notice I'm providing the variable *addr* as an argument to each of these functions. DBRead and DBWrite will use and set the information in this variable. (I'll describe how this works in the next section.)

Here are the new definitions for DBRead and DBWrite, which show how you define parameters for subroutines that you create:

```
Sub DBRead (addr As AddressInfo)
    Get #1, 1, addr                 ' Read first record from file
End Sub
```

```
Sub DBWrite (addr As AddressInfo)
    Put #1, 1, addr                 ' Save changes back to file
End Sub
```

As you can see, these two subroutines are now quite simple (we'll add more to them later to support more than one record in the file).

Finally, change the line with DBRead in Form_Load to this:

```
GetRecord                           ' Get the first record
```

And change the DBWrite in Form_Unload to this:

```
SaveRecord                          ' Write record back to file
```

Save your project, then try to run this new program. Does it work correctly? If it doesn't, check your work carefully to make sure you've made all the changes.

Your program now has a database module that is fairly cleanly separated from the rest of your program. We'll use this fact, after a short detour, to make some changes to the way your database code works. The amazing thing (at least it was to me the first time I ran into it) is that these changes won't affect the rest of your program. By making your program modular, you can make major changes to the way a module works without having to rewrite any other code.

Using Subroutine Parameters

The subroutines DBRead and DBWrite each use a parameter to pass information back and forth. Whenever SaveRecord writes a record to your file, it first sets all the information in the *addr* variable, and then passes this information to the DBWrite subroutine as a parameter. Simple enough.

Now let's look at what happens when you call GetRecord. This subroutine "passes" the *addr* variable to DBRead. DBRead then sets the values in its *addr* variable. But what does this mean? Will the changes DBRead makes to *addr* change the *addr* variable in the GetRecord subroutine? Yes they will, but it may not be obvious why.

The first time I ran into these issues, I found them very confusing. And even today I sometimes get confused. So if you find yourself feeling somewhat confused, finish reading this section, then put the book aside for a while. After a couple of hours, try reading this section again and see if it makes any more sense. Sometimes you just need time to let ideas percolate.

To give you a better idea of exactly what's happening, let's look at a very simple example, using two subroutines called GetInfo and SupplyInfo:

```
Sub GetInfo ()
   Dim info As AddressInfo

   SupplyInfo info
End Sub
```

```
Sub SupplyInfo (addr As AddressInfo)
   addr.address = "My Address"
End Sub
```

These two subroutines actually use two separate names (*info* and *addr*) to refer to the same variable. The reason for this is very simple. Subroutines you create, such as SupplyInfo, need to be able to work with any variables you send to them, no matter what you call such variables. So you can write "SupplyInfo info" to tell SupplyInfo that it should work with the *info* variable. Inside SupplyInfo, any statements that reference *addr* actually use the variable *info*.

This method of passing a variable to a subroutine is called *passing by reference* because Visual Basic passes a reference to a variable, rather than a copy of the variable's data. In other words, any changes you make to the value of *addr* inside SupplyInfo change the value of *info*.

Visual Basic also allows you to pass parameters *by value*. In this case you're sending a copy of the variable to the subroutine, which means the subroutine can't change the value in your main program (see Figure 11.2). To send a copy of a variable, rather than a reference to the variable, you need to place the ByVal keyword in front of the parameter definition. For example, if you want a copy of *info* sent to SupplyInfo, you define SupplyInfo like this:

```
Sub SupplyInfo (ByVal addr As AddressInfo)
```

Figure 11.2:

The top part shows passing a variable by reference (the default), and the bottom part shows passing by value (which requires that you place ByVal in front of the parameter definition).

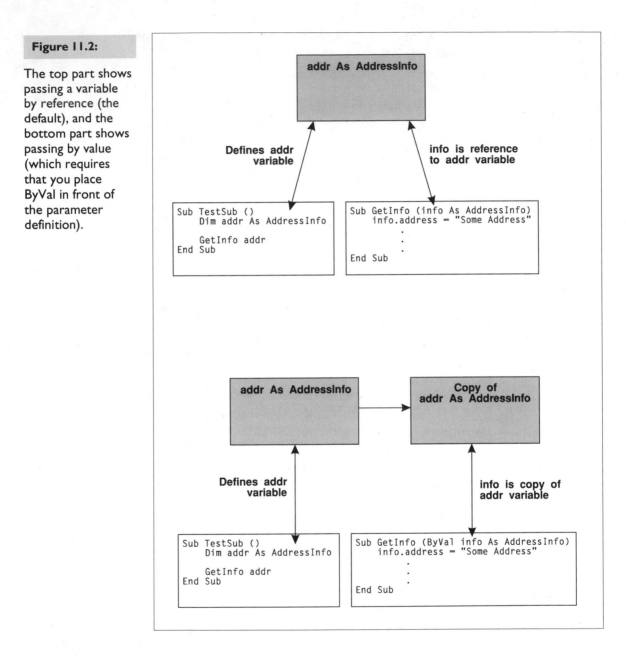

Reference: Subroutine Parameters

Whenever you create new subroutines in your forms and modules, you can also define parameters to pass to these subroutines. Here's how you define parameters:

Sub *SubName(param1* [**As** *typeName*] [,*param2* [**As** *typeName*]]...)
Defines parameters you can pass to a subroutine (this is a simplification of the real definition, which allows more options)

By default, variables are passed to subroutines by reference, which means your subroutines can change the values of variables you pass to them.

If don't want your variables to be modified, you can place the ByVal keyword in front of the parameter definition to tell Visual Basic that you want a copy of variables passed.

Modifying the Database Module

Now that you have a better understanding of subroutines and parameters, let's get back to working on the database module. I mentioned earlier that you can often rewrite a module without affecting any of the code that uses it. Right now your database module does a very simple job. But there is one assumption you should change. If you look again at the DBOpen and other subroutines in your database module, you'll notice they all have the file number hard-wired as #1. This isn't a good idea. What happens if you try to use another module that also uses file number #1? Not good.

These subroutines should not have a fixed file number. Instead, they should use a function in Visual Basic called FreeFile, which will return a file number that's not being used.

Here are the changes you'll need to make to use FreeFile: First, you'll need to create a module-level variable to keep track of the file number. A module-level variable works just like a form-level variable works: You define it in the (declarations) section of your module, and it will be visible to all the subroutines in your module.

Add this line to the (declarations) section of your module:

```
Dim fileNum As Integer          ' The file number used in DB subs
```

Then change the DBOpen subroutine so it looks like this:

```
Sub DBOpen ()
    Dim addr As AddressInfo     ' Used to calc record size

    fileNum = FreeFile          ' Get next file number
    Open "address.dat" For Random As #fileNum Len = Len(addr)
End Sub
```

You'll notice I added a new line that uses FreeFile, and I also changed the #1 to #fileNum in the Open statement.

Finally, change all the #1's in the other subroutines to #fileNum. Now try your program again to make sure it works correctly. You'll notice that we changed the way the database subroutines work, and we only changed code inside the database module. Dividing the code into modules really makes it easy to make changes, because we're working with fairly separate and distinct pieces. As we make changes in this and the next chapter, you'll see this modular approach in action, and you'll see how it simplifies the process of writing Address Book.

Modifying DATABASE.BAS for Multiple Records

In this section I'll present the code that will allow your Address Book program to read and write multiple records. As I mentioned at the start of this chapter, I'll show you the code and explain how it works, rather than show you all the steps you would take to write it.

First, let's look at the changes to the database module to support multiple records.

Adding Multirecord Support to DBOpen

Modifying Database to work with multiple records is actually quite simple, as you'll see in the code below. The first thing you'll want to do is add another form-level variable to keep track of how many records are in the database file.

Strictly speaking, this variable isn't really necessary because you can use the LOF (length of file) function to calculate the number of records in the database. But using a variable instead will speed up your programs.

Add the definition of *numRecords* to the (declarations) section of DATA-BASE.BAS, so it looks like this:

```
Dim fileNum As Integer       ' The file number used in DB subs
Dim numRecords As Integer    ' Number of records in database
```

Next, modify DBOpen so it sets this variable to the number of records in your file:

```
Sub DBOpen ()
    '
    ' This subroutine opens the database file for reading one
    ' record at a time. The length of each record is simply
    ' Len(addr), which is why I've defined the variable addr
    ' below.
    '
    Dim addr As AddressInfo      ' Used to calc record size

    fileNum = FreeFile           ' Get next file number
    Open "address.dat" For Random As #fileNum Len = Len(addr)

    numRecords = LOF(fileNum) / Len(addr)
End Sub
```

You'll notice I also added a comment to the start of DBOpen. It's a good idea to put comments at the start of your subroutines that describe what each subroutine does. As we modify each subroutine in DATABASE.BAS, I'll put such comments at the start of the subroutine.

There are two reasons these types of comments are important. First, if anyone else will ever look at your program, it makes it much easier for that person to understand how your program works because such comments tell why you're doing something, not just what you're doing (which you can often figure out by looking at the code). Second, if you're writing a larger program and you don't work on it for, say, a year, you might not remember yourself why you wrote your program the way you did. By including comments that explain why, as well as what, each subroutine does, it will be much easier for you to go back to your own code several years later. I learned this lesson writing a commercial product called The Norton Commander, a DOS product that I worked on over a period of six years (which covered three versions of the product). The longer I worked on this product, the gladder I was that I wrote detailed comments (and the more comments I wrote).

Testing Your Code

I've mentioned before that it's a good idea to test each part of your code as you write it. But how do you check the changes you've made to DBOpen to calculate the number of records?

Visual Basic has a debugger built into it, which we haven't used so far. Debuggers are programs, or part of environments like Visual Basic, that allow you to run your program one line at a time, which is known as *stepping* through your program. The easiest way to use the debugger in Visual Basic is to set a *breakpoint*. A breakpoint is a line of code that you mark to tell Visual Basic that you want it to stop running (and enter break mode) whenever it tries to run this line. Let's look at an example, using the new DBOpen subroutine.

Make sure DBOpen is visible in your Code window. Then move the insertion point to the last line, which sets the *numRecords* variable. Next select Toggle Breakpoint from the Run menu (or press F9). This last line of code will be in bold type (see Figure 11.3) to indicate that it's marked as a breakpoint.

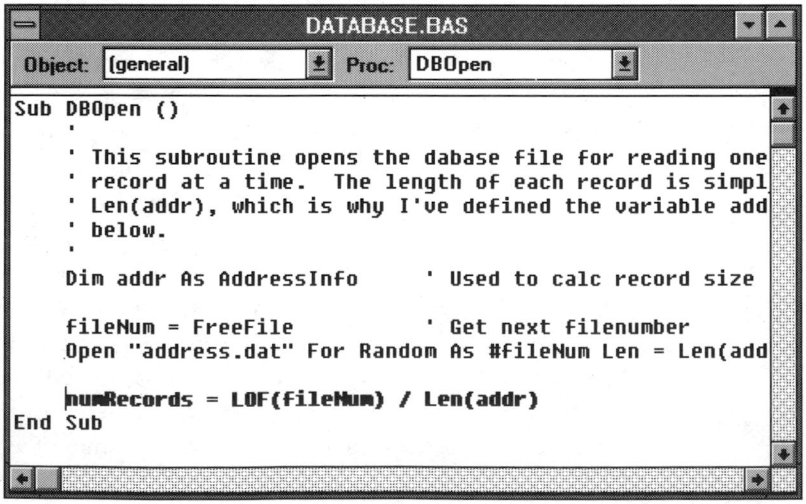
DATABASE.BAS
Object: (general)
Proc: DBOpen
Sub DBOpen ()
'
' This subroutine opens the dabase file for reading one
' record at a time. The length of each record is simpl
' Len(addr), which is why I've defined the variable add
' below.
'
Dim addr As AddressInfo ' Used to calc record size
fileNum = FreeFile ' Get next filenumber
Open "address.dat" For Random As #fileNum Len = Len(add
numRecords = LOF(fileNum) / Len(addr)
End Sub

Figure 11.3:

Lines marked as breakpoints appear in bold type.

Now press F5 to run your program. Visual Basic will run your program until it encounters the line you marked as a breakpoint; it will stop just before running the line you marked. Next press the F8 key or select Single Step from the Run menu. This command runs a single line of code at a time. In this case it will run the code that sets *numRecords*.

After you've run this line of code, you can use the Immediate window to display the value of the *numRecords* variable. Make sure the Immediate window is active (select the Immediate Window item from the Window menu if necessary), then type the following line into the window:

?numRecords
    |

    |

Visual Basic reports that there is just one record in the database, which is exactly what it should report (it will report 0 if you delete the ADDRESS.DAT file).

To "remove" this breakpoint, click on the line in your Code window that sets *numRecords* and press F9 again. The F9 key *toggles* a breakpoint on and off, so pressing F9 again will turn a breakpoint off if it was turned on.

You can continue running your program at any time by pressing F5 again. Using breakpoints to stop your program, along with pressing the F8 key to run your program one line at a time and using the Immediate window to see the values stored in variables, is extraordinarily useful. From time to time, you'll find your programs don't work the way you expect them to, and you can't figure out why they don't. This is when using breakpoints and single stepping (the F8 key) is really useful; you can see exactly what lines of code your program runs, and you can see the values of the variables your program uses.

There is another debugging technique that is also very useful but not used as often by Visual Basic programmers, simply because they're not familiar with it. Add this line to the end of your DBOpen subroutine, just before the End Sub statement:

```
Debug.Print "numRecords = "; numRecords
```

The Debug object actually refers to the Immediate window, so this line of code displays text in the Immediate window. Run your program again (make sure you don't have a breakpoint set). Then select Immediate Window from the Window menu after your program starts. You should see a line like this in your

Immediate window:

numRecords = 1

Using the Debug object to send output to the Immediate window is a very useful method for debugging your program. You can easily track exactly what changes your program makes to variables and when they're made.

Remember to remove the Debug.Print statement before you continue. If you leave it in, your program will continue to work correctly, but since you don't need this statement anymore, it's a good idea to remove it.

Creating a DBLen( ) Function

Now that you know DBOpen is correctly calculating the number of records in a file, let's finish making the changes to support reading and writing multiple records.

Several of the modified subroutines, which you'll see below, use a new function called DBLen( ), which returns the number of records in your database file. You create functions in a module just as you create subroutines (select New Procedure from the Code menu), except that you need to click on the option button called Function in the New Procedure dialog box.

Here is the function called DBLen( ):

```
Function DBLen () As Integer
    '
    ' Returns the number of records currently stored in the
    ' database.
    '
    DBLen = numRecords                ' Return number of records
End Function
```

Notice several things about this function: First, instead of using the word Sub in both the start and end of this definition, it uses the word Function. You'll also notice the As Integer that appears after the function name, which tells Visual Basic that this function returns a number of type Integer.

You'll also notice the line DBLen = numRecords. This line assigns a value to the DBLen function, which is the value that will be returned by DBLen.

Once you have this function in your DATABASE.BAS module, you can test DBLen to make sure it works as follows: Run your program, then press Ctrl+Break to stop your program and display the Immediate window. You can

Reference: Functions

You can create functions just as easily as you can create subroutines. The only difference is that you'll want to define the type of value your function will return.

Function *funcName* **([***parameters***]) [As** *typeName***]**
    [*statements*]
    [*funcName* **=** *value*]
    [Exit Function]
    [*statements*]
    [*funcName* **=** *value*]
End Function

Defines a function called *funcName* that returns a value with the type *typeName*. The default return type, if you don't provide one, is As Single.

funcName **=** *value*

Sets the return value for the function.

Exit Function

This statement stops running the function and returns the current value stored in *funcName*.

then call this function directly to see what number it returns by typing the following line:

```
?DBLen( )
 1
 1
```

DBLen( ) reports that there is one record in the database file, which is what it should return. When you're finished with the Immediate window, press F5 to continue running your program.

There is one thing about using functions that's different from using subroutines. You'll notice the two parentheses after the function name. Visual Basic distinguishes between functions and subroutines by requiring parentheses for functions, but not for subroutines.

Modifying DBRead

The DBRead subroutine, as you can see here, has a lot more code than before, which I'll describe below:

```
Sub DBRead (num As Integer, addr As AddressInfo)
    '
    ' Retrieves a single record from the database. Records
    ' range from 1..DBLen().
    '
    ' On entry:      num      Number of record to read
    ' Returns:       addr     The record just read
    '
    Dim i As Integer                   ' Actual record number

    i = num                            ' Record number requested
    If i < 1 Then i = 1                ' Make sure i >= 1
    If i > DBLen() Then                ' Is i too large?
        i = DBLen()                    ' Yes, use the last record
    End If

    Get #fileNum, i, addr              ' Read record i from the file
End Sub
```

When you modify DBRead in your program, make sure you add the *num* parameter to the first line.

Most of this new code checks and handles boundary conditions. As I mentioned before, boundary conditions are special cases you need to check in your programs. Here, for example, the Get command doesn't allow record numbers less than 1, so you need to make sure you don't pass it a number less than 1. You'll notice I added code that sets the variable $i = 1$ if *num* is less than 1. It's also a good idea to check for numbers that are too large. The Get command can never read records past the end of the file, so I've added code that sets *i* to the number of records if *num* is too large.

Once you've made these changes, you should test your program to make sure these changes work correctly. You can do this by changing the call to DBRead in the GetRecord subroutine:

```
DBRead 1, addr                 ' Read one record
```

Run your program to make sure it works correctly. You can also easily test to make sure DBRead handles the boundary conditions correctly. Change the 1 in the line above to a 0. Does your program still display the first record correctly? Then change this number to 2, which is larger than the number of records in your file. Does your program still work correctly? Make sure you set it back to 1 when you're finished testing.

It's a good idea to perform such simple tests whenever you make changes to a program. I know I've said this before, but it's so important that I wanted to mention it again.

Modifying DBWrite

The changes to DBWrite look very much like the changes to DBRead, except for one small change: DBWrite allows you to create a new record, which requires writing a record past the end of the file. In other words, you need to be able to write a record number equal to DBLen() + 1:

```
Sub DBWrite (num As Integer, addr As AddressInfo)
    '
    ' Writes a single record to the database file. The
    ' record number ranges from 1 .. DBLen() + 1
    '
    Dim i As Integer                ' Number of record to write

    i = num                         ' Record you want to write
    If i < 1 Then i = 1             ' Make sure i >= 1
    If i > DBLen() Then            ' Is this past end of file?
        i = DBLen() + 1            ' Yes, add new record to file
        numRecords = numRecords + 1 ' Keep track of num records
    End If

    Put #fileNum, i, addr           ' Write record to file
End Sub
```

Again, you'll need to make sure you add the *num* definition to the first line above.

All of this code should be clear after you read the description above of DBRead, except for the small change I already mentioned that allows you to add a new record to the file.

To test these changes, you'll need to modify the call to DBWrite in SaveRecord:

```
    DBWrite 1, addr             ' Write record back to file
```

Your program should now run correctly (but remember that SaveRecord won't run until you quit your program). You can test the boundary conditions by changing the 1 here to a 0 or a 2. Remember to set it back to 1 when you're finished testing boundary conditions.

By the way, when you test this with the record number set to 2, you should discover that your file size grew from 584 bytes to 1168 bytes because you just added a second record to your database.

Adding Comments to DBClose

Finally, the DBClose subroutine doesn't require any changes to support multiple records, but I've added comments to the start of this subroutine:

```
Sub DBClose ()
    '
    ' You should call this subroutine when your program is
    ' finished using the database (usually just before it quits).
    '
    Close #fileNum
End Sub
```

These are all the changes you'll need to make to the DATABAS.BAS module. All the other changes will be to the form itself.

Adding Multiple Records to the Form

The form actually needs much more code to support multiple records than you've written in the Database.bas module. Why is this? Many Windows programs you write will have more code to handle the user interface than to do the actual work. Reading and writing multiple records is quite simple, but providing the support behind the user interface is not so simple.

Think about this. There are a lot of functions you'll want to have available while you're viewing or changing records in your database. For example, you'll want to be able to find addresses, sort them, delete them, and so on. The reading and writing of a record is just one small part of the picture. All the other functions are built on top of the database functions.

In this section we'll modify the form so all the basic user-interface functions work, such as adding new records. But I'll leave coverage of printing, searching, and sorting until the next chapter.

Adding Form-Level Variables

Right now your form only reads and writes a single record, and it doesn't remember the creation or modification dates for records. I've used four form-level variables to keep track of information on the current record: whether you've changed it, the number of the current record, and the modification and creation dates. Add these definitions to the (declarations) section of your form:

```
Dim recChanged As Integer     ' True when record's changed
Dim currentRec As Integer     ' Current record number
Dim createDate As Double      ' Date record was created
Dim modifyDate As Double      ' Date record last modified
```

Both *createDate* and *modifyDate* are defined as Double since this is the type of number returned by the Now() function. I've defined *currentRec* as an Integer, which means you won't be able to have more than 32,767 records in your file; I didn't think this would be a problem. If you do want to allow more records, you should redefine all numbers that refer to record numbers As Long rather than As Integer.

Modifying GetRecord

Next we'll modify GetRecord and SaveRecord so they'll have a record-number parameter, which will allow them to read and write any record number. Right now they're both hard-wired to read record number 1. These subroutines contain all the other code you'll need for the rest of this chapter. Here is the new version of GetRecord (make sure you add the parameter *num* in the first line):

```
Sub GetRecord (ByVal num As Integer)
    '
    ' Reads a record from the database and sets all the
    ' controls in this form.
    '
    ' On entry:     num      Number of record, 1..DBLen()
    '
    Dim addr As AddressInfo

    If num > DBLen() Then      ' Is this past end of file?
        num = DBLen()          ' Yes, set to last record
    ElseIf num < 1 Then        ' Is it before first record?
        num = 1                ' Yes, set to first record
    End If
    currentRec = num           ' Remember current record num
```

```
If DBLen() = 0 Then          ' Are there any records?
    ClearRecord              ' No, return a clear record
    UpdateStatus             ' Update the status info
    Exit Sub                 ' We're all done here
End If

DBRead num, addr             ' Read one record

'
' Finally we need to set all the controls based on the
' values of this record.
'
txtAddress.Text = RTrim$(addr.address)
txtNotes.Text = RTrim$(addr.notes)

txtPhone(0).Text = RTrim$(addr.phone1)
txtPhone(1).Text = RTrim$(addr.phone2)
txtPhone(2).Text = RTrim$(addr.phone3)
txtPhone(3).Text = RTrim$(addr.phone4)

cboPhone(0).ListIndex = addr.type1
cboPhone(1).ListIndex = addr.type2
cboPhone(2).ListIndex = addr.type3
cboPhone(3).ListIndex = addr.type4

createDate = addr.created    ' Get creation date into global
modifyDate = addr.modified   ' Get last modify date
UpdateStatus                 ' Update record number display
recChanged = 0               ' Record hasn't changed yet
End Sub
```

Before you can try this new subroutine, you'll need to make three other changes. First, you'll need to change the call to GetRecord in Form_Load so it supplies a record number:

```
GetRecord 1                         ' Get the first record
```

Second, you'll need to create an empty subroutine called ClearRecord. We'll fill in this subroutine later, but for now you need to create it so you'll be able to test the new version of GetRecord. Finally, you'll need to define the subroutine UpdateStatus, which will update the labels at the bottom of your form to show the record number, creation date, and modification date.

Here is the subroutine UpdateStatus:

```
Sub UpdateStatus ()
'
```

```
' Updates the status information, which includes the
' current record counter and the create/modify date
' at the bottom of the input window.
'
    lblPage.Caption = Format$(currentRec) + "/" +
➤ Format$(DBLen())
    lblCreated.Caption = Format$(createDate, "ddddd")
    lblModified.Caption = Format$(modifyDate, "ddddd")
End Sub
```

This last subroutine should be clear, since you've already worked with For-mat$ and the Caption parameter. There are just a couple of new items. First, the formatting string "ddddd" tells Format$ to format a date serial number as a short date. For example, in the United States, a short date is a date like 12/25/92. It may be 1992-12-25 if you have the country setting in Windows set to Sweden. You'll also notice I used the plus operator to combine three strings in the first assignment statement. As you learned in Chapter 2, plus concatenates strings.

Since the new GetRecord is rather long, let's take a quick look at what it does and how it works. You'll notice I put the ByVal keyword in front of the defini-tion of the *num* parameter. Why did I do this? For a couple of reasons. First, defining *num* as ByVal means GetRecord gets a copy of *num,* so you can change the value inside GetRecord without affecting the original number—in other words, without changing the variable used in any subroutine that calls GetRecord. But the real reason is a little more subtle.

Whenever you call a subroutine or function, every parameter has a specific type. In the case of GetRecord, that type is Integer. Without the ByVal keyword, all parameters are passed by reference, which means that the parameter in your subroutine refers to the original variable. This can work only if both the variable and the parameter have the same type.

But if you use a variable, such as *i,* that you haven't defined with a Dim state-ment, its type will be Single. If you try to pass a Single variable by reference to a subroutine that expects an Integer parameter, Visual Basic will stop your pro-gram and display an alert box that says "Parameter type mismatch." Passing a variable by value eliminates this problem.

Parameters defined as ByVal receive a copy of the variable, rather than a ref-erence to the original variable, so the variables don't have to be the same type—provided both the variable and the parameter are numbers (Integer, Long, Single, Double, or Currency type).

The first few lines of code make sure *num* has a valid record number: between 1 and DBLen( ). Then GetRecord saves this record number in the

> ## Reference: Exit Sub Statement
>
> The Exit Sub statement allows you to control when your program will finish running a subroutine.
>
> ### Exit Sub
> Stops running the subroutine, just as if Visual Basic had encountered the End Sub statement

form-level variable *currentRec*. This variable keeps track of what record you're looking at, and it's used by several subroutines, including UpdateStatus.

Next you'll notice five lines of code that start with If DBLen( ) = 0. When you run Address Book for the very first time, the address book file will be empty. In this case you want to make sure you have a new, empty record with all the values set correctly, which is what the ClearRecord subroutine does. Update-Status makes sure all the status displays are correct. The Exit Sub statement exits from the subroutine without running any more commands in the subroutine; you don't need to run the rest of GetRecord after you create an empty record.

GetRecord then calls DBRead to read one record from the file, and the rest of the code transfers the values from the *addr* variable to the controls on the form. The very last line sets the *recChanged* variable to False (0), to mark this record as unchanged. Other subroutines will set this value to True whenever you've made changes to the record, which allows SaveRecord to save a record only when you've made changes to it.

Now run your program to see if it works. The status line at the bottom of the form should now show a record counter as well as the creation and modification dates. You'll notice, however, that the dates aren't correct, because you haven't added any code yet to set them correctly. The creation date will be set correctly by ClearRecord whenever you create a new record, but right now ClearRecord has no code in it.

Creating Empty Records

New records are records that have all the text fields blank, the phone-type combo boxes set up correctly, and the creation date set to the current date. The easiest way to set these fields is with a subroutine called ClearRecord, which "clears" all the fields on the form. Add this code to the empty ClearRecord subroutine you created above:

```
Sub ClearRecord ()
    '
    ' This subroutine clears all the fields in the data entry
    ' screen, which you'll need to do for a new record.
    '
    txtAddress.Text = ""          ' Clear the Address field
    txtNotes.Text = ""            ' Clear the Notes field
    For i = 0 To 3                ' Clear the telephone numbers
        txtPhone(i).Text = ""
    Next i

    cboPhone(0).ListIndex = 0     ' Set 1st type to Home
    cboPhone(1).ListIndex = 1     ' Set 2nd type to Office
    cboPhone(2).ListIndex = 2     ' Set 3rd type to FAX
    cboPhone(3).ListIndex = -1    ' Set 4th type to blank

    createDate = Now              ' Set creation date to today
    modifyDate = createDate

    recChanged = 0                ' Mark as unchanged
End Sub
```

You can test this subroutine by first deleting the ADDRESS.DAT file. Then run Address Book again. This time Address Book will notice there are no records in the file, so it will call ClearRecord to create a new record. You should now see a correct creation and modification date appear at the bottom of your form. However, when you close Address Book and run it again, you'll notice the dates are incorrect. This is because SaveRecord isn't saving this information, so you'll need to modify SaveRecord, which we'll do next.

Modifying SaveRecord

The changes to SaveRecord are really quite simple. It has some extra lines to save the creation and modification dates, as well as a couple of lines that check and set the *recChanged* variable. The new SaveRecord is not short, but it should be fairly clear:

```
Sub SaveRecord ()
    '
    ' Saves the current record if it's been changed
    '
    Dim addr As AddressInfo
```

```
        If Not recChanged Then       ' Did you change record?
            Exit Sub                 ' No, we're all done
        End If

        '
        ' This code sets all the fields in the variable addr
        ' to reflect the values stored in the controls.
        '
        modifyDate = Now             ' Set modify date to today

        addr.address = txtAddress.Text
        addr.notes = txtNotes.Text

        addr.phone1 = txtPhone(0).Text
        addr.phone2 = txtPhone(1).Text
        addr.phone3 = txtPhone(2).Text
        addr.phone4 = txtPhone(3).Text

        addr.type1 = cboPhone(0).ListIndex
        addr.type2 = cboPhone(1).ListIndex
        addr.type3 = cboPhone(2).ListIndex
        addr.type4 = cboPhone(3).ListIndex

        addr.created = createDate
        addr.modified = modifyDate

        DBWrite currentRec, addr      ' Write record back to file

        recChanged = 0               ' We just saved the record
End Sub
```

Testing this code requires some changes we'll make below. If you delete the ADDRESS.DAT file, then run your program, it will show the correct date when you exit, then run again. But this is because the file is empty; SaveRecord won't save any changes because the *recChanged* variable will always be 0. We need some code to set *recChanged* to –1.

Noticing Changes to Records

The way you can keep track of any changes you make is by using an event in text boxes called Changed. This event handler will be called whenever you type any characters into a text box, so you can set the *recChanged* variable to –1 in these event handlers. Add the following code to track such changes:

```
Sub txtAddress_Change ()
    recChanged = -1
```

```
End Sub
```

```
Sub txtNotes_Change ()
    recChanged = -1
End Sub
```

```
Sub txtPhone_Change (Index As Integer)
    recChanged = -1
End Sub
```

Run Address Book and it should now correctly save your record whenever you change the text in any of your text fields.

You'll also want to set the *recChanged* flag whenever you change any of the phone-type combo boxes. But you don't want to use the Change event for combo boxes because this event doesn't apply to the Dropdown List style of combo boxes. Instead, you'll need to use the Click event, which is called whenever you select one of the items from the drop-down list. Add this code to your form:

```
Sub cboPhone_Click (Index As Integer)
    recChanged = -1
End Sub
```

Reference: Change Event

The Change event will be called anytime you change any of the text in a text box.

Sub *ctlName*_Change ( )

This event handler will be called whenever the text in a text box is changed.

There are other controls that also support the Change event (combo boxes, directory list boxes, drive list boxes, scroll bars, labels, and picture boxes), and the meaning is a little different for each control. See the *Language Reference* manual for more details.

Those are all the changes you'll need to make to keep track of when you modify the address information in a form.

Creating the Menu Bar

To add new records to the database, you'll need some way to ask for new records. I've done this by adding a menu bar that includes an item for adding new records to your file, so the next thing you'll want to do is create a menu bar for your program. Table 11.1 shows all the menus, items, and control names for the menu. Add this menu to your program.

Table 11.1:	Caption	CtlName	Accelerator
Menus Used by Address Book	&File	menFile	
	&Print...	miPrint	Ctrl+P
	P&rint Setup...	miPrintSetup	
	–	miFileLine	
	E&xit	miExit	
	&Edit	menEdit	
	&Undo	miUndo	Ctrl+Z
	–	miEditLine1	
	Cu&t	miCut	Ctrl+X
	&Copy	miCopy	Ctrl+C
	&Paste	miPaste	Ctrl+V
	–	miEditLine2	
	&Find...	miFind	Ctrl+F
	&Go to...	miGoto	F5
	&Address	menAddress	
	&New	miNew	Ctrl+N
	&Delete	miDelete	

	Caption	CtlName	Accelerator
Table 11.1:	&Sort	miSort	
	–	miAddressLine1	
Menus Used by	Ne&xt	miNext	F4
Address Book	&Previous	miPrevious	F3
(continued)			

As you can see, this menu bar provides a lot. Most of these menu items require almost no code. But a few of them (the ones for printing, sorting, and searching) require quite a bit of work.

These menu items use a number of Ctrl+*key* shortcuts that may or may not be familiar to you. With the introduction of Windows 3.1, Microsoft changed some of the standard keyboard shortcuts that new programs should use (the recommended and suggested shortcuts are outlined in Table 11.2). You set these *accelerator* keys with the Accelerator combo box inside the Menu Design window.

	Suggested Ctrl+*letter* Shortcuts	
Table 11.2:	**Function**	**Key**
Keyboard Shortcut	Undo	Ctrl+Z
Standards	Cut	Ctrl+X
	Copy	Ctrl+C
	Paste	Ctrl+V
	Suggested Ctrl+*letter* Shortcuts	
	Function	**Key**
	New	Ctrl+N
	Open	Ctrl+O
	Print	Ctrl+P
	Save	Ctrl+S
	Bold	Ctrl+B

Table 11.2:	Suggested Ctrl+*letter* Shortcuts	
	Function	Key
Keyboard Shortcut Standards (continued)	Italic	Ctrl+I
	Underline	Ctrl+U
	Double underline	Ctrl+D
	Small caps	Ctrl+K
	Word-by-word underline	Ctrl+W
	Remove character formatting	Ctrl+spacebar

Before Windows 3.1, the standard shortcut keys for Undo, Cut, Copy, and Paste were Alt+Backspace, Shift+Del, Ctrl+Ins, and Shift+Ins, respectively. I don't know about you, but I found these very hard to remember and often chose the wrong key. I find Microsoft's new shortcuts much easier to work with.

Your program should not use any of the shortcut keys in Table 11.2 for functions other than the ones listed. For example, don't use Ctrl+N for Next record—only use it for New.

Adding New Records

You now have all the pieces you need to be able to add new records to your database, and the code to do this is very simple. Add the following code to the miNew_Click event handler:

```
Sub miNew_Click ()
    '
    ' Create a new record at the end of the file. This
    ' record will be saved only if you type something into it.
    '
    SaveRecord                    ' Save changes to current record
    currentRec = DBLen() + 1      ' Add record to the end
    ClearRecord                   ' Clear the current record
    UpdateStatus                  ' Update record counter display
    txtAddress.SetFocus           ' Put insertion point in address
End Sub
```

This subroutine took only five lines of code! Once you've written the right tools, you'll find you can write some very powerful subroutines simply by calling

How to Choose Keyboard Shortcuts

Microsoft has a number of suggestions on how to choose keyboard shortcuts for different functions. When you have a choice between a function key or Ctrl+*letter*, the Ctrl+*letter* combination is often better because it's easier to remember. Below you'll find suggestions for the use of shifted and unshifted function keys:

- **Unshifted Function Keys.** Assign simple function keys, like F3, to small tasks that you might perform frequently. For example, in the Address Book program, I've assigned F3 to Previous Record and F4 to Next Record, so I can switch records easily.

- **Shift+key Combinations.** Use for actions that either extend or are complementary to actions that have an unshifted function key assigned to them. For example, if you assign Find to F5 (rather than Ctrl+F), you can use Shift+F5 for Search Again.

- **Ctrl+key Combinations.** Use for infrequent, larger tasks that are similar to the task provided by the unshifted function key. For example, Ctrl+F5 might be Search Again Backward when F5 is Search, and Shift+F5 is Search Again. Also use Ctrl+cursor-movement keys to move in larger increments. For example, Ctrl+← moves back by an entire word.

- **Alt+key Combinations.** Microsoft generally recommends against using any Alt+*key* combinations. All Alt+*letter* keys are reserved for use with mnemonic access characters for selecting menus and controls. Some of the Alt+function keys have assignments already in the Control menu.

several existing subroutines. Let's take a quick look at how this works. First, miNew_Click calls SaveRecord to save any changes you may have made to the current record. Next, it changes the form-level variable *currentRec* so it points to an empty slot at the end of the database file. The call to ClearRecord initializes all the controls in the form for an empty record. UpdateStatus updates the status information at the bottom of the form.

Reference: SetFocus Method

The SetFocus method allows you to change which control has the current keyboard focus. In the case of text boxes, the control with the focus is the control that will have the insertion point visible and active.

controlName.**SetFocus**

Causes the keyboard focus to shift to the control named *controlName*

The last statement, txtAddress.SetFocus, uses a new method: SetFocus. This method allows you to change which control has the current keyboard focus. What I'm doing here is moving the insertion point back to the address text box. Without this statement, the keyboard focus will remain where it was before, which isn't the most natural place for it to be. Whenever you ask to create a new record, you expect to be able to start typing a new address immediately. In other words, you expect the insertion point to be in the address text box, and this is why I've included the txtAddress.SetFocus statement in this subroutine.

You can test this out, but you won't be able to look at any of your new records until you make the next set of changes.

Navigating through Records

In this section I'll show you the code I wrote to move between records, using the Next and Previous buttons at the bottom of the form. First you'll need a subroutine called NextRecord, which can move forward or backward through the records in your file. Add this subroutine to your form:

```
Sub NextRecord (delta As Integer)
    '
    ' This subroutine moves between records, either forward
    ' or backward. NextRecord saves any changes to the
    ' current record before it shows a different record.
    '
    ' On entry:
    '    delta       +1      Show the next record
    '                -1      Show previous record
    '
    Dim num As Integer
```

```
    SaveRecord                      ' Be sure to save changes

    num = currentRec + delta        ' Move to "next" record
    If num < 1 Then                 ' Are we past start?
        num = DBLen()               ' Yes, wrap to last record
    ElseIf num > DBLen() Then       ' No, are we past end?
        num = 1                     ' Yes, wrap to first record
    End If

    GetRecord num                   ' Show this new record
End Sub
```

Then you'll need to add code to the cmdNext_Click and cmdPrev_Click event handlers so that clicking on these buttons will move you forward and backward one record at a time. Here's the code to add to each event handler:

```
Sub cmdNext_Click ()
    NextRecord 1                    ' Show next record in database
    txtAddress.SetFocus             ' Put insertion point in address
End Sub
```

```
Sub cmdPrev_Click ()
    NextRecord -1                   ' Show previous record in dbase
    txtAddress.SetFocus             ' Put insertion point in address
End Sub
```

All three of these subroutines should be clear. You'll notice I've used the txtAddress.SetFocus statement in each Click event handler. These statements put the insertion point into the address text box. Without these statements, the keyboard focus will remain in the Next or Previous command button, which probably won't feel as natural as what I've provided here.

You'll notice there are also two menu items for moving to the next and previous records, called Next and Previous on the Address menu. I've put them in the menu bar so that I could attach the F3 and F4 keyboard shortcuts to them. Once you add the code below, you'll be able to move between records using either the keyboard or the mouse. Here are the two event handlers for these menu items:

```
Sub miNext_Click ()
    cmdNext_Click
End Sub
```

```
Sub miPrevious_Click ()
    cmdPrev_Click
End Sub
```

Each of these event handlers simply calls the event handler for the Next or Previous button. Any code inside your form can activate a Click event handler simply by writing its name, as shown here. Now try your program to see how the Next and Previous menu items work.

Enabling the Exit Menu Item

Let's take a look at what code to write for the miExit_Click event handler, which handles the Exit item on the File menu. You might expect that you'd want to put an End statement here. But you don't. An End statement will exit your program immediately, without ever running the Form_Unload event handler. But you want this event handler to run so it will save changes you've made to the current record.

You could duplicate the call to SaveRecord in miExit_Click, but there's a better way. Enter this code into miExit_Click:

```
Sub miExit_Click ()
    Unload Address
End Sub
```

Reference: Unload Command

The Unload command allows you to unload any form from memory, which causes that form's Form_Unload event handler to be called. Your program will quit when all its forms have been unloaded.

Unload *formName*
Unloads the form called *formName* from memory, which results in the Form_Unload event being called

You can use the Load command to load a form back into memory and the Show command to both load and show a form on the screen.

The Unload command *unloads* a form from memory, which means that the form will be removed from your screen, and Visual Basic will run its Form_Unload event handler. Your program will exit automatically as soon as all its forms have been unloaded from memory, so calling Unload *form* will both run Form_Unload and exit your program. You should be careful not to use the End command when any of your forms have a Form_Unload event handler.

Supporting Cut, Copy, Paste, and Undo

You now have a fully functional address book program you can start to use. You might want to delete the ADDRESS.DAT file before you continue, which will remove all your test records. You'll be able to enter addresses and move between them. But you won't be able to delete them (we'll handle that in the next chapter).

Any real Windows program should support the Cut, Copy, Paste, and Undo items on the Edit menu. Many programs that people write for themselves don't support these functions. But as you'll see here, it's very easy to add an Edit menu to any program that includes text boxes. Add the code below to the four event handlers for the Edit menu:

```
Sub miUndo_Click ()
    SendKeys "%{BACKSPACE}"        ' Send Alt+Backspace
End Sub
```

```
Sub miCut_Click ()
    SendKeys "+{DELETE}"           ' Send Shift+Del
End Sub
```

```
Sub miCopy_Click ()
    SendKeys "^{INSERT}"           ' Send Ctrl+Ins
End Sub
```

```
Sub miPaste_Click ()
    SendKeys "+{INSERT}"           ' Send Shift+Ins
End Sub
```

Reference: SendKeys Command

The SendKeys command allows you to send any keystrokes to the control with the current keyboard focus.

SendKeys "*string***" [,***wait%***]**

Sends the characters in *string* to the active control.

wait%

Determines whether SendKeys waits until the keystrokes are processed before returning control. Set it to True (−1) to wait or False (0) to return immediately. By default, SendKeys returns immediately.

Here's how these subroutines work. Visual Basic has a command called SendKeys that sends keystrokes to whichever control has the current keyboard focus. To allow you to send special keys, such as Alt+Backspace, SendKeys uses some special characters: % for Alt, + for Shift, and ∧ for Control. Also, any characters between curly braces, such as {BACKSPACE}, refer to a key, and Send-Keys will send this keystroke rather than the text inside the braces.

All text boxes support these keyboard combinations:

Undo	Alt+Backspace
Cut	Shift+Del
Copy	Ctrl+Ins
Paste	Shift+Ins

All the code has to do is send these keystrokes to the edit boxes.

You now have an address book program that actually works. In the next chapter we'll finish Address Book by adding three new functions: Print, Search, and Sort.

Related Tools

GotFocus and LostFocus Events You can use these two events to tell when a control gains or loses the keyboard focus. The control receiving the focus will have its GotFocus event handler called, while the control that just lost the focus will have its LostFocus event handler called. Don't rely on the order of the GotFocus and LostFocus method calls: Sometimes LostFocus will be called before GotFocus and sometimes after GotFocus. In other words, the old control won't always be notified that it has lost the focus *before* the new control is notified that it has gained the focus.

Debugging Visual Basic has almost an entire menu of commands you might find useful for debugging. They're on the Run menu in two groups: one for setting and clearing breakpoints, and the other for stepping through your program. You might want to read the sections of your manual on these commands to learn how they work. The Immediate window is also very useful for debugging, because you can run any subroutine or function from this window. You can also change the values of variables.

Show and Load Commands The Show command allows you to load a form into memory and make it visible. You'll want to use this command when your program has more than one form (you'll see how this works in the next chapter). The Load command loads a form into memory without showing it first, which is useful if you want to make some changes to the form, such as centering it, before you show it on the screen. You can then call Show after you've made your changes.

Sending Keys to Other Programs You can send keystrokes to other programs using the SendKeys command along with AppActivate, which allows you to activate another program. SendKeys will send keystrokes to whatever program is the current application.

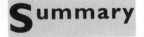

Summary

You learned a lot in this chapter:

Modules. You learned how to add new modules to your programs. Modules can contain subroutines and module-level variables, but not forms or controls. Modules are very useful for containing a group of related subroutines, such as the ones in the database module.

Controls in Other Forms. You can read and write the properties of controls in other forms by putting the form name in front of the control: *formName.controlName.property.*

Defining Parameters. The subroutines you create can have any number of parameters in them. You define the parameters between the parentheses in the first line of the Sub or Function definition.

Passing Parameters. Parameters can be passed either by reference (the default) or by value. Whenever a parameter is passed by reference, any changes you make to the value of the parameter inside the subroutine will change the original value. Also, the type of the variable you're passing to the subroutine must be the same as the parameter in your subroutine. Parameters passed by value (you put the keyword ByVal in front of the parameter definition) have a copy of their value passed to the subroutine, so any changes you make in the subroutine will not change the original value. Also, variables passed by value don't have to have the same type as the parameter, as long as both values are numbers (Integer, Long, Single, Double, or Currency).

FreeFile. This function returns the first available file number. You should call this function rather than hard-wiring a file number into your program. Remember to retain this file number in a form- or module-level variable so you can use it in Get, Put, and Close calls.

LOF. The LOF function returns the length, in bytes, of a file that you've opened with the Open command.

Breakpoints. Visual Basic allows you to set breakpoints in your programs. These are lines you mark (they appear in bold) using the F9 key. Visual Basic will stop running your program whenever it gets to one of these lines. You can then use the Immediate window to display the values of variables, to change values, or to run subroutines and functions. You can also use F8 to run your program one line at a time and F5 to continue running your program until the next breakpoint.

Debug.Print. Another way to debug your programs is to use the Debug.Print command to display information in the Immediate window while your program runs.

Functions. You can create new functions just as easily as you create new subroutines. The only difference is that you'll need to define what type of value your function returns, which you do by placing an As *typeName* at the end of your function definition. You then set the value that this function will return by assigning a value to a special variable with the function's name.

Formatting Dates. The string "ddddd" tells the Format$ function to format a time serial number as a short date—for example, 12/30/92. The actual format used is determined by the country setting in Windows, which could be something like 30.12.92.

Change Event. Every text box has a Change event handler that's called whenever you change any text in the box. Combo boxes also have a Change event, but this event doesn't apply to the Dropdown List style of combo box; for these you'll need to use the Click event to tell when you select an item from the drop-down list.

SetFocus Method. You can set which control has the current keyboard focus by calling the SetFocus method for that control. For example, I've used txtAddress.SetFocus to set the focus back to the address text box after you press the Next or Previous button.

Unload Command. You can remove forms from the screen, and memory, using the Unload command. This command causes the Form_Unload event handler to run. Your program will end after all forms have been unloaded from memory.

SendKeys Command. This command allows you to send keystrokes to the control with the current keyboard focus. You can even use this command to send keystrokes to other programs, using the AppActivate command.

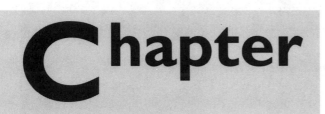

Chapter 12

Featuring

Searching for Strings
Printing the Address Book
Sorting Addresses
Deleting Records

Searching, Printing, Sorting, and Deleting

This is the last chapter in Part II of this book. Part III contains advanced information, including hints, tips, and techniques you can use in the programs you write. You'll find these advanced chapters useful as you continue to learn Visual Basic.

In this chapter I'm going to take a very different approach from previous chapters in this book. All the changes you'll find described in this chapter are in the final version of Address Book on the disk included with this book. But since I don't have room for detailed explanations, this chapter will be a very brief overview of the changes I've made.

The source code on the disk has comments, so along with the descriptions you'll find here, you should be able to figure out what's going on. If you can't, experiment with the source code. Make some changes and see what happens. Doing this kind of experimenting is the best way to learn more about programming, and it's how I first learned to write software.

Searching

The Find item in the Edit menu will allow you to search through your names and addresses for any text. For example, you can search for the word *Great* to find the following address:

    Joe M. Smith
    Great Software Company

238 Somewhere Lane
Imaginary, CI 12345-6789

The Address Book program will allow you to search for any string that appears inside any address. If it finds an address, it will simply display that address for you; otherwise it will beep to let you know it couldn't find the string. The only problem with the searching in Address Book is that it's case-sensitive, so searching for *great* won't find the word *Great*.

Searching the database isn't very difficult. Most of the work is done using Visual Basic's InStr function, which tells you whether a string is inside another string. For example, if you're searching for *Great* in the address above, you can use the InStr function to see if the string "Great" appears inside the address field, the notes field, or any of the telephone-number fields.

There are a couple of other things you'll need. When you select the Find... item from the Edit menu, you'll want to display a dialog box, such as the one shown in Figure 12.1, that allows you to input a search string.

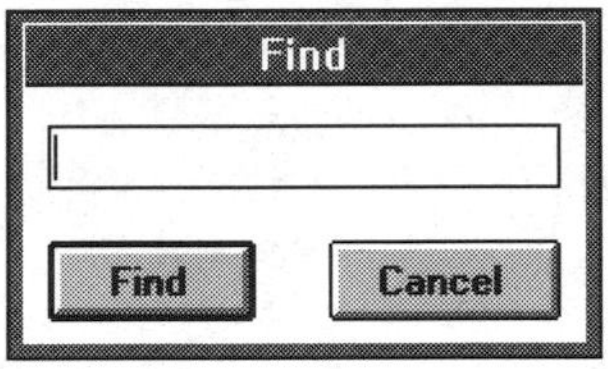

Figure 12.1:

This is what Address Book's Find dialog box will look like.

To create this dialog box, you'll need to create a new form, using the New Form item from the File menu. Then you'll want to add a text box and two command buttons to this form. I've created a *modal* form (with no resizable borders, no Minimize or Maximize buttons, and no Control menu) by setting the following properties:

Property	Setting
BorderStyle	3 - Fixed Double
ControlBox	False
Caption	Find
FormName	FindDialog

You'll also want to set the Default property to True for the Find button, and the Cancel property to True for the Cancel button. This will allow pressing the Enter key to be the same as clicking on the Find button, and pressing the Escape key to be the same as clicking on the Cancel button.

When you display this dialog box, you'll probably want to make it a modal dialog box. Modal dialogs always stay in front of the main window until you click on the Find or Cancel button. To display this dialog box as a modal dialog box, you use the Show method of a form, as follows:

```
FindDialog.Show 1          ' Display modal dialog box
```

Putting a 1 after Show tells Visual Basic that you want the form displayed as a modal dialog box, so the subroutine that calls Show won't continue to run until the new form is no longer visible on the screen (you can hide a form using a method called Hide).

Next you'll need some code in the Find dialog box to send information back to the code that called it. Here's what to do. In the Click event handler for the Cancel button, set the Text field of the text box to an empty string: "". Then in the Click event handler for both buttons, hide the form:

```
Sub cmdFind_Click ()
    Hide                     ' Return to Address Book
End Sub
```

_____

```
Sub cmdCancel_Click ()
    txtFind.Text = ""        ' Indicate cancel
    Hide                     ' Return to Address Book
End Sub
```

Once you hide the Find dialog box, the code in Address Book that called FindDialog.Show will continue to run, so most of the work is done in the miFind_Click event handler. In this event handler you can look at the text in the txtFind button using a statement like this:

```
If FindDialog.txtFind.Text = "" Then
    ' The Find dialog box was canceled
Else
    ' Do the find...
End If
```

The only other thing you should do is remove the Find form from memory when you're done with it. You'll notice in miFind_Click that I use the Unload command to remove FindDialog from memory.

The actual work of searching for an address is reasonably simple. All you have to do is call DBRead to read each address and InStr to search each field until you find a match. Then call GetRecord to retrieve and show the record you found. You'll find all the details in ADDRESS.FRM under miFind_Click and FINDDIAL.FRM.

Printing Addresses

Printing the address book doesn't take a lot of work, but there are a few new concepts and techniques I've used in the program. You'll notice from the menu you created earlier that there are two menu items to support: Print... and Print Setup... The Print... item allows you to print all the addresses in your address book, and most Windows programs show a standard Print dialog box that lets you confirm your choice before printing actually starts. The Print Setup... dialog box allows you to change which printer you'll use and to switch between portrait and landscape modes on your printer.

Both the Print and the Print Setup functions in Address Book use a set of dialog boxes provided by a *dynamic link library* (DLL) in Windows 3.1 called COMMDLG.DLL, along with another DLL called MHDEM200.VBX included with this book. The COMMDLG.DLL file is part of Windows 3.1, but you can also use it under Windows 3.0. The MHDEM200.VBX file provides the glue between Visual Basic and the common dialog box routines. You'll find detailed instructions and documentation on using the common dialog routines in the file MICROHLP.WRI on the disk included with this book.

Implementing these two dialog boxes, as you can see from the miPrint and miPrintSetup event handlers, is very easy. The only tricky part is that you'll need to make sure you include the definitions in your global module for the common dialog routines (again, you'll find details in MICROHLP.WRI).

The actual work of printing records takes a little work, but it's not really difficult. Each address consists of a single string, which has to be broken up into individual lines so they can be printed exactly where you want. The output from the Print routines looks something like this:

Joe M. Smith   Home: (800) 555-1212

Great Software Company   Office: same

238 Somewhere Lane

Imaginary, CI 12345-6789

The left side contains the address (with a 1-inch margin), and the right side contains any phone numbers you've filled in. I also draw a line between each address. You'll find all the details in the PRINT.BAS module, as well as in ADDRESS.FRM.

Sorting Addresses

The Address Book program we have developed in this book stores the addresses in the database in exactly the same order as you type them in, which isn't very useful. A real program should automatically sort addresses as you add them. The Address Book program included with this book, however, takes a slightly simpler approach. Each time you add a new address, it will be added to the end of the list. You'll then need to select the Sort item from the Address menu to explicitly ask Address Book to re-sort all the addresses.

I took this approach because it's simple and fast. It's a little simpler (in terms of the code needed) to sort the address only on request. And by not having the program sort addresses as you add them, Address Book is a lot faster.

There are actually many different approaches to sorting names, so I chose the one that works best for me. The sorting program you'll find on the disk, in SORT.BAS, uses a sort method that I've used for years in a commercial product, The Norton Commander.

The idea behind this sort is that you want to compare two names in the address list, and if they're out of order, you want to "swap" them. You swap two addresses by reading one address, copying the second address to where the first address was, and then writing the first address to where the second address was. Again, you'll find all the details on how this works on the disk.

Deleting Addresses

I chose a very simple method for deleting addresses, but it's not very fast. The first thing I did was change the way the database works so I could use the first record in the file to keep information about the file itself. The first address in the file will then be in the *second* record.

The reason I did this is very simple. Visual Basic allows you to increase the size of a file, but it doesn't provide any way to decrease the size. In other words, you can't make a file shrink if you remove one address from the file.

The problem is that DBLen uses the size of the file to calculate how many addresses are in the file, so it won't know that you've deleted records from the file. By using the first record to keep track of how many addresses are actually in the file, I can remove addresses from the end of the file and then just update the count in the first record to keep track of the number of addresses.

Here's how I remove an address from the file: I move down all the records after the deleted record by one record. For example, if I delete record number 10 from the file, I copy record 11 to record 10, then I copy record 12 to record 11, and so on. Because I copy all the records after the deleted record to move them closer to the start of the file, deleting records tends to be quite slow near the start of the file. But since most people don't delete addresses very often, I decided to use this very simple approach.

You'll find all the details in the miDelete event handler. You'll also notice that I modified the DATABASE.BAS module to use the first record to keep track of how many files are in the address book.

Summary

You should now have enough of an understanding of programming and Visual Basic to start working on your own programs. Part III of this book contains some general-purpose subroutines and functions you can use in your own programs and as a source for inspiration in writing new programs.

Part
three

Toolbox of Advanced Techniques

Chapter 14 provides some very useful information you'll need to know if you want your programs to work on other people's computers. Because there are actually three main types of computer displays in use by Windows (EGA, VGA, and 8514/A), you may discover that your program doesn't look nice on other people's computers. Chapter 14 will show you why, and it will also show you a number of techniques you can use to make your programs look nice on all displays.

Chapters 15 through 19 provide a number of useful functions and subroutines that you can use in your programs, as is. I've tried to write these routines in a general way so you can use them without necessarily understanding exactly how they work inside. I've organized these chapters by Controls, Forms, Drawing, Fonts, and Miscellaneous. The best way to use these chapters is to browse through them, reading the first few paragraphs from each major section. This will give you an idea of what's available when you have a need.

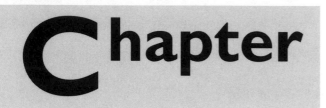

Chapter 13

Featuring

Visual Basic–Only Techniques

Custom Controls

DLLs and Windows Functions

Overview of Advanced Techniques

In this chapter I'll give you a quick overview of more advanced techniques you can use in Visual Basic programs you write. These techniques generally fall into three categories: Visual Basic–only techniques, custom controls, and dynamic link libraries (DLLs) and Windows API functions. I'll cover each topic briefly, and I'll also give you an idea of how the rest of this book is organized and how to use it.

Visual Basic–Only Techniques

Visual Basic is a very rich language and environment, which provides many possibilities without your ever having to leave the environment. We were only able to touch on a few of Visual Basic's abilities in the first two parts of this book.

In Chapters 14 through 19, however, you'll find a number of techniques, subroutines, and functions that you can use in your own programs. Some of these are written entirely in Visual Basic, and some use even more advanced techniques. To name just a few examples from these chapters, you'll find a subroutine for creating progress bars like you see in most installation programs, you'll learn how to draw shadows around controls, and you'll learn how to center forms on the screen before they become visible.

I suggest you browse through these chapters to see what's there, and if you find anything that looks useful, try it out. Some of the functions and subroutines from these chapters use very advanced techniques, which you don't need to understand in order to use the functions or subroutines; I've tried to write each section so you can use the technique without having to understand all the details of how I wrote it.

Custom Controls

There are a number of commercial add-on packages for Visual Basic that include *custom controls*. These are new types of controls that appear in Visual Basic's Toolbox when you add a special file to your project, which usually has the extension VBX.

Three of the top custom-control companies have provided some custom controls on the disk that comes with this book. These controls will give you an idea of what kinds of custom controls you'll find in commercial add-on products. The controls are fully functional—they're not crippled demos!—so you'll be able to use them in any programs you write.

To add a custom-control file to your project, select the Add File... item from the File menu, then double-click on the name of the VBX file you want to add. Once you add a VBX file to your project, you'll see some additional control icons appear in Visual Basic's Toolbox (see Figure 13.1).

DLLs and Windows Functions

Behind every Windows program is the Windows system itself. Windows provides hundreds of functions and subroutines that programs can call to create windows, menus, and controls, to do drawing, and so on. Any Windows program calls a number of these functions and subroutines. And any Visual Basic program you write calls these subroutines and functions indirectly. For example, Visual Basic's Line command is converted into a call to the Windows LineTo command, which draws lines inside a window.

All of these Windows functions are provided through a mechanism known as a *DLL*, an abbreviation for *dynamic link library*, which is a code library that's loaded into memory and connected to your program *on demand*. Windows

Figure 13.1:

The icons added to Visual Basic's Toolbox when you include the three VBX files on this book's disk in a project

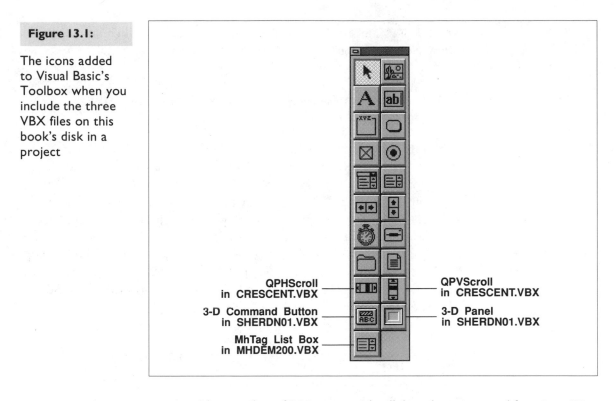

QPHScroll
in CRESCENT.VBX

QPVScroll
in CRESCENT.VBX

3-D Command Button
in SHERDN01.VBX

3-D Panel
in SHERDN01.VBX

MhTag List Box
in MHDEM200.VBX

comes with a number of DLLs to provide all the subroutines and functions Windows programs can call. You can also write your own DLLs in languages like C and Pascal (but not Visual Basic).

One really powerful feature in Visual Basic is its ability to call almost any DLL function or subroutine, both in Windows' DLLs and in other DLLs that you or someone else might write.

The Declare Statement

To call a routine inside a DLL, the first thing you have to do is define the function or subroutine that you want to call. You do this using the Declare statement, which defines a number of pieces of information. Here is the basic syntax for Declare:

Declare Sub *subName* **Lib** *libName$* [**Alias** *aliasName*] ([*argument list*])

This defines the subroutine called *subName* located in the DLL called *lib-Name$*. **Note:** You don't need to include the extension for the DLL, just its file name.

> **Declare Function** *functionName* **Lib** *libName$* **[Alias** *aliasName*]
> (**[***argument list***]**) **[As type]**

This defines a function called *functionName* located in the DLL called *lib-Name$*, which returns a value of *type*. **Note:** You don't need to include the extension for the DLL, just its file name.

In Chapters 15 through 19 you'll find a number of examples of how to use and declare Windows functions and subroutines. These routines are often known as the *Windows API*, where API is short for Application Programming Interface, and defines the functions that all Windows programs are built on top of. The best place to start learning about Windows APIs is with the section in Chapter 17 called "Fast Line Drawing," which shows you how to use a Windows function called Polyline.

Translating between C and Visual Basic Types

Whenever you're working with Windows API calls or with other DLLs, the documentation on the routines will probably be written for C programmers, which means it will use a number of terms and abbreviations you may not be familiar with. Let's take a look at a simple example to see how this works. Here is how the Windows function Polyline is defined in the Microsoft Windows programmer's manuals:

```
BOOL Polyline(hdc, lppt, cPoints)

HDC hdc;                    /* handle of device context */
POINT FAR* lppt;            /* address of array with points */
int cPoints;                /* number of points in array */
```

What does all this mean? The names in all uppercase letters, such as BOOL, are C's version of types. For example, BOOL is a Boolean type, which means it is an Integer that returns either −1 or 0 (in other words, True or False). HDC and POINT are also types. The lowercase *int* is also a type, which is exactly the same as Visual Basic's Integer type.

Since there can be so many different types in C and Windows, I've put together a table that shows how to translate between C and Visual Basic types. Tables 13.1 and 13.2 provide much of the information you'll need. You'll also find all the definitions in the WINAPI.TXT file included with Visual Basic, which defines all the functions and subroutines available in Windows.

When you're ready to start using Windows API calls on your own, you'll find a number of examples in Chapters 15 through 19. You'll find more information in your Visual Basic *Programmer's Guide,* and there also are a number of books that have some excellent examples of using the Windows API calls.

The important thing to realize about the Windows API is that there is really no limit to what you can do in Visual Basic.

Table 13.1:

Translating between C and Visual Basic Types

Windows	C	Visual Basic
BOOL	int	ByVal...As Integer
BYTE	char	ByVal...As Integer †
WORD	int	ByVal...As Integer
DWORD	long	ByVal...As Long
LPSTR	char FAR*	ByVal...As String
BOOL FAR*	int FAR*	...As Integer
BYTE FAR*	int FAR*	...As Integer †
WORD FAR*	int FAR*	...As Integer
DWORD FAR*	long FAR*	...As Long

† The Intel microprocessor treats bytes as words when you pass them to subroutines.

Table 13.2:	Windows	Visual Basic	Comments
Other Types of Variables	H*xxxxx*	ByVal...As Integer	Any type of handle is an Integer.
	ATOM	ByVal...As Integer	
	struct	ByVal...STRUCT	A user-defined type created with the Type statement.

Here are some special notes:

To pass both a string and a NULL pointer to a subroutine, define that parameter as As Any. You can pass a NULL pointer by passing the value 0&.

Define all strings as ByVal when you pass them to DLLs. Visual Basic will automatically convert them to C strings before calling the DLL, and it will convert C strings back to Visual Basic strings when the DLL finishes.

Arrays. Pass the first element in the range that you want to pass. For example, if you have an array of points called *points,* you could send part of this array to a DLL, starting with the fifth element, by using *points(5)* as the "value" you pass to the DLL. See "Fast Line Drawing" in Chapter 17 for an example.

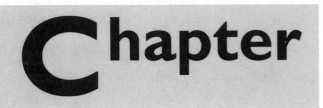hapter

Featuring

Understanding Screen Resolution
and Logical Inches

How Visual Basic's Objects
Change Size

How to Adjust Your Programs

A Clock/Calendar Sample Program

Writing Programs That Work with All Displays

Did you know that your nicely designed program won't always look good? If you've designed it on a VGA screen, then run that same program on an EGA or 8514/A screen (which some people have), you may discover it looks terrible.

In this chapter we'll look at what can cause screens to change their appearance and how to write programs that work well with all kinds of display adapters. We'll start by looking at the issues of *screen resolution* and *dot density,* which are at the root of screen problems. Then we'll move on to the specifics of how Visual Basic's controls change size between different screens. Finally, I'll provide some suggestions for how to write and design your programs so they'll look good on all displays.

Understanding Screen Resolution

The subject of screen resolution can be a little confusing for a couple of reasons. First, not everyone uses the term *resolution* in the same way. Second, Windows introduces a new term, *logical inches,* which further confuses the issue.

I spent some time looking for a good definition of resolution. *Webster's Dictionary,* as it turns out, wasn't much help. None of the definitions was even close. So I looked at a number of computer books to see how they define resolution. What I found is that there are two main definitions in use: one for printer resolution and a completely different one for display resolution.

Printer Resolution

The definition of printer resolution is quite simple and has to do with density. All the characters you see on this page were generated by a computer-driven printer (usually called a phototypesetter), using a number of very small dots. These dots are so small and close together that you can't see them.

Most book publishers use printers that can print 1200 or 2400 dots per inch. Laser printers, like the Hewlett-Packard LaserJet printers, typically print 300 dots per inch. A printer's resolution is measured by the density in dots per inch (dpi) of the characters it produces.

Display Resolution

The resolution of displays, on the other hand, is *not* a measure of dot density. Instead, a display's resolution is measured in terms of the total number of dots that it displays horizontally and vertically. A standard VGA display, for example, is 640 dots wide and 480 dots high, or 640 × 480.

A higher-resolution display simply has more dots on it. For example, the resolution of Super VGA displays is 800 × 600. The display resolution has nothing to do with the physical size of the screen (such as a 14-inch vs. 17-inch diagonal screen)—it refers only to the total number of dots on the screen. This is in contrast to printer resolution, which refers only to the density of dots, not to the total number of dots that a printer can print.

How Screen Size Affects Density

Now that you've seen that display resolution isn't measured by the density of dots, let's look at how the density changes as the resolution and screen

The Two Faces of Resolution

Here is a quick review of the definition of resolution for printers and displays:

Printers	Density of dots (measured in dots per inch, or dpi)
Displays	Total number of dots displayed horizontally and vertically, such as 640 × 480

size change. We'll look at examples using a 14-inch and a 17-inch diagonal monitor (many VGA screens are 14-inch) with several different resolutions (see Figure 14.1).

Figure 14.1:

This figure shows how the size of the screen and the display resolution affect the density of dots displayed on the screen, or dots per inch (dpi). The two arrows in the table show combinations of screen size and resolution that have similar dot densities.

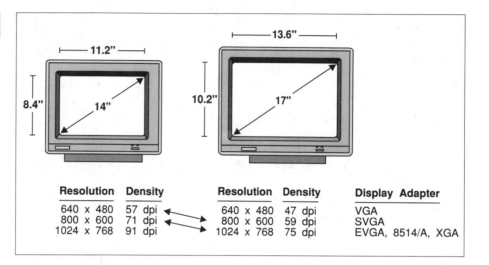

Resolution	Density	Resolution	Density	Display Adapter
640 x 480	57 dpi	640 x 480	47 dpi	VGA
800 x 600	71 dpi	800 x 600	59 dpi	SVGA
1024 x 768	91 dpi	1024 x 768	75 dpi	EVGA, 8514/A, XGA

NOTE

The colors you see on color screens are created by triplets of small phosphor dots. The sizes of these dots depend on your monitor and usually range from 0.28 mm for expensive monitors to 0.39 mm or larger for less expensive monitors. These sizes correspond to densities of 90 to 65 dpi.

You'll notice that the density of dots depends both on the resolution (the total number of screen dots) and the screen size. If you increase the size of your screen without changing the resolution, you'll see a larger picture without any more detail, which is a result of spreading the same number of dots over a larger area. On the other hand, if you increase the resolution without changing the screen size, you'll see a smaller picture. (If you like the sizes of the images on your 14-inch screen at 640 × 480 but you'd like more room on your screen, you can upgrade to a 17-inch screen and change the resolution to 800 × 600 to obtain the same size images with a larger workspace (see Figure 14.2).

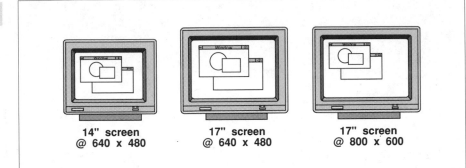

Figure 14.2:

How the screen size and resolution affect the image. Notice that the windows on the 17" screen at 800 × 600 are the same size as the windows on the 14" screen, but there are more dots.

14" screen
@ 640 x 480

17" screen
@ 640 x 480

17" screen
@ 800 x 600

Magazine Advertisements: What Do They Mean?

Advertisements in magazines for monitors muddy the waters somewhat on the issue of resolution. Most companies print two numbers that they never define: *dot pitch* and supported modes.

Dot pitch is a measure of the smallest dot that a color screen can theoretically display. The image you see on your screen is created by a large number of small phosphor dots grouped in triplets (called triads) of red, green, and blue. A shadow mask is used to ensure that the red, green, and blue electron guns light up only red, green, or blue phosphor dots (see Figure 14.3). The more expensive, and higher-quality, monitors used with Windows have a dot pitch of 0.28 mm, which translates into a density of 90 phosphor triads per inch (less expensive color monitors have dot pitches of 0.31 to 0.39 mm, which corresponds to densities of 81 to 65 dpi). This means that if you try to use a resolution and screen size that result in a density higher than these numbers, the image on your screen will be fuzzy because there aren't enough phosphor triads to show the image.

On the other hand, even if you have enough triads, your screen image may still be fuzzy. This is because the maximum screen resolution is dependent on more than just the density of phosphor triads. It is also dependent on how well the electronic circuitry inside the monitor is built.

For example, many 14-inch monitors have a dot pitch of 0.28 mm, but some of these have a maximum resolution of 640 × 480, while other, more expensive ones have a maximum resolution of 1024 × 768. It all has to do with the electronics and quality of the components used to build the monitor.

Even if a monitor is advertised as having a maximum resolution of 1024 × 768, it may not display clear images at this resolution. The supported display

Figure 14.3:

The density of dots on a color screen is limited by the dot pitch, which is a measure of the smallest dot that you can display on the screen. Each dot is created by a combination of up to three colors from the red, green, and blue phosphor dots.

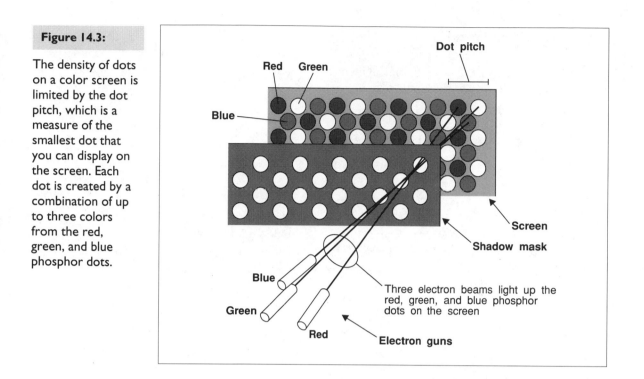

modes define which modes your monitor can display, but they are not an indication of the highest resolution that will be clear enough for your needs.

What Are Logical Inches?

In the last section you saw that the size of an image depends on a combination of things, such as the screen size and the display resolution. But what if you're writing a program and you want an object to be 1 inch square? How does Windows handle this? Does it somehow know the size of the monitor you're using?

Windows has no idea how large your monitor is—it only knows the resolution. Instead of trying to make an image appear exactly 1 inch square on the screen, Windows defines a *logical inch,* which is a certain number of pixels wide and high. Any object that is 1 logical inch wide will be exactly 1 physical inch wide when printed, but its physical width on the screen depends on the size and resolution of your screen.

If you're writing a program that needs to display a ruler, or anything else on the screen that needs to be measured in inches, the best thing to do is to ignore the fact that logical inches are different from real inches. Simply program everything using logical inches and anything you print will come out the correct size.

Defining a Logical Inch

How many pixels should be in a logical inch? And how did Microsoft come up with a number? I'll answer both of these questions in this section. First let's look at the number of pixels per logical inch.

Since Windows doesn't know the size of your screen (it only knows the type of display adapter and the resolution), Microsoft chose to define the size, in pixels, of a logical inch based solely on the screen resolution. Table 14.1 shows the numbers that Microsoft chose for various display adapters and resolutions.

Table 14.1:

The Logical Dot Densities That Windows Defines for Different Display Adapters and Resolutions

Display Adapter	Resolution	X - dpi	Y - dpi	Dot Aspect Ratio
CGA	640 × 200	96	48	2:1
EGA	640 × 400	96	72	1.33:1
VGA	640 × 480	96	96	1:1
SVGA	800 × 600	96	96	1:1
EVGA	1024 × 768	96	96	1:1
8514/A	1024 × 768	120	120	1:1

These densities allow a logical display width of at least 6.5", which is the width of the writing area on an 8.5" × 11" piece of paper with 1" margins. Notice that the dots are square (1:1 aspect ratio) rather than oblong on all display adapters except for the CGA and EGA adapters.

You'll notice that most of these screens have a logical dot density of 96 dots per inch. In order for a real VGA display to have a real (rather than logical) density of 96 dpi, it would have to be 6.7 inches by 5 inches, or 8.3 inches diagonal, in size. On a 8.3-inch diagonal monitor, an object that was 1 logical inch wide would be *exactly* 1 physical inch wide on the screen. But most VGA screens are 14-inch diagonal with densities more like 60 dpi. So why did Microsoft define the density of logical inches to be 96 dpi instead of 60 dpi?

The reason for this has to do with readability. If the logical density is too small (like 60 dpi), you won't have enough dots in a 6- or 8-point font to be able to read it well. In other words, you want as high a density as possible so small characters will be easy to read. A density of 300 dpi, for example, is extremely readable, and this is the density used by most laser printers.

On the other hand, you don't want the density to be too high, because this would limit the size, in logical inches, of documents you could see on your screen. For example, if you chose a logical density of 300 dpi, a 640 × 480 screen would be limited to a logical size of 2.1 × 1.6 inches, which is far too small a display for most programs, like word processors.

Here is where Microsoft's numbers come from. A standard sheet of paper is 8.5 inches wide with a 1-inch margin on each side. This means that the printed area is 6.5 inches wide (8.5 inches minus 2 inches). Microsoft wanted this print area to fit on the screen in any Windows program and wanted to include a vertical scroll bar. Since the width of a vertical scroll bar is 16 pixels, we can calculate the density needed to be able to display both 6.5 inches and a scroll bar as (640 − 16) / 6.5-inch = 96 dpi, which is exactly the number Microsoft chose.

Once again, as long as you work with just logical inches in your programs, everything will print at the correct size. (Most users are used to the rulers on their screens showing inches that appear larger than a real inch.)

Can I Have Sharper Images?

Most people I know would like to have a sharper image on their screen, in which Windows uses more dots to create the same image. Is there any way you can increase the logical density, and therefore the sharpness, of your screen? The answer is yes, and no.

As you'll recall from Table 14.1, the logical dot density is defined by the Windows display drivers, and different display adapters have different logical densities. In particular, notice that the logical density for an 8514/A display adapter is 120 dpi, which is noticeably higher than the 96-dpi density for most other display drivers. So, yes, you can have a sharper display. But you, as the user, don't have control over this sharpness—the dot density is determined by the people who write the display drivers. Of course, in theory someone could write a display driver that allowed you to change the logical dot density, but I'm not aware of any such driver. And, as you'll see in the next section, when I talk about bitmaps and icons, there's a good reason for not writing such a driver.

How Visual Basic's Objects Change Size

Now that you have a firm foundation in how Windows defines a logical inch, you're ready to learn how Visual Basic uses this information—and in particular, how Visual Basic determines the sizes and locations of controls on different display adapters.

Twips and the Height of Text

The first thing you need to know is that Visual Basic uses twips (rather than pixels or inches or any other measure) to store the sizes and locations of all controls you place on a form. This allows Visual Basic to do a reasonable job of keeping a form's appearance on different display adapters. Unfortunately, it can't do a perfect job, for reasons you'll see here.

To understand why Visual Basic has some problems, we need to take a closer look at how a twip is defined in terms of pixels and how this impacts the size of objects.

There are three logical dot densities that Windows currently supports: 96 dpi (which is used for all VGA, SVGA, and EVGA displays), 72 dpi (which is used for EGA displays), and 120 dpi (which is used for 8514/A displays). We'll look at only the EGA, VGA, and 8514/A display modes for the rest of this chapter.

Table 14.2 shows the number of twips per pixel for each of these three displays (recall that a twip is $1/1440$ inch). This table also shows the height of Visual

Table 14.2:				
Twips per Pixel and TextHeight for Displays	**Display**	**X Twips/ Pixel**	**Y Twips/ Pixel**	**TextHeight (Twips)**
	EGA	15	20	200
	VGA	15	15	195
	8514/A	12	12	192

Basic's default Helv font, which is used for all controls unless you change the FontName or FontSize property or both.

Notice that the text heights are very close to one other, but they're not identical. Why? The font used to display characters on the screen (Helv in Windows 3.0 and MS Sans Serif in Windows 3.1) is a bitmap font, which means it has a height measured in pixels rather than twips. Each display mode (EGA, VGA, and 8514/A) actually has its own version of the font that it uses. Since these fonts have sizes measured in pixels, we can't get an exact match in the height of the font—we can only get close. This is why the TextHeight values are close but not exactly the same.

How the Heights of Controls Vary

What does the information above mean for your forms? Some controls will have different sizes, depending on the font and display adapter you're using. Table 14.3 tells most of the story but requires a little explanation.

The first three columns show the minimum size for each type of control, measured in twips. Most of the controls have a minimum size that varies between the different display adapters. These variations are caused by the slight variations in the height of the default font. The last three columns give you an idea of how the heights of the controls vary among the three display modes and require some further explanation:

Keeps Size	These controls will maintain their size, in twips, in the different display modes, as long as their initial height is greater than or equal to the minimum EGA heights.
Fixed Height	You can't change the height for these controls, so they will change in height among the different display modes.
Whole Lines	These controls increase and decrease in size by only a whole number of lines, which means they will vary in size in the different display modes. Table 14.4 shows how to calculate the heights of these controls.

Table 14.3: The Minimum Height for Each Control, in Twips, for Each Type of Display Adapter

Control Type	EGA	VGA	8514/A	Keeps Size	Fixed Height	Whole Lines
Combo Box	320	300	288		✓	✓
Drive Combo Box	360	315	288		✓	✓
List Box	≥240	≥255	≥216			
File List Box	≥240	≥225	≥216			
Directory List Box	≥240	≥225	≥216	✓		
Check Box	≥200	≥195	≥192	✓		
Command Button	≥200	≥195	≥192	✓		
Option Button	≥200	≥195	≥192	✓		
Text Box	≥300	≥285	≥288	✓		
Frame	Any	Any	Any	✓		
Label	Any	Any	Any	✓		
Picture Box	Any	Any	Any	✓*	*	
HScroll Bar	≥240	Same	Same	✓		
VScroll Bar	≥240	Same	Same	✓		

* If AutoSize is False, the size of the picture box will remain the same, in twips, but the picture itself (bitmap or icon) will change in size because the size of a pixel will change. You can set AutoSize to True to keep the picture box same size as the bitmap or icon inside it.

Table 14.4:	Mode	Control Height (in twips)
How to Calculate the Height of List and Dir Boxes	EGA	numLines * 200 + 40
	VGA	numLines * 195 + 15
	8514/A	numLines * 192 + 12

How to Adjust Your Programs

Now let's take a look at what all this means to programs you write, by concentrating on the items that can cause problems. If you look again at Table 14.3, you'll notice that there are only a few controls that can cause problems:

Combo Box

Drive Combo Box

File List Box

Directory List Box

Picture Box

Picture Property of a Form

You can group these controls into three groups: list boxes, combo boxes, and pictures. Of these three groups, the combo boxes tend to cause the fewest problems, while the pictures tend to cause the most problems. We'll look at each group below, and I'll offer suggestions on how to write programs that work well on all displays.

By the way, I've said nothing about widths because, except for pictures, Visual Basic does an excellent job of maintaining the width of all controls. The only thing you'll need to do is to make sure all your strings are visible on 8514/A displays. This is a concern because lines of text on 8514/A displays are often slightly wider (in twips) than the same string on a VGA (or an EGA) display. The width of strings increases slightly because the widths of characters on a 8514/A display are a little different from the widths on a VGA display. As long as you check your programs on an 8514/A display, you shouldn't have a problem.

How to Work with Combo Boxes

You really have no choice about the height of combo boxes since the Height property is read-only (you can't change it). So all you have to do (and all you can do) is make sure you have enough room under each combo box so they won't bump into other controls on an EGA display. Drive combo boxes should have enough room to become 360 twips high on an EGA display, and regular combo boxes need enough room to become 320 twips high.

How to Work with List Boxes

List boxes are a little trickier. There are actually three types of list boxes you can use: List Box, File List Box, and Directory List Box. Only the first two really cause any problems. For reasons that aren't clear, a directory list box will keep its twip height as long as it's greater than 240 twips (the largest minimum size), because the last line in this list box is allowed to show a partial line. The other two list boxes can only change height by multiples of the line height, which means they can only show entire lines.

The result is that list boxes and file list boxes *will* have different heights on different displays, so here's what you have to do. If you want a directory list box and a file list box to have the same height, you'll need to put code like the following in your Form_Load subroutine:

```
Sub Form_Load ()
    Dir1.Height = File1.Height
End Sub
```

In other words, you can change the height of the directory list box to match the height of your file list box, but you can't do the reverse.

Because the height of a list box or file list box can change quite a bit (if you have many lines in the list), you may need to move any controls that appear below such list boxes to keep the list boxes from bumping into your controls. Again, here is the type of code you can write in your Form_Load subroutine to move such controls (Command1 in this example):

```
Sub Form_Load ()
    Command1.Top = List1.Top + List1.Height + 150
End Sub
```

This code will move Command1 so that its top is 150 twips below the bottom of List1.

How Pictures Change

Pictures have by far the most potential for creating problems when you're trying to write a program that will work with all display modes. The reason for this is quite simple (but the solution isn't so simple). Bitmaps and icons are made out of pixels, which means that their actual size will always be measured in pixels rather than twips.

All controls other than picture boxes have their size measured in twips (it doesn't matter what ScaleMode you use; Visual Basic always remembers the size of objects in twips). This difference, then, between picture boxes and all other controls leads to several problems.

First, if you don't set the AutoSize property of a picture box to True, the picture box itself will stay the same size in twips, but the picture inside a picture box will always keep its same size in pixels. For example, when you draw a picture box on a VGA display, then show it on an 8514/A display, the picture box will occupy more pixels on the screen (since the dot density is 120 dpi on an 8514/A display vs. 96 dpi for a VGA display), but the picture itself will use the same number of pixels. The picture will be smaller than the picture box.

On the other hand, if you set AutoSize to True, the picture box will always keep the same size in pixels. This means that its size in twips will change by a large amount. Let's say, for example, you have a picture box with an icon in it (which is 32 by 32 pixels), and you have set AutoSize = True and BorderStyle = 0 (no border). This picture box will have very different heights in twips for the three types of displays, as you can see here:

Display	Height
EGA	640 twips
VGA	480 twips
8514/A	384 twips

To give you a better idea of what this means, Figures 14.4 through 14.6 show a form with a picture box and several controls. As you can see, the controls stay about the same size and remain in about the same location, but the bitmap changes considerably in size.

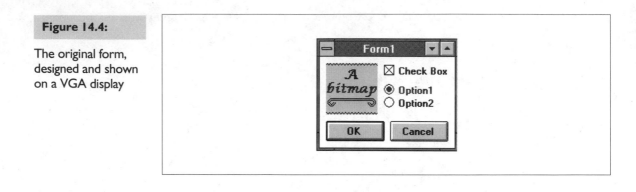

Figure 14.4:

The original form, designed and shown on a VGA display

Figure 14.5:

The same form, but shown on an 8514/A display

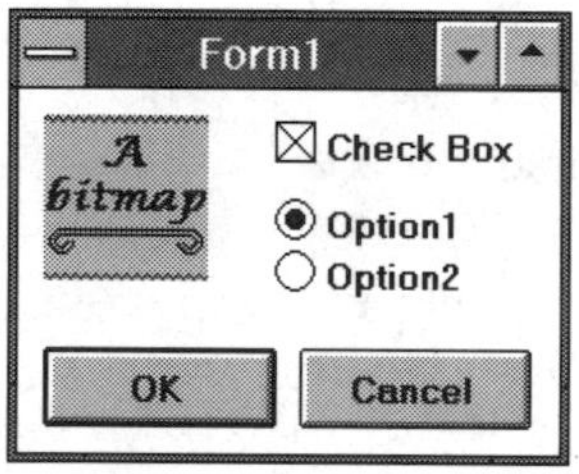

Figure 14.6:

The same form, but shown on an EGA display

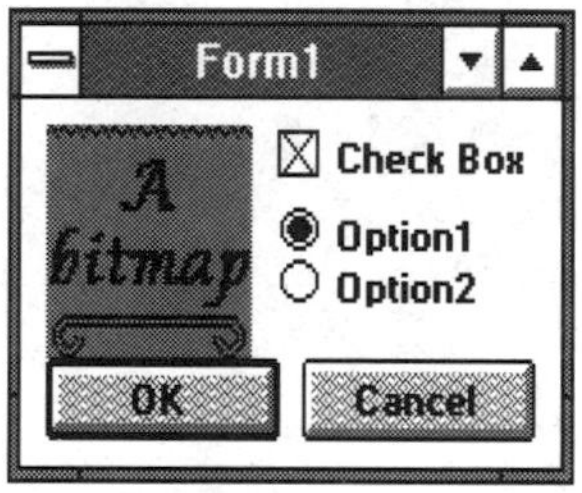

Figure 14.4 shows the original form, designed and shown on a VGA display. Figure 14.5 shows the same form, but shown on an 8514/A display. The bitmap is noticeably smaller, compared with the other controls, than it was on the VGA display. Figure 14.6 shows the same form, but shown on an EGA display. Notice that the bitmap has the same width as on a VGA display, but now it's much taller and is actually cut off at the bottom by the OK button. Also notice how the gray in this picture is now shown as dark gray. This happens on an EGA

display because it can't show light gray. But the button, which should have the same gray, uses a dithered pattern (alternating black and white dots) to show light gray.

How you solve this problem really depends on what you're doing with bitmaps and icons. If you're using a bitmap for a simple application, like displaying a logo, you really don't need to do much, except make sure you have enough room around your icon so it won't bump into other controls on an EGA display.

On the other hand, if you're writing a program that uses a lot of bitmaps, and the locations of these bitmaps are important, you'll definitely have to write some code that positions each bitmap and the controls around these bitmaps. Or, you can have three sets of icons or bitmaps of different sizes: one for EGA displays, another for VGA displays, and the last for 8514/A displays. Then all you have to do is to write code to display the correct icon. The hard part is finding out which mode you're in.

I've written a small function that makes choosing an icon fairly simple. Let's say you have a four-element array of picture boxes, called picLogo. Element 0 is the one you'll show inside your form, and the other three contain the pictures for the EGA, VGA, and 8514/A displays, in that order. The first thing we need, then, is a function that will tell us which bitmap to use, which might look something like this:

```
Function ChooseBitmap (c As Control) As Integer
    '
    ' This function returns the following:
    '
    '     1    Use 8514/A bitmap
    '     2    Use VGA bitmap
    '     3    Use EGA bitmap
    '
    c.ScaleMode = 3                 ' Set to pixel scaling
    c.CurrentY = 1                  ' Move down one pixel
    c.ScaleMode = 1                 ' Set to twip scaling mode
    Select Case c.CurrentY          ' CurrentY = twips/pixel in Y
        Case 12
            ChooseBitmap = 1        ' Use 8514/A bitmap
        Case 15
            ChooseBitmap = 2        ' Use VGA bitmap
        Case Else
            ChooseBitmap = 3        ' Use EGA bitmap
    End Select
End Function
```

You'd use this function with some code like this:

```
Sub Form_Load ()
    i = ChooseBitmap(picLogo(0))
    picLogo(0).Picture = picLogo(i).Picture
    picLogo(0).AutoSize = -1
End Sub
```

Here's how it works. The function ChooseBitmap uses the control you pass to it to figure out the twips-per-pixel ratio. This ratio tells you exactly which type of display is being used. ChooseBitmap then returns the array index for the bitmap you should use on the current display.

Fortunately, you won't often need to use this type of code in your program, because most programs don't make heavy use of pictures.

Text and Pictures

If you're mixing text and pictures—in particular, if you have text on top of pictures—you may need to adjust the size of your text to match the pictures. This is a real problem because pictures change in size (measured in twips) by a large amount among the different display modes, as mentioned in the last section. You'll probably want to adjust the font height so it keeps the same height in pixels, which takes a bit of work.

How do you set the size of a font in pixels? Can you simply supply the size of the font, measured in pixels or twips? The answer is no, for a couple of reasons. First, Visual Basic's FontSize property is *always* measured in points ($1/72$ inch, or $1/20$ twip), so you have to supply the size in points. To compound the problem, you can't always set the exact size of a font. For example, you might find that FontSize = 8.25 after you set it to 1.

And there's still one other problem. The value you get back from TextHeight won't be the same as the font size you set because TextHeight and FontSize refer to different numbers that measure the size of a font. The FontSize property, as it turns out, sets the height of the characters in the font, whereas the TextHeight function reports this height plus the *leading* (or extra spacing) between lines of text. This extra space, by the way, always appears above (rather than below) any text you display in a text box, in a label, or with the Print method.

The problem, then, is how to adjust the TextHeight of a font when all we can set is the FontSize property, and we don't have full control over that.

The solution I chose is to write a small function called FindFontSize that finds the closest font whose size (TextHeight) is less than or equal to the height you want. The following function returns the size of the closest font, and it must be in one of your forms since it uses the FontSize property of a form.

```
Function FindFontSize (f As Form, ByVal high) As Integer
    '
    ' This function returns the first font with a
    ' TextHeight <= high.
    '
    ' Note: If the smallest font has a TextHeight > high, this
    '        function will return a font larger than high.
    '
    Dim i, oldSize, size

    oldSize = f.FontSize              ' Remember old font size
    i = 1                             ' Start with 1-point font
    f.FontSize = i                    ' Set first size
    size = f.FontSize                 ' Keep track of best match

    While f.TextHeight("A") <= high ' Is font too large?
        size = f.FontSize             ' No, remember this size
        If f.FontSize > i Then        ' Is size larger than i?
            i = f.FontSize            ' Yes, adjust i to real size
        End If
        i = i + 1                     ' Try next higher size
        f.FontSize = i                ' Set font to this size
    Wend
    f.FindSize = size                 ' Return size of found font

    f.FontSize = oldSize              ' Restore the old font size
End Function
```

As you can see, this function starts by setting FontSize to 1, which will actually give us the smallest available font. Using Visual Basic's Helv font, this actually gives us an 8.25-point font with a TextHeight of 13 pixels. The While loop keeps increasing the FontSize value until TextHeight is greater than or equal to *high*. We now have the font size we want.

NOTE

You'll find a slightly more complicated (and perhaps better) solution in the Toolbox section of this book. You'll also learn more about the difference between the TextHeight and FontSize values.

You'll notice that the FindFontSize function uses a form for calculating the size of a font, which allows it to use the FontSize property and TextHeight method to do all the work.

Colors

You may also need to think about how colors are used in your programs. For the most part, the colors you use in your programs will translate well among different displays. The light gray color, however, isn't available directly on EGA displays. How Visual Basic handles this is a little different for pictures and for colors set with the BackColor property.

All colors set to light gray using the BackColor property will be shown on the screen as a dithered pattern. Instead of showing a solid color, Visual Basic *simulates* a light gray color by setting alternate pixels to black and white (as you can probably see in the command buttons in Figure 14.6).

For pictures (bitmaps and icons), on the other hand, Visual Basic (actually Windows) converts any colors in the bitmap or icon into the closest *solid* color that matches. Since light gray isn't available on an EGA display, you get dark gray instead (as you can see in Figure 14.6).

As long as you don't use light gray in any bitmaps or icons, you won't have a problem. But if you mix the light gray in pictures with a light gray BackColor, you may want to set BackColor to dark gray on EGA displays so that the Back-Color gray will match the gray shown in bitmaps or icons.

Summary of Rules

Here is a summary of the rules for writing programs that look good on all displays:

- **Widths of Controls.** All controls, except some pictures, will keep the same width, in twips. The only thing to remember is that strings are sometimes wider on 8514/A displays because some of the characters in the font are wider.

- **Upper-Left Corner.** The Top and Left properties of all controls will stay the same, in twips, for all displays.

- **Combo Boxes.** Make sure all drive combo boxes have enough space under them so they can be 360 twips high on an EGA display without bumping into other controls (320 twips high for regular combo boxes).

- **List Boxes.** You normally don't have to do anything for list boxes. But if you have a directory list box next to either a file list box or a regular list box, you'll need to change the height of your directory list box to match the other list box. You need to change the height of the directory list box, rather than the file list box, because the directory list box is the only one you can change by a partial line.

- **Pictures.** If you need other objects located at specific locations on top of a picture, you'll have to write code that moves controls to a specific position. You'll probably want to set ScaleMode = 3 (Pixel), then set the location of controls using pixel values.

NOTE

Setting ScaleMode = 3 (Pixel) while you're designing your program will *not* set the positions of controls to specific pixel locations. Visual Basic stores the sizes and locations of controls internally in twips, not in pixels, so their pixel location and size *will* change among different displays.

- **Picture AutoSize.** You'll usually want to set the AutoSize property on a picture box to True to make sure the picture box will always be the same size as the picture or icon inside it.

- **Multiple Pictures.** You can also have three bitmaps (or icons) for each picture you want to display, with each set tuned for EGA, VGA, and 8514/A displays. Then show the picture for the correct display (using code like that presented earlier).

- **Colors.** If you're mixing the light gray color in bitmaps (or icons) with a light gray set by BackColor, you may want to set BackColor to dark gray whenever your program is running on an EGA display.

- **Testing.** There is no substitute for testing your programs. If your program uses a lot of bitmaps or icons, you'll need to do extensive testing on all three types of displays. The best way to do this type of testing is to have a card inside your computer that supports all three modes. I use an ATI Graphics ULTRA card, and I can switch between the three modes using the Windows Setup program. Setup will change the drivers, then let you restart Windows in a new display mode. This process is reasonably fast under Windows 3.1 (it was quite slow under 3.0).

The ClockCal Example

When I was first learning Visual Basic, I wrote a program just for the fun of it that displayed a clock and a calendar with the current date. I created an icon for each digit using Icon Works so the digits would look like the digits on a digital clock, and I put the current date on top of what looked like a pad of tear-off days, which I created using Paintbrush. Everything looked really nice!

But then I got a new display adapter that allowed me to switch to 8514/A mode, and I discovered that my nice-looking program suddenly didn't look as nice on an 8514/A display. The problem was that the bitmaps I used changed in size much more than anything else in my programs, as you can see in Figure 14.7.

Figure 14.7:

The original program, designed on a VGA display, stays about the same size (in twips) on EGA and 8514/A displays. The bitmaps change considerably in size.

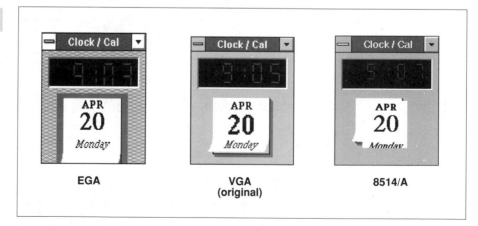

EGA

VGA
(original)

8514/A

I ended up rewriting my Clock/Calendar program using the techniques outlined in this chapter, and as you can see in Figure 14.8, the final program looks very nice on all the different types of displays (although it does change in size quite a bit). In this section I'll present the final program and show you how I

Figure 14.8:

The modified program that adjusts all the sizes to match the bitmap sizes. This program works well with all display adapters, even though the ClockCal window changes in size.

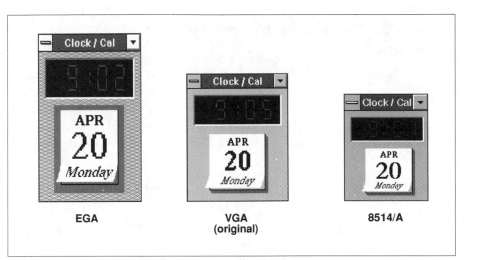

rewrote ClockCal to resize all the objects connected with the bitmaps, which in this example is every object.

Control Arrays

The ClockCal program makes heavy use of a *control array*. Control arrays are groups of controls that all have the same name; we looked at them briefly in Chapter 5, where we used a control array for items in the menu bar. Here we have two control arrays: one for the digits 0 through 9, and the other for the digits in the clock. We can refer to any of the controls in the array simply by giving the index of that control. For example, if we want to look at the digit 7 (which is the eighth element of the Digits array), we write Digits(7).

There are two ways you can create a control array in Visual Basic. First, you can assign a value to the Index property of a control. Second, you can create two (or more) controls and assign the same control name to both controls. As soon as you assign the same name to a second control, Visual Basic will display a dialog box asking if you want to create a control array. Simply answer Yes.

I created a Digits control array using 10 controls with index values of 0 through 9. Then I loaded the correct icon into each of these picture boxes so Digits(n).Picture refers to the icon for the *n*th digit.

Almost all the other techniques I use in ClockCal should be familiar to you after reading Parts I and III of this book.

How Resizing Works

Let's start by looking at the form in design mode. Figure 14.9 shows the ClockCal form with all the controls shown on it. You can see that I have the ten digits plus a colon and a blank icon near the lower part of the form. None of these controls will be visible while ClockCal is running because it makes the form much smaller. But we need these icons so we can change the digits that will be visible, which we can do with a command like this:

```
Digit(0).Picture = Digits(2)
```

This command will display a *2* in the leftmost digit on the screen.

There are really several parts to how ClockCal works. But since this chapter is about resizing objects as needed, let's look first at how ClockCal changes the size of its controls to match the bitmaps we'll be working with.

There are three subroutines and one function that do all the work, called SetupSizes, SizeWindow, SizeCalendar, and FindFontSize. SetupSizes is called once when ClockCal first starts by a single statement in the Form_Load event, as you can see in the program listings at the end of this chapter. SetupSizes does some work, as well as calling SizeWindow and SizeCalendar.

First SetupSizes calls SizeWindow, which changes the size of the ClockCal form so its *inside* dimensions are 136 by 148 pixels. All the properties and methods provided by Visual Basic for changing a form's size work with the outside dimensions (which include the borders and the caption bar), so I wrote a special subroutine called SizeWindow that changes a form's size using inside, rather than outside, dimensions.

Let's take a quick look at how SizeWindow works. The first thing we want to do is to calculate the size of the borders in the X and Y directions. We want to calculate these sizes in twips because the Move method, which we'll use to change the form's size, works only with twips. This is why the first statement changes ScaleMode to twips. The next four statements calculate the width and height of the borders, measured in twips. Next, we change the Scale-Mode back to pixels, and then calculate the twips/pixel ratio in both the X and Y directions; these values are stored in xScale and yScale. We need these values so we can convert the pixel dimensions into twips in the Move command. Finally, the last three statements calculate the new width and height, then change the window's width.

Next we have to set the sizes on the digital clock display. First we set the width and height of the colon placeholder, which is a picture box located between the first two and last two digits inside the ClockFrame picture box. The For..Next loop handles setting the top left of each digit picture box, as well as setting the width and height. We need to set all these values in pixels because Visual Basic tries to keep them constant in twips, rather than in pixels. Finally, we can set the left and top of the colon placeholder after we've positioned all the digits.

The next two lines set the width and height of the clock frame. Then we set the top of the DatePad picture box so it will be 6 pixels below the ClockFrame picture box.

NOTE

Strictly speaking, I should also have set the left and top of the ClockFrame, but I didn't. If you look closely at Figure 14.8, you'll notice that the ClockFrame moves slightly to the right of center in the 8514/A display because I did not set the Left property. For the same reason, I should also have set the Left property for the DatePad picture box.

Finally, SetupSizes calls SizeCalendar, which handles all the resizing of the elements inside DatePad.

The code in SizeCalendar is rather simple: It sets the Top, Left, Width, and Height properties for each label inside the DatePad picture box. The last three statements are the really interesting part, since they're the ones that change the text sizes so they'll fit inside the labels. You can see that I'm using FindFontSize to calculate the correct FontSize to use for each label.

The FindFontSize function I'm using is slightly different from the one outlined previously. The one in ClockCal finds a font that is either the correct size or slightly larger (whereas the one presented earlier may find a font slightly smaller).

How ClockCal Works

Now that you've seen how ClockCal resizes all its controls, let's look at the rest of the program, but first a few cosmetic items. You may have noticed that there is a nice beveled edge on the inside of the ClockFrame. Where did this come from? If you look in ClockFrame_Paint, you'll see the following statement:

```
Sub ClockFrame_Paint ()
    DrawBevel ClockFrame
End Sub
```

DrawBevel is a subroutine I wrote that draws a nice beveled edge inside any picture box. That's all there is to it. You can look at DrawBevel if you're interested in the details of how it works.

Both the clock and the calendar are updated by their own subroutine: UpdateClock for the clock, and UpdateCalendar for the calendar. Let's look at UpdateClock first.

UpdateClock is rather like the clock program we wrote in Chapter 7, but with a couple of differences. Instead of drawing hands on a clock, it shows individual digits. The way we do this, as I mentioned above, is to assign the Picture property from the Digits array (which holds the digits 0 through 9) to the Picture property of a Digit (which is a control array that shows the digits in the form).

I use another small trick to make the colon blink on and off. It will blink every half second, so it will be on for half a second and off for half a second. First, I set the timer Interval to 500, which is half a second, so Ticker_Timer will be called (usually) every half second. Then I created a *static* variable called showColon. A static variable is like a form variable, because it keeps its value even after UpdateClock exits. But by defining it as Static inside UpdateClock, we make it visible only to the UpdateClock subroutine.

Every time UpdateClock is called, I change the value of showColon to Not showColon. In other words, if showColon was True, I set it to False. And if it was False, I set it to True. Then I use the value of showColon to determine whether I should show the colon picture or the blank picture.

UpdateCalendar is really simple, as you can see below. The Format$( ) function does almost all the work of converting dates into names. The only extra thing is the UCase$( ) function, which converts the name of the month into all uppercase letters.

The ClockCal Form

The ClockCal form has a number of controls on it, as you can see from Figure 14.9. Most of the objects, including the form itself, are automatically sized correctly at run time, so these controls don't have to be placed very carefully. Table 14.5 shows the properties for the form, and Table 14.6 shows the controls on the form.

Figure 14.9:

The ClockCal form at design time, with all the controls

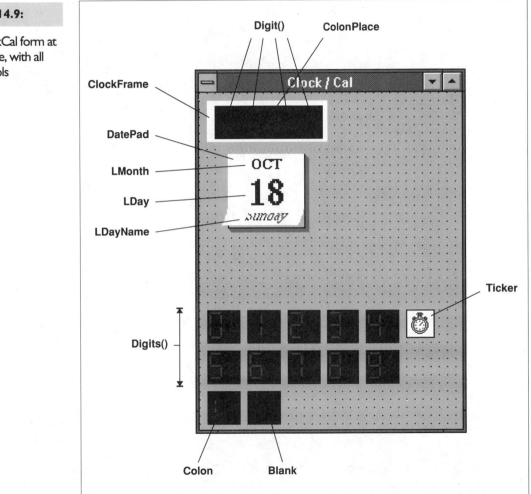

Table 14.5:

Properties for the Form

Property	Setting
BackColor	&H00C0C0C0&
BorderStyle	1 - Fixed
Caption	Clock / Cal
FormName	ClockCal
MaxButton	False
ScaleMode	3 - Pixel

Table 14.6:

Controls on the Form

Control	Property	Setting
Picture Box	CtlName	ClockFrame
	BorderStyle	0 - None
	Left	8
	ScaleMode	3 - Pixel
	Top	8
Picture Box (4)	CtlName	Digit
	BackColor	0
	Index	0, 1, 2, 3—left to right
Picture Box	CtlName	ColonPlace
	BackColor	0
Picture Box	CtlName	DatePad
	AutoSize	True
	BackColor	&H80000005&
	BorderStyle	0 - None
	Left	20
	Picture	(Bitmap)…
	ScaleMode	3 - Pixel

Control	Property	Setting
Table 14.6: Controls on the Form (continued)		
Label	CtlName	LMonth
	Alignment	2 - Center
	FontName	Tms Rmn
Label	CtlName	LDay
	Alignment	2 - Center
	FontName	Tms Rmn
Label	CtlName	LDayName
	Alignment	2 - Center
	FontName	Tms Rmn
Timer	CtlName	Ticker
	Interval	500

The Code for ClockCal

Here are the definitions from the (declarations) area of the ClockCal form:

```
'
' These two variables are used to keep track of the
' last time we updated the clock so we won't flash
' the display when there are no changes.
'
Dim lastHour
Dim lastMin
```

Here is the code that initializes ClockCal:

```
Sub Form_Load ()
    ClockFrame.BackColor = 0     ' Set background to black
    lastMin = -1                 ' Update minutes even if 0
```

```
        lastHour = -1                  ' Update hour even if 0

        SetupSizes                     ' Set all the sizes

        UpdateCalendar
        UpdateClock
End Sub
```

Here are the four subroutines that together take care of changing the size of all the items that are not bitmaps inside the window:

```
Sub SetupSizes ()
    '
    ' First we'll set the size for all the digits in the
    ' digital clock face.
    '
    SizeWindow 136, 148        ' Set form size, in pixels

    ColonPlace.Width = 16
    ColonPlace.Height = 33

    For i = 0 To 3
        Digit(i).Width = 24
        Digit(i).Height = 33
        Digit(i).Top = 5
        Digit(i).Left = 4 + 24 * i
        If i >= 2 Then
            Digit(i).Left = Digit(i).Left + ColonPlace.Width
        End If
    Next i

    ColonPlace.Left = Digit(1).Left + 24
    ColonPlace.Top = Digit(0).Top

    ClockFrame.Width = 120
    ClockFrame.Height = 41

    '
    ' Next we'll set the size and locations for the
    ' calendar.
    '
    DatePad.Top = ClockFrame.Top + ClockFrame.Height + 6
    SizeCalendar
End Sub
```

```
Sub SizeWindow (ByVal pWidth, ByVal pHeight)
    '
```

```
    ' This subroutine sets the inside dimensions of the
    ' window to 148 x 136 pixels.
    '
    Dim xScale, yScale            ' twips/pixel ratio
    Dim xBorder, yBorder          ' Size of border, in twips
    Dim newWidth, newHeight       ' New width, height of window

    ScaleMode = 1                 ' Set to twip scaling
    xScale = ScaleWidth           ' Get width in twips
    yScale = ScaleHeight          ' And height in twips
    xBorder = Width - ScaleWidth  ' Size of x borders
    yBorder = Height - ScaleHeight ' Size of y borders

    ScaleMode = 3                 ' Switch back to pixel
    xScale = xScale / ScaleWidth  ' x twips/pixel ratio
    yScale = yScale / ScaleHeight ' y twips/pixel ratio

    newWidth = xBorder + xScale * pWidth
    newHeight = yBorder + yScale * pHeight
    Move Left, Top, newWidth, newHeight
End Sub
```

```
Sub SizeCalendar ()
    LMonth.Left = 16
    LDay.Left = 16
    LDayName.Left = 16

    LMonth.Width = 64
    LDay.Width = 64
    LDayName.Width = 64

    LMonth.Top = 7
    LMonth.Height = 16

    LDay.Top = 21
    LDay.Height = 42

    LDayName.Top = 58
    LDayName.Height = 16

    LMonth.FontSize = FindFontSize(LMonth.Height)
    LDay.FontSize = FindFontSize(LDay.Height)
    LDayName.FontSize = LMonth.FontSize
End Sub
```

```
Function FindFontSize (ByVal high) As Integer
```

```
'
' This function returns the first font with a
' TextHeight >= high.
'
i = 1
FontSize = i
While TextHeight("Ay") < high
    FontSize = i
    If FontSize > i Then
        i = FontSize
    Else
        i = i + 1
    End If
Wend
FindFontSize = i
End Function
```

The next set of subroutines handles the clock and calendar functions:

```
Sub ClockFrame_Paint ()
    DrawBevel ClockFrame
End Sub
```

```
Sub Ticker_Timer ()
    UpdateClock
    UpdateCalendar
End Sub
```

```
Sub UpdateClock ()
    Static showColon As Integer      ' True when colon visible
    Dim t As Double
    Dim h, m, s As Integer

    t = Now
    h = Hour(t) Mod 12
    If h = 0 Then h = 12
    m = Minute(t)
    s = Second(t)

    If h <> lastHour Then
        If Int(h / 10) = 0 Then
            Digit(0).Picture = Blank.Picture
        Else
            Digit(0).Picture = Digits(Int(h / 10)).Picture
        End If
```

```
            Digit(1).Picture = Digits(h Mod 10).Picture
            lastHour = h
        End If

        If m <> lastMin Then
            Digit(2).Picture = Digits(Int(m / 10)).Picture
            Digit(3).Picture = Digits(m Mod 10).Picture
            lastMin = m
        End If

        If showColon Then
            ColonPlace.Picture = Blank.Picture
        Else
            ColonPlace.Picture = Colon.Picture
        End If
        showColon = Not showColon
End Sub
```

```
Sub UpdateCalendar ()
    t = Now
    d = Day(t)
    LDay.Caption = Format$(d)
    LDayName.Caption = Format$(t, "dddd")
    LMonth.Caption = UCase$(Format$(t, "mmm"))
End Sub
```

Here are two general-purpose subroutines for drawing a bevel around a control, which I use to draw the beveled edges around the digital clock display:

```
Sub DrawBevel (frame As Control)
    bevelWidth = 2

    DrawBevelLine frame, 0, bevelWidth, QBColor(8)
    DrawBevelLine frame, 1, bevelWidth, QBColor(15)
    DrawBevelLine frame, 2, bevelWidth, QBColor(8)
    DrawBevelLine frame, 3, bevelWidth, QBColor(15)
End Sub
```

```
Sub DrawBevelLine (frame As Control, side, wid, color)
    '
    ' This procedure draws a beveled line inside a control.
    ' Side has the following meaning:
    '
```

```
'    side    Meaning
'    ----    -------
'     0      Left side of control
'     1      Right side of control
'     2      Top side of control
'     3      Bottom side of control
'
Dim x1, y1, x2, y2 As Integer

rightX = frame.ScaleWidth - 1
bottomY = frame.ScaleHeight - 1

Select Case side
    Case 0                      'Left side
        x1 = 0: dx1 = 1
        x2 = 0: dx2 = 1
        y1 = 0: dy1 = 1
        y2 = bottomY + 1: dy2 = -1

    Case 1                      'Right side
        x1 = rightX: dx1 = -1
        x2 = x1: dx2 = dx1
        y1 = 0: dy1 = 1
        y2 = bottomY + 1: dy2 = -1

    Case 2                      'Top side
        x1 = 0: dx1 = 1
        x2 = rightX: dx2 = -1
        y1 = 0: dy1 = 1
        y2 = 0: dy2 = 1

    Case 3                      'Bottom side
        x1 = 1: dx1 = 1
        x2 = rightX + 1: dx2 = -1
        y1 = bottomY: dy1 = -1
        y2 = y1: dy2 = dy1

End Select

For i = 1 To wid
    frame.Line (x1, y1)-(x2, y2), color
    x1 = x1 + dx1
    x2 = x2 + dx2
    y1 = y1 + dy1
    y2 = y2 + dy2
Next i
End Sub
```

Chapter 15

Featuring

- Progress Bars
- Drawing Shadows around Controls
- Checking Text Box Input
- Limiting the Numbers of Characters in Text Boxes
- Overtype Mode in Text Boxes
- Password Text Boxes
- Supporting an Edit Menu
- Setting Default and Cancel for 3-D Buttons
- Quickly Clearing a List Box

Toolbox for Controls

Progress Bars

File CTRLTOOL.BAS

Purpose Creates animated progress bars that show the current percentage as both a bar graph and a number.

Many programs display progress bars (like the one in Figure 15.1) while they're doing a lengthy operation. It's actually quite easy to create progress bars, once you know how to do it. You'll find a full explanation below as well as a general-purpose progress bar subroutine you can use in your programs.

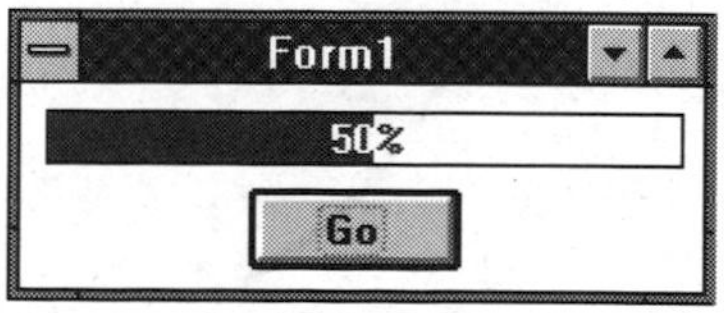

Figure 15.1:

A progress bar

How to Use UpdateProgress

If you want to create a progress bar in your own programs, here's what you have to do:

1. Create a picture box on your form and give it a control name. In the case of Figure 15.1, I created a wide, thin picture box called Picture1.

2. Add the CTRLTOOL.BAS file to your project. You use the Add File... menu item from the File menu to select a file to add.

3. Make a call to UpdateProgress in your program. You need to supply two parameters to this subroutine: the CtlName of the picture box, and a number between 0 and 100.

Below is a sample program that shows you how to use UpdateProgress. I created a picture box called Picture1 and a command button called Command1 (I changed the Caption on Command1 to Go). When you click on Command1, you'll see an animation of the progress bar. You'll also notice that I changed the ForeColor property of the picture box to blue, which changes the color of both the bar and the text.

```
Sub Command1_Click ()
    Picture1.ForeColor = RGB(0, 0, 255)   ' Use blue progress bar
    For i = 0 To 100 Step 5
        UpdateProgress Picture1, i
    Next i
    Picture1.Cls                          ' Clear when we're done
End Sub
```

How UpdateProgress Works

Visual Basic provides several features that make writing UpdateProgress particularly simple.

First, UpdateProgress sets the AutoRedraw property for the picture box to True. This creates an off-screen drawing image where all your drawing actually takes place. Any changes to this off-screen image are transferred to the screen in only three cases: when Visual Basic has some free time, as part of the Paint method, and when you explicitly call the Refresh method.

By using an off-screen image instead of drawing to the screen, the rest of UpdateProgress becomes much simpler. For one thing, you can erase the image and then draw it from scratch without any screen flicker. If you want to see what

I mean, simply remove the line that sets AutoRedraw to True. For another thing, you don't have to write any code for the picture box's Paint method, since Visual Basic will redraw the picture box using the off-screen image. Erasing the image first also makes it easy to draw the number on top of the progress bar, and to handle cases where the percentage drops, causing the bar to shorten.

After UpdateProgress erases the image, it sets ScaleWidth to 100. This allows you to draw a bar with the correct proportions without doing any calculations. Since the variable *percent* can range from 0 to 100, you simply draw the bar from 0 to *percent*.

Next, UpdateProgress changes DrawMode to 10, which is Not Xor Pen. In Chapter 7, I mentioned that this mode allows you to draw erasable lines on top of a white background (you use mode 7 for a black background). Drawing a box over text in this mode "inverts" the text, which gives you the effect shown in Figure 15.1.

The next group of lines displays the current percentage as a number, centered in the picture box. Once you've drawn the text, you can then draw the bar on top of this text. The Line command is quite simple because UpdateProgress already set up the coordinates so 0 is at the left end and 100 is at the right end of the picture box.

Finally, the last line calls the Refresh method of the picture box, which forces Visual Basic to copy the new image to the screen right now. Without this method, you may not see your progress bar updated until much later.

There is one other small detail about UpdateProgress I'd like to mention. You'll notice I defined the argument *percent* to be ByVal. Without ByVal in front of *percent,* you would only be allowed to pass numbers of type Single to UpdateProgress. ByVal allows you to pass *any* number (Integer, Single, etc., as well as properties). It's a good idea to use ByVal in general-purpose subroutines so you have the freedom to pass any type of number to your subroutine.

The Code

Here is the subroutine contained in CTRLTOOL.BAS. This is all the code you'll need to use progress bars in your programs (you'll find it on the disk at the back of this book).

```
Sub UpdateProgress (pb As Control, ByVal percent)
    Dim num$                          ' Used to hold percent string

    If Not pb.AutoRedraw Then   ' Do we have off-screen image?
```

```
        pb.AutoRedraw = -1        ' No, set one up.
    End If

    pb.Cls                        ' Clear off-screen image
    pb.ScaleWidth = 100           ' Set for percentage
    pb.DrawMode = 10              ' Set for erasable drawing

    '
    ' Display the percentage, centered in the picture
    ' box.
    '
    num$ = Format$(percent, "##0") + "%"
    pb.CurrentX = 50 - pb.TextWidth(num$) / 2
    pb.CurrentY = (pb.ScaleHeight - pb.TextHeight(num$)) / 2
    pb.Print num$                 ' Display percentage

    '
    ' Draw box over the percentage.
    '
    pb.Line (0, 0)-(percent, pb.ScaleHeight), , BF
    pb.Refresh                    ' Show changes on screen
End Sub
```

Drawing Shadows around Controls

File CTRLTOOL.BAS

Purpose Draws a drop shadow around any control on your form.

Have you ever wanted your controls to have drop shadows drawn around them, like the shadow around the text box in Figure 15.2? This is very easy to do, requiring only a few lines of code.

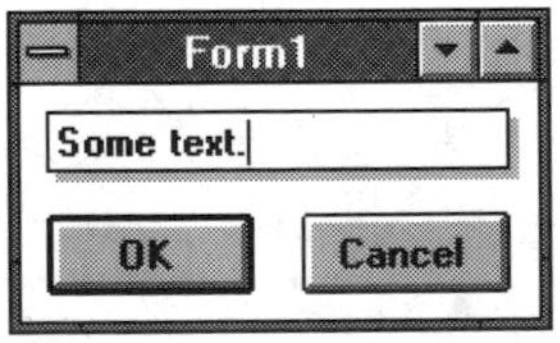

Figure 15.2:

The text box in this figure has a drop shadow drawn around it.

Let's say you have a text box called Text1 on your form, and you want to draw a drop shadow around your text box. How do you do it? Anything you draw on a form will be drawn behind all the controls on your form, so you can draw the shadow by drawing a gray rectangle behind your control. I've put together a subroutine, called Shadow, that you can put into any module, and it does all the work of drawing shadows around controls.

To use this subroutine, simply place a call to it in your form's Form_Paint event handler, with two parameters: the name of your form and the name of your control. For example, if you have a form called Form1 with a control called Text1, you write

```
Sub Form_Paint ()
    Shadow Form1, Text1
End Sub
```

I've included both the form and the control as parameters so you can use this subroutine from any form. This allows you to put Shadow into a general-purpose module you can simply add, without modification, to any form. This subroutine is also included in the CTRLTOOL.BAS module included on the disk that comes with this book.

By the way, you can change the color and width of the shadow by changing the *color* and *shWidth* constants at the start of Shadow.

The Code

Here's the subroutine that you can add to any module, or simply include the CTRLTOOL.BAS module:

```
Sub Shadow (f As Form, c As Control)
    '
    ' This subroutine draws a gray shadow below and to the
    ' right of a control. This subroutine must be in
    ' your form.
    '
    Const color = &HC0C0C0       ' Color of the shadow
    Const shWidth = 3            ' Width of the shadow
    Dim oldWidth As Integer      ' Saves old DrawWidth
    Dim oldScale As Integer      ' Saves old ScaleMode

    oldWidth = f.DrawWidth       ' Remember current DrawWidth
```

```
    oldScale = f.ScaleMode        ' Remember current ScaleMode

    f.ScaleMode = 3               ' Set to Pixel scaling
    f.DrawWidth = 1               ' 1-pixel-wide lines
    '
    ' Draws the shadow around the control by drawing a gray
    ' box behind the control that's offset right and down.
    '
    f.Line (c.Left + shWidth, c.Top + shWidth)-Step(c.Width - 1,
➤   c.Height - 1), color, BF

    f.DrawWidth = oldWidth        ' Restore old DrawWidth
    f.ScaleMode = oldScale        ' Restore old ScaleMode
End Sub
```

Checking Text Box Input

File CTRLTOOL.BAS

Purpose Ensures that you can only type valid numbers or strings into a text box. This section includes subroutines that allow you to limit the input to simple floating-point numbers.

There are a number of cases where you'll want to be able to control what someone can type into your programs. For example, if you have a text box that should only accept numbers, you'll want to make sure someone can't type letters into it.

In this section I'll give you an idea of how to control what someone can type into a text box. I'll describe the techniques and show a few simple examples, but I won't provide any general-purpose subroutines since there are many possible types of input checking. (There are some commercial custom controls that provide very sophisticated input checking and formatting.)

Discarding Characters

The simplest type of input field is a numeric-only input field that accepts only integers. All you have to do is to throw out any characters that aren't numbers. But how do you do this? By using the KeyPress event handler.

Whenever you press a key that will be inserted into a text box, Visual Basic calls the KeyPress event handler *before* actually inserting the character into the text box. This event handler has a parameter, called KeyAscii, that contains the character code for this character. You can keep Visual Basic from inserting this character into a text box by setting KeyAscii = 0.

Here is a version of KeyPress for a text box called Text1 that only accepts the digits 0 through 9:

```
Sub Text1_KeyPress (KeyAscii As Integer)
    If KeyAscii < Asc(" ") Then      ' Is this Control char?
        Exit Sub                     ' Yes, let it pass
    End If

    If KeyAscii < Asc("0") Or KeyAscii > Asc("9") Then
        KeyAscii = 0                         ' Discard character
    End If
End Sub
```

Now the text box will accept any number of digits, but it won't accept any other characters.

There is a bit of extra code in the KeyPress event handler that is very important: Any keys with a KeyAscii less than Asc(" "), which has a numeric value of 32, are control keys, such as the Backspace key. If you don't keep these keystrokes, you won't be able to use Backspace to delete characters from your text box. KeyPress first checks to see if the characters are control characters, and if so, it simply exits.

Limitations of Using KeyPress

There is one problem with using the KeyPress event handler that isn't easy to get around. Even though KeyPress gives you complete control over keys you type, it doesn't give you control over the Paste (Shift+Ins) keyboard combination supported by all text boxes. With the previous example, you can insert *any* text into the text box by copying the text from another text box, then pasting it in. The KeyPress event handler won't be called for any text you paste.

The easiest way to handle this situation, although perhaps not the best way, is to disable the Shift+Ins key combination, which you can do with the following code in KeyDown:

```
Sub Text1_KeyDown (KeyCode As Integer, Shift As Integer)
    '
    ' Disable the Shift+Ins keyboard combination for Text1.
    '
    If KeyCode = 45 And (Shift And 1) = 1 Then
```

```
        KeyCode = 0
    End If
End Sub
```

This code looks for the Shift+Ins key combination. The KeyCode for the Ins key is 45 (note that unlike KeyAscii, KeyCode refers to the actual key on your keyboard rather than to the character). The Shift parameter contains information on which Shift keys are down (you can have, for example, both the Control key and the Shift key down at the same time). Checking to see if Shift And 1 is equal to 1 checks to see if the regular Shift keys are down.

Checking Simple Floating-Point Numbers

Ensuring that the number in a text box is valid takes more work than simply ensuring that only digits can be entered. For example, let's say you want a numeric field where you can type in only valid floating-point numbers. In this case, you need to allow the decimal point as well as digits, but only one decimal point. You also need to support the minus sign and the E notation for large numbers. How do you do this without knowing the exact format for all numbers?

You don't. You really have to know what numbers look like in order to do checking. But to give you an idea of how to go about checking more complex numbers, I've provided a very simple example that allows you to type in a floating-point number with a single minus sign and a single decimal point but no exponent. Below you'll find two general-purpose subroutines called DoKey-Press and CheckPeriod that do all the work of checking a floating-point number, as well as the KeyPress and KeyUp event handlers for a text box called Text1.

First, here are the KeyPress and KeyUp event handlers, along with the Key-Down handler that disables Paste:

```
Sub Text1_KeyDown (KeyCode As Integer, Shift As Integer)
    '
    ' Disable the Shift+Ins keyboard combination for Text1.
    '
    If KeyCode = 45 And (Shift And 1) = 1 Then
        KeyCode = 0
    End If
End Sub
```

```
Sub Text1_KeyPress (KeyAscii As Integer)
    DoKeyPress Text1, KeyAscii
End Sub
```

```
Sub Text1_KeyUp (KeyCode As Integer, Shift As Integer)
    CheckPeriod Text1
End Sub
```

You'll notice that the last two event handlers rely completely on the DoKey-Press and CheckPeriod subroutines, which are shown here:

```
Sub DoKeyPress (t As Control, KeyAscii As Integer)
    '
    ' This subroutine discards any characters that can't be in
    ' a number. Here are the allowed characters:
    '
    '     0..9      All digits are allowed
    '     -         A minus, only if it's the first character
    '     .         Periods are allowed (they're checked in KeyUp)
    '
    If KeyAscii < Asc(" ") Then       ' Is this Control char?
        Exit Sub                      ' Yes, let it pass
    End If

    CheckPeriod t                     ' Remove excess periods

    If KeyAscii >= Asc("0") And KeyAscii <= Asc("9") Then
        ' keep digit
    ElseIf KeyAscii = Asc(".") Then
        ' keep .
    ElseIf KeyAscii = Asc("-") And t.SelStart = 0 Then
        ' Keep - only if first char
    Else
        KeyAscii = 0                  ' Discard all other chars
    End If


    ' This code keeps you from typing any characters in front of
    ' a minus sign.
    '
    If Mid$(t.Text, t.SelStart + t.SelLength + 1, 1) = "-" Then
        KeyAscii = 0                  ' Discard chars before -
    End If
End Sub
```

```
Sub CheckPeriod (t As Control)
    '
    ' This subroutine makes sure your text box never has more
    ' than one period in it.
    '
    Dim i As Integer

    i = InStr(1, t.Text, ".")   ' Look for a period
    If i > 0 And InStr(i + 1, t.Text, ".") > 0 Then
        t.SelStart = t.SelStart - 1
        t.SelLength = 1          ' Select new period
        t.SelText = ""           ' Remove new period
    End If
End Sub
```

Let's take a look at how these subroutines work. Most of DoKeyPress should be clear. It makes sure you can only type digits, the minus sign, and periods. All other characters are discarded. The one new thing you'll notice is that Do-KeyPress allows you to type a minus sign only if the SelStart property is 0, which ensures that the minus sign will only be allowed as the first character. I've also added code to keep you from typing any character in front of a minus sign—the last three lines of DoKeyPress.

The CheckPeriod subroutine does all the work of making sure you don't have more than a single period in your text box. This subroutine is called in two different places. First, it's called in KeyUp to remove the last character if it was a period. But CheckPeriod is also called in DoKeyPress to handle auto-repeat keys. When you hold down a key and it starts to repeat, this generates a number of KeyPress events without generating matching KeyUp events. You'll see the KeyUp event only when you release the period key. If DoKeyPress didn't call CheckPeriod, you'd be able to insert a number of periods into a text box simply by holding down the period key.

Checking Other Types of Inputs

The techniques I've shown here should help you start to write your own input-checking routines. As you've seen, writing a set of input-checking sub-routines takes a lot of work, but if you write them as general-purpose subroutines, such as DoKeyPress and CheckPeriod above, you can use them in any program.

Limiting the Number of Characters in Text Boxes

File CTRLTOOL.BAS

Purpose Places a limit on how many characters you can type into a text box.

If you have input fields, you'll often want to limit the length of text you can type into them. For example, if you have a zip-code field, you might want to limit it to five characters (or ten characters for the five-plus-four zip codes). In this section I'll show you how to do this, using a subroutine called LimitLength.

How to Use LimitLength

The LimitLength subroutine takes just two parameters. The first parameter is the text box that you want to change. The second parameter is the limit on the number of characters you want to allow in the text box.

The only thing you have to ensure is that the text box is actually visible before you call LimitLength. There are two ways to do this: You can call Limit-Length in the Form_Paint event handler, or you can call Show in Form_Load to make the form visible before you call LimitLength. In this example, I use the latter method:

```
Sub Form_Load ()
    Show
    LimitLength Text1, 5
End Sub
```

This code displays the form, then limits the text box called Text1 so it can never have more than five characters in it. If you paste a string longer than this into the text box, Windows will truncate the string to 5 characters (or whatever limit you set).

How It Works

Windows allows you to "send a message" to many of its controls, which is very much like calling a method in Visual Basic. The way you send a message is by using the Windows SendMessage function, which you must first define in the (declarations) section of your form or module. SendMessage also needs a handle to your text box, which you can get using the Windows GetFocus( ) function. You can see all the details in the code shown in the next section.

The Code

These definitions should be in the (declarations) section of your form or module, since they're used by the LimitLength subroutine below.

```
Declare Function GetFocus Lib "User" () As Integer
Declare Function SendMessage Lib "User" (ByVal hWnd As Integer,
➤ ByVal wMsg As Integer, ByVal wParam As Integer, ByVal lParam
➤ As Any) As Long
```

This subroutine can be in any form or module:

```
Sub LimitLength (c As Control, size As Integer)
    '
    ' This subroutine sets the maximum number of characters that
    ' a text box can contain.
    '
    Const WM_USER = &H400              ' The base message number
    Const EM_LIMITTEXT = WM_USER + 21 ' Message to limit length

    c.SetFocus
    i& = SendMessage(GetFocus(), EM_LIMITTEXT, size, O&)
End Sub
```

Overtype Mode in Text Boxes

Purpose Allows you to change a text box so it will work in overtype mode rather than insert mode, which is the default.

In this section I'll show you how to change the way typing characters in a text box works. Normally whenever you type a character, Windows inserts it between two existing characters. But you can easily change this so Windows will replace the character after the insertion point, rather than inserting your new character.

Add the following code to your KeyPress event handler for each text box that you want to support overtype mode:

```
If Text1.SelLength = 0 and KeyAscii >= 32 Then
    Text1.SelLength = 1
End If
```

You should have this code at the end of your KeyPress subroutine in case you do some other type of input checking on characters you type, in which case you might be setting KeyAscii to 0. This code works by selecting the character after the insertion point before Visual Basic actually inserts the character into your text box. In other words, by selecting the character after the insertion point, the character you typed will replace that character.

You need to make sure you change the selection length only if no characters are selected (hence If Text1.SelLength = 0). You also need to make sure you don't select a character if KeyAscii is less than 32. Such character codes are used for control characters, like the Backspace key, which erases characters.

An Example

Here is a simple example of using this technique along with the techniques described previously for limiting the characters you can type to numbers only. The version of KeyPress that follows provides a numeric-input field that allows you to type only digits, and it also supports overtype mode:

```
Sub Text1_KeyPress (KeyAscii As Integer)
    If KeyAscii < 32 Then          ' Is this Control char?
        Exit Sub                   ' Yes, let it pass
    End If

    '
    ' Only allow digits in this text box.
    '
    If KeyAscii < Asc("0") Or KeyAscii > Asc("9") Then
        KeyAscii = 0               ' Discard character
    End if

    '
    ' Use overtype mode to write over the character after the
    ' insertion point.
```

```
        '
        If Text1.SelLength = 0 and KeyAscii >= 32 Then
            Text1.SelLength = 1
        End If
    End Sub
```

Password Text Boxes

File CTRLTOOL.BAS

Purpose Builds a password text box that allows you to type in a password without the password appearing on the screen. Instead you'll see the • character.

When you want a text field to contain a password, you probably won't want the password itself to be visible. After all, if it were visible, someone looking over your shoulder could read your password as you typed it in. You probably want your program to show some character, such as •, for each character in the password field, and to keep all the characters you've really typed hidden. All you have to do is to call a subroutine ToPassword, which will change any text box to a password input box. Figure 15.3 shows what a password field looks like in operation.

Figure 15.3:

A password input field used in a log-in dialog box. The actual text in the box is Hello, but all you see are bullets.

How to Use Password Fields

Using the subroutine presented here is really easy. All you have to do is to call the subroutine and pass the name of your text box as a parameter. For example, if you create a new form and add a text box called Text1, you write this:

```
ToPassword Text1
```

The only question is this: Where do you make this call? As it turns out, the control must be visible on the screen before you can call ToPassword, for reasons I'll explain below. Usually the best place to call ToPassword is in your Form_Load event handler, since this will be called whenever your form is loaded into memory. On the other hand, you'll want to make sure your control is visible before you call it.

The solution I've developed for this problem uses the Form_Paint event handler, since it won't be called until your form actually becomes visible. I've also created a *static* constant in Form_Paint, which is a variable that will keep its value between calls to Form_Paint, but it will be 0 whenever the form is first loaded into memory. By setting this variable to −1 after you've called To-Password, you can make sure you call ToPassword only once.

Here's the code in Form_Paint to call ToPassword:

```
Sub Form_Paint ()
    Static isPassword As Integer

    If Not isPassword Then      ' Have we called ToPassword?
        ToPassword Text1        ' No, call it now
        isPassword = -1         ' Remember that we've done this
    End If
End Sub
```

By the way, the text box will be drawn normally, with the text visible, before Form_Paint is called. This means that any text in the text box will be visible for a brief moment before Form_Paint converts the text box to a password field. As a result, you should set the Text property to an empty string in Form_Load:

```
Sub Form_Load ()
    Text1.Text = ""
End Sub
```

How It Works

The ToPassword function internally uses a total of four Windows functions to do all the work. Windows provides a style of text box that provides a password input field, so the trick is to change the style of a Visual Basic text box so it will be a password input field. This requires using four Windows functions.

Most of the functions ToPassword uses require a window handle for the text box. Here's how ToPassword gets this window handle: First, ToPassword sets the focus to your text box using the SetFocus method. Then it calls the function GetFocus. GetFocus returns the window handle of the control that has the focus, so the variable *hWnd* now contains the window handle for your text box.

Next are three lines of magic. The GetWindowLong function returns a long word from the information that goes along with each control. In this case, the GWL_STYLE parameter asks Windows for the style information, which is information that determines how a control will behave. The ToPassword subroutine then sets the ES_PASSWORD bit in this style number, which will tell the text box to act as a password box rather than as a normal text box. Then, the call to SetWindowLong puts this new style number back into the text box, which changes the way the text box works.

Finally, ToPassword sets the font and character to use in the password field. I've chosen to use the • character (a bullet), which is available in the Symbol font, so the first line sets the FontName property to Symbol. The second line uses the Windows SendMessage function to set the character that your password text box will use. The number 183 is the number for the bullet character. If you want to use a different character, such as * in the regular font, you can use Asc("*") to obtain the number of the character.

The Code

Here are the definitions that must appear in the (declarations) section of your module (or form):

```
Declare Function GetFocus Lib "User" () As Integer
Declare Function GetWindowLong Lib "User" (ByVal hWnd As
➤ Integer, ByVal nOffset As Integer) As Long

Declare Function SetWindowLong Lib "User" (ByVal hWnd As
➤ Integer, ByVal nOffset As Integer, ByVal LParamNew As Long)
➤ As Long

Declare Function SendMessage Lib "User" (ByVal hWnd As Integer,
➤ ByVal wMsg As Integer, ByVal wParam As Integer, ByVal
➤ lParam As Any) As Long
```

This is the subroutine that does the actual work:

```
Sub ToPassword (c As Control)
    '
    ' Changes a text box to a password input field, which
    ' will show a * for each character rather than the
```

```
' actual character.
'
Const ES_PASSWORD = &H20      ' The Password type flag
Const GWL_STYLE = -16         ' Where to get window type
Const WM_USER = &H400         ' Offset for all EM messages
Const EM_SETPASSWORDCHAR = WM_USER + 28

Dim hWnd As Integer           ' Handle to the control
Dim flags As Long             ' Control flags

c.SetFocus                    ' Set focus to this control
hWnd = GetFocus()             ' Get its window handle
'
' Now turn on the ES_PASSWORD flag in the Windows style
'
flags = GetWindowLong(hWnd, GWL_STYLE)
flags = flags Or ES_PASSWORD
flags = SetWindowLong(hWnd, GWL_STYLE, flags)

'
' Set the character to use in the text box to *.
'
c.FontName = "Symbol"         ' Bullet in Symbol font
flags = SendMessage(hWnd, EM_SETPASSWORDCHAR, 183, 0&)
End Sub
```

Supporting an Edit Menu

Purpose Allows you to support the Undo, Cut, Copy, and Paste menu items in a text box.

All Windows programs that use text boxes of any kind should support the standard Edit menu, with the items Undo, Cut, Copy, and Paste. Fortunately, this is extremely easy to do in Visual Basic.

Let's assume you have an Edit menu that's defined as follows:

Caption	CtlName	Accelerator
&Edit	menEdit	
&Undo	miUndo	Ctrl+Z
—	miEditLine1	

Caption	CtlName	Accelerator
Cu&t	miCut	Ctrl+X
&Copy	miCopy	Ctrl+C
&Paste	miPaste	Ctrl+V

To support these menu items, add the following event handlers:

```
Sub miUndo_Click ()
    SendKeys "%{BACKSPACE}"      ' Send Alt+Backspace
End Sub
```

```
Sub miCut_Click ()
    SendKeys "+{DELETE}"         ' Send Shift+Del
    recChanged = -1             ' Record has changed
End Sub
```

```
Sub miCopy_Click ()
    SendKeys "^{INSERT}"         ' Send Ctrl+Ins
End Sub
```

```
Sub miPaste_Click ()
    SendKeys "+{INSERT}"         ' Send Shift+Ins
    recChanged = -1            ' Mark record as changed
End Sub
```

How It Works

Here's how these subroutines work. Visual Basic has a command called SendKeys that sends keystrokes to whatever control has the current keyboard focus. To allow you to send special keys, such as Alt+Backspace, SendKeys uses some special characters, such as % for Alt, + for Shift, and ^ for Control. Also, any characters between braces, such as {BACKSPACE}, refer to a key, and Send-Keys will send this keystroke rather than the text inside the braces.

All text boxes support these keyboard combinations:

Undo	Alt+Backspace
Cut	Shift+Del
Copy	Ctrl+Ins
Paste	Shift+Ins

All the code has to do is send these keystrokes to the edit boxes.

Table 15.1 lists the special symbols you can use in the SendKeys strings. You'll notice these symbols provide both keys and actions.

	Key	String
Table 15.1:	↑	{UP}
	↓	{DOWN}
Special SendKeys Strings	←	{LEFT}
	→	{RIGHT}
	Home	{HOME}
	End	{END}
	PgUp	{PGUP}
	PgDn	{PGDN}
	Break	{BREAK}
	PrtScr	{PRTSC}
	Num Lock	{NUMLOCK}
	Scroll Lock	{SCROLLLOCK}
	Caps Lock	{CAPSLOCK}
	Help	{HELP}
	Clear	{CLEAR}
	Tab	{TAB}
	Enter	{ENTER} or ~
	Backspace	{BACKSPACE} or {BS}
	Del	{DELETE} or {DEL}

Table 15.1:	Key	String
Special SendKeys Strings (continued)	Ins	{INSERT}
	Esc	{ESCAPE} or {ESC}
	F1...F16	{F1}...{F16}
	Shift	+
	Ctrl	^
	Alt	%

Keyboard Shortcuts

Incidentally, you'll notice I've used the Ctrl+Z, Ctrl+X, Ctrl+C, and Ctrl+V keyboard shortcuts for the Undo, Cut, Copy, and Paste menu items. These are the new standard shortcuts that Microsoft suggests all programs use for these items; Table 15.2 lists all of them. This list has two parts: The recommended shortcuts should be used for all programs; the suggested shortcuts are keys that programs should support if they have a similar function.

Table 15.2:	**Recommended Ctrl+*letter* Shortcuts**	
Keyboard Shortcut Standards	**Function**	**Key**
	Undo	Ctrl+Z
	Cut	Ctrl+X
	Copy	Ctrl+C
	Paste	Ctrl+V
	Suggested Ctrl+*letter* Shortcuts	
	Function	**Key**
	New	Ctrl+N
	Open	Ctrl+O
	Print	Ctrl+P
	Save	Ctrl+S

	Suggested Ctrl+*letter* Shortcuts	
Table 15.2:	**Function**	**Key**
Keyboard Shortcut Standards (continued)	Bold	Ctrl+B
	Italic	Ctrl+I
	Underline	Ctrl+U
	Double underline	Ctrl+D
	Small caps	Ctrl+K
	Word-by-word underline	Ctrl+W
	Remove char formatting	Ctrl+spacebar

Setting Default and Cancel for 3-D Buttons

Purpose Provides the Cancel and Default properties for the 3-D buttons or other custom controls that lack the Cancel and Default properties.

There are a number of small quirks in Visual Basic, and one of them has to do with buttons and the Default and Cancel properties. These properties allow you to determine which button will be "clicked" when you press the Enter or Escape key, which is really useful for building dialog boxes in Visual Basic. When you set a button's Default property to True, it will receive a Click event when you press the Enter key (as long as another button doesn't have the keyboard focus). When you set a button's Cancel property to True, it will receive a Click event when you press the Escape key (no matter what control has the focus).

The problem is that not all buttons have a Default or Cancel property. In particular, any buttons that are supplied by an add-in (also known as a custom control, and provided by a file with the VBX extension) will *not* have the Default and Cancel properties. Only the standard command buttons have these properties.

But what if you want, for example, a 3-D button to have the Cancel or Default property set? What do you do? There is a very simple workaround you can use in all your programs. The idea is this: You create a standard command button that has the Cancel or Default property set, but you place it outside the visible part of your form.

Let's look at an example of how this works. Figure 15.4 shows a simple test program that has two 3-D buttons, each with an icon inside. (These buttons are supplied by the SHERDN01.VBX file on the disk accompanying this book.) The goal is to have the Open button respond to the Enter key, and the Cancel button respond to the Escape key.

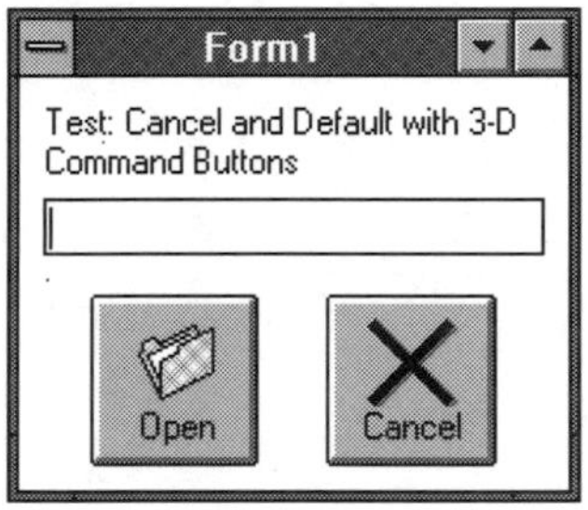

Figure 15.4:

The form looks like this when it's running. The two standard command buttons aren't visible because they're off the right side of the screen.

Here are the steps you can follow to solve this problem (see Figure 15.5 for control names and properties):

1. Create your form with all the controls you want. In this example, these include a label, a text box, and two 3-D buttons.

2. Enlarge your form either to the right or the bottom so you'll have room for two buttons. You'll reduce your form later to hide these buttons.

3. Create two standard command buttons, called cmdoOpen and cmdoClose in this example.

4. Set the Default property of cmdoOpen to True and set the TabStop property to False (to keep this button from ever receiving the keyboard focus). Set the Cancel property of cmdoCancel to True and set TabStop to False.

5. Add the following code to each of these controls (I've assumed your two 3-D buttons have the control names cmdOpen and cmdClose):

```
Sub cmdoOpen_Click ()
    cmdOpen_Click
End Sub
```

```
Sub cmdoCancel_Click ()
    cmdCancel_Click
End Sub
```

6. Reduce the size of your form so the two standard command buttons won't be visible again (your program will look like Figure 15.4).

Figure 15.5:

This form shows the two off-window command buttons, cmdoOpen and cmdoCancel, that will provide the Default and Cancel properties for the two 3-D command buttons called Open and Cancel.

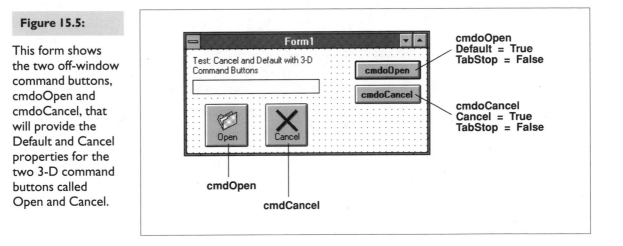

Hiding the Controls on the Left Side

If your form is resizable, hiding the controls off the right side of the window won't work very well, since the controls will appear again as soon as you enlarge the window. Fortunately, you can easily move the controls off the left side of your form as part of the Form_Load process. For the example in the previous section, you could use this code:

```
Sub Form_Load ()
    cmdoOpen.Left = -1000
    cmdoCancel.Left = -1000
End Sub
```

This code moves both of the controls well off the left side of the form to ensure they'll never be visible. You can then place the controls anywhere inside your form at design time, with the knowledge that they won't be visible when your program runs.

Quickly Clearing a List Box

File MHDEM200.VBX or CTRLTOOL.BAS

Purpose Quickly removes all the items from a list box.

The normal method for clearing all the items from a list box, which calls RemoveItem for each item, can be very slow. Fortunately, there are two ways you can fix this problem. You can use the MhTag custom list box on the disk that comes with this book, which allows you to clear all the items in a list box with a single assignment. (The MhTag list box has many other features that make it better than Visual Basic's list box.) Alternatively, you can call the subroutine below, which will clear any list box with a single call (using some Windows functions for speed).

Using RemoveItem, removing a thousand items from a list box on a 25-MHz 386 takes about 6 seconds, whereas using either of the methods described in this section clears the list box in a fraction of a second!

Using MhTag

To create a MhTag list box, you'll need to add the file MHDEM200.VBX file to your project, using the Add File... item from the File menu in Visual Basic.

Once you have an MhTag list box created, you can clear all the items in the list box with this line of code:

```
MhTagBox1.ClearBox = 0
```

Setting the ClearBox property to any number clears all the items in the list box.

Using Windows Functions

The other way to clear a list box is to call a Windows function that can do it. Using the function below, which is in the file CTRLTOOL.BAS, you can remove all the items from a list box called List1 with this line of code:

```
ClearList List1
```

ClearList uses a Windows function called SendMessage that allows you to send a *message* to a control asking it to perform some function. In this case ClearList sends the list box the LB_RESETCONTENT message, which removes all the items from a list box. To use SendMessage, you also need to use the Get-Focus( ) function, which returns a window handle to the control with the current focus. The line that has lb.SetFocus sets the focus to the list box before the call to SendMessage.

Here are the definitions that appear in the (declarations) section of the form or module that contains the ClearList subroutine:

```
Declare Function GetFocus Lib "User" () As Integer
Declare Function SendMessage Lib "User" (ByVal hWnd As Integer,
➤ ByVal wMsg As Integer, ByVal wParam As Integer, ByVal lParam
➤ As Any) As Long
```

Here is the ClearList subroutine:

```
Sub ClearList (lb As Control)
    '
    ' This subroutine very quickly removes all the items
    ' from a list box.
    '
    Const WM_USER = &H400            ' The base message number
    Const LB_RESETCONTENT = WM_USER + 5

    lb.SetFocus                      ' Make this active control
    i& = SendMessage(GetFocus(), LB_RESETCONTENT, 0, 0&)
End Sub
```

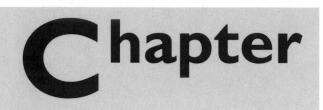

Chapter 16

Featuring

Adding Lines to a Form

Centering Forms

Sizing Forms

Resizing a Form's Controls

Showing a Start-up Screen

Toolbox for Forms

Adding Lines to a Form

Purpose Adds lines to your form in design mode. This is useful for adding lines between groups of controls in your programs.

There is a very simple trick you can use to add vertical or horizontal lines to any form while you're designing it, without having to write a Line command that draws the line. Here's how it works:

1. Create a new picture box, and set its height (or width) to the height (or width) you want your line to be. For example, you could set it to 30 twips to have a line 2 pixels high on a VGA screen.

2. Select the BackColor property, then click on the button with three dots (...) on the Properties bar to display the color palette. Select the color you want your line to be (usually black or gray).

3. Select the BorderStyle property and set it to 0 – None.

You will now have a line in your form that you can move around at design time so it will be exactly where you want it. See Figure 16.1 for an example of how this works. The first image shows what the picture box looks like when you create it. The next image shows the picture box with a BackColor of light gray. The last image shows the picture box with BorderStyle set to 0.

Figure 16.1:

The line in three stages.

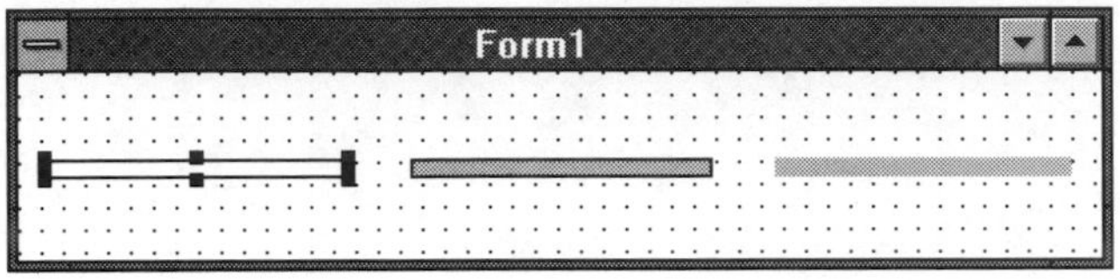

Notes

Adding a number of controls to a form will cause the form to take longer to load into memory. If you find your form takes too long to load, you have two choices: Instead of using a picture box to draw lines, you can use a Line command in your Form_Paint event, or you can display a start-up screen while your form loads (this technique is described later).

Centering Forms

File FORMTOOL.BAS

Purpose Centers a form on the screen.

When you're writing programs that use multiple forms, where some of your forms act as dialog boxes, you might want to center the forms on the screen when they're displayed. This is often better than using the positions you set during design time, since centered forms tend to stand out better. In fact, most commercial programs center dialog boxes on the screen.

Centering a form is really very simple and takes only a single line of code. But I've written a general-purpose subroutine that will do all the work for you. It's much easier to use than typing in the code each time you want to center a form.

How to Use CenterForm

To use CenterForm, all you have to do is make a call to it, then show your form. For example, if you have a form called OpenDialog, you might use

CenterForm like this:

```
CenterForm OpenDialog        ' Center but don't display form
OpenDialog.Show              ' Display the form on screen
```

You don't have to do anything special before you call CenterForm. In other words, you don't have to explicitly load the form using the Load command. If you actually want to use the Load command, you can call CenterForm either before or after the Load command.

It is, however, a good idea to call CenterForm *before* you use Show to display the form, for two reasons. First, if you display the form on the screen before you center it, you'll see your form move on the screen. Calling CenterForm before you call Show does all the moving before you see anything appear on the screen. Second, if you want to show your form as a modal form (using OpenDialog.Show 1), you'll need to center the form before you call Show because Visual Basic won't return to the next command after Show until your new form is removed from the screen.

Notes

- *Center in Resize Method.* If you want your window to always be centered, even when the user changes the size of your form, you can call CenterForm inside your Form_Resize event.

- *Center on Form_Load.* You have two choices about where you can put the code that centers a form: You can call CenterForm before you call the Show method, as described above, or you can put a call to CenterForm in your Form_Load event. This will cause your form to be centered each time it's loaded.

- *Note about CenterForm on Form_Load.* If you put the call to Center-Form in your Form_Load method, and you hide the window using the Hide rather than the Unload method, your form won't be centered automatically the next time it's shown using the Show method.

How It Works

The first two lines (x = and y =) calculate the new left and top values for the form. The number Screen.Width is the width in twips of the screen, and aForm.Width is the width, also in twips, of the form you want to center. The difference of these two numbers divided by 2 is the space you'll want between the left side of the screen and the left side of the form when the form is centered. The Move method then does the work of actually moving the window to this new location.

The Code

Here's the subroutine that centers a form:

```
Sub CenterForm (aForm As Form)
    Dim x, y                        ' New top left for the form

    x = (Screen.Width - aForm.Width) / 2
    y = (Screen.Height - aForm.Height) / 2
    aForm.Move x, y                 ' Change location of the form
End Sub
```

You can place this subroutine in any module or form. I suggest placing it in a module so you can call it from anywhere in your program.

Sizing Forms Using Inside Dimensions

File FORMTOOL.BAS

Purpose Allows you to set the size of the inside of a form.

The only tools Visual Basic provides for changing the size of a form (the Height and Width properties and the Move method) refer to the outside dimensions of a form. If you want to resize a form to have specific inside dimensions, you need to know the size of the borders and the title bar, or you can simply use the ResizeInside subroutine presented here.

How to Use ResizeInside

Using ResizeInside is very simple. Let's say you have a form called Form1 and you want its inside dimensions to be 2880 by 1440 twips (2 inches by 1 inch). You would then make the following call to ResizeInside:

```
ResizeInside Form1, 2880, 1440
```

There are only a couple of things you should be aware of when you use this subroutine:

- ResizeInside changes the ScaleMode of your form to 1 – Twips. If you want to use some other scale mode with your form, you'll need to change it when you're finished resizing the form.

- ResizeInside doesn't change the Top and Left properties of your form: It only changes the Width and Height properties. If you want to center the form, you can call CenterForm, also in FORMTOOL.BAS, *after* you call ResizeInside.

To use this subroutine, you must add the file FORMTOOL.BAS to your project, or type the code shown later into any form or module.

Notes

- *ResizeInside in Form_Load.* A good place to call ResizeInside is in your form's Form_Load event, which allows you to change your form's size before it's shown on the screen.

- *ResizeInside in Form_Resize.* Be careful not to call ResizeInside from within your form's Form_Resize event handler. Doing so can result in an "Out of stack space" message from Visual Basic. The reason this happens is that any code that changes a form's size, which ResizeInside may do, results in Form_Resize being called again.

How It Works

ResizeInside is fairly simple, once you figure out how to write it. The secret behind ResizeInside is to calculate the size of the borders in both the X and Y directions. In the X direction, the borders will be the resize borders (or just lines if you've set the BorderStyle to Fixed). In the Y direction, the borders also include the height of the title bar, if you have one. In Figure 16.2, there are resize borders and a title bar with the caption Form1.

Figure 16.2:

The Height and Width properties refer to the outside dimensions of a form, in twips, while ScaleHeight and ScaleWidth refer to the inside dimensions when ScaleMode = 1 – Twips.

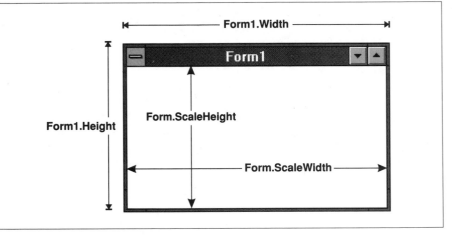

The way I calculate the size of the borders is by using some knowledge about how the Height, Width, ScaleHeight, and ScaleWidth properties work. You can see in Figure 16.2 that the Height and Width properties of a form *always* measure the outside dimensions of a form, in twips. The ScaleHeight and ScaleWidth properties, on the other hand, measure the inside dimensions of the form, but not necessarily in twips. So in ResizeInside the first thing I do is set ScaleMode = 1, which sets the units for ScaleHeight and ScaleWidth to twips.

Then subtracting ScaleHeight from Height gives the height of the Y borders in twips, including both the resize borders and the title bar. Similarly, subtracting ScaleWidth from Width gives the width, in twips, of both resize borders.

Finally, I use the Move method of the form to change both the width and height of a form at the same time. If you were to set Width and Height separately, rather than using Move, you'd see your form change in size twice, once for each dimension. Using Move results in a snappier response on the screen because it changes both dimensions of a form at once.

By the way, I'm using the ByVal keyword in front of the *w* and *h* parameters so you can pass properties in calls to ResizeInside. Normally Visual Basic passes arguments by reference, which means you can change the values in variables you pass to a subroutine from inside that subroutine. But you can't change properties this way, so you have to use the ByVal keyword. ByVal tells Visual

Basic to send a copy of the value to the subroutine, which works with properties, as well as any other value.

The Code

Here is the code you'll find in FORMTOOL.BAS. You can also type it into any module or form.

```
Sub ResizeInside (f As Form, ByVal w As Integer, ByVal h As
➤ Integer)
    '
    ' This subroutine changes the size of a form so the
    ' inside of the form will be w twips wide, and h twips
    ' high.
    '
    '    Note: Sets ScaleMode = 1
    '
    Dim yBorders                        ' Size of vertical borders
    Dim xBorders                        ' Size of horizontal borders
    Dim x, y                            ' Location of the form

    f.ScaleMode = 1                     ' Switch to twips
    xBorders = f.Width - f.ScaleWidth
    yBorders = f.Height - f.ScaleHeight
    x = f.Left                          ' Get location of form
    y = f.Top

    f.Move x, y, w + xBorders, h + yBorders
End Sub
```

Limiting a Form's Size

Purpose You want to limit how small a form can be resized, or you want to fix the width of a form but allow the height to change.

I have a program I've been working on that has a window with a fixed width, but I want to be able to change its height by dragging on the size borders. The problem is that Visual Basic doesn't provide any way to put limits (either upper or lower) on the size of a form. So how do you do this?

It turns out to be not that difficult, and it doesn't require very much code. It just requires knowing how to do it.

Keeping the Width Constant

Let's first look at how you'd keep the width of a form constant, while letting the height be anything you want. All you have to do is to change the Width property of the form inside the Form_Resize event. For example, if you want a form to always be 4000 twips wide, put the following line into Form_Resize:

```
Sub Form_Resize ()
    Width = 4000                    ' Set width back to 4000 twips
End Sub
```

If you try this, you'll notice that your form's width is always the same, and you can change the height to anything you want.

Setting a Minimum Size for a Form

The next example shows how to set a minimum size for a form. Let's say you want to make sure your form is never smaller than 4000 by 3000 twips, but it can be any size larger than this. The following Form_Resize code does just that:

```
Sub Form_Resize ()
    If Width < 4000 Then Width = 4000
    If Height < 3000 Then Height = 3000
End Sub
```

Try this out and you'll see how it works. You can also set upper limits for the width or height exactly the same way: Just use an If..Then statement with the > operator, rather than the < operator used in this example.

Notes

Visual Basic calls the Form_Resize event *after* Windows changes the size of your form on the screen. This means that you'll see your form change its size twice when you use the methods in this section. Commercial programs, on the other hand, manage to limit the size of a window as you're dragging the new window size. The solution provided here is the best you can do in Visual Basic.

Resizing a Form's Controls

Purpose If you have a resizable form, you may have controls inside the form that you want to move or resize when you change a form's size.

The best way to see how resizing works is with an example. Figure 16.3 shows a small program that has a single text box that takes up most of the window and has two buttons at the bottom of the window. You'll want to change the size of the text box whenever you change the size of this window. You'll also need to move the two buttons so they'll always be near the bottom of the window and nicely centered.

Figure 16.3:

The sample program shown below. The text box will change in size whenever you resize this window, and the two buttons will always be centered at the bottom of this window.

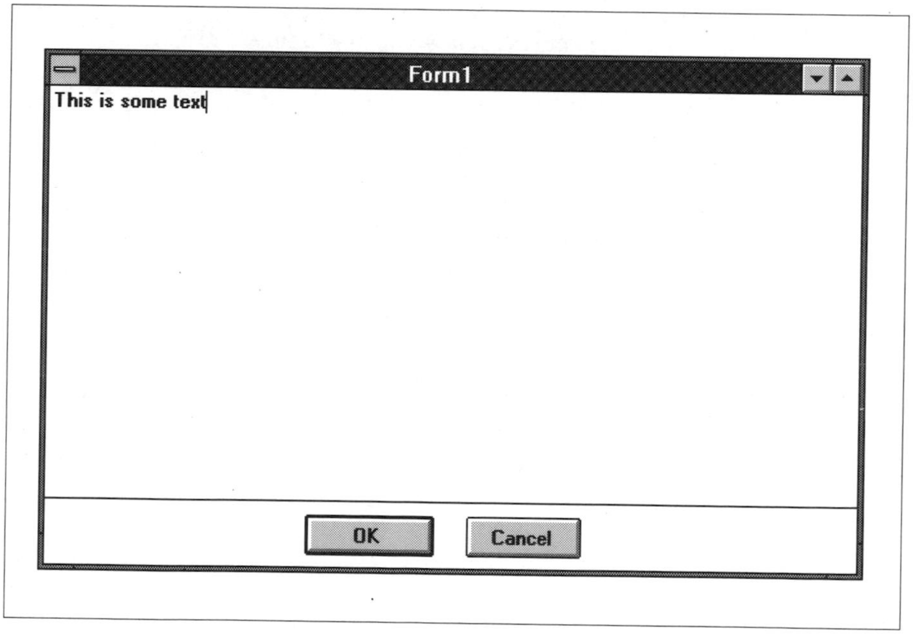

There are two ways you can change the size of a control (or move it): You can either change the properties (Width, Height, Left, and Top) or use the Move command. The Move command is the best command to use if you want to change more than one property, since Move will make all the changes at once. If you change the individual properties, you'll see your control redrawn at the new size or location each time you change a property, whereas Move will change all the values at one time.

Resizing a Text Box

In this example the text box will always be 2 pixels wider than the width of the form. The reason for this is quite simple: Text boxes have a 1-pixel-wide box drawn around them (unless you set BorderStyle to 0 – None), so you have to make the text box wider by 2 pixels if you want the left and right lines to be outside the form. Here is the code that will change the width of a text box to fill the entire form:

```
ScaleMode = 3                    ' Switch to pixel mode
Text1.Left = -1
Text1.Width = ScaleWidth + 2
```

The first line sets the form so the units will be pixels instead of twips. You need to do this to set Left to −1 pixels in the next line, which moves the line on the left side of the text box off the left side of the screen.

NOTE

Some programmers use −15 twips rather than switching to pixel mode, but this won't always work. On VGA (and Super VGA) screens, 1 pixel is always 15 twips wide and high. But on EGA screens, 1 pixel is 20 twips high and 15 twips wide, and on 8514/A screens, a pixel is 12 twips wide and high.

The third line moves the line at the right side of the text box off the right side of the screen.

Changing the text box's height is very much the same, except that you'll want to make the text box a little shorter than the form to make room for the two buttons at the bottom of the screen. Here is the code to do this:

```
Text1.Top = -1
Text1.Height = ScaleHeight + 1 - 30
```

These two lines should be fairly clear. I've written the second line so you can see the individual pieces. The +1 adds 1 to the height because the top line around the text box is off the top of the screen (Top = −1). I've subtracted 30 pixels to leave room at the bottom for the buttons.

When to Resize Controls

Each time you change the size of your form, the form will receive a Form_Resize event. Putting your resizing code into this event handler will then allow your program to correctly resize your controls every time the form's size changes. This event will also be called the first time your program starts.

There is one small problem with sizing your controls only in the Form_Resize event. This event will be called the first time you run your program after all the controls have been drawn on the form, so you'll see all the controls resize after your program starts. The easiest way to get around this, which I'll show in the last section below, is to also resize the controls in Form_Load, which is called before your program draws any of the controls.

Moving Controls

Now let's look at how you would move the two buttons in the window. Here are the commands that move the two buttons, called cmdOK and cmdCancel:

```
cmdOK.Top = Text1.Top + Text1.Height + 8
cmdCancel.Top = cmdCancel.Top
cmdOK.Left = ScaleWidth / 2 - cmdOK.Width - 10
cmdCancel.Left = cmdOK.Left + cmdOK.Width + 20
```

The first two lines move the buttons down so they'll be 8 pixels below the bottom of the text box called Text1. Then the last two lines center these controls, with 20 pixels between the two controls.

Sample Program

The sample program shown here uses all the methods described above, as well as the Move command, to make all the resizing as fast and unobtrusive as possible. You'll notice both Form_Load and Form_Resize call the same subroutine, MoveControls, to actually move the controls. The call in Form_Load resizes and moves all the controls before your window appears.

```
Sub Form_Load ()
    MoveControls
End Sub
```

```
Sub Form_Resize ()
    MoveControls
End Sub
```

Here is the MoveControls subroutine. You'll notice I've used the Move command instead of setting the properties, which is faster and doesn't cause as much screen flicker. I've also written the code so that the controls will be centered vertically in the gap left by the text box.

```
Sub MoveControls ()
    Dim newTop                      ' The new Top for the buttons
    Dim center                      ' Used to position the buttons

    ScaleMode = 3                   ' Switch to pixel mode
    Text1.Move -1, -1, ScaleWidth + 2, ScaleHeight + 1 - 40

    newTop = Text1.Top + Text1.Height
    newTop = newTop + (ScaleHeight - newTop) / 2
    newTop = newTop - cmdOK.Height / 2

    center = ScaleWidth / 2
    cmdOK.Move center - (cmdOK.Width + 10), newTop
    cmdCancel.Move center + 10, newTop
End Sub
```

Showing a Start-up Screen

Purpose Your program takes a long time to load before you see the first form, so you'd like to display a start-up screen while your program loads.

If you have a large Visual Basic program, or even a small one that has a complicated form, you may have noticed that your program takes a long time to load, which makes it seem very slow. Fortunately, there is a trick you can use to make your program *feel* like it's loading faster—you can display a start-up screen while the rest of your program loads into memory.

Using a Start-up Screen

There are several things you'll need to do to create a start-up screen:

1. *Create a Form*. You'll need to create the form you'll display as the start-up screen. This can be anything you want, but it's usually a form without a caption—with MaxButton, MinButton, and Control-Box all set to False, and BorderStyle set to 1 – Fixed Single.

2. *Create a Sub Main*. You'll find instructions for creating a Sub Main below. If you already have a Sub Main, you'll want to add the code below to this subroutine.

3. *Add Code to Sub Main*. You'll find a full description below of the code you'll want to add to Sub Main.

4. *Make Sub Main the Start-up Form*. Select Set Startup Form from the Run menu, then click on Sub Main and press Enter.

Creating a Sub Main

If you don't have a Sub Main already in your project, you'll need to create one, following these steps:

1. Select New Module from the File menu (or you can use an existing module if you have a .BAS module other than your Global.bas module).

2. Click on the View Code button in your Project window to display the Code window for this module.

3. Select New Procedure... from the Code menu.

4. Type Main into the New Procedure dialog box, then press Enter. This will create a subroutine called Main.

You should now see a blank Main subroutine, like this one:

```
Sub Main ()

End Sub
```

Adding a Start-up Screen to Sub Main

Now that you have a start-up form and a Sub Main, you can add the lines of code that show the start-up screen while your program loads. Let's say, for example, that your main form is called MainForm, and your start-up form is called StartupForm. Here is the simplest (but not the best) way to display this start-up screen while your program loads:

```
Sub Main ()
    StartupForm.Show         ' Show start-up form
    StartupForm.Refresh      ' Force everything to draw
    MainForm.Show            ' Show program
    Unload StartupForm       ' Remove start-up form
End Sub
```

The first line displays your start-up screen, but without all of your form being drawn. Your form won't be redrawn completely until all your forms finish loading, unless you explicitly call the Refresh method, which is why I have the second line here. The third line then loads your main form. Finally, when your main form finishes loading, Main unloads the start-up form from memory, since it won't be needed anymore.

The code above works quite well, but there are a few extra touches you can add to make your program even more professional in the way it feels:

```
Sub Main ()
    Screen.MousePointer = 11      ' Set to wait cursor
    CenterForm StartupForm        ' Center start-up screen
    StartupForm.Show              ' Show start-up form
    StartupForm.Refresh           ' Force everything to draw
    MainForm.Show                 ' Show program
    Unload StartupForm            ' Remove start-up form
    Screen.MousePointer = 0       ' Restore mouse pointer
End Sub
```

The first line sets the mouse pointer to a wait cursor (an hourglass) while your program loads into memory. You set it back to its default shape at the end of Sub Main by setting Screen.MousePointer back to 0.

You'll also notice I added a call to CenterForm to center the start-up screen. This is a nice touch, and you'll find the CenterForm subroutine described elsewhere in this chapter (it's also in the file FORMTOOL.BAS on the disk included with this book).

Chapter 17

Featuring

Fast Line Drawing

Fast Ruler Drawing

Drawing Filled Polygons

Adjusting DrawWidth on Printers

Printing Using the Screen
Pixel Mode

Using Twip Scaling with API Calls

Toolbox for Drawing

Fast Line Drawing

Purpose A very fast way to draw lines (it's about six times faster than using Visual Basic's Line command).

There are times you'll find that the Line command is much too slow, such as when you're drawing a complex graph or figure. In such cases, you can use a Windows API function called Polyline. The Polyline command draws a number of lines with a single call. All you have to do is create an array of points, then send these points to Polyline.

To give you an idea of how fast Polyline can be, I wrote two programs, one using Polyline and one using Line −(x, y), to draw a spiral with 3000 points (see Figure 17.1). The Polyline function took approximately 0.5 seconds, while Line took 2.9 seconds, which means using Polyline is about six times faster than using Basic's Line command.

NOTE

The default mapping mode for all Windows API calls inside Visual Basic is the pixel mapping mode. But if you also want to draw on a printer, the twip mapping mode is a better choice. See the section "Using Twip Scaling with API Calls" for some subroutines that will allow you to use Polyline in the twip scaling mode, both on your screen and on your printer.

Figure 17.1:

This is the output you'll see from the Polyline sample program. Drawing this screen with 3000 line segments (which is more than you need) takes less than $1/2$ second.

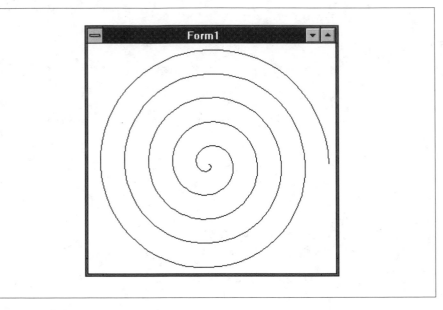

You might also want to use Polyline if you're planning to draw a complex curve with a line style like dashed. In such cases, the Line command won't always produce very good results (see Figure 17.2), whereas Polyline always will.

Figure 17.2:

This figure shows you the difference between using Line and Polyline with the dashed drawing style (DrawStyle = 1). You can see that Line doesn't do a very good job dashing a complex curve, whereas Polyline does.

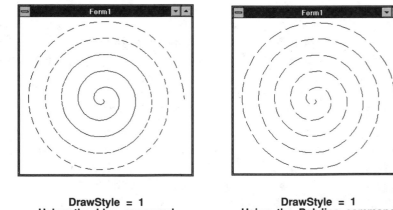

The reason for this is quite simple: When you use a pattern with the Line command, Line always begins at the start of the pattern. This means you'll never get very far into the pattern if you have very short lines (like near the center of the spiral). Visual Basic applies the line pattern individually to each short line you draw, whereas Polyline applies the line style to the entire curve, not just one line segment.

How Polyline Works

The Polyline routine draws a number of connected lines, where the points in the lines are in an array of type POINTAPI. You must have at least two points (one line) to use the Polyline routine. There are three parameters to this API call: hDC, lpPoints, and nCount. Here is what these arguments mean:

Function Polyline (ByVal hDC As Integer, lpPoints As POINTAPI, ByVal ➤ nCount As Integer) As Integer

hDC	A handle to the *device context* of the current form. API calls use the DC for permission to write on a form or picture control. Use the hDC property of a form, a picture box, or Printer.
lpPoints	The points you want to display. This should be the first element of the array you want to send, such as points(0). Note that you can also start with the fifth element, for example, by writing points(4).
nCount	The number of points in the array, which is one more than the number of lines.
returns	0 if no lines were drawn; some other number (Microsoft doesn't say what) if the lines were drawn.

Global Definitions

The following definitions should be in your global module:

```
Type POINTAPI
    X As Integer
    Y As Integer
End Type
```

```
Declare Function Polyline Lib "GDI" (ByVal hDC As Integer,
➤ lpPoints As POINTAPI, ByVal nCount As Integer) As Integer
```

The last two lines should be entered as one line.

Sample Program

Here is a small sample program that uses Polyline to draw a spiral using 300 line segments. The first two lines should be in the (declarations) section of your form.

```
Dim numPoints
Dim points(3000) As POINTAPI


Sub Form_Load ()
    numPoints = 300
    dTheta = 3.14159 / numPoints * 10
    dR = 150 / numPoints
    For i = 0 To numPoints - 1
        points(i).X = i * dR * Cos(dTheta * i) + 150
        points(i).Y = i * dR * Sin(dTheta * i) + 150
    Next i
End Sub


Sub Form_Paint ()
    j% = Polyline(hDC, points(0), numPoints)
End Sub
```

You'll notice that this program "jumps" onto the screen once it finishes running Form_Load. If you minimize and then restore this screen, you'll see that it takes almost no time at all to redraw the screen. Figure 17.1 shows the output from this program.

Drawing on a Printer with Polyline

It's very easy to use Polyline to draw on your printer. Use Printer.hDC as the first argument:

```
Printer.Print " "
j% = Polyline(Printer.hDC, points(0), numPoints)
Printer.EndDoc
```

The Printer.Print command makes sure Visual Basic starts the printing process so the Polyline command will work correctly. Without this Print command, Polyline may not work with all printer drivers.

There is one small problem, however. Since Polyline is working with pixels, and since pixels are much smaller on printers, the image drawn on your printer will be much smaller than the one you see on your screen. As explained next, there is a way you can use twips, rather than pixels, with the Polyline command.

Using Nonpixel Scaling Modes

Polyline, like all other Windows API functions, uses the scaling mode that's being used underneath Visual Basic, which is usually the pixel scaling mode (called MM_TEXT in Windows jargon). You have two choices: Use the pixel scaling mode for all your work (see the section "Printing Using the Screen Pixel Mode"), or use the twip scaling mode (see the section "Using Twip Scaling with API Calls").

Notes

Color	You can change the color of lines drawn with Polyline simply by setting the ForeColor property to whatever color you want. Polyline, as it turns out, uses the current ForeColor when it draws.
Width	The DrawWidth property will change the width of the lines drawn by Polyline.
Dash/Dot	If you want to draw dashed or dotted lines, the DrawStyle property works much better with Polyline than it does with Line. This is because Windows restarts the dashing for each new line drawn with Line, but not with Polyline. Thus, a number of very short lines drawn with Line will be solid rather than dashed. To see how this works, add the line DrawStyle=1 in Form_Paint before the Polyline command. Note: DrawStyle applies only if DrawWidth=1.
Mode	DrawMode has the same effect on Polyline as it does on lines drawn with the Line command.

Fast Ruler Drawing

Files RULER.BAS and APISCALE.BAS (used by RULER.BAS)

Purpose Draws rulers, with inch marks, on the screen. (You can also modify the code to draw rulers with any mark spacing.)

It's not hard to draw a set of rulers, like the ones shown in Figure 17.3, using Visual Basic's Line command. Such a program, however, will be somewhat slow at drawing the ruler. For a full-screen form on my 16-MHz laptop, it takes about 1.5 seconds to draw both rulers. But if you use the Polyline function to draw the lines, you can cut this time to about a quarter of a second, which is nearly instantaneous!

Figure 17.3:

The output of the Ruler sample program. These rulers are drawn almost instantaneously using Polyline to draw the lines. Writing the same program using the Line command takes about five times longer to draw the rulers.

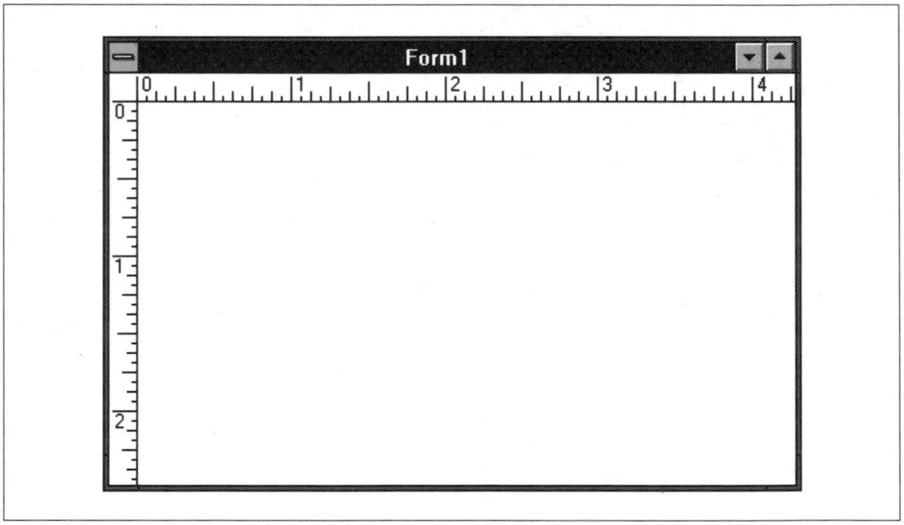

How Ruler Works

The trick to using the Polyline function to draw the ruler is to turn the ruler into a list of lines that are all connected. But instead of defining the entire length of the ruler, we'll define just 1 inch (see Figure 17.4). This 1-inch section, as you'll see shortly, requires a total of 51 points, or three points for each tick mark.

Figure 17.4:

The algorithm stores 51 points— enough to define 1 inch.

Figure 17.5 shows how to define the points that will draw this 1-inch segment of the ruler. You'll notice that you actually need to draw two lines for each tick mark, one going up and the second returning to the baseline, so Polyline doesn't have to lift the pen while drawing the ruler.

Figure 17.5:

To draw the ruler, you'll need to draw all the lines without lifting the pen. You can see how each tick mark consists of two lines: one going up and the second going back to the baseline.

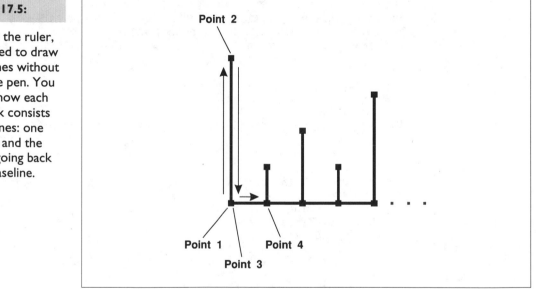

The final trick is to use the SetWindowOrg function in Windows to change the starting point of the coordinate system. This will let you draw a 1-inch section of the ruler anywhere inside a window without changing the points that define the ruler.

The RULER.BAS Module

The ruler-drawing code is actually in a Visual Basic module, called RULER.BAS. By putting this code into a module, you can add a ruler to any program simply by loading RULER.BAS, adding a global definition for POINTAPI to your global module, and calling DrawXRuler or DrawYRuler.

```
Type POINTAPI
    x As Integer
    y As Integer
End Type
```

Here are the definitions and the code in RULER.BAS:

```
Declare Function Polyline Lib "GDI" (ByVal hDC As Integer,
➤ lpPoints As POINTAPI, ByVal nCount As Integer) As Integer
Declare Function SetWindowOrg Lib "GDI" (ByVal hDC As Integer,
➤ ByVal x As Integer, ByVal y As Integer) As Long

Dim xPoints(51) As POINTAPI
Dim yPoints(51) As POINTAPI
Dim numPoints As Integer
Dim validData As Integer                  ' True when we have points
```

```
Sub DrawXRuler (theForm As Form, x As Integer, y As Integer,
➤ wid As Integer)
    If Not validData Then InitRuler
    SetFormToTwips theForm
    For i = 0 To wid
        l& = SetWindowOrg(theForm.hDC, -x, -y - 1440 * i)
        j% = Polyline(theForm.hDC, xPoints(1), numPoints)
    Next i
    l& = SetWindowOrg(theForm.hDC, 0, 0)
    ResetFormScale theForm
End Sub
```

```
Sub DrawYRuler (theForm As Form, x As Integer, y As Integer
➤ wid As Integer)
    If Not validData Then InitRuler
    SetFormToTwips theForm
    For i = 0 To wid
        l& = SetWindowOrg(theForm.hDC, -x, -y - 1440 * i)
        j% = Polyline(theForm.hDC, yPoints(1), numPoints)
```

```
      Next i
      l& = SetWindowOrg(theForm.hDC, 0, 0)
      ResetFormScale theForm
End Sub
```

```
Sub InitRuler ()
    Dim x As Integer, n As Integer

    n = 0                              ' No points yet.
    bot = 250
    For x = 0 To 1440 Step 90
        n = n + 1                      ' Next free point
        xPoints(n).x = x               ' Bottom of this line
        xPoints(n).y = bot
        yPoints(n).x = bot
        yPoints(n).y = x

        tick = 0                       ' Reset tick height
        If x = 1440 Then tick = tick + 1
        If (x Mod 720) = 0 Then tick = tick + 1
        If (x Mod 360) = 0 Then tick = tick + 1
        If (x Mod 180) = 0 Then tick = tick + 1
        If (x Mod 90) = 0 Then tick = tick + 1

        n = n + 1                      ' Next free point
        xPoints(n).x = x               ' End of tick mark
        xPoints(n).y = bot - tick * 45
        yPoints(n).x = xPoints(n).y
        yPoints(n).y = x
        n = n + 1
        xPoints(n).x = x               ' Back at bottom
        xPoints(n).y = bot
        yPoints(n).x = bot
        yPoints(n).y = x
    Next x
    numPoints = n
    validData = -1                     ' Now have points
End Sub
```

Sample Program

This simple program draws the rulers you see in Figure 17.4:

```
Sub Form_Paint ()
    Dim iWidth As Integer, iHeight As Integer
    Dim wid As Integer
    Dim i As Integer
```

```
      Const offset = 250

      iWidth = ScaleWidth / 1440   ' Size of form, in inches
      iHeight = ScaleHeight / 1440
      DrawXRuler Form1, offset, 0, iWidth
      DrawYRuler Form1, 0, offset, iHeight

      FontBold = 0                 ' Don't use bold
      wid = iWidth                 ' Set wid to widest dimension
      if iHeight > wid Then wid = iHeight
      For i = 0 To wid
          CurrentX = offset + i * 1440: CurrentY = 0
          Print i
          CurrentX = 0: CurrentY = offset + i * 1440
          Print i
      Next i
End Sub
```

See Also SetFormScaling: The DrawRuler subroutines use this subroutine, which you'll find in the APISCALE.BAS module, to change the scaling mode for the Polyline function.

Drawing Filled Polygons

Purpose Draws polygons that can be filled with any color.

Visual Basic allows you to create filled boxes and ellipses, but not polygons, such as the one shown in Figure 17.6. For that, you need to use a Windows function called Polygon, which, as you'll see here, is very easy to use.

NOTE

The mapping mode used by default for all API calls inside Visual Basic is the pixel mapping mode. But if you also want to draw on a printer, the twip mapping mode is a better choice. See the section "Using Twip Scaling with API Calls" for some subroutines that will allow you to use Polyline in the twip scaling mode, both on your screen and on your printer.

Figure 17.6:

A filled polygon drawn using the Polygon API call. Notice how the line width, color, and fill color are all set using Visual Basic properties.

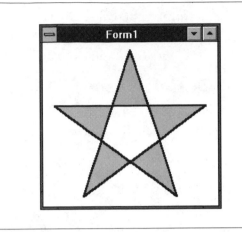

How Polygon Works

The Polygon routine draws a number of connected lines, where the points in the lines are in an array of type POINTAPI. You must have at least three points (two lines, which will be connected automatically by a third, closing line) to use the Polygon routine. There are three parameters to this API call: hDC, lpPoints, and nCount. Here is what these arguments mean:

Function Polygon (ByVal hDC As Integer, lpPoints As POINTAPI,
➤ByVal nCount As Integer) As Integer

hDC	This is a handle to the *device context* of the current form. API calls use the DC for permission to write on a form or picture control. Use the hDC property for a form, a picture box, or Printer.
lpPoints	Pointer to the points you want to display. This should be the first element of the array you want to send. Note that you can also start with the fifth element, for example, by writing points(4).
nCount	The number of points in the array, which is 1 more than the number of lines.

returns   0 if no lines were drawn; some other number (Microsoft doesn't say what) if the lines were drawn.

Global Definitions

Put these definitions for the Polygon function in your global module (the last two lines should be entered as one line):

```
Type POINTAPI
    X As Integer
    Y As Integer
End Type

Declare Function Polygon Lib "GDI" (ByVal hDC As Integer,
➤ pPoints As POINTAPI, ByVal nCount As Integer) As Integer
```

Sample Program

Here is a small sample program that uses Polygon to draw a pentagon with a 2-pixel-wide black border and filled with light gray. The first two lines should be in the (declarations) section of your form.

```
Dim points(10) As POINTAPI
Dim numPoints As Integer


Sub Form_Load ()
    numPoints = 5
    dTheta = 4 * 3.1415926 / 5
    For i = 0 To numPoints
        points(i).X = 100 * Sin(dTheta * i) + 110
        points(i).Y = -100 * Cos(dTheta * i) + 110
    Next i
End Sub


Sub Form_Paint ()
    ForeColor = RGB(0, 0, 0)            ' Draw lines in black
    FillColor = RGB(192, 192, 192)     ' Fill with light gray
    FillStyle = 0                      ' Use a solid fill
    DrawWidth = 2                      ' Set line width to 2
    j% = Polygon(hDC, points(0), numPoints)
End Sub
```

The code in Form_Load calculates the points for the polygon in Figure 17.6. Calculating these points at form load time allows redraws (Form_Paint) to be very fast.

Polygon Fill Modes

You may be wondering why there's a hole inside the star drawn by the sample program. By default, Polygon only fills areas that can be reached from outside the figure by crossing an odd number of lines. Consequently, the branches of the star are filled (you only need to cross one line), and the interior isn't (because you have to cross two lines).

Fortunately, as you can see in Figure 17.7, you can tell Polygon to fill the entire figure, using another Windows call. The SetPolyFillMode function tells Polygon which mode to use. Here are the global definitions:

```
Global Const ALTERNATE = 1
Global Const WINDING = 2

Declare Function SetPolyFillMode Lib "GDI" (ByVal hDC As
➤ Integer, ByVal nPolyFillMode As Integer) As Integer
```

Add the following line just before the Polygon call to change the fill mode:

```
j% = SetPolyFillMode(hDC, WINDING)
```

Figure 17.7:

The effects of setting the polygon fill mode. The ALTERNATE fill mode only fills areas that can be reached by crossing an odd number of lines, while WINDING fills the entire inside of a figure.

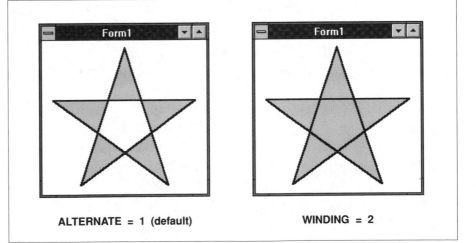

ALTERNATE = 1 (default)   WINDING = 2

Drawing on a Printer with Polygon

It's very easy to use Polygon to draw on your printer when your coordinates are in pixels. Use Printer.hDC as the first argument:

```
Printer.Print " "
j% = Polygon(Printer.hDC, points(0), numPoints)
Printer.EndDoc
```

The Printer.Print command makes sure Visual Basic starts the printing process so the Polygon command will work correctly. Without this Print command, Polygon may not work with all printer drivers.

Using Nonpixel Scaling Modes

Polyline, like all other Windows API functions, uses the scaling mode that's being used underneath Visual Basic, which is usually the pixel scaling mode (called MM_TEXT in Windows jargon). You have two choices: Use the pixel scaling mode for all your work (see the section "Printing Using the Screen Pixel Mode"), or use the twip scaling mode (see the section "Using Twip Scaling with API Calls").

Notes

Fill Color	Polygons will be filled with the color set by the FillColor property. You'll also need to set FillStyle to 0 (solid).
Color	You can change the color of lines drawn with Polygon simply by setting the ForeColor property to whatever color you want. Polygon uses the current ForeColor when it draws on the screen.
Width	DrawWidth will change the width of the lines drawn by Polygon.

Dash/Dot	If you want to draw dashed or dotted lines, the DrawStyle property works much better with Polygon than it does with Line. This is because Windows restarts the dashing for each new line drawn with Line, but not with Polygon. Consequently, a number of very short lines drawn with Line will be solid rather than dashed. Note: DrawStyle applies only if DrawWidth=1.
Mode	DrawMode has the same effect on Polygon as it does on lines drawn with the Line command.

Adjusting DrawWidth on Printers

File APISCALE.BAS

Purpose Allows you to draw lines on your printer that will have the same width as the lines you draw on your screen.

Some of Visual Basic's commands work with the current ScaleMode (such as twips or inches), but other commands don't. The DrawWidth property, for example, is *always* measured in pixels. But there are times when this presents problems: When you're printing on a printer (where pixels are much smaller), you'll discover that the lines are narrower because pixels are smaller than on your screen (see Figure 17.8).

Figure 17.8:

Setting DrawWidth to 4 will result in nice, fat lines on the screen. But on a laser printer, these 4-pixel lines will be much narrower for the same size image, as in the picture on the right.

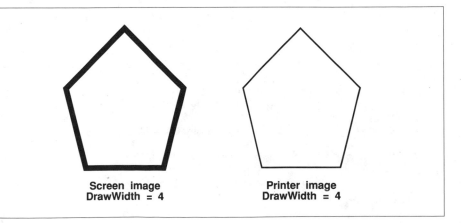

Screen image
DrawWidth = 4

Printer image
DrawWidth = 4

You'll find two functions here to help you solve these problems. The first function returns a number that is the width of a pixel, measured in twips, and the second function returns the ratio of the screen to printer pixel size (which is 3 for a VGA screen and a 300-dpi printer).

NOTE

If you're using the pixel scaling mode, another solution to this problem (which is actually easier) is to use the subroutines described in the section "Printing Using the Screen Pixel Mode."

Calculating the Width of a Pixel

It's very easy to calculate the width of a pixel using just a few commands:

```
ScaleMode = 3          ' Switch to pixel mode
CurrentX = 1000        ' Move 1000 pixels from origin
ScaleMode = 1          ' Switch to twip mode
```

The idea is that you set CurrentX so it's 1000 pixels away from 0. Then when you switch to twip mode (or any other scale mode), CurrentX will have a new value, measured in the new coordinate system. Since it's exactly 1000 pixels away from 0, CurrentX / 1000 will tell you the width of a pixel in twips (or inches if you set ScaleMode to 5).

To turn these lines of code into a general-purpose function, you need to add a few lines that save and restore the ScaleMode so it won't be changed by this function. Here is the finished function that calculates the width of a pixel in twips:

```
Sub UnitsPerPixel (xUnits As Single, yUnits As Single)
    '
    ' Returns the number of scale units (twips, inches, etc.)
    ' per pixel in the X and Y directions.
    '
    ' Usually 15 for a VGA display adapter.
    '
    Dim oldMode

    oldMode = ScaleMode              ' Remember current screen mode
```

```
          ScaleMode = 3              ' Switch to pixel mode
          CurrentX = 1000            ' Move 1000 pixels from origin
          CurrentY = 1000
          ScaleMode = oldMode        ' Switch back to old mode
          xUnits = CurrentX / 1000   ' Size in scale units of
          yUnits = CurrentY / 1000   '    one pixel.
      End Sub
```

You can easily modify this subroutine to return the same information for the printer:

```
Sub PrinterUnitsPerPixel (xUnits As Single, yUnits As Single)
      '
      ' Returns the number of scale units on the current printer
      ' (twips, inches, etc.) per pixel in the X and Y directions.
      '
      ' Usually 4.8 for a 300 dpi printer.
      '
      Dim oldMode

      oldMode = Printer.ScaleMode        ' Remember current screen mode

      Printer.ScaleMode = 3              ' Switch to pixel mode
      Printer.CurrentX = 1000            ' Move 1000 pixels from origin
      Printer.CurrentY = 1000
      Printer.ScaleMode = oldMode        ' Switch back to old mode
      xUnits = Printer.CurrentX / 1000   ' Size in scale units of
      yUnits = Printer.CurrentY / 1000   '    one pixel.
End Sub
```

Table 17.1 shows the values returned by this function for a number of common devices (using the default twip scale mode).

Table 17.1:	Device	xUnits	yUnits
Twips per Pixel on Common Devices	EGA screen	15	20
	VGA screen	15	15
	8514/A screen	12	12
	300-dpi laser printer	4.8	4.8
	2400-dpi phototypesetter	0.6	0.6

Ratio of Screen to Printer Pixel Size

If you want to calculate the ratio of the width of pixels on your display and printer, you can use the following code:

```
Function PrinterToScreenRatio () As Single
    '
    ' Returns a multiplier that reports the number of
    ' printer pixels per screen pixel.
    '
    ' Usually 3.125 for a VGA screen and a 300 dpi printer.
    '
    Dim xUnits As Single        ' Width of pixel on screen
    Dim yUnits As Single        ' Height of pixel on screen
    Dim xUnitsP As Single       ' Width of pixel on printer
    Dim yUnitsP As Single       ' Height of pixel on printer

    UnitsPerPixel xUnits, yUnits
    PrinterUnitsPerPixel xUnitsP, yUnitsP

    PrinterToScreenRatio = xUnits / xUnitsP
End Function
```

Call this once near the start of your program and assign the result to a global (or module) variable. Then calculate the printer DrawWidth by multiplying by this number:

```
Printer.DrawWidth = PrinterToScreenRatio * DrawWidth
```

Printing Using the Screen Pixel Mode

File APISCALE.BAS

Purpose Allows you to draw on your printer using the pixel mapping mode used by your screen. The subroutines given here adjust the size and spacing of your printer pixels to match the size and spacing of your screen pixels.

If you've written programs using the pixel mapping mode on your screen, you've probably discovered that these images appear much smaller when you print them on your printer, and they use thinner lines. For example, if you're using a VGA screen and a 300-dpi laser printer, anything you print will be about a third the size of your screen image. This happens because a VGA screen is defined as having a pixel density of 96 dpi, so a 100-pixel-long line will be about 1 inch on your screen and ⅓ inch long when printed.

You can easily reprogram any Windows printer so it will have larger pixels, which is what the SetPrinterToScreenPixels subroutine does. You can then draw anything you want, both on the screen and on your printer, and it will be the correct size in both cases.

How to Use APISCALE.BAS

To use the subroutines described here, you'll first need to add the API-SCALE.BAS file to your project, using the Add File… item from the File menu. Next, you'll need to call these subroutines at the correct times. There are two subroutines you'll want to use:

SetPrinterToScreenPixels

This subroutine changes the size of pixels on your printer so they will match the size of pixels on your screen. After calling this subroutine, anything you draw in pixel mode will be about the correct size when printed.

ResetPrinterScale

This subroutine restores the pixel size on your printer so the pixels will be as small as possible. Call this subroutine after you're finished drawing in pixel mode on your printer.

How Pixel Scaling Works

SetPrinterToScreenPixels allows you to tell Windows to multiply each pixel coordinate by some scale factor. For example, if your screen has a dot density of 96 dpi and your printer has a density of 300 dpi, you have 3.125 printer pixels per screen pixel. You want to multiply all coordinates by 3.125.

But there's a problem with this. For reasons of speed, Windows uses Integer numbers for coordinates and scaling factors, which means that you can't use the number 3.125. But you can tell Windows to multiply by 3125 and divide by 1000. This is what we'll do.

Let's now take a look at the code to see how it actually does this. The code uses several Windows API calls that you may not be familiar with. The first call,

GetDeviceCaps, is a function that reports various pieces of information on a particular device (like the screen or printer). In this case I use it to get the number of pixels per inch in the X and Y directions for both the screen and the printer. I get this information using a *device context,* which is the hDC property of a form or the Printer object (this is why you must pass a form to the SetPrinter-ToScreenPixels subroutine).

The first three lines (after the Dim statements) calculate the printer-to-screen-pixel ratio, and save this number in *xRatio.* For the example above, *xRatio* would be 3.125 (notice that I've defined *xRatio* as type Single). The next three lines calculate this ratio in the Y direction. It's important to calculate the ratio independently in both directions because some devices have a different number of pixels per inch in the X and Y directions (for example, an EGA screen has 96 dpi in the X direction, but only 72 dpi in the Y direction).

The next line uses the SetMapMode API call to change the mapping mode on the printer. By default, the printer uses a mapping mode of MM_TEXT, which is its internal pixel scale mode. I've changed the mapping mode to MM_ANISOTROPIC, which allows you to define a custom scale.

The next four lines actually define the scale. The first call, SetViewportExt, sets the multiplier for the coordinates. Windows will multiply each coordinate by these numbers (one for X and one for Y), then divide by the numbers in SetWindowExt. I've used a very large, even integer for the multiplier (30,000) so I can keep as much information as possible in the divider. The divider, then, is this number, 30,000, divided by the printer-to-screen-pixel ratio. For the example above, we get 30,000 / 3.125 = 9600.

The Code

Place these lines in the (declarations) area of the module, where you'll put the two subroutines below:

```
Const MM_TEXT = 1           ' Pixel scale mode
Const MM_ANISOTROPIC = 8    ' Custom scale mode

Declare Function SetMapMode Lib "GDI" (ByVal hDC As Integer,
➤ ByVal nMapMode As Integer) As Integer
Declare Function SetViewportExt Lib "GDI" (ByVal hDC As Integer,
➤ ByVal X As Integer, ByVal Y As Integer) As Long
Declare Function SetWindowExt Lib "GDI" (ByVal hDC As Integer,
➤ ByVal X As Integer, ByVal Y As Integer) As Long
```

```
Const LOGPIXELSX = 88        ' Logical pixels/inch in X
Const LOGPIXELSY = 90        ' Logical pixels/inch in Y

Declare Function GetDeviceCaps Lib "GDI" (ByVal hDC%, ByVal
➤ nIndex%) As Integer
```

This subroutine does all the work of changing the size of pixels on your printer:

```
Sub SetPrinterToScreenPixels (f As Form)
    '
    ' This subroutine enlarges the pixels on your printer so
    ' they will match the size of your screen pixels. You
    ' can then use Windows API calls to draw on the printer.
    '
    Dim screenRes As Integer        ' Screen pixels/inch
    Dim printerRes As Integer       ' Printer pixels/inch
    Dim xRatio, yRatio              ' Printer/screen ratio
    Dim extX As Integer             ' X printer/screen ratio
    Dim extY As Integer             ' Y printer/screen ratio

    screenRes = GetDeviceCaps(f.hDC, LOGPIXELSX)
    printerRes = GetDeviceCaps(Printer.hDC, LOGPIXELSX)
    xRatio = printerRes / screenRes

    screenRes = GetDeviceCaps(f.hDC, LOGPIXELSY)
    printerRes = GetDeviceCaps(Printer.hDC, LOGPIXELSY)
    yRatio = printerRes / screenRes

    i% = SetMapMode(Printer.hDC, MM_ANISOTROPIC)

    k& = SetViewportExt(Printer.hDC, 30000, 30000)

    extX = 30000 / xRatio
    extY = 30000 / yRatio
    k& = SetWindowExt(Printer.hDC, extX, extY)
End Sub
```

Call this subroutine to restore the size of your printer's pixels to their normal size:

```
Sub ResetPrinterScale ()
    '
    ' This subroutine restores the printer's scale so each
    ' pixel will be as small as possible.
    '
    i% = SetMapMode(Printer.hDC, MM_TEXT)
End Sub
```

Using Twip Scaling with API Calls

File APISCALE.BAS

Purpose Allows you to use Windows API calls to draw on the screen and/or printer in the twip scaling mode. Also changes DrawWidth so it measures line widths in twips, rather than pixels.

All Windows API calls, such as Polyline, use the scaling mode that underlies Visual Basic, the pixel scaling mode (Visual Basic does all the work of scaling itself, rather than using Windows' scale modes). If you want to use API calls with coordinates in twips, you'll need to use the subroutines in this section.

How to Use APISCALE.BAS

To use the subroutines described here, you'll first need to add the API-SCALE.BAS file to your project, using the Add File... item in the File menu. Next, you'll need to call these subroutines at the correct times. There are two subroutines you'll want to use:

SetPrinterToTwips
SetFormToTwips *formName*

These subroutines change the underlining scale mode of a form or the printer to use twip scaling. After calling these functions, any API calls you make will use twip scaling.

ResetPrinterScale
ResetFormScale *formName*

These subroutines restore the underlining scale mode of a form or the printer to pixel mode, which is what Visual Basic uses (since it does its own scaling). Call this subroutine after you finish drawing with Windows API calls.

NOTE

The SetPrinter... and SetForm... subroutines have one small side effect, which may or may not be desirable: They both change the meaning of the DrawWidth property, which is the width of lines and is normally measured in pixels. After you call SetPrinterToTwips or SetFormToTwips (and before you call one of the reset functions), DrawWidth will measure line widths in *twips*. If you'd like to work with twips and always have both coordinates and line widths measured in twips (for Visual Basic commands as well), you can set ScaleMode to Pixel, then do all your drawing using coordinates measured in twips after calling SetFormToTwips.

How Twip Scaling Works

These subroutines allow you to tell Windows to multiply each pixel coordinate by some scale factor. For a standard VGA screen, which is defined by Windows to be 96 dpi, this scale factor will be 1440 / 96 = 15 (since there are 1440 twips per inch).

These two subroutines each take only five lines of code to do all the work. The first line, SetMapMode, sets the Windows mapping mode (which is similar to Visual Basic's scaling mode)—in this case, to MM_ANISOTROPIC, which means that we can set the scaling to anything we want.

The next two lines of code (which use GetDeviceCaps) calculate 10 times the number of twips per pixel in the X and Y directions. I'm multiplying by 10 to increase the accuracy of the scaling. The actual scaling is done by multiplying the coordinates by 10 and dividing by *extX* or *extY*.

The line SetViewPortExt sets the multiplier for the X and Y parts of the coordinates, and SetWindowExt sets the divider. Windows uses these two numbers, rather than a single number of type Single, in the interest of speed—working with integers is much faster than working with numbers of type Single.

The Code

Place these lines in the (declarations) area of the module, where you'll put the four subroutines below.

```
Const MM_TEXT = 1            ' Pixel scale mode
Const MM_ANISOTROPIC = 8     ' Custom scale mode

Declare Function SetMapMode Lib "GDI" (ByVal hDC As Integer,
➤ ByVal nMapMode As Integer) As Integer
```

```
Declare Function SetViewportExt Lib "GDI" (ByVal hDC As Integer,
➤ ByVal X As Integer, ByVal Y As Integer) As Long
Declare Function SetWindowExt Lib "GDI" (ByVal hDC As Integer,
➤ ByVal X As Integer, ByVal Y As Integer) As Long


Const LOGPIXELSX = 88        ' Logical pixels/inch in X
Const LOGPIXELSY = 90        ' Logical pixels/inch in Y

Declare Function GetDeviceCaps Lib "GDI" (ByVal hDC%, ByVal
➤ nIndex%) As Integer
```

Here are the four subroutines that do all the work:

```
Sub SetFormToTwips (f As Form)
    '
    ' This subroutine sets a form to Twip scaling mode
    ' for all Windows API calls. You'll need to call
    ' ResetPrinterScale before you use any Visual Basic
    ' drawing commands.
    '
    i% = SetMapMode(f.hDC, MM_ANISOTROPIC)
    extX = 14400 / GetDeviceCaps(f.hDC, LOGPIXELSX)
    extY = 14400 / GetDeviceCaps(f.hDC, LOGPIXELSY)
    l& = SetViewportExt(f.hDC, 10, 10)
    l& = SetWindowExt(f.hDC, extX, extY)
End Sub
```

```
Sub SetPrinterToTwips ()
    '
    ' This subroutine sets the printer to Twip scaling mode
    ' for all Windows API calls. You'll need to call
    ' ResetPrinterScale before you use any Visual Basic
    ' drawing commands.
    '
    Dim extX As Integer                ' Windows extent
    Dim extY As Integer

    i% = SetMapMode(Printer.hDC, MM_ANISOTROPIC)
    extX = 14400 / GetDeviceCaps(Printer.hDC, LOGPIXELSX)
    extY = 14400 / GetDeviceCaps(Printer.hDC, LOGPIXELSY)
    l& = SetViewportExt(Printer.hDC, 10, 10)
    l& = SetWindowExt(Printer.hDC, extX, extY)
End Sub
```

```
Sub ResetPrinterScale ()
    '
    ' This subroutine restores the printer's scale so each
    ' pixel will be as small as possible.
    '
    i% = SetMapMode(Printer.hDC, MM_TEXT)
End Sub
```

```
Sub ResetFormScale (f As Form)
    '
    ' This subroutine restores a form's API scale back to
    ' MM_TEXT (pixel) scale mode.
    '
    i% = SetMapMode(f.hDC, MM_TEXT)
End Sub
```

Chapter 18

Featuring

Font Name Problems

Asking for a Font by TextHeight

Setting Font Names Reliably

Toolbox for Fonts

Font Name Problems

Purpose Writing programs that work under both Windows 3.0 and 3.1, using standard font names. In particular, how to use the names "Tms Rmn" and "Helv" under Windows 3.1, which doesn't have fonts with these names.

See Also "Setting Font Names Reliably"

Visual Basic checks to ensure that the names you use for the FontName property are valid. For example, if you try to set FontName = "!@#&", which isn't a valid font name, Visual Basic will display an "Invalid property value" error dialog box.

This can be a real problem when you want to write a Visual Basic program that works correctly under both Windows 3.1 and 3.0. How can you choose font names? What if the font name exists in one version of Windows but not in another?

Using Standard Names

The best solution to these problems is to use "standard" Windows fonts. Windows has a set of *font families*, which are a set of font types supported by all versions of Windows. These families have the names Courier, Helv, Tms Rmn, and Symbol (I'm ignoring the three vector font families that most programs never use: Roman, Modern, and Script).

The problem is that Microsoft renamed two of these standard fonts in Windows 3.1. Here is a list of the standard bitmapped fonts supported in both versions of Windows, with the old and new names:

Windows 3.0	Windows 3.1
Courier	Courier
Helv	MS Sans Serif
Tms Rmn	MS Serif
Symbol	Symbol

Because changing these font names could have created problems with existing programs, Microsoft introduced a new section into the WIN.INI file, for the sole purpose of *mapping* old names into the new font names. Your Windows 3.1 WIN.INI file should contain the following lines:

```
[FontSubstitutes]
Helvetica=Arial
Times=Times New Roman
Tms Rmn=MS Serif
Helv=MS Sans Serif
```

What this means it that when you write FontName = "Helv" in a Visual Basic program running under Windows 3.1, Windows will actually set the current font to MS Sans Serif (although your program will never know this).

As long as your WIN.INI file has these font substitutions (added during Windows 3.1 Setup), you won't have any problems assigning the names "Helv" and "Tms Rmn" to any FontName property. The bottom line is this: As long as you use only the names Courier, Helv, Tms Rmn, and Symbol in your programs, you won't have any problems.

Putting Helv and Tms Rmn Back into the FontName List

There is one case where you may have problems using the names Helv and Tms Rmn under Windows 3.1 (fortunately there is an easy fix). If you change the FontName property using the Properties bar, you won't be able to reset it to Helv or Tms Rmn. Why not? Visual Basic obtains a list of the fonts actually installed in your computer, rather than a list of all the fonts that will work. Since Helv and Tms Rmn aren't real fonts under Windows 3.1, they won't appear in this list.

You can, however, put these two font names back into the font list in the Properties bar. The trick is to use a little-known area of Windows 3.1's WIN.INI file. After following the steps outlined below, Visual Basic will again show the Helv and Tms Rmn font names in the FontName combo box in the Properties bar:

1. Create a backup copy of the WIN.INI file in your Windows directory (use the File Manager).

2. Start the Write accessory.

3. Select Open... from the File menu and type **WIN.INI**. Then press the Enter key to load this file into Write.

4. Search for the word *compatibility* (use the Find... item from the Find menu).

5. Look through the list of names until you find VB. You should see a line like this one: VB=0x0200.

6. Change this line to the following (or add this line if it doesn't appear in the list after [Compatibility]): VB=0x1200.

7. Save your changes.

The next time you run Visual Basic, you should see the names "Helv" and "Tms Rmn" appear in the combo box for the FontName property.

The Compatibility section of your WIN.INI file is designed to "turn off" features new to Windows 3.1 so that older programs will work correctly. The numbers are designed so you can turn individual features on and off. In this case, changing the first 0 to a 1 tells Windows that you want the Helv and Tms Rmn fonts to appear whenever you run a program called VB.

NOTE

You only need to make this change on your computer. Any programs you write will work on other computers, even if the WIN.INI file hasn't been changed. The only reason to change WIN.INI is so the Helv and Tms Rmn fonts will appear in the FontName combo box in design mode.

Asking for a Font by TextHeight

File FONTTOOL.BAS

Purpose Finds the largest font whose TextHeight is less than or equal to a given height.

Whenever you set the FontSize property of a form or control, you're always setting the height of the font in points. But what if you want the height of the font to be a certain size in twips. How do you do that?

It turns out that you can't simply convert the height to points and use that number. This is because the size of a font (in points) never includes the font's *leading,* which is a measure of the extra space between lines. Although this may not seem like much of a problem, it is a little trickier than you might guess. To understand all these issues, let's take a short look at fonts, and how the Text-Height and FontSize values are related (they don't measure the same thing).

A Brief Primer on Fonts

Any font includes some extra space above it that's used to separate lines. But, as you can see in Figure 18.1, this extra space is also used for displaying diacritical marks on international characters, such as umlauts over characters, like ü.

You can also see from this figure that TextHeight and FontSize measure different sizes in a font. FontSize refers to the height of characters, without including the extra space for leading. TextHeight, on the other hand, includes both the FontSize height *and* the leading between lines. If you want a font to have a certain size, including the leading, you can't simply set FontSize to this number. Instead, you'll need some way to find a slightly smaller font whose Text-Height is the height you want.

I've provided the function FindFontSize for just this need.

Figure 18.1:

This figure shows how the TextHeight and FontSize values refer to different heights because the leading between lines is included in Text-Height but not Font-Size. Also notice that diacritical marks (such as the caret) appear in this leading area.

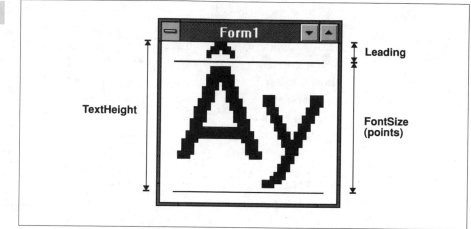

How to Use FindFontSize

Using FindFontSize is really quite simple. Let's say, for example, that you have a form called Form1. Let's also say that you want to create a label (called Label1) that is no more than 18 pixels high. Here's the kind of code you would use:

```
ScaleMode = 3                    ' Set to pixel scaling
Label1.FontSize = FindFontSize(Form1, 18)
```

The first line makes sure you're using pixel scaling in the form that you'll pass to FindFontSize (this function uses the form's FontSize property and Text-Height method to do all the work). The second line then calls FindFontSize to find the largest font size (in points) that has a TextHeight of no more than 18 pixels (because we set ScaleMode = 3).

How It Works

How do you set the size of a font in pixels? Can you simply supply the size of the font, measured in pixels or twips? The answer is no, for a couple of reasons. First, Visual Basic's FontSize property is *always* measured in points ($1/72$ inch, or $1/20$ twip), so you have to supply the size in points. To compound the problem, you can't always set the exact size of a font. For example, you might find that FontSize = 8.25 after you set it to 1.

There's still one other problem. The value you get back from TextHeight won't be the same as the font size you set, because TextHeight and FontSize refer to different numbers that measure the size of a font. The FontSize property sets the height of the characters in the font, whereas the TextHeight function reports this height plus the leading (or extra spacing) between lines of text. This extra space, by the way, always appears above (rather than below) any text you display in a text box, in a label, or with the Print method.

The problem, then, is how to adjust the TextHeight of a font when all you can set is the FontSize property, and you don't even have full control over that.

The solution I chose is to write a function called FindFontSize that finds the closest font whose size (TextHeight) is less than or equal to the height you want. It does this by first converting the height to points, then setting FontSize to this value. Finally, it looks for fonts smaller and smaller than this initial size until it finds one with a small enough TextHeight.

Let's take a closer look at the function (the code is shown in the next section). The first line of code saves the current FontSize so it can be restored at the end. Next, this function converts the size from whatever units you're using to points, and it sets the initial FontSize value to this number. This number will be too large, since the actual text height includes some extra leading. Finally, Do..Loop looks for smaller and smaller fonts until it finds a font whose TextHeight is less than or equal to the height you want. This is the number it returns to you.

You'll notice that this function uses a form for calculating the size of a font, which allows it to use the FontSize property and TextHeight method to do all the work.

The Code

Here is the code that you can put into a module or a form:

```
Function FindFontSize (f As Form, ByVal high)
    '
    ' This function returns the first font with a
    ' TextHeight <= high.
    '
    ' Note: If the smallest font has a TextHeight > high, this
    '          function will return a font larger than high.
    '
    Dim i, oldSize, size
    Dim oldScale

    oldSize = f.FontSize                ' Remember old font size
```

```
'
' Convert starting height to points.
'
oldScale = f.ScaleMode          ' Remember scale mode
CurrentY = high                 ' Set Y to height we want
ScaleMode = 2                   ' Switch to points
f.FontSize = CurrentY           ' Set to size, in points
f.ScaleMode = oldScale          ' Restore the scale mode

i = f.FontSize                  ' Size we'll start at
Do
    If f.FontSize < i Then      ' Is size smaller than i?
        i = f.FontSize          ' Yes, adjust i to real size
    End If
    i = i - .5                  ' Try next smaller size
    f.FontSize = i              ' Set font to this size
Loop While f.TextHeight("A") > high And i > 1
FindFontSize = f.FontSize       ' Return size of found font

f.FontSize = oldSize            ' Restore the old font size
End Function
```

Setting Font Names Reliably

Files　FONTNAME.BAS and FONTNAME.H

Purpose　You'll need the subroutines in this section if you plan to work with both screen and printer font names. For example, if you use MhChooseFont (included on the disk that accompanies this book) to choose a font, you won't always be able to assign the name you get back to the FontName property. This is because the font name may not be supported by both the screen and the printer. The routines described here fix this problem in much the same way Word for Windows does—by substituting a font that is as close as possible to the one you want.

There are a number of problems with the way fonts work with Visual Basic. For one thing, not all versions of Windows and not all printers support the same font names. In fact, sometimes the same font has several different names. For example, the Helvetica font may be called Helv or Helvetica.

The real problem is what happens when you try to assign one of these names to the FontName property and it's not supported. Visual Basic will generate a run-time error. To give you an idea of just how much of a problem this is, one of my computers uses Helv for the screen font, but Helvetica for the printer font. I got a run-time error when I tried to set my printer to print with the same font, using Printer.FontName = "Helv".

So what do you do? How can you know what name to use when the name keeps changing? And what do you do to make sure it will work on all computers? Visual Basic doesn't have a solution for this problem. But there is a solution, which is rather complicated. Fortunately you can use this solution without knowing anything about how it works.

The Simple Solution

The simple solution is to use MhChooseFont to bring up a dialog box that allows you to select fonts. Then you can call MhSetFont to start using this font on the screen. Both these functions are part of the MHD-EM200.VBX file on the disk included with this book. If you use these functions, you'll have an easy-to-use interface, and you won't have to know all the details that are described below.

For the printer you'll need to use the hard solution, which is written entirely in Visual Basic, using Windows functions to do all the work.

Background Information on Fonts

There are some simple concepts you need to know about to effectively use the solutions provided here. Windows defines a set of five standard font families for all devices. (These font names aren't always the names you'll be able to use with Visual Basic, which is why you'll need the solution provided here.) Here are the standard Windows fonts:

Courier	A fixed-pitch, typewriter-style font.
Helv	A proportionally spaced font without serifs.
Tms Rmn	A proportionally spaced font with serifs.
Symbol	Contains a number of special characters, including the letters of the Greek alphabet.

Roman, Modern, Script	These fonts are a throwback to the early days of Windows, when computers had little memory or hard-disk space. These fonts were designed to be scalable to any size, without using much disk or memory space. All three fonts tend to look rather crude, especially compared with TrueType fonts.

Under Windows 3.1, there are also three new TrueType fonts. These fonts will always be available on both your screen and printer, in any size:

Courier New	A fixed-pitch, typewriter-style font.
Arial	A proportionally spaced font without serifs.
Times New Roman	A proportionally spaced font with serifs.
Symbol	Contains a number of special characters, including the letters of the Greek alphabet.

As long as you're working with these fonts, everything is really quite easy.

If, however, you also want to be able to use fonts that are defined on your printer but not on your screen, such as AvantGarde, you need to be a little more careful. Such fonts are available only if you have a printer that supports them, or if you've installed such a font on your computer.

The problem is, what happens when you ask for the AvantGarde font on someone's computer and that person doesn't have either a display or a printer font with that name? The best solution is to allow the user of your program to select a font. The easiest way to do this is by using the MhChooseFont function, which can be found on the companion disk.

Figure 18.2 shows a list of similar fonts on my display and printer. For this figure, I used Windows 3.1 for the display and a PostScript printer. You can see that the font names aren't always the same, and in one case (ZapfChancery), Windows wasn't even able to find a font that was close.

Adding FONTNAME.BAS to Your Project

The most reliable way to set a font name is to use the functions described here: SetFormFont, SetControlFont, and SetPrinterFont. Simply supply each of

Font Names			
Family	Display	Printer	Sample text
Courier	Courier	Courier	Sample text
Helv	Helv	Helvetica	Sample text
Tms Rmn	Tms Rmn	Times	Sample text
Symbol	Symbol	Symbol	Σαμπλε τεξτ
Modern	Modern	Modern	Sample text
Roman	Roman	Roman	Sample text
Script	Script	Script	Sample text
System	System	Courier	**Sample text**
Terminal	Terminal	Courier	**Sample text**
Arial	Arial	Arial	Sample text
AvantGarde	MS Sans Serif	AvantGarde	Sample text
Courier New	Courier New	Courier New	Sample text
NewCenturySchlbk	MS Serif	NewCenturySchlbk	Sample text
Palatino	MS Serif	Palatino	Sample text
Times	Times New Roman	Times	Sample text
Times New Roman	Times New Roman	Times New Roman	Sample text
ZapfChancery	Fixedsys	ZapfChancery	**Sample text**
ZapfDingbats	MT Symbol	ZapfDingbats	Σαμπλε τεξτ

these functions with the name of the font you want to use, and they'll look for the closest font that matches the name you provide. For example, if you call SetFormFont with the name AvantGarde and this font is only available on your printer, SetFormFont will set the form's font to MS Sans Serif (since this is the closest match).

To use these subroutines, you'll have to do two things: First, you'll need to include the FONTNAME.BAS module in your program, which you can do using the Add File... item in the File menu. Second, you'll need to include the contents of the FONTNAME.H file in your Global.bas module. Follow these steps:

1. Open the Code window for your Global.bas module.

2. Choose Load Text... from the Code menu.

3. Select the file FONTNAME.H (but do **not** double-click on it).

4. Click on the Merge button. This will add the contents of FONTNAME.H to your Global.bas module without replacing the contents of Global.bas.

Using **FONTNAME.BAS**

The FONTNAME.BAS module has three subroutines you'll want to use. They're all identical, except we need one to handle forms, one to handle controls, and one to handle the Printer object. We need three subroutines because Visual Basic doesn't allow us to write a single subroutine that works with all three types of objects.

Here is the definition for the three subroutines:

SetFormFont(*form*, *fontName$***)**
SetControlFont(*control*, *fontName$***)**
SetPrinterFont(*someForm*, *fontName$***)**

These three subroutines change the font on a form, a control, or the printer to fontName$. They set the font to one that matches fontName$ as closely as possible, using the following method.

If SetFormFont and SetControlFont don't find a screen font that matches fontName$, they look for a printer font with this name, then use a screen font that is as close as possible to this printer font. If SetPrinterFont, on the other hand, can't find a printer font called fontName$, it uses the form someForm to find a screen font with this name, then it sets the printer font to one that matches this screen font as closely as possible.

The name of the font you want to use, fontName$, should be one of the following:

- A screen font.

- A printer font.

- One of the names Courier, Helv, Tms Rmn, Symbol, Modern, Roman, or Script. These names are *always* supported.

For example, let's say you want to use the Helvetica font on both your screen and printer, and you're drawing on a form called MyForm. You can use these two commands to change both the screen and printer font to Helvetica:

```
SetFormFont MyForm, "Helv"
SetPrinterFont MyForm, "Helv"
```

As you can see, these subroutines are quite easy to use, and they're much more reliable than Visual Basic, since it won't always let you write

```
Printer.FontName = "Helv"          ' Not!
```

This line will work on some printers but not on others. My printer is a Post-Script printer, which doesn't support the name Helv.

How Font Matching Works

The first thing that the Set*xxx*Font subroutines do is to try to set the font. If they're successful, they don't need to do anything else. But if there is an error, you have to resort to using some more advanced Windows functions (the API calls). Here is the code that tries to set the font in SetFormFont:

```
On Error Resume Next
f.FontName = fName
if Err = 0 Then Exit Sub
```

The first line turns on error trapping. If Visual Basic generates an error when you set the FontName property, it will simply move on to the next statement. At this point the Err function will return a number other than 0. If Err returns 0, you know that Visual Basic changed the FontName property, so you don't have to go any further.

If the Err function returns a number other than 0, it means that Visual Basic didn't allow the font name you tried to use. In this case all the Set*xxx*Font subroutines call a function I wrote called GetMatchingFont$, which returns the name of a font as close as possible to the name you've provided.

How GetMatchingFont$ Works

The secret behind GetMatchingFont$ is very simple: All Windows fonts, both screen and printer, have a number of characteristics associated with them. You can use these characteristics to find, for example, a printer font that is as close as possible to a screen font, even if these fonts have different names.

My PostScript laser printer, for example, doesn't have a font called Helv, but it does have a font called Helvetica with exactly the same characteristics as my screen's Helv font. The GetMatchingFont$ function I wrote returns the name

Helvetica for my printer when I ask it for a printer font that matches my screen's Helv font.

When you ask Windows, as opposed to Visual Basic, for a font, you have to do so in two steps. In the first step you create what's known as a *logical font,* which is simply a set of information that describes the font (it's not the font itself, just some information about the font, and it can be as little as just the font's name). In the second step you create a *real font* (which is a font actually available on either the display or your printer), based on the information in the logical font.

Let's use SetFormFont as an example. In this case the Err function will be nonzero whenever there's no screen font with the name you asked for. But there could be a printer font with this name, so you need to look for a printer font with the name you asked for and get its characteristics. You can then use these characteristics to find a similar screen font.

As an example, my printer has a font called AvantGarde, which is a nice, clean sans-serif font, but I don't have an AvantGarde font on my screen. When I create a logical font called AvantGarde, realize this font on my printer, and then use this font information to realize a font on my screen, the name I get back (under Windows 3.1) is MS Sans Serif, which is a sans-serif font that's as close as possible to Avant Garde. Now let's look at how to do all this using the Windows API functions.

The CreateFont function is a Windows function that creates a logical font. The first call to CreateFont in GetMatchingFont$ has all the values except the name set to 0, which tells CreateFont to use default values for the other characteristics. The next step realizes this font on the device context of the "other" device (which is Printer.hDC for SetFormFont); you do this using the Select-Object function. Next the GetTextMetrics function returns a number of pieces of information about this font in the *metrics* data structure (a variable of type TEXTMETRIC). GetMatchingFont$ then calls SelectObject again to restore the previous font, and finally calls DeleteObject to delete the logical font it created.

Once you have this font information in the variable *metric,* you call Create-Font again to create a new font on the first device context (*hDC,* which for Set-FormFont is the form's hDC property) using the information you just got from the *matchDC* device context. GetMatchingFont$ again realizes the font, but this time on the first device, so GetTextFace returns the name of a screen font. That's about all there is to this function, except for one case having to do with Windows 3.1.

There are some major differences between the way Windows 3.0 and 3.1 handle fonts. When Microsoft introduced TrueType fonts, they also introduced a new section in the WIN.INI file, called FontSubstitutes, which creates alternate names for some of the font names that were supported by Windows 3.0, as you can see here:

```
[FontSubstitutes]
Helvetica=Arial
Times=Times New Roman
Tms Rmn=MS Serif
Helv=MS Sans Serif
```

The name Times now refers to the Times New Roman font, which is a True-Type font. It doesn't refer to a real font, so Visual Basic won't let you use it. However, CreateFont will create a font with this name, and GetTextFace will return this name, which you still can't use in Visual Basic (VB only lets you use the names of real fonts—it doesn't allow substituted names). Consequently, I had to add some code to handle cases where GetTextFace returns the same name as we started with (if you don't use such code, you'll just get an error again when you try to set the FontName property). This is handled by the function called GetMetricMatch$, which searches through all the fonts actually on the device, looking for a real font with a close match. You can see all the details in GetMetricMatch$, shown in the next section.

The Code

The following Type definition *must* appear in your global module (usually called Global.bas). This defines the data structures used by the GetTextMetrics call in Windows. (You'll find these definitions in the file FONTNAME.H.)

```
Type TEXTMETRIC
    tmHeight As Integer
    tmAscent As Integer
    tmDescent As Integer
    tmInternalLeading As Integer
    tmExternalLeading As Integer
    tmAveCharWidth As Integer
    tmMaxCharWidth As Integer
    tmWeight As Integer
    tmItalic As String * 1
    tmUnderlined As String * 1
    tmStruckOut As String * 1
    tmFirstChar As String * 1
```

```
      tmLastChar As String * 1
      tmDefaultChar As String * 1
      tmBreakChar As String * 1
      tmPitchAndFamily As String * 1
      tmCharSet As String * 1
      tmOverhang As Integer
      tmDigitizedAspectX As Integer
      tmDigitizedAspectY As Integer
End Type
```

Here are the definitions that appear in the (general) section of the FONT-NAME.BAS module:

```
Declare Function SelectObject Lib "GDI" (ByVal hDC%, ByVal
➤ hObject%) As Integer

Declare Function DeleteObject Lib "GDI" (ByVal hObject%) As
➤ Integer

Declare Function GetTextFace Lib "GDI" (ByVal hDC%, ByVal
➤ nCount%, ByVal lpFacename$) As Integer

Declare Function CreateFont Lib "GDI" (ByVal h%, ByVal W%, ByVal
➤ E%, ByVal O%, ByVal W%, ByVal i%, ByVal U%, ByVal S%, ByVal
➤ c%, ByVal OP%, ByVal CP%, ByVal Q%, ByVal PAF%, ByVal f$) As
➤ Integer

Declare Function GetTextMetrics Lib "GDI" (ByVal hDC As Integer,
➤ lpMetrics As TEXTMETRIC) As Integer
```

Finally, here are all the subroutines and functions in this module. The first three are the ones you call, and the rest support functions used by the first three subroutines.

```
Sub SetFormFont (f As Form, fName As String)
    '
    ' This subroutine sets the font for the current form
    ' to the name you provided. Here is what happens.
    '
    '         If Name exists
    '              Set FontName using this name
    '         Else
    '              Look for a font that matches a printer font
    '
    On Error Resume Next
    f.FontName = fName                ' Try setting font name
    If Err = 0 Then Exit Sub          ' It worked, we're done
```

```
      f.FontName = GetMatchingFont$(f.hDC, Printer.hDC, fName)
End Sub
```

```
Sub SetControlFont (c As Control, fName As String)
    '
    ' This subroutine sets the font for the current form
    ' to the name you provided. Here is what happens.
    '
    '       If Name exists
    '           Set FontName using this name
    '       Else
    '           Look for a font that matches a printer font
    '
    On Error Resume Next
    c.FontName = fName                 ' Try setting font name
    If Err = 0 Then Exit Sub           ' It worked, we're done

    c.FontName = GetMatchingFont$(c.hDC, Printer.hDC, fName)
End Sub
```

```
Sub SetPrinterFont (f As Form, fName As String)
    '
    ' This subroutine sets the font for the printer to the
    ' name you provide. Here is what happens.
    '
    '       If Name exists
    '           Set FontName using this name
    '       Else
    '           Look for printer font that matches screen font
    '
    On Error Resume Next
    Printer.FontName = fName           ' Try setting font name
    If Err = 0 Then Exit Sub           ' It worked, we're done

    Printer.FontName = GetMatchingFont$(Printer.hDC, f.hDC,
fName)
End Sub
```

```
Function GetMatchingFont$ (ByVal hDC As Integer, ByVal matchDC
➤ As Integer, matchName As String)
    '
    ' This subroutine looks for a font called matchName on the
    ' device matchDC (which will be the hDC property from a
    ' form, control, or Printier). It then returns the closest
```

```
    ' font on the hDC device with the same characteristics.
    '
    '   hDC        The device you're setting FontName on
    '   matchDC    The "other" device (Printer or form)
    '   matchName  The font name you're looking for
    '
Dim tempName As String * 32      ' Matching font name
Dim hFont As Integer             ' Handle to font info
Dim hOldFont As Integer          ' Handle to old font info
Dim metrics As TEXTMETRIC        ' Information about the font
Dim i%


    '
    ' First we'll get information about the font from the
    ' device that has the font (matchDC).
    '
hFont = CreateFont(0, 0, 0, 0, 0, 0, 0, 0, 0, 0, 0, 0, 0,
                    matchName)

hOldFont = SelectObject(matchDC, hFont) ' Set to this font
i% = GetTextMetrics(matchDC, metrics)   ' Get info on font
i% = SelectObject(matchDC, hOldFont)    ' Restore old font
i% = DeleteObject(hFont)                ' Delete font info


    ' Now we'll look for a font on hDC that matches the info
    ' we just got from matchDC.
    '
hFont = CreateFont(0, 0, 0, 0, 0, 0, 0, 0,
                    Asc(metrics.tmCharSet), 0, 0, 0,
                    Asc(metrics.tmPitchAndFamily), matchName)

hOldFont = SelectObject(hDC, hFont)     ' Select this font
i% = GetTextFace(hDC, 128, tempName)    ' Get matching name
newName$ = Left$(tempName, i%)          ' Remove spaces
i% = SelectObject(hDC, hOldFont)        ' Restore old font
i% = DeleteObject(hFont)                ' Delete new font

GetMatchingFont$ = newName$

If newName$ = matchName Then
    GetMatchingFont = GetMetricMatch$(hDC, matchName)
End If
End Function


Function GetMetricMatch$ (hDC As Integer, matchName$)
    '
    ' This code handles the case in Windows 3.1 where you
    ' can have a font name returned that isn't a real font.
```

```
' For example, 3.1 defines Times=Times New Roman, so if
' you select Times, you'll get Times back even though
' it's not a real font. This code searches for a real
' font that has the same metrics as Times.
'

Dim hFont As Integer              ' Handle to font info
Dim hOldFont As Integer           ' Handle to old font info
Dim hiIndex As Integer            ' Index of highest font
Dim hiValue As Integer            ' Highest match
Dim metrics As TEXTMETRIC         ' Information about the font
Dim newMetrics As TEXTMETRIC      ' Metrics of enumerated font

'

' First we get the metrics for the font matchName$.
'

hFont = CreateFont(0, 0, 0, 0, 0, 0, 0, 0, 0, 0, 0, 0, 0,
                    matchName)

hOldFont = SelectObject(hDC, hFont)
i% = GetTextMetrics(hDC, metrics)
i% = SelectObject(hDC, hOldFont)
i% = DeleteObject(hFont)

'

' Next we walk through all the fonts actually on the
' device, looking for the closest match of real fonts.
'

If hDC = Printer.hDC Then          ' Is this for printer?
    count = Printer.FontCount      ' Yes, use printer
Else
    count = Screen.FontCount       ' No, use screen
End If
count = count - 1                  ' Fonts is zero-based

For j = 1 To count
    If hDC = Printer.hDC Then       ' Get a font from device
        aFont$ = Printer.Fonts(j)
    Else
        aFont$ = Screen.Fonts(j)
    End If

    hFont = CreateFont(0, 0, 0, 0, 0, 0, 0, 0, 0, 0, 0, 0, 0,
                        aFont$)

    hOldFont = SelectObject(hDC, hFont)
    i% = GetTextMetrics(hDC, newMetrics)
    i% = SelectObject(hDC, hOldFont)
    i% = DeleteObject(hFont)
    value = 0                       ' Calculate matching value
    If metrics.tmCharSet = newMetrics.tmCharSet Then value =
                                        value + 4
```

```
➤           If metrics.tmPitchAndFamily = newMetrics.tmPitchAndFamily
                                     Then value = value + 6
            If value > hiValue Then      ' Is this a new high match?
               hiValue = value           ' Yes, save the new hi value
               hiName$ = aFont$          ' Remember best match name
            End If
         Next j
         GetMetricMatch$ = hiName$       ' Report best match
      End Function
```

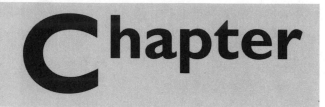 

Chapter 19

Featuring

Multimedia Sound

Running DOS Programs

Building Very Large Programs

Checking the DOS and Windows Versions

Finding a Program's Directory

Toolbox: Miscellaneous

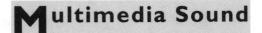Multimedia Sound

Purpose Playing the .WAV files that are supported by Windows 3.1.

With version 3.1, Windows added multimedia sound support to the system, which allows you to play recorded sound (.WAV) files on your computer. To use these features, your computer must have a sound board, such as Sound Blaster, installed. If your computer makes a "symphony" sound when it first starts, chances are very good that your computer has a sound card.

The Windows 3.1 function that plays .WAV files is called sndPlaySound and is very easy to use. All you have to do is to make sure you're using Windows 3.1 or later, which you can do using the WindowsVersion function described later in this chapter.

How to Use sndPlaySound

The sndPlaySound command takes just two parameters: the name of the .WAV file and a flags value, which gives you control over how sndPlaySound works.

The simplest call to sndPlaySound looks like this:

```
i% = sndPlaySound("chord.wav", 0)
```

This will play the chord sound you hear when Windows 3.1 first starts.

NOTE

If your computer doesn't have a sound device installed, this function will return 0, which indicates that the computer wasn't able to play the sound.

Instead of using 0 for the second parameter, you can set a number of flags to control how sndPlaySound works. You set flags by using the Or operator to combine flags, for example,

```
flags = SND_ASYNC Or SND_LOOP
```

Here are descriptions for each of the flags you can use with the sndPlaySound function:

SND_SYNC	Waits until the sound finishes playing before returning from the call to the sndPlaySound function.
SND_ASYNC	Returns immediately to your program; the sound plays while your program continues to run. You can stop the sound by calling sndPlaySound (0&, 0).
SND_NODEFAULT	Normally sndPlaySound will play the default sound if it can't find the .WAV file name you provided. This flag tells sndPlaySound to remain silent if it can't find the sound file.
SND_LOOP	Keeps playing the sound file over and over until you stop it. Calls sndPlaySound(0&, 0) to stop playing the sound file. You must use SND_ASYNC along with this flag.
SND_NOSTOP	Returns False immediately if a sound is currently playing, rather than starting to play the new sound file.

This single line of code will play the "chord.wav" file over and over:

```
i% = sndPlaySound("chord.wav", SND_ASYNC Or SND_LOOP)
```

You can then stop the sound with this command:

```
i% = sndPlaySound(O&, 0)
```

The Definitions

Here are the definitions for the sndPlaySound function and its constants, which you must put in the same form or module as the code that uses sndPlaySound:

```
Const SND_SYNC = 0
Const SND_ASYNC = 1
Const SND_NODEFAULT = 2
Const SND_MEMORY = 4
Const SND_NOSTOP = 16

Declare Function sndPlaySound Lib "MMSYSTEM.DLL" (ByVal WavFile
➤ As Any, ByVal wFlags As Integer) As Integer
```

Running DOS Programs

File   MISCTOOL.BAS

Purpose   Runs a DOS command then allows you to continue with your Visual Basic program.

See Also   "Checking the DOS and Windows Versions"

Visual Basic has a command called Shell that allows your programs to launch DOS programs. In this section I'll show you a few things about Shell that aren't documented, and I'll also show you how to do more than you can do with the Shell command.

The Basics of Shell

The Shell command has two parameters (the second is optional): the command you want to run, and how you want Windows to run the program (such as full screen or windowed). To run the Format command, for example, to format a floppy disk in drive A, you use this command:

```
i = Shell("format.com a:")
```

You'll notice that I've included the extension .COM. Shell needs to know both the name of the command and its extension. This means that you can't use the Shell command to directly run any of DOS's internal commands, such as DIR or DEL (use the Visual Basic Kill command to delete files instead).

Shell can run any type of program that has the .COM, .EXE, .BAT, or .PIF extension; the last one, .PIF, gives you more control over how DOS programs are run. I'll talk about this option next.

Running Special DOS Commands

There are cases where you can't run a command directly (when you are using internal commands) or use a command line directly (when you are using command redirection). Some DOS commands aren't programs on your disk. Instead, they're built into a file called COMMAND.COM. Also, you can't use the DOS redirection characters (<, >, and |) as the command line for most commands. How do you get around these limitations?

You can use the COMMAND.COM program to run *any* DOS command. All you have to do is run COMMAND.COM with a /c followed by your DOS command:

command.com /c *any DOS command*

The next section shows an example using the Format command with input redirection.

Running DOS Programs in the Background

Normally when you use the Shell command to start a DOS program, the Shell command will return to your program almost immediately, then the DOS program will start to run as a full-screen program. But what if you want the DOS program to run in the background as an icon? And what if you want your Visual Basic program to wait until the DOS program is finished? In this section I'll show you how to run a DOS program in the background, and in the next section I'll show you how to wait until the DOS program finishes.

Windows has a type of executable file called a .PIF file. PIF stands for *program information file*, and it contains information on how Windows should run your DOS programs. One of the options (available only in 386 enhanced mode) allows you to set up a DOS program so it will run in the background while Windows continues to run. You create a new .PIF file using a program called PIFEDIT, which you can run using the Run command from the File menu in the Program Manager (see Figure 19.1).

Figure 19.1:

The PIFEDIT program allows you to create a .PIF file that will let a DOS program run in the background. Here I've created a .PIF file to run a command in the background.

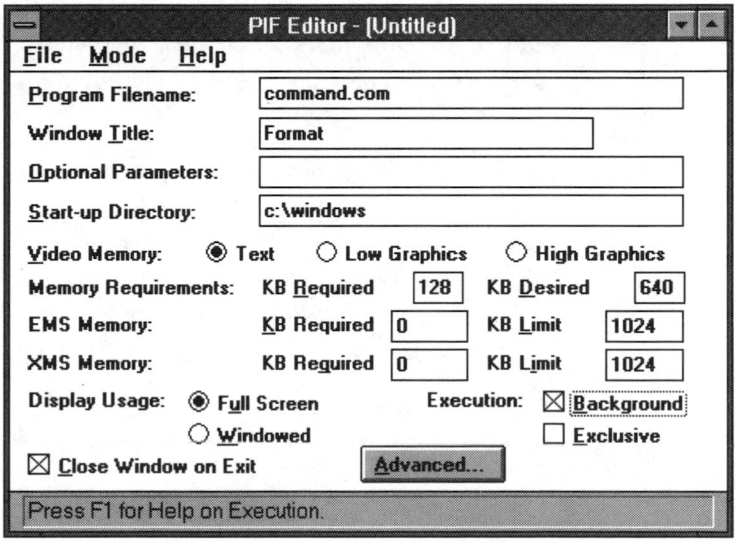

NOTE

The Windows 3.0 version of PIFEDIT doesn't have as many options available in its main window as the 3.1 version, but all the options you'll need to set are available in Windows 3.0.

There are several fields you'll need to fill in. First, you'll need to fill in the name of the program you want this .PIF file to run. In this case it will be COM-MAND.COM, which can run *any* DOS command. The next field, Window Title, is the name that will appear under the minimized DOS icon. You should leave the next field, Optional Parameters, blank so that you can send parameters to COMMAND.COM using the Shell command. The start-up directory can be any directory; I've set it to the WINDOWS directory, which is where I put the .PIF file. Finally, check the Background box to allow your DOS program to run in the background while Windows continues to run.

You'll also need a text file called FORMAT.TXT, which provides keyboard input to the Format command. When you run Format, it asks you to press any key before it starts to format the disk. Then when it's all finished, it asks if you want to format another disk. The FORMAT.TXT file contains four keystrokes: Enter, another Enter, an *n,* and a final Enter.

Now when you write

```
i = Shell("format.pif /c format a: /u <format.txt", 7)
```

your program will start the Format command, then continue running while DOS formats a floppy disk in the background. The second parameter, 7, in the Shell command tells Windows to minimize your program and to keep the keyboard focus in your Visual Basic program (rather than switching to the new DOS program).

NOTE

The /u switch is required with the DOS 5 and later versions of the Format command to make sure Format won't ask whether you want to format the disk when there is information already on the disk. If you want to use Format for all versions of DOS, you'll need to include the /u switch only if the DOS version is 5 or higher. You'll find the code to get the DOS version number in the section called "Checking the DOS and Windows Versions."

Waiting Until a DOS Program Finishes

Normally the Shell command returns to your program as soon as it has started the program you want to run, which means your program will continue running before your DOS program finishes. How can you have your program wait until the DOS program finishes?

It turns out to be fairly easy, thanks to some help from a Windows function called GetModuleUsage, which you can use to tell if a program is still running. The Shell command returns an ID (identification) number of the program that you've started, and GetModuleUsage tells you how many copies of that program are running. The code below waits, using a Do…While loop, until GetModuleUsage returns 0. You'll notice that DoEvents( ) is called before the first call to GetModuleUsage. This is absolutely necessary to make sure Windows has a chance to finish starting the program before you see if it's still running.

```
Declare Function GetModuleUsage Lib "Kernel" (ByVal hInst As
➤ Integer) As Integer

Sub RunDOS(prog As String)
    Dim hInst As Integer

    hInst = Shell(prog, 7)
    Do
        i = DoEvents()
    Loop While GetModuleUsage(hInst) > 0
End Sub
```

Building Very Large Programs

If you're building very large programs, there are some things you'll need to know about how Visual Basic uses memory and the limitations this places on your applications. Much of this information isn't well documented, so you're not likely to find it anywhere else. Also, this information was gleaned from Visual Basic version 1.0 and is subject to change in future versions. Still, it should give you a better understanding of how to structure your programs so you'll have as few problems as possible when you write very large programs.

A Quick Introduction to Memory

To really understand the limits in Visual Basic, there are some basic things you'll need to understand about Windows's use of memory inside your computer. Here are two terms you'll see in the discussions that follow:

Segment   Memory in Windows is organized into a number of small chunks called *segments*. Each segment can be anywhere from 16 bytes to 64K bytes in size. You can never have more than 8192 segments at one time (4096 in standard mode).

P-Code   All Visual Basic programs are "compiled" into a form that's very fast to run, called *p-code*. P-code is a compact form that's fairly fast to run, but not as fast as programs written in languages like C.

The most important detail, as you'll see below, is that Visual Basic uses a number of different segments for its programs, and there are a limited number of segments available in your computer. This means that it's possible for Windows to run out of segments before you've used all the available memory in your computer. If this happens, Windows will probably display an Unrecoverable Application Error (in 3.0) or a General Protection Fault (in 3.1) and quit working correctly. You're likely to see this problem only if you have a very large program that uses a number of segments.

You can also have other memory problems, such as getting an "Out of Memory" error message, that have nothing to do with the amount of memory free in Windows. Instead, as you'll see below, a memory problem may have to do only with the amount of memory available inside a single segment. If your program happens to need any one segment to be larger than 64K, you may see the "Out of Memory" message.

Finally, you'll find a discussion of other types of scarce memory that are consumed by any Visual Basic program.

Error Messages

When you start to write very large programs, there are a couple of error messages you might see. Here's a short explanation of what can cause these errors and how to fix them:

"Out of Memory"   When you see this message, it means you
                          have a large module or form that has too
                          many names defined in it. You'll need to
                          split this module or form into smaller mod-
                          ules or forms, or you'll need to use the
                          technique described below under "Module
                          and Form Name Tables" to fix the problem.

"Out of Stack Space"   This message usually occurs only when you
                          have recursion, which means you have one
                          or more subroutines calling themselves in a
                          loop. For example, you might have Sub A
                          calling Sub B, which in turn calls Sub A.
                          This is a loop with no end. Each time you
                          call a subroutine or function, it uses some
                          stack space. Since stack space is limited
                          to 16K, you'll eventually run out of stack
                          space. The solution is to trace through
                          your code looking for cases like this, then
                          figure out how to rewrite your code to
                          eliminate the loop.

Visual Basic's Limits

Below you'll find a list of the memory limits in Visual Basic as I know them.
This list may not be complete; it was gleaned from information provided by
Microsoft personnel on CompuServe.

- **Subs and Functions.** Each subroutine and function gets its own
  segment, which means that a subroutine can be as large as 64K of
  p-code.

- **Module and Form Variables.** Each module and form gets its own
  data segment, which can be up to 64K. This segment is used for all
  constants, strings, and simple variables (variables that aren't arrays)
  that are defined in the (declarations) part of the module or form. It's
  also used to save Declare statements.

- **Array Variables.** Each array gets its own data segment, which means that an array can be up to 64K in size. Arrays larger than 64K will cause a "subscript out of range" error.

- **Controls.** Each form gets a single data segment (up to 64K) that's used to save all the properties for controls you include in a form, except for the lists in list and combo boxes, and the text in text boxes. The Caption property of controls is limited to 1K in size. Any captions longer than this will be shortened to 1K by truncating them. The Tag property is limited to 32K.

- **List and Combo Boxes.** Each list and combo box gets a single data segment (up to 64K) that's used to save the list( ) property of the list or combo box. Also, each item in a list can be up to 1K in size. Any items longer than 1K will be shortened to 1K by truncating them.

- **Text Boxes.** The text from a text box is stored in its own data segment, which can normally be up to 32K in size. You can, however, use an API call to increase the upper limit to 64K.

- **Global Module.** The global module has its own segment (up to 64K), which is used for storing global constants and variables, as well as templates for Type definitions and Declare statements.

- **Module and Form Name Tables.** Each module and form has a name table (up to 32K) that includes information on every label, variable name, subroutine, and function name, and on line numbers. These entries (one for each item) consist of the characters in the name plus four bytes. There are several things you can do to avoid "Out of Memory" errors: 1) move subroutines/functions out of your form and into a module; 2) use shorter variable names; 3) avoid using fixed-length strings when at all possible; 4) split your program into smaller modules/forms.

NOTE

Out-of-memory errors occur when the name table grows larger than 32K. If you see such an error, you'll need to use the Save..Load Text commands (described next), or you'll need to break up a module or form into smaller modules or forms. **Workaround:** The name table will never shrink under normal use, even if you remove variables and subroutines from your program. The only way to reduce the size of this table is to use the Save Text... menu item in the Code menu to save the code as a text file. Then load this text back into your module or form by using the Load Text... menu item. This forces Visual Basic to create a new name table based solely on the actual code.

Limits in the Debug Version of Windows

If you're using a special debugging version of Windows, which you get by copying some special dynamic link libraries (DLLs) from the Windows SDK into your SYSTEM directory, the memory limits described above change rather dramatically for the worse: All of a form's properties, *including list( ) and text,* are stored in a single segment, up to 64K in size. This means you'll have much less memory available for your list and text boxes. Other memory limits may also change, and they'll probably be smaller.

The Valuable System Resources

In addition to having a limited number of segments available, Windows has some other limited system resources. A number of objects, such as menu bars, menu items, windows, and so on, use space from two areas in memory that are limited to a mere 64K in size. These are the GDI and USER *heaps,* which are used by *all* Windows programs.

Visual Basic tends to use a large number of these system resources, which means that you can easily write programs that consume large chunks of this shared space. If you have several such programs running, it's even possible to run out of available resources. When that happens, you're likely to see the dreaded Unrecoverable Application Error (UAE) dialog box appear (in Windows 3.0), which will terminate your program and perhaps even Windows.

You'll need some understanding of what kinds of resources Visual Basic programs consume and how you can minimize the amount of resources your program will use. It's actually very difficult to calculate how much space will

Usage by Forms and Picture Boxes

You may have noticed that both forms and picture boxes use about 300 bytes of GDI space. What is all this memory used for? It's used for several objects that Windows (and Visual Basic) needs in order to draw inside a form or picture box.

The first piece is something called an hDC, which is the same thing as the hDC property for a form or picture box. The letters hDC are an abbreviation for *handle to a Device Context*. A handle is a number used by Windows to refer to its objects. Every window and control has a handle, as do many other objects inside Windows.

A device context is something like permission for drawing to an object on the screen. Both forms and picture boxes allow you to use Windows API (Application Programming Interface) calls to draw inside your forms and picture boxes, in addition to using Visual Basic commands. All the Windows functions for drawing need an hDC so they'll know where you want them to draw. This is very much like writing Picture1.Line in Visual Basic, where you have to specify where you want the line drawn. Each device context consumes about 200 bytes of GDI space. Every control needs to use an hDC when it draws, but it can borrow it from Windows whenever it needs to draw. But because forms and picture boxes have a public hDC property, they need dedicated device contexts—hence the 200 bytes only for forms and picture boxes.

Along with the hDC are several other pieces of information: the current brush (used to fill circles and boxes), the current pen (which is used to draw lines and has a color, width, and style), and the current font.

be used by different objects in your Visual Basic programs. But there are some numbers that will help give you a better idea of how your programs are using the valuable GDI and USER data. Here are some rough numbers:

- **Forms.** Each form you add to your program uses some GDI and USER space whenever it's loaded into memory (whether it's visible or hidden). You can recover the memory a form uses by unloading it. Empty forms consume about 300 bytes of GDI space and 100 bytes of USER space (these are very rough numbers).

- **Picture Boxes.** Picture boxes, like forms, consume about 300 bytes of GDI space and 100 bytes of USER space.

- **Combo Boxes.** Combo boxes consume about 350 bytes of USER space for Dropdown Combo and Simple Combo boxes, and about 280 bytes of USER space for Dropdown Lists.

- **Timers.** Each timer consumes about 330 bytes of GDI space and 100 bytes of USER space.

- **Other Controls.** Most other controls consume little or no GDI space, and between 70 and 100 bytes of USER space.

- **Menus.** Each menu and menu item is also a control, but under Windows 3.1, the menus and menu items are stored in their own segment, so they won't consume any of the USER and GDI space. Under Windows 3.0, menus consume USER space: about 80 bytes for the first menu, 80 bytes for the first menu item, and about 25 bytes for each additional menu or menu item.

Table 19.1 provides a summary of GDI and USER usage.

As you can see, picture boxes can consume GDI resources very quickly. For example, 10 picture boxes will use about 3000 bytes of GDI space, which could be about 10 percent of the available resources in GDI. For the most part, you'll

Table 19.1:	Control	GDI	USER
Summary of GDI and USER Usage (in bytes)	Form	300	100
	Picture box	300	100
	Combo box		350 (280 for drop-down list)
	Timer	330	100
	Other controls		70 to 100
	Menus *		80 for first menu, item; 25 for all others

* Only in Windows 3.0. Menus have their own segment in Windows 3.1.

probably want to keep the number of controls in a form down in the range of 10 to 20 controls.

Your programs will probably use more memory than you might guess from the numbers in Table 19.1, because other parts of Visual Basic also allocate some space from both USER and GDI.

Other Limited Resources

There are also some other limits you might run into from time to time when you're writing programs. For example, Windows has a fixed number of timers that are available to all running programs. The limits are 16 for Windows 3.0 and about 29 for Windows 3.1.

Checking the DOS and Windows Versions

File MISCTOOL.BAS

Purpose Sometimes you'll need to know which version of DOS or Windows your program is running under. For example, if you're using a Windows function or DOS command that isn't available in all versions, you should make sure you're running under a recent enough version before you use that function or command.

Every new version of DOS or Windows has some new commands or features you can use. But if you want your program to run under previous versions, you'll need to make sure you can tell when you can and when you can't use these new commands. In this section you'll learn about two functions: DOSVersion( ) returns the DOS version number (such as 5.0), and WindowsVersion( ) returns the Windows version (such as 3.1).

Normally, you use these functions like this:

```
If WindowsVersion() >= 3.1 Then
    ... do new stuff
Else
    ... do it the old way
End If
```

You might use this kind of test, for example, before you try to use any of the new multimedia functions in Windows 3.1 (such as the new sound routines).

How It Works

Each of these two functions uses a Windows API function called GetVersion. This function returns both the Windows and the DOS version information in a number of type Long, which can easily contain all the information. Version numbers actually consist of two parts: a major and a minor number. For example, Windows 3.1 has a major number of 3 and a minor number of 10 (each part has two digits, so Windows 3.1 is actually version 3.10).

Each part of the version number can be any number between 00 and 99, which means each part of the version number fits into a single byte (a byte can contain numbers between 0 and 255). A number of type Long contains four bytes, which allows exactly enough room to contain two version numbers, each with a major and a minor number.

Here is the exact equation Windows uses to encode both version numbers into a Long number:

GetVersion = ((DOS major version) * 256 + (DOS minor version)) * 65536 +

(Windows minor version) * 256 + (Windows major version)

There's one interesting thing about this equation. You'll notice that Windows isn't consistent in how it reports the major and minor version numbers: For DOS, the major number is multiplied by 256, but for Windows the *minor* version number is multiplied by 256. Strange, huh?

The DOS Version( ) and Windows Version( ) functions pull out the major and minor version numbers, then put both parts back together again in a single number, where the major part appears to the left of the decimal point, and the minor part appears to the right. For example, the version number 3.31 will be returned as the number 3.31.

The DOSVersion( ) function begins by dividing the number from GetVersion( ) by 65,536, which removes all the Windows version information, leaving only the DOS version information. Next it gets the major part of the version number by dividing by 256. Finally, DOSVersion() adds the minor version divided by 100 to the major number. The Mod 256 extracts a single byte (the minor version number) from a larger number.

The WindowsVersion( ) function works in very much the same way as the DOSVersion( ) function. The main difference is that WindowsVersion( ) uses Mod 65536 to extract the lower two bytes, which contain the Windows version information, from the Long number returned by GetVersion( ).

The Code

Here are the two functions that return version information. Both of these functions use a Windows API call that must be defined in the (declarations) section of your module:

```
Declare Function GetVersion Lib "Kernel" () As Long
```

Here are the two functions:

```
Function DOSVersion () As Single
    '
    ' This function returns the DOS version number as a
    ' floating point number, such as 3.31 for DOS 3.31.
    '
    Dim ver As Long
    Dim DOSVer As Single

    ver = GetVersion()                  ' Get DOS/Windows version
    ver = ver / 65536                   ' Get just the DOS version
    DOSVer = ver / 256                  ' Get major version number
    DOSVer = DOSVer + (ver Mod 256) / 100
    DOSVersion = DOSVer                 ' Return version
End Function
```

```
Function WindowsVersion () As Single
    '
    ' This function returns the Windows version number as a
    ' floating point number, such as 3.1 for Windows 3.1.
    '
    Dim ver As Long
    Dim WinVer As Single

    ver = GetVersion()                  ' Get DOS/Windows version
    ver = ver Mod 65536                 ' Get just the Win version
    WinVer = ver Mod 256                ' Get major version
    WinVer = WinVer + (ver / 256) / 100
    WindowsVersion = WinVer             ' Return version
End Function
```

Finding a Program's Directory

File MISCTOOL.BAS

Purpose Finds a program's full path name or the home directory of your program. This is very useful when you need to find your program's directory so your program can find its other files (to read and/or write).

If your program is very simple, you won't be interested in this section. But if you have other files you need to access, such as help files, INI files, etc., you'll want to find the directory where your program resides. The functions in this section will do the trick.

Let's look at an example. Say you have a program called MyCalc located in the directory C:\PROG\MISC, and you want to display on-line help using a help file in this directory. As long as the current directory is C:\PROG\MISC, there's no problem. But a number of programs, including Windows 3.1, allow you to set a default start-up directory different from the program's directory. In such cases, your program won't be able to find its help file unless you know which directory it's in.

All you have to do to find a program's directory is call GetProgramDir$( ), which returns your program's directory, such as

C:\PROG\MISC

NOTE

There is one exception that you should be aware of: When you're running your program from within Visual Basic (run mode), Get-ProgramDir$( ) will return the name of Visual Basic's directory, such as C:\PROG\VB, rather than your program's. This happens because Visual Basic is actually the current EXE program running.

How to Use It

The two functions here are very easy to use. Each function takes a single argument and returns a string. The argument is the hWnd property from any form in your application.

fileName$ = GetProgramName$(Form1.hWnd)

This returns the full path name of the current program, such as C:\PROG\MYCALC.EXE.

dirName$ = GetProgramDir$(Form1.hWnd)

This returns the drive and directory where your program resides. For example, it would be something like C:\PROG if your program were in the \PROG directory on drive C. The hWnd is the hWnd property from any form in your program. If you're calling these functions from inside a form, you can write hWnd without a form name; otherwise you must use something like Form1.hWnd.

The Code

You'll need the following definitions in the (declarations) section of any module or form:

```
'  Window field offsets for GetWindowLong() and GetWindowWord()
Const GWL_WNDPROC = (-4)
Const GWW_HINSTANCE = (-6)
Const GWW_HWNDPARENT = (-8)
Const GWW_ID = (-12)
Const GWL_STYLE = (-16)
Const GWL_EXSTYLE = (-20)

Declare Function GetWindowWord Lib "User" (ByVal hWnd As
➤ Integer, ByVal nIndex As Integer) As Integer
Declare Function GetModuleFileName Lib "Kernel" (ByVal hModule
➤ As Integer, ByVal lpFilename As String, ByVal nSize As
➤ Integer) As Integer
```

The following function, which you can put into either a module or a form, returns the full name of your program (such as C:\PROG\MISC\MYCALC.EXE). The sample program in the next section shows how to use this function.

```
Function GetProgramName$ (ByVal hWnd As Integer)
    Dim fullName As String * 255
    Dim hInstance As Integer

    hInstance = GetWindowWord(hWnd, GWW_HINSTANCE)
    i% = GetModuleFileName(hInstance, fullName, 255)
    GetProgramName$ = Left$(fullName, i%)
End Function
```

This function finds your program's directory by removing the file name at the end of the string returned by GetProgramName$( ). Load this function into the same module as GetProgramName$( ).

```
Function GetProgramDir$ (ByVal hWnd As Integer)
    Dim fullPath As String
    Dim lastSlash As Integer

    fullPath = GetProgramName$(hWnd) ' Get full path + name
    i = 1                             ' Start with first char
    Do                                ' Look for last \
        lastSlash = i                 ' Remember last location
        i = InStr(i + 1, fullPath, "\")
    Loop While i < > 0                ' Go until no more \'s
    If lastSlash > 2 Then             ' Did we find a \?
        GetProgramDir$ = Mid$(fullPath, 1, lastSlash - 1)
    Else
        GetProgramDir$ = ""           ' No, return empty string
    End If
End Function
```

Sample Program

The following sample program displays the full path name of your program, as well as its directory:

```
Sub Form_Paint ()
    CurrentX = 0                      ' Move to upper-left corner
    CurrentY = 0
    Print "Full path: "; GetProgramName$(hWnd)
    Print "Program dir: "; GetProgramDir$(hWnd)
End Sub
```

To run this program, you'll need to use the Make EXE File... option in the File menu, then run this program as an EXE file (rather than from within Visual

Basic). You'll then see output something like this:

Full path: C:\PROG\MISC\TEST.EXT
Program dir: C:\PROG\MISC

Notice that GetProgramDir$( ) returns the path name without a \ at the end. This is the form used by DOS for directory names.

Notes

These functions will return information on VB.EXE rather than your program when you use them in Visual Basic's run mode. In other words, they'll only return information on your program when you run your program as an EXE file.

How It Works

First we'll look at how GetProgramName$( ) works. You'll notice that this function uses two Windows functions, GetWindowWord( ) and GetModuleFile-Name( ).

The GetModuleFileName( ) function returns the full path name of any program currently running in Windows. A full path name, in this case, is a drive letter followed by a path and the program's name with an extension. In the example above, GetModuleFileName would return a string like this:

C:\PROG\MISC\MYCALC.EXE

You'll notice that the name is returned as all uppercase letters. You'll almost certainly see uppercase letters in your programs, but you shouldn't assume this will always be the case: Microsoft reserves the right to change such small things.

The GetModuleFileName function takes three parameters: an *instance handle,* a string, and a number that tells Windows how long the string is.

Whenever you use an API call like GetModuleFileName that returns information in a string, you must make sure the string will be large enough to hold any string returned by Windows. We'll use a 255-character string to make sure we have more than enough room for any path name. In current versions of DOS, full names are limited to 2 characters for the drive letter (C:), 64 characters for the path, and 13 characters for the name, so a full path name will never be longer than 80 characters. But this could change in future versions of Windows (such as Windows NT), so we'll reserve 255 characters.

The GetModuleFileName function needs to know which program we're interested in, since it can report information on any program running in Windows. To tell this function that we're interested in *our* program, we use the Windows GetWindowWord function to retrieve something called the instance handle. This is a unique number that identifies one of the programs currently running. In this case, GetWindowWord retrieves the instance handle from any form in your application, which is why we need to pass an hWnd to the GetProgram-Name$( ) function.

GetProgramDir$( ), as you can see, is written entirely with Visual Basic commands and functions. All it does is remove the program name and \ (such as \MYCALC.EXE) from the end of the string returned by GetProgramName$( ). We do this by looking for the last \ in the string, then removing it and everything after it.

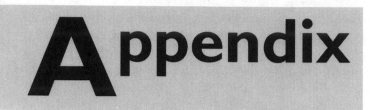 

Installing Visual Basic and the Companion-Disk Files

This appendix will lead you through the steps involved in installing Visual Basic on your computer and installing the files from the disk included with this book.

Installing Visual Basic

To use Visual Basic, you'll need to already have installed Microsoft Windows version 3.0 or later. Then you'll want to start Windows because the installation program for Visual Basic runs as a Windows program. Also, the instructions here apply to Visual Basic version 1.0. Later versions may have slightly different dialog boxes, but most of what you'll find here should apply.

Once you have Windows running, follow these steps to start the installation program:

1. Pull down the File menu and choose the Run... command. You'll see a dialog box like the one shown in Figure A.1.

2. Type **a:\setup** in the Command Line text box, then press Enter (if you're installing from a floppy disk in drive B rather than A, enter **b:\setup**).

Your computer will grind away for a while as it reads the Setup program from your floppy disk, then it will display a screen like the one shown in Figure A.2.

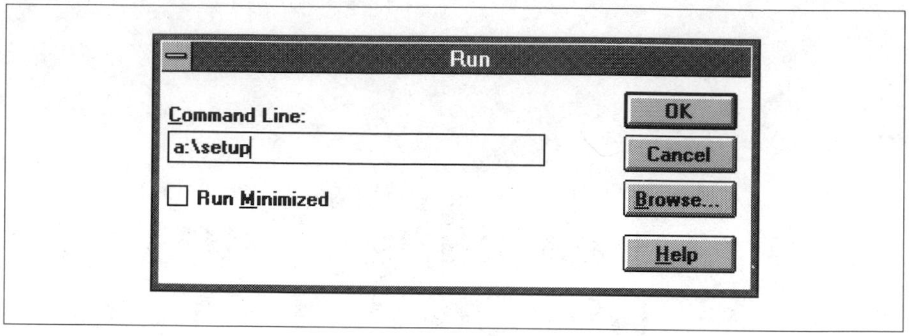

Figure A.1:

The Run dialog box that you'll use to start Visual Basic's Setup program

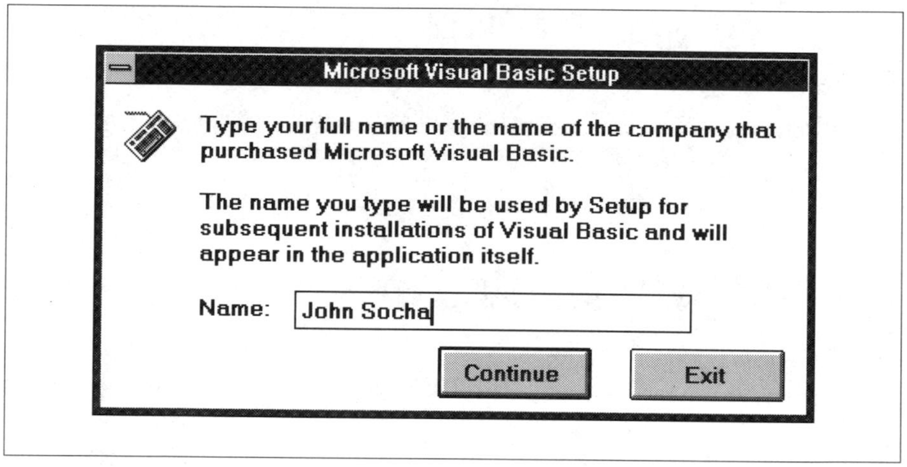

Figure A.2:

The registration dialog box asks for your name (or the name of the company that purchased the product).

3. Type your name, or your company's name, then press Enter or click on the Continue button.

4. You'll see another dialog box that contains the information you just entered. You can either click the Continue button again to continue or press the Change button to change the name you typed in.

After you've entered your name (or your company's name), you'll see the dialog box shown in Figure A.3. It asks you where you'll want Visual Basic itself to be installed on your hard disk. By default, Setup suggests a directory called C:\VB. I personally don't like to have a lot of directories that appear at the top of my hard disk, so I've created a directory on my computer called PROG where I store all my programs. So in my case, I type C:\PROG\VB into this dialog box.

Figure A.3:

In this dialog box, type the name of the directory where you want Visual Basic's files to be installed. If the default directory C:\VB is acceptable, simply press Enter or click on the Continue button.

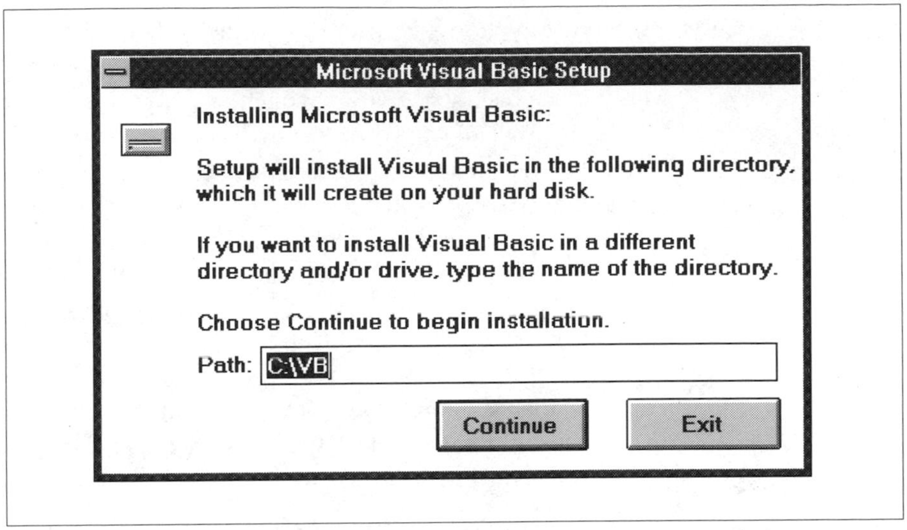

Microsoft Visual Basic Setup

Installing Microsoft Visual Basic:

Setup will install Visual Basic in the following directory, which it will create on your hard disk.

If you want to install Visual Basic in a different directory and/or drive, type the name of the directory.

Choose Continue to begin installation.

Path: `C:\VB`

> [Continue]   [Exit]

5. Type the directory where you want Setup to store Visual Basic's files. I personally like to use C:\PROG\VB rather than the default (you'll need to make sure the C:\PROG directory exists before you enter C:\PROG\VB).

The next dialog box, shown in Figure A.4, gives you a number of choices about what to install. Visual Basic comes with a number of optional add-ons

Figure A.4:

This is the last dialog box you'll see before Setup begins to install files on your hard disk. You can select which parts of Visual Basic you want Setup to install.

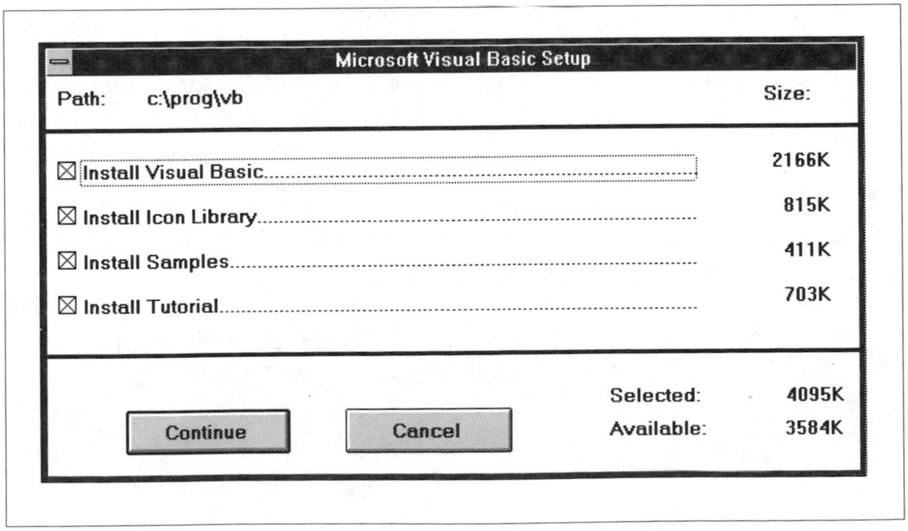

Microsoft Visual Basic Setup

	Size:
Path: c:\prog\vb	
☒ Install Visual Basic...	2166K
☒ Install Icon Library...	815K
☒ Install Samples...	411K
☒ Install Tutorial...	703K
	Selected: 4095K
[Continue] [Cancel]	Available: 3584K

that you can choose to install on or leave off your hard disk, depending on how much free disk space you have left. You'll also notice that Setup shows you both how much disk space you have left and how much disk space you'll need in order to install all parts of Visual Basic. (In this example there isn't enough room to install the entire Visual Basic package, but there is enough room to install everything except for the Tutorial.)

Before continuing, let's take a quick look at each of these options so you can decide what to install and what not to install. By the way, if you don't install everything now but you later decide to install other parts of the package, you can always run Setup again later to install, for example, just the Icon Library.

- **Visual Basic.** You'll definitely want to keep this item checked. It accounts for about 2MB of disk space, including all the files you'll need to run and use Visual Basic. All the other items are optional.

- **Icon Library.** This library contains about 400 icons that you can use in your programs. You'll use some of these icons in this book, so you can either install them now or you can run Setup later to add them. You'll find pictures of all the icons that come with Visual Basic in Appendix B of the *Microsoft Visual Basic Programmer's Guide* that comes with Visual Basic.

- **Samples.** These are sample programs that come with Visual Basic, designed to give you examples of what you can do with Visual Basic. You can modify them for your own use. Version 1.0 of Visual Basic comes with three sample programs: Calc, which is a simple calculator program; Cardfile, which looks and works just like the Windows Cardfile program, except that this version is written in Visual Basic; and Iconwrks (Icon Works), which is a program you can use to edit existing icons or to create your own icons.

- **Tutorial.** This is an interactive tutorial on Visual Basic. You probably won't want to look at this now since all the same ground is covered in this book.

Once you've chosen which parts of Visual Basic you want to install (I suggest at least Visual Basic and the Icon Library), press Enter or click Continue to start the installation. Setup will start to copy files to your computer and will prompt you each time you need to insert a new floppy disk into drive A (or B). When Setup finishes, it will display one last dialog box to let you know that it's all done. Simply press Enter to exit Setup.

Installing the Companion-Disk Files

This book comes with a disk at the back that includes a number of files on it. Some of these files are sample programs you'll find in this book, some are general-purpose tools you can use in your own programs, and some are custom controls and dynamic link libraries, or DLLs (these are add-ins that extend Visual Basic) that were provided by Crescent Software, MicroHelp, and Sheridan Software Systems. These add-ins are fully functional commercial tools that you can use in your own programs.

To make installing these files simpler, I've included a setup program you can run from Windows to install all these files on your computer. Choose the Run… item from the File menu and type **a:\setup** in the Run dialog box (or **b:\setup** if your floppy disk is in drive B). Your computer will grind away for a while as it reads the Setup program from your floppy disk, then you'll see a dialog box that will explain all the steps. Follow the directions and you'll have all the files installed on your hard disk.

Using the Commercial Software on the Companion Disk

The disk at the back of this book includes the following custom-control files:

CRESCENT.VBX	Provided by Crescent Software, Inc. The documentation is in the file CRESCENT.WRI, which is a formatted Windows Write file you can print out.
MHDEM200.VBX	Provided by MicroHelp, Inc. The documentation is in the file MICROHLP.WRI, which is a formatted Windows Write file you can print out.
SHERDN01.VBX	Provided by Sheridan Software Systems, Inc. The documentation is in the file SHERIDAN.WRI, which is a formatted Windows Write file you can print out.

You'll also find three files with the same names as these files, except they have the extension VBR instead of VBX. These files are run-time versions of the VBX files. The license agreements from Crescent, MicroHelp, and Sheridan **permit you to redistribute ONLY the VBR files, royalty-free**. You're not allowed to redistribute the VBX files.

If you write a program using any of the custom controls, and you want to give it to someone else, you'll need to do the following:

- Copy the EXE file that you made to another disk, and copy all other related files except for the VBX files.

- Copy the VBR file with the same name as the VBX file you used.

- Rename the VBR file you copied, changing its extension to VBX. You will now be able to run this program using the run-time version of the custom control.

The only difference between the run-time file and the VBX file is that you can't use the VBR file (even after you rename it VBX) to design new programs. You'll find more details on how to use these custom controls in the documentation included on the disk.

Where to Put the VBX Files

For Windows to find the VBX files, they must be in the correct directory. Windows will search for your VBX files in the following directories (in this order):

1. The current directory.

2. The Windows directory (which contains the WIN.INI file).

3. The Windows system directory (which contains the system files, such as KERNEL.EXE).

4. *Windows 3.1 and later:* The directory containing your program.

5. Directories listed in the PATH statement.

6. The list of directories mapped in a network.

You should be aware of several things. First, you can place the VBX files in the same directory as your program, and Windows will always find them if you have Windows 3.1 or later. But if you have Windows 3.0, it may or may not, depending on what shell program you use to run your program. The Windows Program Manager will always set the current directory to the same directory as your program. However, Norton Desktop 2.0 will not, which means your program may not run correctly if you use Norton Desktop 2.0 under Windows 3.0, unless you put the VBX files in the path or in the Windows or system directory.

Microsoft recommends putting all VBX files into the Windows system directory. The Setup program on the disk will copy VBX files to your system directory when you check the last option: *Installing VBX's in SYSTEM directory*.

Crescent Software Files

The custom controls and DLL functions provided by Crescent Software are a sample of their QuickPack Professional for Windows product. Their actual product contains far more custom controls and DLLs, and you'll find an advertisement with more details near the back of this book. Crescent Software has also agreed to offer QuickPack to readers at a special price. For more information, contact

> Crescent Software, Inc.
> 32 Seventy Acres
> West Redding, CT 06896
> (203) 438-5300

These are the functions provided by the Crescent Software custom-control file:

- *Instant Change Scroll Bars*. These scroll bars allow you to update your screen as you drag the scroll box on the scroll bar. The standard Visual Basic scroll bars only inform your program after you release the scroll box.

- *Play Command*. This command allows you to play melodies on your computer. You'll hear songs come out of your speaker. If you're familiar with the DOS versions of Basic (such as QBasic), this command is almost exactly like DOS Basic's Play command.

- *Financial Functions*. There are a number of functions, provided as a Visual Basic module, for doing financial calculations.

There are a number of Crescent files included on the disk at the back of this book:

CRESCENT.VBX   The custom-control file that you can use for both run-time and design-time. This is the file you'll use when you're building your program. **DO NOT give this file to other people—you do not have a license to distribute it.**

CRESCENT.VBR   Run-time-only version of CRESCENT.VBX. When you want to give your program to other people, give them a copy of this file, and rename it CRESCENT.VBX. Crescent allows you to freely distribute only this file, and you do *not* need to display a Crescent copyright notice or pay royalties to Crescent.

SOUND.DRV   This is an updated sound driver for Windows 3.0 (don't use this with Windows 3.1). You are free to distribute this driver with any programs you create.

FNSPREAD.BAS   This file contains a number of financial functions. You're free to distribute programs you create using this module **as long as you do not distribute the source code**.

DEMOPLAY.*   This is a demo program, with source code, that shows how to use the Play command.

DEMOSCRL.*   This is a demo program, with source code, that shows how to use the instant-change scroll bars.

To use the instant-change scroll bars, you'll need to add the CRESCENT.VBX file to your project:

- Add CRESCENT.VBX to your program by selecting the Add File... item from the File menu in Visual Basic. Then double-click on the CRESCENT.VBX file.

MicroHelp Files

The custom controls and DLLs provided by MicroHelp are a sample of their VBTools product. Their actual product contains far more custom controls and DLLs, and you'll find an advertisement with more details near the back of this book. MicroHelp has also agreed to offer VBTools to readers at a special price. For more information, contact

> MicroHelp, Inc.
> 4359 Shallowford Industrial Parkway
> Marietta, GA 30066
> (404) 516-0899

There are two functions provided by the MicroHelp custom-control file:

- *MbTag Custom List Box*. This list box behaves exactly like Visual Basic's list box, but it has some very useful additions. Here are some of the improvements: You can select multiple items, you can use tab stops, and you can have multiple columns.

- *Common Dialog Routines*. MicroHelp has provided a number of subroutines and functions you can call to use the standard dialog boxes introduced in Windows 3.1 for such common tasks as Print, Print Setup, Open File, Save File As, etc. I've used these routines in the Address Book program that you'll find on the disk for the Print and Print Setup dialog boxes. You're allowed to redistribute the COMMDLG.DLL file and the MHDEM200.VBR file (which you'll need to rename MHDEM200.VBX when you give copies to other people).

There are three MicroHelp files included on the disk at the back of this book:

MHDEM200.VBX The custom-control file that you can use for both run-time and design-time. This is the file you'll use when you're building your program. **DO NOT give this file to other people—you do not have a license to distribute it.**

MHDEM200.VBR   Run-time-only version of MHDEM200.VBX. When you want to give your program to other people, give them a copy of this file, and rename it MHDEM200.VBX. MicroHelp allows you to freely distribute only this file, and you do *not* need to display a MicroHelp copyright notice or pay royalties to MicroHelp.

MHDEM200.BI   This file contains the definitions you'll need to add to your Global.bas module in order to use the Common Dialog routines.

To use any of these functions, you'll need to do the following:

1. Add MHDEM200.VBX to your program by selecting the Add File... item from the File menu in Visual Basic. Then double-click on the MHDEM200.VBX file.

2. If you're going to use the common dialog routines, you'll also need to include the MHDEM200.BI file in your global module. You can do this by selecting Load Text... from the Code menu. Type ***.bi** and press Enter, then click once (don't double-click) on MHDEM200.BI, and click on the Merge button. This will add all the definitions to your global module without replacing it.

Sheridan Files

The custom controls and DLL functions provided by Sheridan Software Systems are a sample of their 3-D Widgets product. Their actual product contains far more custom controls and DLLs, and you'll find an advertisement with more details near the back of this book. Sheridan Software Systems has also agreed to offer 3-D Widgets to readers at a special price. For more information, contact

Sheridan Software Systems, Inc.
65 Maxess Road
Melvill, NY 11747
(516) 753-0985

These are the functions described in this chapter that are provided by the Sheridan custom-control file:

- *3-D Panel.* This custom control allows you to add three-dimensional borders to your program. You can place these borders anywhere, including around other controls.

- *3-D Button.* This is a special version of the command button that allows you to put a picture inside a command button. The standard Visual Basic command button allows only text inside the button.

There are two Sheridan files included on the disk at the back of this book:

SHERDN01.VBX   The custom-control file that you can use for both run-time and design-time. This is the file you'll use when you're building your program. **DO NOT give this file to other people—you do not have a license to distribute it.**

SHERDN01.VBR   Run-time-only version of SHERDN01.VBX. When you want to give your program to other people, give them a copy of this file, and rename it SHERDN01.VBX. Sheridan allows you to freely distribute only this file, and you do *not* need to display a Sheridan copyright notice or pay royalties to Sheridan.

To use the 3-D Panel and 3-D Button, you'll need to add the SHERDN01.VBX file to your project:

- Add SHERDN01.VBX to your program by selecting the Add File... item from the File menu in Visual Basic. Then double-click on the SHERDN01.VBX file.

Index

A

accelerator keys, 281–283, 361–362, 364–365
AddItem method, 210–212
addition, 10, 17, 21
additive colors, 155, 164
Address Book program, 176
  adding records in, 272–277, 282–284
  changed records in, 278–280
  combo box setup for, 209–214
  compound variables in, 238–242
  controls for, 191–203, 280–282
  deleting addresses in, 298
  Edit menu support by, 287–288
  empty records for, 276–277
  exit handler for, 286–287
  feature list for, 178–181
  icon for, 201–203
  initial design for, 177–178
  menu bar for, 182, 280–282
  modules for, 255–260
  for multiple records, 264–272
  navigating records in, 284–285
  passing variables in, 260–263
  printing addresses with, 296–297
  reading records in, 229–230
  saving records in, 277–278
  searching with, 293–296
  sketching screens for, 181–182
  sorting addresses with, 297
  subroutines for, 244–250
  tab order for, 207–209
  user-defined type for, 234–240
  writing records in, 229–230

AddressInfo type, 234–240
alert boxes, 8–9
Alignment property, 204, 206
alpha testing, 183–184
Alt key as accelerator, 283
ALTERNATE fill mode, 399
ampersands (&)
  for long type, 37, 107
  in menus, 89–90
And operator, 81
APISCALE.BAS file, 392, 401, 404, 408
arguments, 12–13
  for event handlers, 70
  vs. expressions, 15–16
  parts of, 96
Arial fonts, 421
arithmetic, 17–22
arrays, 103–107
  control, 94–98, 194–201, 331
  dynamic, 127
  files as, 220
  indexes for, 105, 127
  limits on, 442
  for lines, 113–114, 116–121
  for points, 107–111, 113–114
  in types, 236
Art of Human-Computer Interface Design, The (Laurel), 187
As keyword, 106–107, 222
ASCII characters, 225
aspect ratios, 316
assignment operator, 28–29, 38
asterisks (*)
  for multiplication, 17–18, 21
  for string length, 236–238

at signs (@), 37, 107
AutoRedraw property, 346–347
AutoSize property, 323, 329

B

BackColor property, 205–206, 328
background, running DOS
    programs in, 436–439
backslashes (\), 17–18, 20–21
Backspace key, 8
Beep command, 7–8
beta testing, 184–185
beveled edges, 334
binary files, 251
bitmaps, display adjustments for,
    323–326, 330
bitwise operators, 81
Black DrawMode value, 165
blank lines, displaying, 16
blocks of code, 111
bold letters
    for event handlers, 112
    in syntax descriptions, 14–15
Boolean expressions, 38, 77–82
borders
    size of, 376
    style for, 205, 207
    three-dimensional, 467
BorderStyle property, 205
boundary conditions, 157, 270
bounds, array, 127
braces ({}), 14–15, 288
break mode, 9–10
breakpoints, 266–267, 289
Brooks, Frederick P., Jr., *The
    Mythical Man-Month*, 187
brushes, system resources for, 444

bugs, 183–184
bytes, 36
ByVal keyword, 261–263, 275

C

C programming language, 5, 306–308
calculator functions, 17–18
calendar. *See* ClockCal program
Cancel property, 295, 365–367
Caption property, 74, 136, 204, 206
captions, 95, 125, 280–281
    for command buttons, 204, 206
    displaying time in, 142, 147
    for forms, 74
    for icons, 136–137
carets (^), 17, 19–21
case-sensitivity
    in searches, 294
    in variable names, 31
cboPhone_Click event handler, 279
CCur function, 41
CDbl function, 41
CenterForm subroutine, 372–374
Change events, 278–280
characteristics. *See* properties
Checked property, 98–100
CheckPeriod subroutine, 352, 354
ChooseBitmap function, 325–326
CInt function, 41
Circle command, 56
clearing
    list boxes, 368–369
    screen, 49, 92–93
ClearList subroutine, 368–369
ClearRecord subroutine, 274, 276–277
CLng function, 41
clock, reading, 137–138

clock faces, 147. *See also* Icon
  Clock program
  erasing lines on, 155–160
  hour and minute hands for, 160–161
  icon for, 148–149
  second hand for, 149–152, 154
ClockCal program, 330
  code for, 337–342
  control arrays for, 331
  form for, 335–337
  operation of, 333–334
  resizing in, 332–333
ClockFrame_Paint event handler, 334
Close command, 222, 229
closing files, 222, 228–229
Cls command, 49, 92–93, 135–136
cmdCancel_Click event handler, 295
cmdFind_Click event handler, 295
cmdNext_Click event handler, 285
cmdoCancel_Click event handler, 367
cmdoOpen_Click event handler, 366
cmdPrev_Click event handler, 285
Code window, 61–62
colons (:), 116
color
  additive, 155, 164
  for background, 205–206
  on displays, 313, 328–329
  for lines, 50, 56, 154–155, 391
  for polygons, 400
  subtractive, 155
combining strings, 34–35
combo boxes, 204–205
  control arrays of, 196–197, 200
  display adjustments for, 321–322,
    328–329
  limits on, 442
  properties for, 205

setting up, 209–214
  system resources for, 445
command buttons, 204
  for Address Book, 199–200
  properties for, 206
command lines for program
    items, 202
COMMAND.COM file, 436, 438
commands, 4–5
  in Immediate window, 6–9
  multiple, 116
  with objects, 50–51
  syntax of, 11–16
commas (,)
  as delimiters, 12–13, 16
  in numbers, 39
COMMDLG.DLL library, 296, 465
comments, 100, 265, 272
common dialog routines, 465
companion-disk files, 459, 461–467
[Compatibility] section (WIN.INI), 415
complex equations, 20–22
compound variables, 231–232,
    238–242
concatenating strings, 34–35
conditions and conditional
    commands, 72, 76–82
Const keyword and constants,
    151–152, 359
control arrays, 94–98
  for ClockCal program, 331
  creating, 194–201
control keys in text box input, 351
ControlBox property, 215
controls. *See also* control arrays
  for Address Book, 191–194,
    280–282
  captions for, 95, 125, 280–281

character limits in, 355–356
clearing, 368–369
for ClockCal, 335–337
custom, 304–305, 461–467
default and cancel, 365–367
display adjustments for, 321–330
Edit menu support by, 361–365
fonts for, 423
height of, 319–321
hiding, 367
input checking for, 350–354
limits on, 442
moving, 381–382
names for, 89–91, 94–96, 99, 140
overtype mode in, 356–358
passwords in, 358–361
progress bars, 345–348
properties for, 203–206
referencing, 258
shadows around, 348–350
size of, 193–194, 319–322, 326, 328, 379–382
on Sketch menu, 124–125
system resources for, 444–445
tab order for, 207–209
text in, changing, 226–227
converting
time and dates, 167
types, 41
coordinate systems, 46, 48, 150–151, 393
Copy command, 287–288, 361–365
Cos function, 143
Courier fonts, 413–414, 420–421
CreateFont function (Windows), 425–427
CRESCENT.VBX file, 461, 463–465
CSgn function, 41

Ctrl key as accelerator, 283
CTRLTOOL.BAS file, 345–346, 348, 350, 355, 358, 368
curly braces ({ }), 14–15, 288
Currency type, 37, 41, 107
current directory, 203, 229–230
CurrentX property, 53–56, 74, 82–83
CurrentY property, 53–56, 74, 82–83
custom controls, 304–305, 461–467
Cut command, 287–288, 361–365

D

dashed lines, 388, 391, 401
database programs and files, 179, 237
Date$ function, 167
dates, 144–147, 167, 182, 275, 334
DateSerial function, 167
DateValue function, 167
Day function, 167
DBClose subroutine, 248, 272
DBLen function, 268–269, 298
DBOpen subroutine, 244–246, 256–257, 264–268
DBRead subroutine, 248–249, 258–261, 270–271, 296
DBWrite subroutine, 248–250, 258–260, 271–272
Debug object, 267–268
debugging, 183–184, 266–268, 289, 443
decimal points, 35, 352
Declare statement, 305–306
declaring
procedures, 305–306
variables, 108
Default property, 295, 365–367

DeleteObject function (Windows), 425, 427
deleting
  addresses, 298
  files, 250
delimiters, 12–13, 16
density and screen resolution, 312–313
descriptions for program items, 202
design mode, 6, 9–10
Design of Everyday Things, The (Norman), 186
designing
  evaluation of, 186–187
  programs, 173–174
  user interfaces, 176–182
design-time properties, 74
detailed specifications, 174
device contexts, 389, 397, 406, 425, 444
Dim statement, 105–106, 232–233
directories
  for Address Book, 229–230
  finding, 449–453
  for installation, 456–457
  for opening files, 221
  for program items, 202
  for saving projects, 74–75
  for VBX files, 462–463
  working, 202, 229
directory list boxes, 322
disk files, 219
  binary and sequential, 251
  closing, 222, 228–229
  creating, 221–223
  deleting and renaming, 250
  modes for, 220, 222
  opening, 75–76, 221–223
    random-access, 220–223, 237
    reading, 226–228
    size of, 250–251, 265
    writing to, 223–225
displays. *See also* ClockCal program; screens
  color on, 328–329
  for combo boxes, 321–322, 328–329
  for list boxes, 321–323, 329
  and logical units, 315–317
  for pictures, 323–329
  pixel size on, 403
  resolution of, 311–315
  rules for controls on, 328–330
  sharp images on, 317–318
  size of, 312–315
  and twips, 318–319
division, 17–18, 20–21
division by zero, 40
Do.. loops, 128–129
DoEvents subroutine, 439
DoKeyPress subroutine, 352–354
dollar signs ($), 33, 37, 107
DOS programs, running, 435–439
DOS versions, checking, 446–448
DOSVersion function, 446–448
dot pitch, 314–315
dotted lines, 391, 401
double quote marks ("), 19, 32
Double type, 37, 41, 107
DrawBevel subroutine, 334, 341
DrawBevelLine subroutine, 341–342
drawing
  clock hands, 149–152, 154, 160–161
  with color, 154–155
  filled polygons, 396–401
  in icons, 135–136
  interface screens, 181–182

lines, 45–50, 68, 113–114, 387–391
mouse for, 68, 72
points, 83
on printer (*See* printers and
    printing)
properties for, 53–56
ruler, 392–396
Step keyword with, 52–53
with twip scaling, 408–411
in windows, 45–50
DrawMode property, 156–157,
    163–166, 347, 391, 401
DrawWidth property, 56, 97, 120,
    122–123, 401, 404, 409
DrawXRuler subroutine, 394
DrawYRuler subroutine, 394–395
drives, finding, 450
drop-down lists, 209
drop shadows, 348–350
duplicate variable names, 33–34
dynamic arrays, 127
dynamic link libraries (DLLs), 296,
    304–308, 443

E

Edit menu support
  by Address Book, 287–288
  by controls, 361–365
elements
  of arrays, 105–106
  of compound variables, 231–232
*Elements of Friendly Software
    Design, The* (Heckel), 187
ellipses (…) in syntax descriptions,
    14–15
Else keyword, 79–80
ElseIf keyword, 80
empty records, creating, 276–277

End command, 9, 65–66, 92
End Function statement, 269
End If statement, 110
End Sub statement, 63–66
EndDoc command, 49
endpoints for lines, 50
Enter key in Immediate window,
    7–9, 28–29
equal signs (=)
  for assignment, 28–29, 38
  as Boolean operator, 38, 79–82
equations, complex, 20–22
Eqv operator, 81
Erase command, 127
erasing
  arrays, 127
  lines, 155–160
Err function, 424
error messages, 440–443
event-driven programs, 66–67
events and event handlers, 63–65,
    68–70
evolutionary programming approach,
    174–175
exclamation marks (!), 37, 107
exclusive Or operator, 81
EXE programs, 123–124
Exit Function command, 269
Exit item
  for Address Book, 286–287
  for menu bars, 91–92
Exit Sub statement, 276
exiting Visual Basic, 4
Exp function, 23
exponentiation, 17, 19–21
exponents, 35
expressions, 15–16
  Boolean, 38, 77–82

in equations, 20–22
in syntax descriptions, 14
extended ASCII characters, 225

F

F1 key, 243
fast line drawing, 387–391
features
list of, 178–181
testing, 183–186
file list boxes, 322
file numbers, 223, 263–264
files. *See* disk files
fill modes, 399
FillColor property, 56
filled polygons, drawing, 396–401
FillStyle property, 56
financial functions, 464
Find dialog box, 294–295
FindFontSize function, 327–328,
332–333, 339–340, 416–419
Fix function, 41
Fixed Height display mode, 319–320
fixed-length strings, 236–238
flicker, 143, 145, 154, 160
floating-point numbers, 35–36, 40–
41, 352–354
focus, 207–209, 284–285, 288–289
font families, 413, 420–421
FontBold property, 205
FontName property, 415, 419
FONTNAME.BAS file, 419–431
FONTNAME.H file, 419, 422, 426
fonts
names for, 413–416, 419–431
in pictures, 326–328
properties for, 205, 215, 326–328,
415–419

requesting, by height, 416–419
TrueType, 421, 426
FontSize property, 326–328, 416–418
[FontSubstitutes] section
(WIN.INI), 426
FONTTOOL.BAS file, 416
For..Next loops, 113–116, 118–119,
127–128
ForeColor property, 56
Form_Click event handler, 62–65
Form_Load event handler, 240–242,
249
for ClockCal, 337–338
for compound variables, 238–240
for control height, 322, 326
for hiding controls, 367
for Icon Clock, 153, 159, 161
for opening files, 221
for polygons, 398
for reading records, 226, 230
for resizing controls, 381–382
for saving records, 224
for spirals, 390
Form_MouseDown event handler,
82–83, 124–125
for saving lines, 117–118
for saving points, 110, 113–114
Form_MouseMove event handler,
68–70, 110, 125
code for, 71–72
for saving lines, 118–119
Form_Paint event handler, 125–126
for passwords, 359
for path names, 451
for polygons, 398
for redrawing forms, 111–113
for redrawing lines, 113–114
for rulers, 395–396

for saving lines, 119–120
for shadows, 349
Form_Resize event handler, 153,
    378, 381–382
Form_Unload event handler, 240–242,
    249, 286–287
  for closing files, 229
  for compound variables, 238–240
  for saving records, 227–228, 230
Form1 window, 45, 51, 61–62,
    134–135
Format command (DOS), 438
Format$ function, 23, 144–145,
    167, 275, 334
FORMAT.TXT file, 438
forms, 51
  adding lines to, 371–372
  for Address Book, 196
  centering, 372–374
  for ClockCal, 335–337
  fonts for, 423
  modal, 294
  multiple records on, 272–277
  properties for, 205–207
  redrawing, 111–113
  referencing controls on, 258
  resizing controls on, 379–382
  saving, 192
  size of, 56–57, 207, 332–333,
    374–378
  for start-up screens, 382–385
  system resources for, 444
  unloading, 227–228, 286–287
  variables for, 107–109, 247, 273
FORMTOOL.BAS file, 372, 374
FORTRAN programming language,
    115
FreeFile function, 263–264

.FRM extension, 72
function keys as accelerators, 283
Function keyword, 268–269
functions, 84, 143–144, 268–269
  limits on, 441
  as procedures, 69

G

GDI heap, 443–446
Get command, 226–227, 251, 270
GetDeviceCaps function (Windows),
    406, 409
GetFocus function (Windows), 356,
    360
GetInfo subroutine, 261
GetMatchingFont$ function, 424–426,
    428–429
GetMetricMatch$ function, 426,
    429–431
GetModuleFileName function
    (Windows), 452–453
GetModuleUsage function
    (Windows), 439
GetProgramDir$ function, 449,
    451–453
GetProgramName$ function, 450–453
GetRecord subroutine, 258–261,
    273–276
GetTextFace function (Windows),
    425–426
GetTextMetrics function (Windows),
    425–427
GetVersion function (Windows),
    447–448
GetWindowLong function
    (Windows), 360, 450
GetWindowWord function
    (Windows), 450, 452–453

global module, 233–234, 237, 256, 442
global variables, 109, 234, 256
Global.bas file, 233, 237
GotFocus event handlers, 289
greater-than signs (>), 81, 147

H

handles
  to device contexts, 444
  instance, 452
  on objects, 139
hands, clock, 149–152, 154, 160–161
heaps, 443–446
Heckel, Paul, *The Elements of Friendly Software Design,* 187
height
  of combo boxes, 322
  of controls, 193–194, 319–322, 326
  of forms, 374–378
  requesting fonts by, 416–419
  of text, 318–319
Height property, 193–194, 322, 374–376
help, 243–244
Helv fonts, 413–416, 420, 423–424
hiding controls, 367
Hopper, Grace, 183
Hour function, 145
hour hands, drawing, 160–161
hyphens, 94

I

Icon Clock program
  clock-face icon for, 148–149
  clock hands for, 149–152, 154, 160–161
  designing clock for, 133–134

displaying time in, 142–147
erasing lines in, 155–160
icons for, 135–137
minimizing icon for, 152–153
reading clock for, 137–138
timers for, 138–142
Icon Works program, 148, 330
icons, 134
  for Address Book, 201–203
  captions for, 136–137
  for clock face, 148–149
  display adjustments for, 323, 325
  drawing in, 135–136
  library for, 458
  minimizing, 152–153
If..Then command, 72, 76–80, 110–111
Immediate window
  for debugging, 267–268, 289
  Enter key in, 7–9, 28–29
  showing, 6–7
  typing in, 7–9
Imp operator, 81
indenting
  menu items, 91, 95
  program lines, 61–62, 111
Index property, 194–197, 200, 331
index variables for controls, 94–98, 125, 194–197, 200, 331
indexes for arrays, 105, 127
initialization of variables, 30
InitRuler subroutine, 395
input
  checking characters for, 350–354
  limiting number of characters for, 355–356
insertion point, 8

inside dimensions, sizing forms using, 374–377
installing Visual Basic, 455–459
instance handles, 452
instant-change scroll bars, 463
InStr function, 42, 294, 296
Int function, 41
integer division, 17–18, 20–21
integers, 36–39, 41, 107
Interval property, 141–142
Inverse drawing modes, 163–166
inverting lines, 156
italics in syntax descriptions, 14

K

Keeps Size display mode, 319–320
Kemeny, John G., 11
KeyAscii parameter, 351
keyboard focus, 207–209, 284–285, 288–289
keyboard shortcuts, 281–283, 361–362, 364–365
keywords, 12, 16
  capitalization of, 63
  in variable names, 31
Kill command, 250
Kurtz, Thomas E., 11

L

labels, 204
  for Address Book, 198–199
  for ClockCal, 337
  properties for, 206
large programs, 439–446
Laurel, Brenda, *The Art of Human-Computer Interface Design,* 187
LB_RESETCONTENT message, 369
LBound function, 127

LCase$ function, 42
leading, 326, 416–417
Left$ function, 42
Left property, 194, 328, 333, 375
left side, hiding controls on, 367
Len function, 42, 240–241
length
  of records, 222
  of strings, 36, 42, 225, 228, 236–238
  of variables, 240–241
length bytes, 36
less-than signs (<), 81, 147
LimitLength subroutine, 355–356
limits
  on memory, 441–443
  on numbers, 37–40
  on text box input, 355–356
Line command and lines
  color with, 50, 56, 154–155, 391
  drawing, 45–50, 68, 113–114, 387–391
  erasing, 155–160
  on forms, adding, 371–372
  in icons, 135–136
  mouse for, 68, 72
  with objects, 51
  on printer, 49, 121–123, 401–407
  for progress bars, 347
  saving, 116–120
  Step keyword with, 52–53
  width of, 56, 96–99, 120–121, 391, 401–407
list boxes
  clearing, 368–369
  display adjustments for, 321–323, 329
  limits on, 442–443
ListCount property, 215

ListIndex property, 212–214
Load command, 286, 289
Load Icon dialog box, 148–149
Loc function, 250
LOF function, 250, 265
logical fonts, 425
logical inches, 311, 315–317
Long type, 37, 41, 107
loop counters, 115
Loop statement, 128–129
loops, 113–116, 118–119, 127–129
LostFocus handlers, 289
LTrim$ function, 42, 251

M

Main subroutine, 383–384
major version numbers, 447
.MAK extension, 72
mantissas, 35
mapping font names, 414
mapping modes, 387, 396, 406, 409
Mask drawing modes, 163–165
MaxButton property, 153, 205
memory, 439–440
    error messages for, 440–443
    limits on, 441–443
    for system resources, 443–446
    for variables, 30
Menu Design window, 87–88
menus and menu bars, 87
    adding code for, 92
    adding items to, 92–93
    for Address Book, 182, 280–282
    checking items on, 98–100
    control arrays for, 94–98
    controls for, 89–91, 124–125
    Exit item for, 91–92, 286–287
    separating lines in, 94

system resources for, 445
    titles for, 88–89
Merge drawing modes, 163–166
messages, 66–67, 111, 355–356, 369
methods, 210
metrics data structure, 425
MhChooseFont function, 421
MHDEM200 files, 296, 368, 420,
    461, 465–466
MhTag list box, 368
miCopy_Click event handler, 287,
    362
MICROHLP files, 296, 461, 465–466
*Microsoft Windows User Interface
    Style Guide,* 187
miCut_Click event handler, 287, 362
Mid$ function, 42
miErase_Click event handler, 93,
    121, 126
miExit_Click event handler, 92,
    126, 286
MinButton property, 215
miNew_Click event handler, 282
miNext_Click event handler, 285
minimizing icons, 152–153
minor version numbers, 447
minus signs (–)
    for negative numbers, 12, 17,
        21–22
    with Print, 12
    for subtraction, 17, 21
Minute function, 145–146
minute hands, drawing, 160–161
miPaste_Click event handler, 287,
    362
miPixel_Click event handler, 96–98,
    126
miPrevious_Click event handler, 286

miPrint_Click event handler, 122–123, 126

MISCTOOL.BAS file, 435, 446, 449

miUndo_Click event handler, 287, 362

mnemonic access characters, 89–90

Mod operator, 17–19, 21

modal dialog boxes, 295

modal forms, 294

Modern fonts, 421

modular design, 256

modules, 246
  creating, 255–260
  global, 233–234, 237, 256, 442
  limits on, 441
  variables for, 263

monitors, 314–315. *See also* displays

Month function, 167

mouse, drawing lines with, 68, 72

mouse-click events, 63, 72

Move commands and methods, 332, 374, 376, 379–380

MoveControls subroutine, 382

moving controls, 381–382

MS Sans Serif fonts, 414

MS Serif fonts, 414

multiline programs, 65

MultiLine property, 203, 206

multimedia sound, 433–435

multiplication, 17–18, 20–21

Mythical Man-Month, The (Brooks), 187

N

Name command, 250

name tables, limits on, 442–443

names
  for arguments, 96
  for controls, 89–91, 94–96, 99, 140
  for event handlers, 63–65
  for files, 223, 250
  for fonts, 413–416, 419–431
  for projects, 72–73
  for subroutines, 64–65, 246–247
  for variables, 28, 30–34, 104, 115

navigating records, 284–285

negative numbers
  minus signs for, 12, 17, 21–22
  with Print, 12
  representation of, 78

New Procedure dialog box, 245

NewPage command, 57

NextRecord subroutine, 284–285

nonpixel scaling modes, 391, 400

Norman, Donald A., *The Design of Everyday Things,* 186

Not operator, 78, 81

not-equal-to operator, 147

NotXorPen drawing mode, 157

Now function, 144–145

number signs (#), 37, 107

numbers. *See also* values
  for files, 223, 263–264
  formatting, 23
  limits on, 37–40
  rounding, 39
  scientific notation for, 40–41
  and types, 32–37

O

Object combo box, 108, 110, 245–246

object-oriented programming, 210–211

objects, 50–51, 64–65, 139–140

On Error command, 424

on-line help, 243–244

Open command, 221–223
Open Project dialog box, 75
opening files, 75–76, 221–223
Option Base statement, 127
optional items in syntax descriptions, 14–15
Or operator, 81
origins of coordinate systems, 46, 48
"Out of Memory" error message, 440–442
"Out of Stack Space" error message, 441
overflow, 40
overtype mode, 356–358

P

p-code, 440
packaging variables, 231
Page property, 57
paint messages, 111
Paint methods for progress bars, 346–347
parameters for subroutines, 260–263, 275
parentheses
  for arrays, 103, 105–106
  for functions, 269
  for operator precedence, 21–22, 82
passing information, parameters for, 260–263, 275
passwords in text boxes, 358–361
Paste command, 287–288, 361–365
path names, finding, 449–453
Pen Color DrawMode value, 166
pens
  properties of, 53–56
  system resources for, 444
percent signs (%), 37–39, 107

periods (.), 51
PgDn and PgUp keys, 110–111
phone numbers
  in Address Book, 180, 195–197, 204–205
  combo boxes for, 209–214
  as strings, 234–235
picture boxes
  for ClockCal, 336
  system resources for, 444–445
Picture property, 334
pictures
  display adjustments for, 321, 323–326, 329–330
  text in, 326–328
.PIF files, 437–438
PIFEDIT program, 437
pixel mapping mode, 387
pixels (picture elements), 48–49
  and logical inches, 316
  scaling, 405–406
  width of, 402–404
Play command (Crescent), 463
plus signs (+)
  for addition, 17, 21
  for concatenation, 34–35
POINTAPI type, 389, 394, 397–398
points (drawing)
  drawing, 83
  with Polygon, 397
  with Polyline, 389
  restoring, 113–114
  saving, 107–111
points (measurement), 49
Polygon function (Windows), 396–401
Polyline function (Windows), 387–391, 394

powers functions, 19–21, 23
precedence of operators, 20–22, 82
Print command, 10–12. *See also*
    printers and printing
  syntax of, 15–16
  variables with, 28
Print # command, 251
Print dialog box, 296
Print Setup dialog box, 296
Printer command, 49, 390–391, 400
printers and printing, 57
  addresses, 296–297
  drawings, 49, 121–123
  fonts for, 419, 423
  line width for, 401–407
  with Polygon, 400
  with Polyline, 390–391
  resolution of, 312
  using screen pixel mode, 404–407
PrinterToScreenRatio subroutine, 404
PrinterUnitsPerPixel subroutine, 403
printing. *See* printers and printing
Proc combo box, 69, 112, 246
procedures, 69
program groups, 3, 201
program information files, 437–438
Program Item Properties dialog
    box, 201–202, 229
Program Manager for icons, 201–203
programming, 4–5
programs. *See also* Address Book
    program; ClockCal program;
    Icon Clock program; Sketch
    program
  building, 183–185
  debugging, 183–184, 266–268,
    289, 443
  designing, 173–174

DOS, 435–439
  evaluating design of, 186–187
  event-driven, 66–67
  event handlers for, 63–65
  EXE, 123–124
  large, 439–446
  multiline, 65
  opening, 75–76
  starting, 61–63
stepwise refinement process for,
    104, 134
progress bars, 345–348
projects, saving, 72–75
properties
  accessing, 99–100
  for controls, 203–206
  for drawing, 53–56
  Properties bar for, 73, 193, 195
  run-time and design-time, 74
  scale-related, 56–57, 167
Properties bar, 73, 193, 195
PSet command, 83
pseudo-code, 157–158
Put command, 223–225, 231, 251

Q

quit messages, 66–67

R

random-access files, 220–223, 237
reading
  with Address Book, 229–230
  clock, 137–138
  compound variables, 238–242
  disk files, 226–228
real fonts, 425
records, 220
  adding, 272–277, 282–284

calculating number of, 265, 268–269

changes in, 278–280

empty, 276–277

length of, 222

multiple, code for, 264–272

navigating, 284–285

reading, 226–230

writing, 223–225, 229–230, 277–278

rectangles, drawing, 50

ReDim command, 127

redrawing

  forms, 111–113

  lines, 113–114

  windows, 52

reference, passing variables by, 261–263

Refresh method, 346, 384

registration dialog box, 456

remainder operation, 17–19, 21

RemoveItem method, 215, 368

renaming files, 250

ResetFormScale subroutine, 408, 411

ResetPrinterScale subroutine, 405, 407–408, 411

ResizeInside subroutine, 374–377

resolution

  of printers, 312

  of screen, 311–315

resources, system, 443–446

RGB function, 56, 154–155

Right$ function, 42

RmDir command, 250

Roman fonts, 421

rounding numbers, 39

RTrim$ function, 42, 242

ruler, drawing, 392–396

RULER.BAS module, 392–396

Run dialog box, 456

run mode, 6, 9–10, 62

RunDOS subroutine, 439

running commands, 5

run-time properties, 74

S

sample programs, 458

Save Project As dialog box, 75

SaveRecord subroutine, 258–260, 277–278

saving

  forms, 192

  line widths, 120–121

  lines, 116–120

  points, 107–111

  projects, 72–75

  records, 223–225, 229–230, 277–278

Scale command, 57, 150–151

ScaleHeight property, 56, 167, 376

ScaleLeft property, 56, 167

ScaleMode property, 57, 329, 332, 375, 409

ScaleTop property, 56, 167

ScaleWidth property, 56, 167, 347, 376

scaling

  changing, 57, 150–151, 329, 332, 375

  pixels, 405–406

  properties for, 56–57, 167, 347, 375–376

  twips, 332, 391, 400, 408–411

scientific notation, 40–41, 352

screen pixel mode, printing using, 404–407

screens. *See also* displays

  clearing, 49, 92–93

  font names for, 419

interface, 181–182
start-up, 382–385
Script fonts, 421
scroll bars
  instant change, 463
  in text boxes, 203–204, 206
ScrollBars property, 203–204, 206
searching
  for addresses, 293–296
  in help system, 244
Second function, 145
second hand, drawing, 149–152, 154
segments, 440
Select Case command, 84
SelectObject function (Windows),
  425, 427
SelStart property, 354
semicolons (;), 12–13, 16
SendKeys command, 288–289,
  362–364
SendMessage function (Windows),
  355–356, 369
separating lines in menus, 94
sequential files, 251
SetControlFont subroutine, 421,
  423–424, 428
SetFocus method (Windows), 284,
  360
SetFormFont subroutine, 421–425,
  427–428
SetFormToTwips subroutine,
  408–410
SetMapMode function (Windows),
  406, 409
SetPolyFillMode (Windows), 399
SetPrinterFont subroutine, 421,
  423–424, 428

SetPrinterToScreenPixels subroutine,
  405, 407
SetPrinterToTwips subroutine,
  408–410
Setup program, 455–459
SetupSizes subroutine, 332–333, 338
SetViewportExt function (Windows),
  406, 409–410
SetWindowExt function (Windows),
  406, 409
SetWindowLong function (Windows),
  360
SetWindowOrg function (Windows),
  393
Shadow subroutine, 348–350
Shell command, 435–439
SHERDN01 files, 366, 461, 466–467
SHERIDAN.WRI file, 461
Shift key as accelerator, 283
Shift parameters, 352
Show command, 286, 289, 295
single-line text boxes, 203
single quote marks ('), 100
Single type, 37–38, 41, 107
size
  of arrays, 127
  of borders, 376
  of controls, 193–194, 319–322,
    326, 328, 379–382
  of display, 312–314
  of files, 250–251, 265
  of fonts, 326–328
  of forms, 56–57, 207, 332–333,
    374–378
  of objects, 139
  of pixels, 48–49
  of twips, 47–49

SizeCalendar subroutine, 332–333, 339

SizeWindow subroutine, 332–333, 338–339

Sketch program, 67, 82–84
arrays for, 103–111, 113–114, 116–121
conditional commands in, 76–80
events for, 68–70
EXE file for, 123–124
form variables for, 107–109
Form_MouseMove event handler code for, 71–72
line widths in, 120–121
listing of, 124–126
menu bar for, 87–101
opening, 75–76
printing in, 121–123
redrawing forms in, 111–113
redrawing lines in, 113–114
saving lines in, 116–120
saving points in, 109–111

slashes (/), 17–18, 21

SND_ flags, 434

sndPlaySound function, 433–435

SORT.BAS program, 297

sorting addresses, 297

sound, 7–8, 433–435, 463–464

spaces
in commands, 18, 29
as delimiters, 12–13, 16
removing, 42, 242, 251

special symbols with SendKeys, 363–364

speed of floating-point numbers, 36

spirals, drawing, 390

square brackets ([ ])
for active mode, 9–10

in syntax descriptions, 14–15

stack space, 441

standard fonts, 413–414, 420–421

starting points for lines, 50

starting Visual Basic, 3–4

start-up screens, 382–385

static constants, 359

static variables, 334

Step keyword
in For..Next loops, 118
with Line, 50, 52–53

stepping through programs, 266–267, 289

stepwise refinement process, 104, 134

Str function, 41

strings, 19, 32–33, 107
concatenating, 34–35
converting, 41
fixed-length, 236–238
functions for, 42
length of, 36, 42, 225, 228, 236–238
phone numbers as, 234–235
searching for, 293–296
suffix for, 37
variable-length, 237

Style property, 205

styles for borders, 205, 207

Sub statement, 64–65

subroutines, 64–65
creating, 244–247
limits on, 441
moving between, 110–111
parameters for, 260–263, 275
as procedures, 69
variables in, 109, 247–248

subtraction, 17, 21

subtractive colors, 155

SupplyInfo subroutine, 261
Symbol fonts, 413–414, 420–421
syntax of commands, 11–16
system resources, 443–446

T

Tab function, 23
Tab key, 61, 207–209, 215
tab order for controls, 207–209
tab stops, 12–13, 23, 215
TabIndex property, 208–209
TabStop property, 215
testing
   display adjustments, 329–330
   Immediate window for, 7
   programs, 72, 183–186, 266–268
text
   height of, 318–319, 416–419
   in pictures, 326–328
text boxes
   for Address Book, 196–198,
      200–201
   changing text in, 226–227
   character limits in, 355–356
   Edit menu support by, 361–365
   input checking for, 350–354
   limits on, 442–443
   overtype mode in, 356–358
   passwords in, 358–361
   properties of, 203–204, 206
   resizing, 380–381
Text property, 201, 206, 226
Text1_KeyDown event handler,
   351–352
Text1_KeyPress event handler,
   350–353, 357–358
Text1_KeyUp event handler,
   352–353

TextHeight property, 326–328,
   416–419
TEXTMETRIC structure, 426–427
3-D buttons, Cancel and Default
   properties for, 365–367
3-D Widgets product, 466–467
Tick_Timer( ) subroutine, 141,
   161–162
   for captions, 143, 145
   for color in lines, 155
   for erasing lines, 157–159
   for formatting time, 146–147
   for hour and minute hands,
      160–161
   for second hand, 151
Ticker_Timer event handler, 334, 340
time. *See also* ClockCal program;
      Icon Clock program
   displaying, 142–147
   reading, 137–138
Time$ string, 137–138, 143
timers, 138
   creating, 139–140
   setting, 140–142
   system resources for, 445
TimeSerial function, 167
TimeValue function, 167
titles for menus, 88–89
Tms Rmn fonts, 413–416, 420–421
To keyword, 105, 115–116, 118
toggles, 267
toolbox (subroutines)
   for controls, 345–369
   for directories, 449–453
   for DOS programs, 435–439
   for drawing, 387–411
   for fonts, 413–431
   for forms, 371–385

for large programs, 439–446
for multimedia sound, 433–435
for versions, 446–448
Toolbox (Visual Basic)
  for controls, 194, 304–305, 345–369
  objects in, 140
  for timers, 138
Top property, 194, 328, 375
ToPassword subroutine, 358–361
trailing spaces, removing, 42, 242
Transparent DrawMode values, 166
triangles, drawing, 54–56
trigonometric functions, 143, 167
TrueType fonts, 421, 426
tutorial, 458
twips, 47–49
  and displays, 318–319, 323
  mapping mode for, 396
  scaling with, 332, 391, 400, 408–411
txtAddress_Change subroutine,
    278–279
txtNotes_Change subroutine, 279
type mismatches, 33
Type statement, 231–233
types, 32–37, 107
  for arguments, 96
  for array variables, 106
  in C, 306–308
  converting, 41
  for functions, 268–269
  mismatched, 33
  user-defined, 231–240
typing in Immediate window, 7–9

U
UBound function, 127
UCase$ function, 42, 334

underlined characters in menus,
    89–90
underscore characters (_), 64–65
Undo command, 287–288, 361–365
UnitsPerPixel subroutine, 402–403
Unload command, 251, 286–287
unloading forms, 227–228, 286–287
Until statement, 128
UpdateCalendar subroutine, 334, 341
UpdateClock subroutine, 334,
    340–341
UpdateProgress subroutine, 346–348
UpdateStatus subroutine, 274, 276
USER heap, 443–446
user interfaces
  designing, 176–182
  feature lists for, 178–181
  sketching screens for, 181–182
user-defined types, 231–240

V
Val function, 41
values, 27, 41. *See also* numbers
  passing variables by, 261–263, 275
  and types, 32–37
variable-length strings, 237
variables, 27–29. *See also* arrays
  compound, 231–232, 238–242
  for counters, 115
  for forms, 107–109, 247, 273
  global, 109, 234, 256
  length of, 240–241
  limits on, 441
  location of, 109
  memory for, 30
  module-level, 263
  names for, 28, 30–34, 104, 115

passing, 260–263, 275
with Put, 224
static, 334
in subroutines, 109, 247–248
types for, 32–37
VBRUN100.DLL file, 124
VBTools product, 465
versions
checking, 446–448
font names in, 414
vertical bars (|), 14–15
visibility
of controls, 258
of variables, 247–248

W

.WAV files, 433–435
Weekday function, 167
Wend statement, 128
While statement, 128
White DrawMode value, 166
Whole Lines display mode, 319–320
width
of controls, 194, 328
of forms, 374–376
of lines, 56, 96–99, 120–121, 391,
401–407

of pixels, 402–404
of printer lines, 401–407
Width property, 194, 374–376
WIN.INI file (Windows), 414–416,
426
WINDING fill mode, 399
windows (objects)
drawing in, 45–50, 52
state of, 152–153
Windows (program)
API for, 306
system functions for, 304–308
versions of, 414, 446–448
WindowState property, 152–153
WindowsVersion function, 446–448
working directories, 202, 229
Write # command, 251
writing
compound variables, 238–242
records, 223–225, 229–230, 277–278

X

Xor DrawMode values, 165–166
Xor operator, 81

Y

Year function, 167

SYBEX

FREE BROCHURE!

Complete this form today, and we'll send you a full-color brochure of Sybex bestsellers.

Please supply the name of the Sybex book purchased.

_____

How would you rate it?

_____ Excellent   _____ Very Good   _____ Average   _____ Poor

Why did you select this particular book?

_____ Recommended to me by a friend

_____ Recommended to me by store personnel

_____ Saw an advertisement in _____

_____ Author's reputation

_____ Saw in Sybex catalog

_____ Required textbook

_____ Sybex reputation

_____ Read book review in _____

_____ In-store display

_____ Other _____

Where did you buy it?

_____ Bookstore

_____ Computer Store or Software Store

_____ Catalog (name: _____)

_____ Direct from Sybex

_____ Other: _____

Did you buy this book with your personal funds?

_____ Yes   _____ No

About how many computer books do you buy each year?

_____ 1-3   _____ 3-5   _____ 5-7   _____ 7-9   _____ 10+

About how many Sybex books do you own?

_____ 1-3   _____ 3-5   _____ 5-7   _____ 7-9   _____ 10+

Please indicate your level of experience with the software covered in this book:

_____ Beginner   _____ Intermediate   _____ Advanced

Which types of software packages do you use regularly?

_____ Accounting   _____ Databases   _____ Networks

_____ Amiga   _____ Desktop Publishing _____ Operating Systems

_____ Apple/Mac   _____ File Utilities   _____ Spreadsheets

_____ CAD   _____ Money Management   _____ Word Processing

_____ Communications   _____ Languages   _____ Other _____
                                                                    (please specify)

Which of the following best describes your job title?

_____ Administrative/Secretarial   _____ President/CEO

_____ Director   _____ Manager/Supervisor

_____ Engineer/Technician   _____ Other _____
                                             (please specify)

Comments on the weaknesses/strengths of this book: _____

_____

_____

_____

_____

Name _____

Street _____

City/State/Zip _____

Phone _____

PLEASE FOLD, SEAL, AND MAIL TO SYBEX

SYBEX, INC.
Department M
2021 CHALLENGER DR.
ALAMEDA, CALIFORNIA USA
94501

SYBEX

SEAL

Sheridan Software

Sheridan Software provides two custom controls that let you add a 3-dimensional look to your program, as well as icons to the buttons in your programs.

3-D Panels

This custom control allows you to add various 3-dimensional borders to your programs:

- Add 3-D borders around other controls
- Use as a 3-D progress indicator
- Display 3-D text

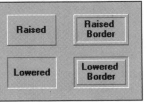

3-D Command Buttons

If you need to put an icon inside a button, this is the custom control for you. Visual Basic's own control only supports text.

- Add icons to your buttons
- Change the width of the bevel
- Add a 3-D effect to the caption

Sheridan Files on the Disk:

SHERIDAN.VBX	Design-time file
SHERIDAN.VBR	Run-time version

Socha's Software

You also get the full source code to the programs and general-purpose subroutines in this book:

Sketch

This simple program is a simple sketch program you'll develop in this book.

Clock/Calendar

This small program shows you how to write a program that will look good on all display adapters.

Icon Clock

Icon Clock is a small program that displays the current time as an icon, near the bottom of your screen.

11:50 AM

Address Book

You'll build a simple address book program in this book.

Features: Type in addresses and phone numbers, searching, printing address books, alphabetizing addresses, deleting addresses.

Subdirectories on the Disk:

SKETCH	Files for Sketch
ICONCLCK	Files for Icon Clock
ADDRESS	The Address Book
CLOCKCAL	Files for Clock/Calendar